The Living Stage

The
Living Stage

A Step-by-Step Guide to
Psychodrama, Sociometry and
Experiential Group Therapy

Tian Dayton, Ph.D., TEP

Health Communications, Inc.
Deerfield Beach, Florida

www.hci-online.com

Library of Congress Cataloging-in-Publication Data is available from the Library of Congress

©2005 Tian Dayton, Ph.D., TEP

ISBN 0-7573-0212-2

Publisher: Health Communications, Inc.
            3201 S.W. 15th Street
            Deerfield Beach, FL 33442-8190

Cover photo by Anetta Andres
Cover design by Larissa Hise Henoch
Inside book design by Lawna Patterson Oldfield

To Zerka Toeman Moreno
for being a true and guiding light.

The Way Out

*The Moment is the loophole through which man will fare on his way.
And though it may sound like a paradox, the intellectual [and] the artist
will be the first carriers of a revolution which in the end will satisfy also the biological
pride of man. Races of man adhering to conserved production will die out. Thus
Darwin's "survival of the fittest" will be found to be too narrow. It will be replaced
by the survival of the creator.*

—J. L. Moreno
Psychodrama, Volume 1

Contents

Acknowledgments

Psychodramatically speaking, everyone's life is played out on a living, inter-personal stage. The stage on which this book has come to life has many platforms. The most immediate of these platforms are my own training and therapy groups. These are my primary source of inspiration, exploration and practice, and I thank each and every one of those involved for the vitality, heart and professionalism that you have breathed into every exercise throughout this book.

Another is the movable stage of the addictions field in which I have trained nationally for the past two decades through my consulting, conferences, addic-tions institutes and workshops far too numerous to mention here. These have given me ever-evolving feedback on what therapists across the United States are really looking for, a kaleidoscopic view of the evolving needs in treatment cen-ters from literally thousands of clinicians. They are a demanding, exciting and invigorating group who do not hesitate to tell you if you have gotten it right (or wrong).

Another is the eight years I spent teaching psychodrama at New York University, in the drama therapy program directed by Dr. Robert Landy. There I needed to develop a clear and user-friendly training approach that could be understood and put into practice by students just entering the mental health and creative arts therapy fields.

And finally, this book also evolved from the specific program development and consulting I have done at addictions facilities throughout the country. Over the six years I've served as the director of program development at the Caron Foundation and consultant at Freedom Institute, Sierra Tucson; SAMSHA/ CSAT; Hazelden and Onsite. I have had the opportunity to put much of what is in this book into programming. Recently, I started the New York Psychodrama Training Institute at Caron, New York, to which therapists in the five state area come for training in psychodrama, sociometry and group psychotherapy. The techniques in this book have been used and found effective in those venues, as well as in the treatment centers of those of my trainees who have adapted them for their own facilities.

The field of psychodrama, sociometry and group psychotherapy has two creators: J. L. Moreno, who is the father of psychodrama, sociometry and group psychotherapy, and Zerka Toeman Moreno, who cocreated it with him throughout their marriage and continued to usher it forward after his death in 1974.

I came to psychodrama after years of using experiential therapy with adults in the addictions field and, before that, creative dramatics and forms of drama therapy with children. Living in New York City and upstate New York, I had easy access to the Mecca of psychodrama, where I spent eight very wonderful years doing my own training in psychodrama with Zerka Moreno and Dr. Robert Siroka. I could not have asked for more talented and knowledgeable people to learn from.

I need to say a special thank-you to Gary Seidler and Peter Vegso, who as publishers of Health Communications and U.S. Journal Training Conferences have been in a position to be very important friends to me and to psychodrama through publishing books and allowing psychodrama and experiential therapy to be presented at their conferences for the last twenty-five years. More recently Gary personally funded a docudrama called *The Process* on psychodrama and the issues that people in recovery face and overcome. Being such a believer in psychodrama both personally and professionally, Gary wanted this powerful method of healing to reach a wider audience.

After certifying as psychodramatists from the American Society of Psychodrama, Sociometry and Group Psychotherapy (ASGPP), Onsite director Ted Klontz and I wanted to provide training in psychodrama for addictions counselors who were ineligible for psychodrama certification, which requires a master's degree. We also provided the training for those counselors with master's and doctorate's who didn't wish to go for full certification in psychodrama but wanted further training in the method and wanted to recognize the importance of both addictions theory and psychodrama in treating addiction or those touched by addiction. To this end we created the, CET, or certification for experiential therapists. I never lose sight of, or respect and gratitude for, those creative souls in the addictions field who breathed new life, spontaneity and creativity into our method. They extended Moreno's vision into new territories, furthering his belief that any worthwhile method should have as its goal the healing of all mankind.

Allison Janse and Christine Belleris, as editors of this book, have been their usual wonderful selves. Their job is not an easy one, and as any author knows, the luck of working with talented editors who know what they're doing and have that extra breadth of mind to be able to get into the wide variety of subjects their jobs call for is a great boon to a book. A thousand thank-yous to each of them and to Bret Witter for seeing this as a worthy project. His words guided this project to its current form.

And, as always, I thank my husband, Brandt, for being my partner in personal growth and my dearest friend. Together, as ACOAs trying to figure the whole thing out, we have been each other's mainstays, guides and challengers. We are ever mindful of the gift of our beloved children, Marina and Alex, the lights and inspirations of our lives who give us more than we could ever give them. They have grown from children filling our home with love and ebullience to independent, intelligent and thriving adults. So, again, as always, I thank Alex and Marina for their love and friendship and for giving my life meaning, purpose and joy. And an added note of appreciation to Alex for his help in creating "Romance with Addiction."

As with many in the mental health field, most especially the addictions field, I feel as if I have been in the field from a very young age. The memory of visiting my father at Hazelden's treatment program when I was fourteen, of having him back sober and clear-eyed, lives in my mind in a bittersweet way. I remember virtually tripping up the stairs to greet him when he returned home (early) and finding him in his chair, vowing to stick with only the glass of water in his hand, and hoping against hope that this might finally be true. But it was not to be. The years leading to this, and the years that followed, taught me very sobering lessons on life—that the people you love the most can and do slip away, especially with the introduction of alcohol or drugs that drag them, and eventually everyone, into a world alienated from self and other. A world with no windows. It was recovery that opened a window in my life. Not recovery from drugs and alcohol, but recovery from the effects of living with them and seeing what they do to the best of people—what they did to my father and those of us close to him. It is the combination of this deeply personal learning and my professional learning that informs this book. Perhaps this book, in addition to being the culmination of my professional life, is also a sort of letter to my father. If it is, it probably says something like, "Look, Dad, I found a way out, and I have spent my professional life helping other people find a way out, too. I never stopped seeing the man who was good in you; and this, in a funny way, is my victory. Today I see you everywhere in the sober, good and restored people, in those who make it to the other side, in the loss and the redemption."

So I acknowledge you, Dad, as inspiring all of this in one way or another. Love, it seems, finds a way. And you were rich in love.

Dad died in 1973. In 1974, I got my family to try therapy, which helped me very much to recognize that we were suffering from something that others were not experiencing and that I, at least, needed help in dealing with it. In 1980 I again asked my mother if she would consider rallying the family for some kind of therapy. She knew of Sharon Wegscheider-Cruse from her work on the Hazelden board, and we met, as a family, for two days to take a deeper look. I had heard of Virginia Satir's work with psychodrama while using improvisational drama with children and from our friends Wheelock and Irene Whitney, two of her great supporters. I met up with it in person through Sharon Wegscheider-Cruse's experiential work with our family. Not only did I feel freer from the grip of an addicted family system than I had felt to date, but it led to training with Sharon and my entry into experiential therapy and psychodrama, sociometry and group psychotherapy. The rest, as they say, is history.

Foreword

Tian Dayton is an indefatigable worker in the area of mental health. She writes, teaches, trains and practices the art of psychodrama with a special focus on addiction, a field in which she has much experience and to which she is devoted as well. This book is but one among many on which she has spent a great deal of energy and interest, using the philosophy and ideas of J. L. Moreno in a broad context.

J. L. Moreno is the originator of psychodrama and sociometry and a pioneer of group psychotherapy; he was my husband for twenty-five years and my co-worker for thirty-three years. I have continued to develop psychodrama and role theory since his death in 1974 up until the present time.

Moreno's career was burdened by being a pioneer in a field already dominated by the teaching of another older genius, Sigmund Freud. Moreno found barriers whenever he declared his opposition to many of Freud's ideas, the major one being that he did not believe that language was the royal route to the human psyche. He found an older, more primeval underlying level, namely that of action and interaction between humans. He declared that the psyche is an open system, constantly influenced and shaped—or misshaped—by the interactional environment in which the human being develops. He knew that to reach this level, words were not enough, that it required action and interaction, that it is the area "in-between" people that demands our attention.

He also stated clearly that spontaneity and creativity are the major forces of human beings—replacing the idea that it is merely instincts which drive us—and that these can work for good or ill. He proclaimed that the human being is a player of roles; these roles bring with them their natural expression in interaction. He described psychodrama as "Shakespearean" psychiatry, as we are all improvisational actors on the stage of life.

So he created instruments to uncover, explore, and if need be, change that area "in-between" humans, such as sociometry, the measurement of interpersonal relations, and psychodrama, the individual psyche put into action through improvisational drama. Out of these grew sociodrama, the interaction of social beings in a dramatic context. The latter has become generally known as role-playing.

It is clear from these descriptions that Moreno never intended for his approach to the field of human interaction to be limited to the clinical setting. It has taken him a lifetime to be accepted, and although he is becoming more recognized as a seminal thinker, and his influence at large is growing, there are still vast areas of need. The sociologists would say that he "has been absorbed by the culture," but that is only superficially true.

Tian Dayton is helping to correct that and to bring his work to deeper and broader layers of our culture with this penetrating and far-reaching book.

Zerka T. Moreno
Charlottesville, Virginia

Introduction

I grew up in an alcoholic family. As the youngest of four children I had the advantage of being born into a family that was well established, with siblings who had already staked out their territory (mostly) and parents who were relaxed and well broken in. I thought that I had the best family in the whole world. I felt sorry for people who weren't as lucky as I was. The disadvantage of being the youngest was that I had fewer years with my family and my alcoholic father, than I wanted and needed. By the time I was nine, alcohol had come to be the most powerful member of our family. We were slowly collapsing from within; trying with all our might to hold on to the happiness that was now, daily slipping away; using all means at our disposal, cajoling, enabling, denying, minimizing and generally lying to ourselves and the outside world about what was really going on within our walls. The one thing we never seemed to do was talk about it. We simply had no language. We were caught in that downward spiral, each frozen in our own pain that, as a psychologist, I have come to recognize is the direct result of relationship trauma. At the time we had stomach aches, back aches, bouts of rage, hysterical fun, chaos, isolation, despair, but rarely, if ever, did we put into words what might have helped us understand what was happening to each of us as individuals and to our family as a unit. In short, we were a fairly typical alcoholic family system of the fifties. A boat without a rudder, or rather a boat with a rudder, alcohol.

As I became an adult I had a growing recognition that I was carrying burdens into my life, marriage and parenting that needed addressing. I knew perfectly well that I was married to the man I loved, I had two children I adored and all that I desired materially. But I knew something was missing and I felt that what was missing was inside of me. In spite of having everything I wished for, I felt an emotional numbness that prevented me from relaxing and enjoying it and I was incessantly worried about something going wrong, I was hyper vigilant, constantly waiting for the roof to cave in as it had done before. I recognized that if I didn't figure out why this was, I was putting everything I loved at risk i.e. bringing pain that belonged to the past into the present and recreating it through unconscious, dysfunctional relationship dynamics. I needed a way out, a way through to the other side, a way to remember in service of healing rather than repeating; a direct experience with my own inner world that would allow me to develop an emotional language through which I could talk about my inner dimensions as fluently as I could talk about the three dimensional world around me. I found that way through the dramatic therapies.

Psychodrama touched my soul, giving shape and meaning to what had lived in a shapeless, wordless state. Standing at the epicenter of my inner world and speaking out from that place was like living from the inside out. I could actually meet parts of my self and others from my life through casting them as role players in my own drama. This approach of personalizing a dramatic form with therapeutic goals was everything at once, profound, intriguing, relieving, reconnecting, creative and funny. There was my queasy stomach standing before me, wearing earrings and a necklace, telling me what was going on inside her, my inner child tugging at my shirt sleeve, trying to get my attention to tell me how sad she felt, and my beloved father, reconstructed and sober again, blessing the marriage he never lived to see, meeting the grandchildren he would have so adored, had he lived to know them. My world turned inside out in all of its meagerness and majesty. A second chance at living

Even though these experiences didn't take place in "reality" they occurred in the reality that lived inside of me, They changed me on the inside. As J.L. Moreno, the father of psychodrama said to Sigmund Freud when encountering him in Vienna, "You interpret their dreams, I give them courage to dream again."

I understood from my own experience and later those of countless clients that there was great healing potential in role play where one could experientially engage in and take direct responsibility for his or her own healing in a relational context. This meant that as a therapist, rather than directly interpret reality to my clients, I used my interpretation to inform the direction and structuring of the dramas clients wanted to do so that they could come to the threshold of their own awareness and feel their truth from within.

For some time I had been witnessing psychodrama's almost mysterious power to gain access to hidden selves and relationships in one's personal and social world and bring them onto the therapeutic stage for exploration and examination. The degree of healing I was seeing in clients inspired me to embark upon what turned into a twenty-year research journey in which I tried to understand why psychodrama seemed able to go where talk therapy could not. Experiential therapies provide a much-needed bridge, an experience so that both conscious and unconscious aspects of the inner world of both body and mind, can be brought forward to be reflected upon in their concrete form. Because what we don't know, can hurt us, it lives within the self-system, perhaps out of mind, but not out of being. In fact, it's power to influence our lives is made even greater because it has not been processed and understood.

GESTURE: OUR FIRST LANGUAGE

Gesturing is our first language. It is the mind-body communication upon which all subsequent language is built. Before language formally enters the picture, we have learned a rich tapestry of gestures to communicate our needs and desires. This gesturing comprises a nonverbal communication that informs our ability to express ourselves and understand others throughout our lives. The expression of concern or alarm on a mother's face, for example, causes the child to feel "held" or alerted to danger. The child's screech accompanied by an arm motion may signal a wish to be picked up, cuddled or command the mother to hand over a favorite toy. All of this body language is part and parcel of gestural communication and contains important connotation. Each tiny gesture is double coded with emotion and is stored by the brain and body with emotional purpose and meaning attached to it. Through this interactive process of communicating our needs and desires, we build emotional intelligence and literacy as surely as we learn math in a classroom.

Because gesturing is our first form of communication, much of this language becomes part of our unconscious and surfaces in the form of "automatic emotion." Alan Schore, in his research on affect regulation writes, "This 'automatic emotion' operates in infancy and beyond at nonconscious levels (Hansen & Hansen 1994), and . . . shape[s] subsequent conscious emotional processing" (Dimberg & Ohman, 1996). Our emotional unconscious, so to speak—this web of gesture, meaning and word—is formed through our interactional environment with our family and caregivers (our first social atom) and lays a foundation for later emotional growth and language development.

What occurs between people as subtle exchange of emotionally laden signals occurs so quickly, we hardly know it is happening because evolution has made the processing of emotions and their communication to others, very rapid. "The transmission of facially expressed emotion, occurs in "as little as two milliseconds (Niedenthal, 1990), far beneath levels of awareness." Nature has favored this speed synch for obvious reasons. The mother who could "feel fast," sense danger and communicate that to her child in order to get him out of harm's way, was "naturally selected" to be the DNA strain that led to us. "Because the unconscious processing of emotional information is extremely rapid, the dynamic operations of the 'transmission of nonconscious affect' (Murphy et al., 1995) and the spontaneous communication of 'automatic emotion' cannot be consciously perceived" (Schore, in press). One might liken this form of instantaneous emotional communication between people, to the hot synch between computers. Significant information gets transferred from one system to another, but it happens in what feels like an invisible realm.

All of these unconscious processes help us to walk, digest, self regulate and remain grounded within the self, in relationships and our environment. They allow us to operate on automatic. This automatic operating also has meaning already woven into it. "Many adults in therapy have a difficult time identifying some of their intentions and emotions. Sometimes therapists make the mistake of trying to help them label their feelings—"Were you happy?" "Are you feeling sad?" etc.—working under the assumption that patients can understand their own actions and feelings. As therapists attempt to help their patients understand the relationship between the past and the present and achieve "insight," they may inadvertently overestimate their patients' ability to experience a wide range of feelings. The therapist may assume that the patient has already "mastered" the relationship between words, action and affect. If our patients' words aren't connected with feelings and with the memories of actual interactive emotional experiences, the abstract words ("happy", "sad") that we so glibly use in therapy can have no deep meaning. During the course of therapy, we discover that some patients have more interactive experience with certain emotions than with others. They may recall warm exchanges with their parents when they were young, but remember very few discussions around aggression and assertiveness. Their families may have thought that such feelings were dangerous of frightening and avoided expressing them with their children or with each other. These former toddlers have grown into adulthood without developing much of a gestural repertoire or comfort level in displaying these avoided or "constricted" feelings."(Greenspan 2000) The result of this is that when patients try to talk about these emotions in therapy there is no real feeling tone or expressiveness on their faces or in their bodies. Adults who have not engaged in adequate gestural communication as toddlers frequently have trouble with certain abstract concepts." (Greenspan 2000). The result of this lack of early experience with the language of gesturing is that gesture (or this meta communication), along with its embedded meaning, becomes detached from word, which makes self-reflection difficult, if not impossible. Many adults have a hard time identifying some of their emotions and their intentions when they enter therapy. They have a lack of awareness about why they do what they do or why they feel what they feel. Or perhaps they experience something in their body, like chronic muscle stiffness or pain in their stomach, back or head, but they are unable to make any connections as to emotional feelings that may be being somatized rather than felt. They may misread or not pick up on the subtle signals from others that are a part of nonverbal communication.

Psychodrama, with its ability to include all of this rich, gestural interactive, language, to, in fact, begin there if necessary, e.g. "Show us don't tell us," can recreate the relational context and conditions necessary to attach feeling to gesture at the appropriate developmental level. The roles we learn in childhood and later play, have a web of unconscious, associated meanings from gesture and word, embedded into them. Roles have physical, mental and relational components. When we work with the roles, we enter into the somatic, intrapersonal and interpersonal world of the client. In the heat of the psychodrama, thinking, feeling and behavior emerge along with its web of associated meaning. Psychodrama reawakens the sleeping child inside the adult, who used to communicate in body language. As clients experience this real life enactment unfolding around them, or witness a protagonist with whom they identify, they feel along with them into a forgotten world. They become purposeful and attending. Through clinical role-play, we can modify our early emotional and psychological language and experience. The function of the role, according to Moreno, is to enter the unconscious and give it shape and definition. By using clinical role-play and group dynamics, "The unconscious can continue to expand through new and ongoing, affectively charged relational or regulatory experiences" (Schore 2004). As we do, undo and redo experience we move toward "more complex psychobiological states and higher levels of self-reflection" (ibid). Initially, we *do*, the wounded part of us emerges into the here and now physically, mentally and emotionally, we feel in the here and now, as we felt then. As we *undo*, we allow that part of us to find its form of expression, to cry the tears that were numbed or thwarted, express the anger or helplessness or shiver with the fear that became frozen. We reempower the self and restore our sense of integrated action as our thinking, feeling and behavior emerge through role-play. Then we *redo*, as the client, having unfrozen and expressed their pain and fear, or even love or excitement, begins to spontaneously experience things differently, to see, as Marcel Proust so elegantly put it, "The same landscape through new eyes." The lens through which the client sees the world changes ever so slightly or very significantly. We replace or at least add insight and understanding, to the knee jerk reaction and the client is able to respond to life differently.

The process of learning this gesturing and attaching language uses both the left and right brain. The interaction between the more emotional right, and the logical left, brain is central to emotional intelligence and literacy. The cortex, or logical brain, is able to modify intense feeling states, associated with the right brain, through the use of reason and words. The right hemisphere is also centrally involved in not just the reception but the expression and transmission of emotional signals and affective states. "Right cortical functions mediate the expression of facial displays of emotion (Borod, Haywood, & Koff, 1997), thereby facilitating "spontaneous emotional communication" (Buck, 1994) and "spontaneous" gestural communication (Blonder et al., 1995). These rapid communications are not only sensed by another face, they trigger motor responses in the facial musculature of the recipient." There is an emotional contagion between us that is part of how people tune in on another person's unconscious communication and regulate their own behavior accordingly.

Research has long recognized that in virtually any form of therapy it is the "relationship" that heals. By developing trusting, long term healing relationships that can create new experience and act as new, external regulators, clients learn a new emotional language along with the skills of regulation and balance both within themselves and their relationships. Psychodrama extends, expands and deepens both the gestural and relational component of that learning.

The Body Comes to Therapy

An increasingly significant aspect of psychodrama in light of the neurological research that has given depth and meaning to the body-mind movement, is psychodrama's ability to allow the body to be a part of the therapeutic process. No longer the dichotomy between nature *versus* nurture, scientific studies substantiate that nature *and* nurture work in exquisite symmetry to lay down the neural wiring that forms the template from which we operate throughout our lives. Each tiny interaction the growing child has with their primary caretakers, actually lays down new neural wiring and this wiring is constantly evolving. As parents, we literally participate in wiring our children's emotional system.

Generally, if the environment is what D.W. Winnecott, British psychoanalyst, might call, "good enough" all goes relatively smoothly and children get what they need to continue on their developmental path with relative ease. "If, however, the developing individual is exposed to an early growth-inhibiting environment which deprives the child of nutritional and/or emotional supplies, this . . . level of maturation will not be achieved," and developmental deficits may occur.

Our right brains, which are associated with our more emotional selves, develop first. At around three and a half, the left brain begins to reach greater maturity and to, in a sense, use it's "critical intelligence" to inhibit some of the more basic drives that are a natural part of toddlerhood. The smooth transfer of emotional information from the right or emotional brain to the left, thinking brain, is part of what allows us to integrate emotion into our thinking and planning. In order for adequate communication to occur between the two hemispheric processors, "the late-acting verbal left must have access to the emotional outputs of the nonverbal early right . . . which it can then in turn inhibit." This process of inhibition is part of becoming socialized to live in the world and develop language that continues to be meaningfully integrated with emotion. But if the early experience of the child is "non optimal," that is, if it doesn't adequately support good brain growth, "the interhemispheric transfer of affective information is inefficient." This can result in anything from mild developmental deficits to alexithymia, or "no words for feelings." (Dewarja & Sasaki, 1990), (Schore 2004). Being able to attach words to feeling states is a corner stone of developing emotional literacy and consciously regulating behavior. We need to think about what we're feeling in order to understand what is occurring inside and outside of us and to use that "understanding" to modulate our thinking, feeling and behavior. A growing child needs what Winnecott referred to as a positive "holding environment" or an affective atmosphere in which he can feel "held" and secure enough to unfold or develop naturally. Homes that are constantly chaotic or chaos's dark underbelly, excessively rigid and controlling, are "non-optimal" for growth and development.

THE FEAR FACTOR: HOW TRAUMA AFFECTS US

Neurobiological research also provides a much-needed window into treating clients whose neurological systems have become deregulated through "less than optimal" relational experiences, such as the relational trauma that comes from familial neglect, abuse or living with addiction.

The body can't tell the difference between an emotional emergency and physical danger. When triggered, it will respond to either by pumping out stress chemicals designed to impel someone to quick safety or enable them to stand and fight. In the case of childhood problems, that is where the family itself has become the proverbial saber-toothed tiger or source of stress, there may be no opportunity to fight or flee. Children and adults in these systems may find escape impossible. And so they do what they can. They freeze. They shut down their inner responses by numbing or fleeing on the inside through dissociating. Though this strategy may have helped them to get through a painful situation, perhaps for a period of many years, they suffered within.

The ability to "escape" or take one's self out of harm's way, is central to whether or not one develops long-term trauma symptoms or PTSD (vander Kolk 2004). If escape is not possible, the intense energy that has been revved up in their bodies to enable them to fight or flee, boils up inside or becomes thwarted or frozen (Levine 1997). Years later these people may live as if the stressor is still present, as if a repeated rupture to their sense of self and their world lurks just around the corner, because their body/mind tells them it does. Early childhood trauma can have long lasting effects.

Children do not have a fully developed capacity to understand what is happening around them and to regulate their intense emotional responses accordingly. That is why kids can get so exited or so scared. They depend upon the adults around them to help them to "contain" their excitement or "calm and soothe" their intense fear. And the child's limited brain development can put them at risk if they are living in a chaotic environment, especially if the adults who they would normally go to for comfort are the source of the stress. "The amygdala, our fight/flight/freeze part of the brain, is fully formed at birth. This means that infants and children are capable of a full-blown stress response from birth on. When frightened, their bodies will go into fight/flight/freeze mode"(Aram 2004). However, the hippocampus or the part of the brain that interprets sensory input as to whether or not it is a threat, is not fully functional until between four and five years of age. So children have no way of assessing whether or not they need to be scared and how scared they need to be. And to make matters even more complicated, the prefrontal cortex, which is where we have the ability to think and reason, is not fully developed until around age eleven (Seifert 1990). Therefore, when small children get frightened and go into fight/flight/freeze, they "have no way of interpreting the level of threat nor of using reason to modulate or understand what is happening. Their limbic system becomes frozen in a sensory fear response and can remain so, without intervention from a caring adult . . . and because of the child's natural egocentricity the threat feels personal, it goes to their core self" (Aram 2004). Whatever is going on, the child is likely to interpret as being "about them," they may feel they are the cause. Because they lack the developmental equipment to modulate this experience themselves, their only way out of this state is through an external modulator, i.e. the parent, who can hold, reassure and restore them to a state of equilibrium. If this modulating occurs at the time painful circumstances are occurring, the child is unlikely to become symptomatic because their parent is wooing them back toward balance and a sense of safety. But if the parent or family environment are the primary stressor and unavailable to the child for reassurance, the child is left to live through repeated ruptures to his developing sense of self, his fundamental learning processes and his relational world, with little ability to make sense of it, interpret the level of threat or use reasoning to regulate and understand what is going on. And later in life, when that memory gets triggered, it is the same, unmodulated sensory memory that was locked down to begin with. And they may still, as adults, be unconsciously living by the meaning they made of it at the time, "I am bad, I cause trouble, I am at fault. Being close to someone is scary."

When seeking treatment as adults, memory or recallability of traumatic events may be minimal and whatever memories there are, may have little insight or cognitive understanding associated with them because of the level of brain development at the time of the incidents. This is also why it can be hard to talk about traumatic experiences, part of us just wasn't there, we were frozen in fear or dissociated and when, in therapy we search for the memory, it doesn't necessarily come. What comes instead is a sensorial and emotional content (shakes, fear, shivers, heart pounding, etc.) and a sense of danger. Because this is how the memory was locked down in the first place. Trauma is a body-mind phenomenon, not just mind. This is why a mind /body approach to trauma therapy is critical to full healing. Adults who were traumatized as children don't tend to remember things well or in order. They simply lacked the developmental capability to understand what was happening to them as frightened children. So a recitation of the traumatic events can be difficult for them. Oftentimes, the body needs to lead the mind to the truth. The body needs to speak in its own voice, to show rather than tell. Then, as the truth emerges through action of some kind, the adult mind, i.e. the observing ego, can witness what is emerging through the mature eyes of adulthood and make new meaning out of the events.

Traumatized people are often emotionally and psychically glued to scenes and dynamics from the past. Trauma sears the painful scene into the brain/body where it may live, relatively unchanged, for a period of many years. The traumatized person's inner world can become characterized by extremes and their outer world may mirror that dynamic. They may tend to cycle between extremes of black and white thinking, feeling and behavior with few shades of gray. This reflects the intense and overwhelming fear response, when a person becomes flooded with pervasive feelings of fear and then shuts down, numbs out or dissociates. These client's limbic systems may have become deregulated, they may become hyper-reactive or hyper vigilant, perceiving danger, whether or not it exists because their limbic system is regularly geared up for fight/flight and their ability to assess levels of threat is impaired, i.e., everything feels threatening. Issues with regulation, both within the self and in the family system seem ever present in this population. Rather than living in the present and tuning into the natural give and take of the moment, their hyper-reactivity may make traumatized clients feel safer living in their heads, in their sets of conclusions, stories about what happened, ideas and ideals about life and relationships rather than the day to day reality. Because they have trouble with self-regulation, their ability to actually tolerate the visisicitudes of the moment is interfered with. They may have trouble "sitting with" strong emotion without acting out, blowing up, withdrawing, dissociating or shutting down. They may lose spontaneity, or the ability to respond "adequately" to a given circumstance, that is they tend to over respond or to under respond. They become caught in a body/mind bind, where their fearful thoughts trigger states of physiological arousal and their physiological arousal triggers more fearful thoughts and emotions. This internal body/mind combustion may lead them to respond with behavior that is equally unconsciously driven. They may function, in some ways, through a false self because they have lost access to large pockets of their real selves. And the more they do this, well, the more they do it. It becomes initially a defensive strategy and eventually a quality of personality.

For the traumatized person, the past may feel as if it is ever present, even if beneath the level of their conscious awareness. These clients often become caught in repeating, dysfunctional relational dynamics, locked in a cycle of unconscious triggering where even small gestural cues, such as a raised eyebrow or flashing eyes, can send them into states of physiological and emotional fear associated with previous painful experiences. And when memories get triggered, they may feel as if they are about the situation that triggered them because the nature of traumatic memory is not fully understood. In this way, our painful past gets projected into our present unconsciously and becomes self-perpetuating.

A similar phenomenon can occur in times of war or intensely frightening experiences. The survival parts of our brain override the prefrontal cortex and we operate from the limbic brain. In other words, we are in fight/flight mode so that the terrifying experience becomes frozen in the brain/body.

One of the symptoms of PTSD is to "self-medicate with drugs or alcohol" (Van der Kolk 1987) or other addictive substances or behaviors. Though these synthetic solutions may effectively quell their inner storm, in the long run, they create a bigger one.

THE STAGE IS ENOUGH

Moreno believed that each individual's internal world was co-created and required healing relationships to restore equilibrium and spontaneity. He felt that giving someone "the stage" that is by making space a dynamic principal in the therapeutic process, people could allow their life stories to emerge into space through action where memories could, through the dynamics of role-play, be reworked and transformed. With its emphasis on interactive role-play, psychodrama offers a method through which the body, mind and relational ability can heal. The body/mind memories can come to the forefront in what Fritz Perls, creator of Gestalt Therapy, referred to as a "safe emergency" a clinical situation in which, if powerful affect emerges or is triggered, it can be worked through toward resolution rather than blindly reenacted. And the all too frequent loss of ability to receive on an emotional level can be broken through as clients slowly learn to accept caring and support into their most vulnerable, open selves.

Moreno believed that what was learned in action, must be unlearned in action, and toward this end, he created his methods of action therapy. Allowing the body to participate in the therapy process means that when the state of frozen physiological sense memories or impulses is accessed or triggered, escape is finally possible. An example of this is a social atom with a woman named Andrea. We were in a very large room. Once her family was up in place, I asked her how it felt to look at them. She said, "I want to run." "So run," I replied, at which point she fled for the corner and safety. Before running, she was experiencing body shivers, heart pounding and sweating palms, after running, she felt calmer, her body stopped "betraying " her or, in fact, telling her the truth that she couldn't make sense of or integrate. Once she could take the physical action she felt moved to take, she could integrate rather than numb or dissociate from her intense reaction. In addition, Andrea began to realize that she had put distance between herself and her stressor. She had reconfigured something on the outside that had inner resonance. Psychodrama allows for "spatial mapping" to enter the therapeutic process. In experiments done on rats, reported in 1983 by R.G.M. Morris, a rat is placed in a tank filled with milk. There was enough milk so that the rat's feet could not touch the bottom. The milk kept the rat from seeing a platform that was located somewhere in the tank, where he could stand safely. The rat swam in concentric, gradually decreasing circles until he finally located the platform, at which point, he stood on it. When he was again placed in the same tank he swam straight to the platform. Researchers postulate that he had developed a cognitive map, or an internal representation of the spatial features of his surroundings. This implies "a direct connection between the representational system and the sensory motor system that is between thought and action". Psychodrama, with its ability to incorporate space into the therapeutic process, would logically provide a healing opportunity that incorporates more of the psychobiological system and thus offers a fuller experience of healing and sensory integration for the entire organism. It helps the client who has been traumatized to overcome the feeling they may have of being lost in space, it provides a new, physical context in which the memories can be reworked and re "placed" with new insight and understanding. It is holistic.

Trauma need not be a life sentence. With proper treatment, suffering can transform into insight, understanding, wisdom and a new and deepened appreciation for life and relationships. Being humans, we often appreciate what we either have to work hard for or have somehow lost and found again. Working through pain toward liberation holds the ingredients for allowing us to master not only trauma, but life itself. The lessons that we learn through losing the self and finding it, are spiritual at their core. It is the age-old story of loss and redemption that opens the doors of our own perception to the spiritual meaning of life. Not only do we not need to leave the traumatized self behind, we bring it forward renewed and revitalized with wisdom and passion sewn into its lining. We learn how to spin straw into gold.

The combination of one to one talk therapy, psychodrama groups and twelve step programs, along with other body-mind healing and relational experiences such as yoga, massage and creative or hobby experiences or spiritual communities, I have found to be very effective in resolving issues related to trauma, grief and addiction. It is also a clear path toward emotional literacy or the ability to feel, label, categorize and discuss one's emotional and psychological states and attend to those of others.

Man as Creator

Moreno, felt that the stage of life was confining, largely because of adherence to social norms and what he termed "cultural conserves" (conserved and repeated aspects of human activities such as the play, a symphony, a book, a ritual or any idée fixe or conserved set of responses or behaviors) that large and very significant parts of ourselves often go unexplored and unexpressed. He felt that this repetition of conserved forms sometimes squelched our personal spontaneity and creativity, which in turn affected personal vitality and mental and emotional health. He was deeply concerned at the increasingly robotic nature of our culture as we continued to spend significant time with mechanical devises that could not feel, think and respond in the affective moment. He offered the living stage as a therapeutic alternative: a safe place where a person might freely, and without excessive restraint, live out his or her fears and fantasies. A stage on which we might act out, in positive service of healing, those issues not only close to our lives but close to our hearts; that press upon our inner worlds. A therapeutic space where we might meet ourselves, including the parts of ourselves that may be held out of consciousness in daily life, even though they powerfully impact and inform who we are. In doing so Moreno felt we could explore and resolve wounds from the past, deepen our actual knowledge and experience of the present and peer into and practice future roles that we might fear, fanaticize about or wish to consider undertaking. By providing a safe space, or stage, for the exploration of personal and social issues, he sought to increase and train our personal spontaneity and creativity, qualities that he felt enhance our ability to respond to life more fully and are crucial to psychological and emotional health.

Moreno felt that we live at a unique period in human evolution, one in which there are more potential roles available to us than at any previous time in history. The task then, he felt, was to find and play the roles that best suit us. Searching out, choosing and playing a set of roles that will allow us to grow, is part of a therapeutic process. Just as a plant needs to have the proper conditions in order to grow and flower, people need to find their proper conditions, too; to plant themselves firmly in the ground that is best for their particular needs and wishes. Part of helping people to recover is to identify those conditions, outside of the therapeutic situation, and slowly integrate them into the client's life so that they can take root, grow and bear fruit.

The "Living Page": Psychodramatic Journaling

I began to translate the basic theoretical concepts of psychodrama into a journaling method about fifteen years ago. I call this "psychodramatic journaling." My frustration, constantly presenting psychodrama to clinicians who lived in parts of the country where further training was scarce, who wished to learn something they could incorporate into their practices now rather than later, coupled with my respect for fundamental psychodramatic concepts such as doubling, role development and role reversal, made me want to find a way to adapt psychodramatic thinking to the written page. I have found through years of clinical trial and application that role theory can be successfully translated into paper and pencil explorations in which clients can gain insight and perspective on their life roles, their role development and place emotional and psychological issues into a developmental framework. Reawakening of the self along developmental lines can occur through psychodramatic journaling as well as psychodrama. Thinking, feeling and behavior that is role specific, can emerge through psychodramatic journaling to be worked with toward meaningful and healing outcomes. Breaking down the journaling process into roles, allows for many of the advantages of role-play to be had through journaling. As, for example, the six-year-old child is given a voice through writing, she opens her heart and says what she may have needed to say then but was, for some reason, thwarted in doing so. As she speaks, the adult mind looks on and can begin to think about what the feeling child is saying. At six, the child did not have the brain capacity to apply reason to what she was feeling, but by journaling out her emotions in the here and now, the adult within her can make sense and meaning out of what may have been living within her in a senseless and confusing state. As a result, this perhaps split off or numbed part of self can be experienced and reintegrated into the current, functioning self. This same process can be done for the self at any stage of development from birth to present day.

In this way, psychodramatic journaling fits neatly into the developmental model that we discuss in our closing chapters and can be an extension of therapy that can be integrated into recovery or programming on its own. It is, in a sense, role-play on paper. And experiential work, in a much more limited fashion can extend from it through, for instance, reading a letter to an empty chair or role player or experiencing a letter being read to the self by an auxiliary role player. Or the client can share her journaling from a developmental perspective, for example, read the journal entry "as" the six-year-old from one chair and reverse roles into the adult self and offer comfort and advice from the adult self back to the child self. In this way the child self can be given a voice and the adult self can comfort, regulate and guide the inner child. These are examples of ways to provide very meaningful therapeutic moments that do not require the kind of training that full psychodrama requires. Throughout the book are exercises that can be done with paper and pencil alone or extended as indicated.

The social atom one of psychodrama's most brilliant contributions can be done entirely on paper. I have devoted an entire chapter to the social atom as it can stand on its own as a therapeutic tool that helps to focus treatment and aftercare planning in a manner that is both practical and healing. I have also developed other approaches of my own that I've adapted and found useful such as mind mapping, self tests, timelines, journaling with photographs and "The Living Genogram." The loss chart, for example, has been very helpful in illustrating for clients how one current loss may bring up many unresolved losses that can complicate the process of mourning. Psychodramatic journaling can also extend the use of psycho educational spectrograms and locograms (see section two) for those who feel able to do some basic, sociometric exercises but are not comfortable moving into enactments. I have integrated theory from the research and practice I've done over the years in, for example, grief and trauma, into these sociometric processes. This combination of psycho educational/ sociometric exercises and psychodramatic journaling is a very full and sufficient way of incorporating focused experiential therapy into existing treatment programming without adding psychodrama per se. Indeed, one of its advantages and my impulses for creating this combination was that the journaling component offered an extended avenue for psycho-educational exploration. It became especially useful when managed care took over and clinicians were continually faced with large groups of clients looking for both a group and individualized experience.Psychodramatic journaling allows group members to continue to unravel their feelings and thoughts that get warmed up through sociometric, psycho educational exercises and then to deconstruct those feelings in terms of the self. It combines educational material with avenues for connecting with the group and connecting with the self in the presence of others.

The process of psychodramatic journaling is fully outlined in chapter 12, Psychodramatic Journaling" and exercises that use psychodramatic journaling have been interwoven throughout the book. They constitute a "book within a book" that outlines the use of journaling in treatment. I have used a symbol

(✐) to indicate which exercises can be used as both experiential exercises and psychodramatic journaling exercises. I explain how to adapt the experiential exercise for psychodramatic journaling in the "variations", though many of the exercises have paper and pencil components embedded in the steps as well. Those trained in psychodrama can combine psychodrama with psychodramatic journaling, but those who don't feel comfortable conducting psychodramas are able to work experientially through the use of psycho educational exercises, which are outlined in each section of this book with "goals," "steps" and "variations."

MAKING OUR METHOD RELEVANT

Picasso's early drawings are brilliantly precise, revealing a highly disciplined and skilled hand. His drawings have the genius and power to inspire the greatest artists. They are as breathtaking as Ingra's work, the neoclassical master draftsman who epitomized the perfection of line. This command of the fundamentals of drawing allowed Picasso in his later work to alter what was previously considered art. His work asked the viewer to see the world anew through his eyes; to play with reality and reveal the unconscious workings of the inner world through the medium of painting. When asked, "What is art?" Picasso replied, "What is not art?" For better or worse, this is the mind of the creator.

When I asked Zerka Moreno, J.L.'s wife and co creator of the field, to offer her vision of the potential depth and breadth of Moreno's vision of psychodrama, sociometry, group psychotherapy and sociodrama she replied , " it can encompass whatever is dramatically focused, whether applied to groups or to an individual, and which can also embrace all forms of art, including music. It can include everything that is possible within the guided action model. Our method is so relevant and such a powerful tool for education that it should be employed equally outside of the therapeutic format as within it. J.L. Moreno never intended it merely as a tool of therapy. He felt, as I do, that it should be made available to a larger population. Based on the twin principle of spontaneity and creativity, it is possible to use this method to mediate in interpersonal and intercultural conflicts. We need to train more people to use this tool, to go out into the world, in every situation to help make people's lives fuller and more complete; to help people to fulfill themselves in positive rather than destructive ways. Indeed, it is used this way effectively far more in other countries than in the USA, where role-playing is still limited to closed institutions, although it is growing in measure, as in police academies, administration, business, schools. It needs to come out into the larger world."

The Morenos encourage us to make our method relevant to those who need it; to avoid becoming caught in a conserved form of a once-spontaneous process. They invite us to bring forth our own spontaneity and creativity to keep our method vital. They encourage us to experiment with line and form, to expand on the classical and adapt it to the pressing needs of today and incorporate into it the new knowledge and creativity at our disposal. To move from role-taking and role-playing into role-creation. We are in a creative evolution in the field of psychodrama, sociometry and group psychotherapy. Our methods have been so mainstreamed that we don't even know we're seeing what originated as the triadic system some of the time. Role-play has been adapted by police academies, businesses, schools and treatment centers and countless other venues throughout the world. Moreno felt that any method worth its salt should have as its goal the "healing of all mankind." He laid down a brilliant basic system that has been adapted into countless venues and inspired inventiveness and creativity.

WHAT YOU WILL DISCOVER IN THIS BOOK

The Living Stage represents my own synthesis of a variety of theory bases along side and into Moreno's triadic system of psychodrama, sociometry and group psychotherapy. I've interwoven into role play, theoretical concepts from addictions, grief and trauma theory; ideas from psychoanalysis, and the neurobiological research that has stimulated so much interest in mind-body therapies over the past decade.

In training clinicians throughout the United States over the past two decades, a few themes and concerns constantly emerge. While clinicians are often riveted by psychodrama and sociometry and recognize its benefits, they don't feel sufficiently trained in the method and are appropriately concerned about using it.

Another question is when it is appropriate to use experiential approaches and when it is not. For the highly trained clinician, the power of the method is less a concern because we understand how to adapt it to the situation in which it is being used.. This book offers a variety of ways of incorporating experiential work into therapy without, necessarily mounting a full psychodrama and guidelines when and how to use it. Throughout the book and especially in sections two and three on special issues and special populations, I have adapted psychodrama, sociometry and sociodrama in creating a psychoeducational approach to use in treatment. And I have developed psychodramatic journaling to extend these forms. This has been a popular approach with clinicians because it bonds and connects group members naturally and quickly, it helps groups to become curious about, engage in and take responsibility for their own healing process and it educates groups on subjects relevant to their healing such as trauma, grief, depression, resilience to name a few.

I have divided this book into three parts:

Part I describes the triadic system of psychodrama, sociometry and group psychotherapy that forms the basis of Moreno's therapeutic vision.

Psychodrama is a concrete method and so I have begun, in section one, with the concrete aspects of the method and worked my way toward the therapeutic underpinnings. I have tried to help the reader to walk from the concrete towards the abstract. We begin by outlining what is sometimes referred to as the classical form of psychodrama, the exquisitely streamlined method that is the personification of "less is more." Zerka Moreno often points out that one of psychodrama's strengths is the teachability of its method.

After outlining the classical or basic action method with its structures, techniques and theoretical underpinnings, we move into chapters on sociometry and group psychotherapy. Sociometry is, on its own a separate science that deals with the nature and quality of connectedness from person to person, group to group or culture to culture. It is also involved with examining the choice making process. How and why do we choose a particular partner, friend or career? What are our criteria for choosing or not choosing and how do we find what best suits us? How does it feel to be highly chosen, under chosen, accepted or rejected. Are we part of the group, isolated from it or does our status rest upon the needs and wishes of a particular system? Does our life represent choices that suit us or that do not? Sociometry offers a clear system through which to concretize and examine these and other choices. It is considered to be one of Moreno's most significant contributions. I break out the "social atom" into its own chapter because it stands on it's own as a diagnostic exploration of the family system. It influenced the genogram (Zerka Moreno 2004) and provides a map for diagnosis and treatment.

Following, I include a chapter on group psychotherapy, of which Moreno is considered the father. Moreno was the pioneer who began to conceive of treating people in groups rather than exclusively in a one to one situation. It was this desire to understand group process that gave birth to the underlying science of sociometry. Next, I have included a chapter on role theory as part of the theory base of the triadic system. Moreno developed his own approach to role theory in order to give further theoretical support to his method of role play. Moreno felt that "the role is the tangible form the self takes" and that the role "enters the unconscious and gives it shape and definition." Because of this and the fact that role development begins at or even before birth, when we work with the role we enter both the unconscious of a person and their full range of life long development. Thinking, feeling and behavior tends to be role specific (Siroka 1988) that is we think, feel and behave in ways that are specific to the roles we play. Working with the role then gives us natural access to the thinking, feeling and behavior attached to the role and its over all development.

Following, we have a brief chapter on sociodrama. While psychodrama deals with the personal role, sociodrama deals with the collective aspects of a role; e.g. one role player may be chosen to represent all nurses, all politicians, all mothers, all daughters, all victims all abusers, all alcoholics, all enablers and so on. Sociodrama is widely used in the psychoeducational components of treatment facilities and the educational programs of police institutions, workplaces and schools.

Lastly in section one, I include a chapter on psychodramatic journaling, my method of translating the theoretical underpinnings of psychodrama into a format to use in journaling along with near-psychodramatic techniques such as letter writing, working with photographs, mind mapping, charting and self tests.

Part II is entitled "Special Issues" and represents my own approach to using experiential methods, such as psychodrama, sociometry and psychodramatic journaling, to address issues that come up again and again throughout recovery. I have outlined experiential approaches that can be added to an overall treatment plan in working with some of the fallout from PTSD, addiction and codependency. I wrote Trauma and Addiction to offer a clear description of how clients self medicate PTSD symptoms with drugs, alcohol, food, sex and spending etc. and Heartwounds to address the impact of unresolved trauma and grief on relationships. I have adapted that material along with recent advances in neurobiological research for experiential use in sections two and three of The Living Stage.

Part III is entitled "Special Populations" and is my own adaptation of the triadic system in the treatment of addicts, ACOAs, codependents and couples.

In the beginning of our chapter on Addicts and ACOAs I have created "The Experiential Model for the Addicted Traumatized Family." When I do program development there is often times a hole in this area. Sharon Wegscheider-Cruse's model for the roles in an addicted family has become an industry standard and helps client's to conceptualize their role or roles in the system. My model addresses the dynamics and organizing principals within that family system that get internalized and become organizing principals of both the self and the system that are at the root of personal and interpersonal issues with dysregulation and generational dysfunction. The swings between numbness/shut down and high/intense affect that characterize the trauma response get internalized into each family member, all too often become the operating style of the family and the individuals within it. For example, the addicted/traumatized family characterized by extremes in functioning may evidence alternating patterns of chaos vs. rigidity. Families may adopt primarily one outward manifestation while its opposite underlies it. That is the there will be a rigidity to the chaotic family and a chaotic underworld to the rigid family. The model is designed to help clients to get a succinct and user friendly picture of what happened to their family and what happened to themselves

The last chapter in the book is entitled Program Development and lays out ways of incorporating these exercises throughout the book into program development.

In the appendix I have included many exercises that are either commonly used in the field or that have been created by myself., students or colleagues.

Throughout the text and on gray pages I have embedded many direct quotes from Moreno, so that the reader can get a real flavor of his own thinking and process of creation.

It is my hope that, after reading this book, you will have a clear overview of psychodrama, sociometry and experiential group therapy and a sense of the theoretical concepts that underlie it. I also hope to make my own, unique contribution to the field through the approaches I have developed that integrate sociometric, psycho educational role play processes and psychodramatic journaling. Incorporating theoretical advances in the area of trauma, grief and neurobiology I have developed practical, step-by-step exercises that you can follow in incorporating this material into your own practice or facility. Outlined and implicit in all of this, is my own sense of the journey clients go through as they heal and the issues that most commonly arise along the path of recovery. It is my wish that the beauty and discovery of experiential healing methods be used far and wide, that these approaches be available to all who need or wish for them.

Drama and the written word have spoken to the soul for centuries. Throughout humanity, theater, ritual and prose have been among the most powerful forms of, education and healing. Experiential learning is core to us as humans; it reaches into our most private worlds and brings them forward so they can find expression and fulfillment. It connects us with those around us in deep and meaningful ways. We need this today, as we have needed it always. Role play therapies are the intelligent and inspired modern adaptation of these ancient forms.

Part I:

The Essence of Psychodrama

The Living Stage

THE THERAPEUTIC THEATER

The "theatre for spontaneity" was the unchaining of illusion. But this illusion, acted out by the people who have lived through it in reality, is the unchaining of life. . . . This mad passion, this unfolding of life in the domain of illusion, does not work like a renewal of suffering, rather it confirms the rule: every true second time is the liberation from the first. One gains towards his own life, towards all one has done and does, the point of view of the creator—the experience of the true freedom, the freedom from his own nature. . . . Every living figure denies and resolves itself through psychodrama. . . . One speaks, eats, drinks, procreates, sleeps, is awake, writes, fights, quarrels, earns, loses, even dies a second time in psychodramatic ways. But the same pain does not affect the player and spectator as pain, the same want does not affect him as want, the same thought does not affect him as thought. It is painless, consciousless, thoughtless, deathless. . . . It is the self-produced and self-created recurrence of itself.

—J. L. Moreno
Psychodrama, Volume 1

Psychodrama uses action and role play as a means to study behavior in its concrete form. The therapeutic stage allows for the natural condensations and expansions of time that exist in both the conscious and unconscious mind to emerge into the therapeutic moment. On the living stage our worlds can be produced in a manner that more closely imitates the way in which they are stored in our surplus reality. Psychodrama accesses that part of us that, though invisible, provides the script from which we live—our psychological and emotional world, with all of its uniquely personal meaning, logic and significance. The world that drives and defines us.

In psychodrama we "unchain the illusion." The usual instruction in psychodrama is "show me, don't tell me." Psychodrama as a method of action uses the body *in situ* to warm up to the contents of the mind and heart. It differs from talking methods not so much in its theoretical approach but in its use of action or role play, in addition to words, to tell a story. Indeed, many therapeutic approaches—psychoanalysis, object relations, trauma and grief theory, self psychology, and some cognitive/behavioral approaches, to name a few—fit tongue-and-groove as a theoretical base for the flexible, action method of psychodrama. Psychodrama's genius is its recognition that in order to find the right words we have to find the right feeling, and in order to find the right feeling we may need to gently reenter in body as well as mind, the time and space in which that feeling was germinated.

Psychodrama might also be seen as "the royal road" to right-brain functioning. The right brain plays a central role in organizing the psychobiological processes that underlie a number of vital functions that occur beneath levels of awareness. The control of vital functions that support survival and enable the organism to cope with stressors (Wittling and Schweiger 1993), the storage of early attachment experiences and internal working models that encode strategies of affect regulation and guide the individual in his interaction with others (Schore 1994), the processing of socioemotional information that is meaningful to the individual (Schore 1998), the ability to empathize with the emotional states of other human beings (Voeller 1986, Schore 1996) . . . the cerebral representation of one's own past and the activation of autobiographical memory (Fink et al., 1996), the establishment of a 'personally relevant universe' (Van Lancker 1991), and the capacity to self-reflect and 'mentally travel through time' (Wheeler et al., 1997). These basic coping mechanisms reflect the right mind's essential role in primary process cognition and affective and motivational phenomena. It is undoubtedly true that adaptive internal and external functioning involves the activation of both left and right brain processes. Freud felt that centrality of unconscious processes in everyday pointed to the fact that the right brain is 'dominant' in humans, and that the most fundamental problems of human existence cannot be understood without addressing this primordial realm" (Schore 2004).

One recognizes in the previous paragraph the qualities that are part of psychodrama, along with why it is a method that integrates right and left brain functioning. Simply put, it accesses right brain functioning and the left brain makes conscious sense out of the material that emerges. Through role play, one can recreate one's "personally relevant universe," tap into "early attachment experiences and internal working models that encode strategies of affect regulation and guide the individual in his actions toward others" and concretize "socioemotional information that is meaningful to the individual" and train people to "empathize with the emotional states of other human beings" and expand the client's ability to "self-reflect" and "mentally travel through time."

THE FULLY ARTICULATED SELF

Recent studies reveal that our neural patterning is set up through myriad tiny interactions. The child, in conjunction with his or her primary caretakers, lays down a psychological and emotional template that gets built on throughout his or her life. This seems to be a phenomenon that continues to occur throughout life but is especially pronounced in childhood when the child's brain and body are in a rapid state of development. Each tiny interaction between child and caretaker affects the child's neural wiring, which is also part of the limbic system. Nature and nurture are exquisitely intertwined within the development of the growing child. And this seemingly personal imprint is, in part at least, relational. Accordingly, our limbic system is the part of our body/brain that has primary jurisdiction over our emotional selves. Altering deep emotional patterns is slow and painstaking work. Limbic bonds imprint themselves onto our emotional systems. The limbic system "sets the mind's emotional tone, filters external events through internal states (creates emotional coloring), tags events as internally important, stores highly charged emotional memories, modulates motivation, controls appetite and sleep cycles, promotes bonding and directly processes the sense of smell and modulates libido" (Amen 1998). Childhood imprints lay down a foundation for how we process our emotions that we work from throughout our lives. Our neural networks are not easily altered, for "early emotional experiences knit long-lasting patterns into the very fabric of the brain's neural networks, changing that matrix calls for a different kind of medicine all together" (Lewis 2002). Our emotional life is therefore physical; it imprints itself on our bodies and it is changed through therapeutic and relational experiences. (I'll discuss this further in our chapter on group psychotherapy).

We learn through all of our senses, and the quality of our sensory integration affects our ability to process life's experiences in a coherent, emotionally intelligent manner. The more senses that are involved in learning, the more the brain records and remembers. In the case of trauma, the more senses involved at the moment the trauma occurred, the greater the risk for developing post-traumatic stress disorder (PTSD) symptoms. For example, the first responder at Ground Zero on September 11, 2001, is more likely to develop PTSD symptoms than the person who watched the events unfold on television because more senses were involved (Golden 2002).

Traumatic experiences from childhood, within the home, involve many senses and are powerfully recorded on the brain/body. They also occur at the hands of caretakers who, in relation to children, have the power in the relationship. A pain-filled relationship where there is a power imbalance coupled with reduced access to support from the outside world can set up a traumatic bond. These are the sorts of bonds that tend to recreate themselves throughout life if they remain unexamined. Psychodrama allows for a reversal of that power imbalance by placing the protagonist at the center of her own experience, in charge of the material to be explored. She operates as a sort of coproducer in her own drama and engages in the psychodramatic moment with all of her senses. This allows her to put the pieces of her world together in a more efficient manner, as many of those pieces are not only encapsulated in word but also in body, action and senses.

Clients who have been traumatized, who have spent too much time on high alert in a fight/flight mode, have likely experienced some deregulation of their limbic system, which governs moods. For example, they may be physically tight and tense, depressive, anxious, moody, or impulsive. Psychodrama, sociometry and group psychotherapy allow clients to slowly create new neural imprints, to repattern their limbic system. Traumatized people may view everyday life in black and white terms. They may cycle back and forth between intense feeling states that overwhelm them and a sort of emotional and psychological numbness. As a result, their inner world comes to mirror this pattern, and it gets projected onto their experience of life. Therapy provides a slow remodulation and, over time, can allow them to renter their bodies and their lives. Their hyperreactivity can slowly calm down and eventually reach a less volatile level.

Psychodrama allows for a level of sensory, intellectual, emotional and behavioral integration that is the foundation of its unusual therapeutic efficacy and healing power. It incorporates all of the senses along with language, concrete behavior and affect. It provides for an integration of both left and right brain.

ROLES PEOPLE PLAY

The role, according to J. L. Moreno, "is the tangible form the self takes," the concrete expression of the living, breathing inner world. By studying the role, we have a way of studying the self, and by working with the role, we have a way of working with the self. Man, according to Moreno, is fundamentally a roleplayer. "The function of the role is to enter the unconscious from the social world and bring shape and order into it." Through working with the roles that a person plays in his or her life, both on the healing stage of psychodrama and in the client's actual life, we have a way to enter a person at a fundamental level and reshape the unconscious. This is, in part, why working through roles goes so deep, because it enters the unconscious and accesses the thinking, feeling and behavior that have developed alongside the role since its beginnings. Psychodrama concretizes, explores, reviews and revises the person *in vivo*, in all his complexity and power. It strengthens and empowers the self.

One of psychodrama's fundamental tasks, according to Zerka Moreno "is to put the client in touch with their own internal healer." She describes that "we all must touch the autonomous healing center of our clients no matter which particular approach we use" (Blatner 1987). As part of the psychodramatic method the protagonist is encouraged to make and remake life choices and expand his or her role repertoire by adding new roles, either within the self or in relation to other people, while reducing others. This can facilitate the learning and mastery of new coping skills (role training) and provide a corrective, socially supportive network or a reworking of object relations through surrogates (role repair). All people have a variety of roles that they constantly play. The process of repairing some roles, adding new ones and allowing others to move from the foreground to the background is part of how psychodrama uses role-play to heal. Protagonists can learn self-directed problem-solving skills using their own and their auxiliaries' resources to help solve issues and experience the self-esteem related to task completion. We are all people living within a context, and all of our problems cannot be adequately addressed by looking only at the inner person. We need a method that looks at the social atom of a person, or a concrete representation of the nucleus of the client's relational world. Through sociometry we address the *inter*personal aspect of healing as we work to bring a client's social atom into balance and harmony (social atom repair).

SPONTANEITY AND CREATIVITY

Moreno felt that man was fundamentally a creator, that our lives suffer when we lose our ability to be creative, spontaneous and in the moment. When we are ruled by fixed images, or *cultural conserves* rather than the experience of living in the here and now, we lose access to our personal sense of empowerment. Moreno believed, as do certain Eastern philosophies, in the sacredness of the present moment. "The greatest challenge in life is to be present, in the here and now, and to act" (Hale 1981). The science of action, both psychodrama and sociometry, "is concerned with the preparation for action (warm-up), barriers to action (resistance), inability to be in the moment and therapeutic methods designed to assist the creative process in life." The task of action is to explore those life events and situations in which a person has learned attitudes and behaviors preventing spontaneity and creativity.

Spontaneity and creativity are twin principles of psychodrama. Psychodrama places the protagonist at the center of his own drama. This empowers him to both show and tell his own story, to restore his position as the creator. In embracing the concepts of spontaneity and creativity, and in understanding and stepping into the role of "the creator," Moreno's concepts become important cornerstone ideas on which to build a life and a world.

We are steeped in the scientific, which is one of our great strengths as a society and helps fuel our curiosity and enhance and inform our relationship with life, the world and ourselves. But we need to be more than objective witnesses in life. We need to engage in the spontaneous process of living. We cannot "Google" our way into self-knowledge; we need a method that will allow us to work from the inside out and the outside in. As we reach, through role exploration, into deeper layers of self, we expand into a new universe—the universe of self. And we find, to our surprise, that it is in connecting with the self that we connect with others, and in connecting with both we delve into our spiritual natures and recognize the pulse of life vibrating within and around us. We see what's already there with new and deepened vision.

Psychodrama believes that "joy, creativity and laughter are vital to the human experience and as such are to be part of psychotherapy" (Siroka and Gershoni 2004).

THE WARMING-UP PROCESS

Moreno felt that what was learned in action must also be unlearned in action, that in action we can do, undo and redo, thus freeing ourselves from blocks and barriers that keep us from being present in the here and now, that block our spontaneity.

Each of us has a warm-up to the various activities of our day, a warm-up to going to work or school, to doing written work, to returning home, to going out with friends and so on. The warm-up is what moves us toward action. Some warm-ups can lead toward positive, nourishing action, while other warm-ups might get us in trouble or cause us to go down a less-than-helpful road. "The science of action begins with the crucial concern of the warming-up process. This phase begins in the here and now and involves externalizing the encounter one has with him/herself, and the unspoken dialogue one has with another." (Hale 1986)

The body, too, has a warm-up. How many times I have listened to clients talk about being in a difficult moment, perhaps at work or home with a spouse or child, when their bodies became flooded with stress hormones, their hands began to sweat, their hearts pound, and soon they were in the middle of intense actions, explosions or withdrawals that seemed to come out of nowhere. But they don't come out of nowhere. Through role-play, we can get in back of the moment, so to speak, and examine the situations that set up the complex to begin with through action. Once we concretize those beginnings on stage, once we go to the *status nascendi,* or the situation from which the conflict took root and grew, we can reflect on behavior in its concrete form. From this we can extract meaning and insight.

2

The Triadic System:
Psychodrama, Sociometry and
Group Psychotherapy

Drama is a transliteration of the Greek Θράμα which means action, or a thing done. Psychodrama is a transliteration of a thing done to and with the psyche, the psyche in action. Psychodrama can be defined, therefore, as the science which explores the "truth" by dramatic methods.

—J. L. Moreno
1964 *Psychodrama*, Volume 1

J L. Moreno believed that full healing involved the combined approach of psychodrama, sociometry and group psychotherapy. He referred to this as his triadic system, and he is considered to be the creator of all three.

If psychodrama explores the inner world of the person, sociometry explores the social world of the person. Psychodrama is intrapersonal, and sociometry is interpersonal. The two approaches marry in the context of group therapy to investigate not only the person but also the person within the system in which they operate, as represented by what we call, in psychodrama and sociometry, a person's "social atom" (see page 106).

Moreno writes in reflection on his early attempts at group psychotherapy, "The merely analytic and verbal method of group psychotherapy very soon led to difficulties. As long as group psychotherapy was practiced only *in situ*, that is, within the family, the factory, etc., where life is lived, in all dimensions of the present, in action, in thought and speech, as monologue, dialogue, or drama, the psychomotor element of the organism and the creative meaning of the encounter remained unconscious and uninvestigated. When, however, the moment came to move from a natural to a synthetic place—for instance, from the family to the clinic—it was necessary to restructure life in all its dimensions in order to carry out therapy in the actual meaning of the word. All relationships which occur in everyday life had, therefore, to be constructed anew; we had to have a space in which the life of the family could be lived in the same fashion as it occurred in reality as well as symbolically. The bedroom, the kitchen, the garden, the *dramatis personae* of the family—father, mother, child—the discussions, conflicts, and tensions between them just as they occur in everyday life, all that which is taken for granted and remains unconscious had to be reconstructed but reduced to the truly symbolic elements. What before appeared as problematic and unfortunate became an asset. Group psychotherapy was forced to enter into all dimensions of existence in a depth and breadth which were unknown to the verbally oriented psychotherapist. Group psychotherapy turned into action psychotherapy and psychodrama."

THE FIVE MAIN ELEMENTS OF A PSYCHODRAMA

The five main elements of a psychodrama are the *stage*, the *protagonist*, the *director* (the therapist), the *auxiliary ego* or egos, and the *audience* (the group). Here we take a closer look at each of these elements.

The Stage

Psychodrama incorporates space into the therapeutic process. The stage is offered as a concrete situation within which a protagonist's story can be brought to life. Life happens *in situ* (in place or situation), and psychodrama allows resolution to occur through simulated role-play that mirrors real life. The hunger to act is as old as humanity, to demonstrate who we are in some dramatic form. While writers get to "live twice," once through living and once through writing about life, so protagonists also live twice—once through living and once through distilling and demonstrating the context of a situation in the form of a model scene deconstructing the depth and meaning as it relates uniquely to them. Alvin Toffler, in his landmark book, *Future Shock,* recommended that every home of the future should have a psychodramatic stage on which to heal the daily wounds that are a natural part of the "slings and arrows" that our "flesh is heir to."

Moreno said, "The stage is enough." The stage is any space that has been designated as a working space. To give someone the stage is to give her the opportunity to meet herself, to take a journey inward with the support of the director, auxiliary egos and audience. It is to provide a place or a platform where her story can be told, shown and witnessed by others.

The Protagonist

The protagonist is the person whose story is being enacted or told, the person who, *de facto,* represents the central concern, or emerging themes in the group. Protagonists work with the director in identifying and warming up to their own scene or story and concretizing it on the stage. Their willingness to fully engage with the auxiliaries in their own drama, and to move with the action and the director, will influence where and how deep the work will go for all participants. Protagonists are responsible for staying true to their own stories and engaging in the action as honestly as possible.

The role of the protagonist is to delve into his or her internal world with the intention of resolving inner conflicts. She has the responsibility to engage in her own healing process and the opportunity to share her story with support, to have it witnessed and become aware of the emotions and thought processes and behaviors that are attached to it. It is the protagonist who assigns group members to play each role in her drama. This choosing process is part of her warm-up to the material being explored. It may take time. She may even, after making a choice, wish to change it for someone who feels closer to the role, and this can occur at any point throughout the process.

Another part of the protagonist's warm-up is scene setting, either through the use of props or by describing the scene to therapist and group.

Due, at least in part, to psychodrama's full sensory involvement, protagonists often feel "a weight being lifted"; emotions that have been held in the musculature release; the body as well as the eyes get a chance to cry. It is not unheard of for protagonists to have an outburst of anger, a high-pitched vocal moment of rage followed by a river of tears as the body releases long-held emotion. It is not expulsion for expulsion's sake, which would be no more healing than acting-out behavior; it is a release in the service of linking and understanding. Often they report a tremendous release and sense of overall calm as they come into a very receptive state for taking in support and caring from others through reformed auxiliary work, group sharing or both. All of this slowly lays the groundwork for new neural patterning.

The Director

The director of a psychodrama is the professional therapist who leads the warm-up, action and sharing. He also facilitates the choice-making process of the protagonist, the decisions involving what material will be examined psychodramatically and how that enactment will take shape in time and space.

The role of director is to aid the protagonist in actualizing his or her own story so that it can be reconstructed, shared and examined in concrete form. The protagonist is allowed to lead the way in choosing what material to explore, with the director empowering the protagonist to take ownership of his or her own healing process. The job of the director is to follow the lead of the protagonist in the production of the protagonist's surplus reality, always allowing the protagonist to define that reality as he sees it and being willing to go where the protagonist feels internally led. The particular associative process that represents the unique internal journey of the protagonist, along with the sense and meaning he has made of the events of his life, is what will most likely yield the most useful insights and "ahas" for the protagonist.

One of the safeguards against retraumatizing clients is to leave the reins in their hands; they have the choice of when to stop and when to go. The goal isn't to unearth each and every detail or to reexperience all feelings, particularly when a protagonist feels forced to constantly go over what a well-meaning therapist feels will be useful for him to recollect. It seems to be more useful to follow the associative path of the protagonist as it unwinds through the labyrinths of his mind and heart, to tease out the way in which the events of his life affected *him*. What meaning did he make out of relationships and circumstances that he is still living by today, and what core beliefs about the self does he carry that affect how he sees and operates within his world?

The Auxiliary Ego

The role of the auxiliary ego is to represent the people in the protagonist's life or other aspects of the protagonist's inner world as accurately as possible, using information shared by the protagonist as well as her own experience of what thinking, feeling and behavior appear to be a part of the role. This allows the protagonist to view her own reality as it is stored within her, whether it be distorted, illusionary or grounded in reality, and to identify the manner in which she experienced her own relationships and the meaning she made out of the nature of those connections. "The auxiliary ego brings the protagonist into the situation, interprets for the absentee figure . . . auxiliaries work on two levels: the role they take and the experience they bring to it. There are regional or cultural differences regarding appropriate behavior of a "father, mother, child, etc." (Z. Moreno 1986–87)

In psychodrama we explore the protagonist's subjective reality and offer the opportunity to deal with the real rather than the imagined. Reality is brought to life through the use of auxiliary egos or improvisational actors chosen by the protagonist to represent particular people in her life. These auxiliaries have, according to Zerka Moreno, five functions: (1) to represent the role required by the protagonist, (2) to approximate the protagonist's perception of the person being portrayed, (3) to find out what is really going on within the interaction, (4) to reverse roles and understand the inner world of the protagonist, and (5) to provide contact with real people rather than imagined people, thereby enabling the protagonist to begin making a connection that is real.

Auxiliary ego work is also a part of spontaneity training. In a split second, auxiliaries are asked to come up with an adequate response to the situation emerging around the protagonist, to put their own needs aside so they can work in service of the needs of the protagonist while simultaneously drawing on their own histories, learning and creativity in order to best approximate the role as it was originally experienced by the protagonist.

Roles that lie dormant within the self system of the auxiliary may reemerge in the psychodramatic moment to be played out through the auxiliary role which, as long as it is tailored to the needs of the protagonist that is, as long as they are playing out the protagonist's version and not their own, can be healing for all involved. The auxiliary who had a critical father, for example, stands for a moment in the shoes of the protagonist's critical father, both playing out the role at a safe distance from their own past experience and viewing the role from within the position of the self, gaining insight as to the motivations, needs and drives that are a part of that role. "Feel free to remove the auxiliary if s/he gets in the way of the action. The auxiliary is a helper, so keep them helpful" (Z. Moreno 1986–87).

Reformed Auxiliary Ego

Once the protagonist psychodramatically works through her issues sufficiently for this session, offering a corrective experience in the form of a reformed auxiliary ego can sometimes be useful. Until this point the protagonist may have used the auxiliary ego to live out the aspects of the situation that have led to problems in their own life. Next, the auxiliary ego can be given back to the protagonist in a reformed sense; that is, as she "wishes it had been." Here, too, the protagonist lets us know how she would like to experience the auxiliary. She may also reverse roles and become the auxiliary, giving herself the experience she longed for.

Paradoxically, finally receiving what has long been wished for can be very anxiety-provoking or even painful. The reformed auxiliary ego is a useful model for the protagonist to take into life so that she can begin to know what it feels like to have what she wants and learn to accept it in small doses within a safe structure. It may also be useful for the protagonist to interact with the reformed auxiliary as a form of role training. Psychodrama allows for the direct involvement of what Moreno refers to as the "therapeutic actor." He explains, "On portraying the role it is expected that the ego will identify himself privately with the role to the best of his ability, not only to act and pretend but to 'be' it. The hypothesis here is that what certain patients need, more than anything else, is to enter into contact with people who apparently have a profound and warm feeling for him.

For instance, if it happens that he, as a child, never had a real father, in a therapeutic situation the one who takes the part of the father should create in the patient the impression that here is a man who acts as he would like to have had his father act; that here is a woman, especially if he never had a mother when he was young, who acts and is like what he wishes his mother to have been, etc. The warmer, more intimate and genuine the contact is, the greater are the advantages, which the patient can derive from the psychodramatic episode. The all-out involvement of the auxiliary ego is indicated for the patient who has been frustrated by the absence of such maternal, paternal, or other constructive and socializing figures in his lifetime.

The Audience (The Group)

The group is the therapeutic context and the safe container through which healing occurs in all roles: protagonist, auxiliary ego and audience (witness) or group member. Out of the group emerge protagonists who represent their own and other group members' inner dramas. Deep healing work can take place within the audience role. Through the process of identification, those watching an enactment may experience feelings as powerful as those of the protagonist. Good group members learn to use those portions of the enactment with which they identify to concretize their own internal dramas so related feelings can become conscious and available to them. Sometimes the heat of the psychodramatic stage is too much for a client, while the audience role offers access to the material being explored from a "safe distance." The opportunity for profound healing exists through this identification. Group members may feel themselves alternately pulled, repelled, moved or shut down as the scenes unravel before them in the psychodramatic moment. They can cultivate the ability to deconstruct the scene *as it relates to them*. Because a scene is occurring in a safe clinical situation, the audience members can afford the luxury, so to speak, of observing their own reactions to it. For instance, why do they identify so strongly here, shut down there, feel their stomachs tighten and their hearts race, wish to cry at still another point, or feel liberated at some other juncture?

It is important that audience members have plenty of time to share what emerged for them during the enactment in order to deconstruct the scene as it relates to their own lives through sharing with the protagonist in the presence of one another. Sharing, in the psychodramatic form, is *not* feedback. It is sharing what emerged in the witness role from one's own self and life. It is heart-to-heart and mind-to-mind identification. This sharing from such a deep place gives the group members the opportunity to understand themselves with greater awareness and depth and allows them to connect with another person (the protagonist) at that level—to share a moment of truth, so to speak, and create an authentic connection. When the audience members share what came up for them with the protagonist, it also reduces the isolation of the protagonist, reconnects the protagonist to the group through support and identification, and allows new connections to be made.

The notion that dramatic representation of tragedy produces a catharsis of pity and fear goes back to the fourth century B.C., to Aristotle's *Poetics*. The plays focused on a few deep concerns and complexes central to all people. Through identification with the action people could experience a spectator catharsis, effecting a purge of their own painful feelings and deepening their understanding of a life dynamic or situation.

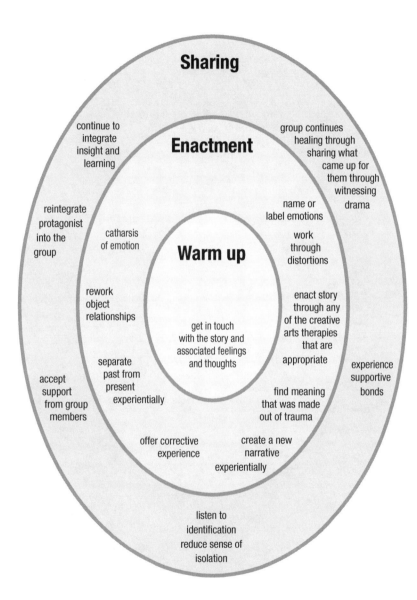

3 The Techniques of the Classical Psychodramatic Enactment

The psychoanalytic interview in its orthodox form, tried to be pure and objective, by reducing the involvement with the analyst to a minimum. In the psychodramatic situation, a maximum of involvement with other subjects and things is not only possible but provoked. . . . All degrees of involvement take place from a minimum to a maximum. The patient is enabled, not only to meet parts of himself, but other persons who are part of his mental conflicts. These persons may be real or illusions.

—J. L. Moreno
Psychodrama, Volume 1

THE STAGES OF PSYCHODRAMA

Moreno delineated three principal stages of a psychodrama: warm-up, enactment and sharing. Here we examine them further.

Warm-Up

The warm-up describes the internal and external processes that both the protagonist and the group go through to ready themselves for actual role-play. The protagonist's warm-up may have begun anywhere: in a previous group, on the way to therapy, in the hallway while encountering various group members or in the privacy of his own imagination. The warm-up allows the work to focus and flow smoothly. It can consist of a structured exercise, such as a locogram, spectrogram or social atom to name just a few, a guided imagery, a check-in, or a spontaneous occurrence in the group.

Scene-setting, through descriptive words or even props, can also function as a warm-up as the protagonist goes through the motions and narrates what he is doing. As long as it is engaging the protagonist in the psychodramatic moment, scene-setting can take as much time as needed or desired. Setting a scene can feel very transporting to a protagonist as he begins to recollect the details of something he wishes to explore. Grounding what has lived in the imagination can feel evocative and stimulate memories that need to be recognized and respected by the director and group members.

The sociometric task of the warm-up phase is to clarify the structure of the group through observation and exploration of its role relationships. The group may or may not have a sociometric center or be capable of choosing one member to represent a drama with which most group members can identify. Sometimes groups will easily choose a protagonist and sometimes they will not. The "Sociometric test" or "Sociometric choosing" (see page 106 in "Sociometry") can provide a method to selecting a protagonist. Groups are not always warmed up to watching one drama. Vignettes, monodramas, dramas with only one role-player, e.g., the empty chair, or autodramas, dramas without a director, can provide variety in the format of group work. I also find it important to reserve some groups for purely psychodynamic work so group members learn to confront and deal with each other directly.

On a scale of one to ten, the degree to which a protagonist is sufficiently warmed up to enter psychodramatic work is somewhere between four and seven. The protagonist who is not sufficiently warmed up may drag the work out by not engaging on an emotional level, while the protagonist who is all action with no engagement of thought may be reenacting or reinforcing that type of behavior. In each case, there may be an inability to stay in the moment with the emotions and thoughts that are coming up.

For example, Jay has had a hard time warming up to doing the work with his mother that he so needs and wishes to do. He felt so deeply traumatized by the combination of both his mother's and father's alcoholism and all of their abusive behavior of each other, himself and his sister, that he learned as a child, to go numb, to feel as little as possible. Actually confronting his family on the stage, even though only through surrogates, makes him go numb all over again. He shuts down his feelings and even his mind goes numb, just as he did in childhood. It's easier for Jay to feel from the audience role, to identify with other people's dramas then deconstruct their particular meaning as it relates to him during the sharing phase. Jay's mere participation in the group, as a group member and role-player in other people's dramas, affords him a smoother entry into his inner world than direct confrontation of his own history. This will likely change over time as he becomes more able to tolerate the strength of his own emotions, but witnessing and identifying allows him space to grow into that while still doing profound healing work.

Martina, a forty-two-year-old woman from Russia, illustrates the other extreme. She is always warmed up, always wanting to dominate the group or the stage with her own dramas. Frequently she feels there is not enough time or space for her to get as much as she wants or feels she needs. She has a terrible time just sitting and experiencing the intensity of her inner world without acting it out in some way or another.

Neither case here illustrates emotional modulation. One extreme reads as emotionless while the other reads as intensely emotional. What both extremes have in common is that neither represents an ability to stay present and experience emotion as it arises within the self. Neither extreme allows for the inner witness to observe and access the emotions that are emerging within the self. One of the tasks of the director is to meet the protagonist where she is and to gradually bring her toward a more modulated position from either direction or allow her to internalize the skill of modulation from being around those who can model it. (See chapter 13.)

Enactment

The action or enactment phase is one of concretization. Through role-play, the protagonist brings aspects of his inner or outer life to the psychodramatic stage to be explored. Concretizing and role-playing allows the protagonist to reveal his inner and outer worlds through action, to externalize hunger for action, to concretize open tensions. This hunger for action that humans feel is at the core of psychodrama. Allowing action to be lived out on a psychodramatic, clinical stage, where his deep need to physicalize his emotional and psychological world can be met before he is asked to reflect upon it, recognizes this need.

Essentially, the enactment phase is one in which the protagonist's object relational world is concretized. Her transferences and projections will reveal themselves on the stage where they can be explored through the devices built into the method, such as doubling, role reversing, interviewing and soliloquizing. Psychodrama's magic exists in these opportunities to stretch the boundaries of everyday life and explore not only reality but surplus reality. It is a journey through the inner space that influences so much of who we are and what we do. Experiencing the self in all of its complexity, giving voice to the rumblings, wishes and concerns of the inner person, answering questions in a way that reveals what is living inside the protagonist, standing in the shoes of others, and experiencing them and staring back at the self through their eyes make this method unique among all others. This is where the psychodramatic stage becomes a path into another world, where it allows a protagonist to time-travel out of the narrow dimensions of her everyday life. It is a moment carved out of time that allows one to live twice and to use that second layer of life to point the way toward another chance at living, an "open sesame" into and out of another world that allows us to partner in our seeing of the self. The sense of identity consolidation can be compared with coming to your home country after a voyage away from it and seeing it as if for the first time, with new perspective and understanding. It takes on a different meaning.

The enactment need not be showy or even especially intense to be very effective. It is the integrative experience that offers long-term shifts in thinking, feeling and behavior as a result of experiencing the parts of self that have been warded off or banished from consciousness and reincorporating them with new insight and understanding. Jay experiences the parts of himself that he has shut down and sees them through new, more mature eyes with the help of others who can assist him in putting the pieces together. Martina experiences her own intensity in the context of a modulated group of people. The group, because they are not so wrought up, act as external modulators, bringing Martina into an awareness of where she is out of balance. As Martina slowly structures and moves through a psychodrama, setting the scene, choosing auxiliaries, role-playing and role reversing, and listening to doubling, she learns the skills of modulation. If she needs to experience a strong catharsis of emotions as part of the drama, it should not be all of the drama, but in service of integrating the split-off affect that may be fueling the overintensity.

Sharing

The importance of the sharing phase should not be underestimated. This is when the group has the opportunity to continue its healing by genuinely sharing how its members experienced the drama from their own chairs, from their own lives. By identifying with the protagonist or reflecting on which parts of the drama warmed them up, shut them down, brought them to tears, or made them wish to flee or stand and fight, the group members can use the protagonist's enactment as a tunnel into their own inner worlds, a mirror into their own selves. Those who played roles should be encouraged to de-role. They can do this by saying, "I'm Cathy, not your mother, but playing your mother I felt . . ." and they can share their experiences of that role and also what playing the role brought up for them from their own lives. Some role-players also like to "brush off the role" physically so they can concretize letting it go. De-roling should always be a part of the sharing process so that transferences from someone playing a role don't carry over in the mind of the protagonist, and so there is not a "role hangover" for an auxiliary who may have played a difficult role.

The sharing phase also allows the protagonist to integrate his own intense feelings that often follow a psychodrama and to reintegrate himself into the group. During an enactment, protagonists often feel "out on a limb," as if they are saying and showing things that no one else can understand. The discovery that group members may have been riveted to the action, watching their own lives flash across their minds, can be very healing to the protagonist. This helps break the powerful and historical feelings of isolation that people often carry. It can help people who have felt that no one can understand or identify with them accept support from others. This will, over time, build a sense of trust and the ability to reach out to others. Emotional literacy builds as clients learn to describe their inner worlds in words. Seeing the enactment allows concrete thinkers, or those frozen at particular stages of development, either through addiction or trauma-arresting development, to see emotion or interpersonal dynamics in their concrete form and then identify and name them.

For both Jay and Martina, sharing will help them reconnect with the group. Having experienced the parts of themselves that they normally banish out of consciousness, or having experienced themselves in new and different ways, they will feel somewhat disequilibrated. Sharing will help them to feel seen, understood and held by the group. It will allow them to come slowly back to earth, back into the here and now. And it will allow them to ground their learning and feel the support and caring of others.

During both the sharing and enactment phases, the past and present are gradually separated as the present-day transferences and projections reveal themselves to have many of their origins in the past (see Spiraling, this chapter). When Jay can ask Betty to play his mother, he can come to realize that the somewhat negative feelings he has harbored toward her have as much to do with the unresolved feelings he has toward his mother as his present-day reaction to Betty, who is the same age and reminds him somewhat of his mother. When Martina can ask Martin to play her father, she can come to identify that her feelings of wanting him to pay more attention to her, and being constantly disturbed that he doesn't, have to do with her historical wish that her father give her more love.

All three stages, warm-up, enactment and sharing, are important not only to give full venue to personal and group issues, but also in order to keep the work safe, grounded and anchored.

SELECTING A PROTAGONIST

The four most common ways in which protagonists can be selected are: by the group (sociometric selection), by the director, by self-announcing a wish or need to work, or by a system in which the client is receiving treatment, such as a hospital, clinic or treatment facility.

Sociometric Selection: Selection by the Group

Groups have their own preferences as to who they might like to see work and what work they would like to have done in group. Sociometric selection allows the individual preferences within the group to be expressed so that the individuals within the group rather than, for example, the director, can choose the protagonist. In sociometric selection, the entire group selects the protagonist. After the group is warmed up, the director invites the group members wishing to work to identify themselves. The director might say, "Give us a couple of sentences on what you would like to explore or the scene you have in mind." Afterwards, the director can say to the group at large, "Walk up and place your hand on the shoulder of the person whose work pulls or draws you." Essentially, this is a choice through identification. Group members choose the person whose drama resonates for them in some way. At times, groups will also choose a group member they wish to see work in order to know them more fully or one who seems in a state of high need, but identification is the most driving force. In all cases, group selection allows the group to cast their own vote, so to speak, and take ownership of the direction in which the work is going.

Sociometric selection allows the group to go through a warm-up process toward the work being explored both individually and as a group. The warm-up contributes to the depth of the work, as does the level of sociometric identification with the particular work being explored. The more identification with a particular drama, the more that drama represents the central concern of the group. It can take courage to put one's self forward for work. This is an important part of the protagonist's warm-up, to declare his wish and need to work, to take the stage. If possible, it may be useful to check in with those not selected to see how they're doing and how they feel after putting themselves forward but not being selected to work. Another possibility, if time permits, is to allow a few moments for those choosing the people who put themselves forward to share with them why they chose them before moving into work with the most highly selected protagonist. Issues around being chosen and not chosen often surface during this selection process.

Note that some people are too shy or blocked to put themselves forward, and some groups develop cliques that repeatedly choose each other and collude in leaving others out. If these situations arise, they can be called to attention by the group leader or explored verbally by any member of the group. This may be explored through a spectrogram (use spectrogram page 117). Criterion questions like "How warmed up are you to work?" or "How much of a chance do you feel you have at being selected?" can be helpful in exploring the issue. The director can also exert her authority by simply asking those who work less if they would like to work (see Director Selection, this chapter). However, it is important for group members, at least eventually, to summon up the strength to put themselves forward, and the director should find ways to support the group members doing just that.

Sociometric selection isn't always the best alternative. Over the years, I've found that sociometric selection can be overwhelming for groups who will not be seeing each other again, such as at conferences or public workshops. Much sensitivity needs to be exercised in protagonist selection so that the person who works has the ego strength to open up in this sort of situation. People entering treatment are oftentimes very vulnerable. Sociometric selection can allow the stronger in the group to dominate the process. In an ongoing group this is grist for the mill and useful to the group. In a treatment setting, it needs to be thought through in terms of treatment goals, length of treatment and the specific needs of the treatment population.

Another cautionary note is that if someone puts himself forward and becomes highly warmed up, not being chosen may feel like being thwarted in their intention or act hunger. He may be warmed up for action but unable to act. This is something to weigh and be aware of when deciding where to use sociometric selection.

Director Selection

In this method the director may facilitate a selection by asking a group member if she would like to work or be willing to give it a try. The advantages of this method of selection are twofold. One, the director can support exploration of particular issues that she feels are important to the growth of the group member, and two, the director can bring isolates (people who tend to isolate themselves in a group) forward and provide an arena in which they can self-disclose so people can come to know and identify with them. True self-disclosure tends to elevate a person's sociometric position or sociometric status within a group as more people can identify with her and have compassion or empathy for her.

The disadvantage of this method is that the director's selection may not represent a central concern of other group members, or the protagonist may shut down or not be present throughout the process, sabotaging the enactment. Pushing someone into work is not a good idea, in my experience, unless you have a very good reason for doing so. It is important to realize that for some people, particularly those new to psychodrama, simply sitting through other people's work is very stimulating, challenging and enlightening. The audience role is a powerful one and not to be underestimated. Witnessing the enactments of others and sharing what comes up may be more than enough for some, at least for a while. In addition, playing auxiliary roles can provide another way of adjusting to the process of psychodrama.

Self-Selection

In self-selection, group members announce their own desire to work. Someone may say they feel very warmed up and in need of working, or they feel they haven't worked in a long time, or they feel they should be exploring a particular issue for their own growth. This is very much in line with psychodrama's philosophy of fostering autonomy and allowing clients to be in charge of the material they wish to explore.

The advantage of this method is that it allows someone who wishes to or feels warmed up to work the freedom to declare that, and the person himself is taking responsibility for his request and the responsibilities to himself and the group that go along with it. The disadvantage is that the group members may not support the self-selected person during the enactment because his issues may not represent the central concern of the group or they may fear a dominant member using self-selection to take up too much space.

Systems/Institutional Selection

When a client is referred to psychodrama by the caregiving system or by an individual who deems it necessary, such as a supervisor or referring therapist in a treatment center, clinic or hospital situation, he may come with what is essentially a prescription or receive one during the course of treatment. For example, a therapist may ask the director, "Could you please help John work on his issues with his father? Or could you work with Susan around her quitting smoking?"

The advantage of this method is that it allows the client a safe space in which to experientially work through an important issue. The disadvantage is that any time work is prescribed there is the risk that it does not truly come from within the protagonist—that it does not arise from the inner depths and wisdom of his psyche. Prescribed work also runs the risk of retraumatizing if the protagonist feels pushed beyond his capacity. It also precludes selection by the group, which, depending on the cohesion of the group, may or may not feel identification and support.

SELECTING AUXILIARY EGOS

The protagonist, with the support of the director, always selects auxiliary egos to play roles in their drama. The director facilitates the choosing but the choices are made entirely by the protagonist, who uses her own tele, or unspoken sense of connection, to reach out toward her choice. Allowing the protagonist to drive this selection process enhances her autonomy and helps or allows her to take ownership of her own drama and the material being explored. Selecting auxiliaries is a significant part of the protagonist's warm-up to the role interactions. The protagonist may seem to go into the beginnings of a psychodramatic trance mode as she uses her tele to feel out who would be the right person to play a particular role for her. She may know immediately; she may need to feel her way slowly to her choices; she may even need to choose and rechoose as she slowly approaches the tele connection and gets closer to the choice that feels right to her. I recall one client who chose her father four or five times, each time shaking her head, and even shaking off a shiver as she said, "No, not him. I think him." As she was working with issues of sexual abuse and was very blocked about approaching the material, for obvious reasons, the choice-making process became her path in. By her fifth choice she said assuredly, "Yes, him. Definitely him." Later in the week the man she chose self-disclosed as a pedophile. She had made the right telic connection.

Though tele drives the choice-making process, a protagonist may have other reasons for making a particular choice. Protagonists may choose people they like and trust to play negative roles because they know they are capable of getting into the role or they trust them to play the role as they need it to be played. Sometimes a group member will not wish to take on a role, especially if there is significant negative transference associated with it by either side. As groups progress, however, members come to value role-playing as a way to explore and express the self and even recognize that they may get a lot out of playing a negative role just to experience what may be behind it or vent their own shadow sides. The person chosen is free to accept or reject the choice. If the person rejects the role, the protagonist moves on to another choice.

Choosing auxiliaries is a very sensitive moment in the drama, an important part of the protagonist's warm-up, and can be done in a variety of ways:

- The director may invite the protagonist to reverse roles and show us Mom, asking, "How is she standing? What's her attitude?" This provides a moment of role training for the group members and allows them to see and warm up to the role being selected. It is the most classical approach. If this approach is used, Zerka's advice is, "Don't call up the auxiliaries until you're actually ready to have them enter the scene. Present the roles involved in a scene first by having the protagonist role-reverse with others in the scene. But don't appoint who in the group will be the auxiliaries for each role until you're ready to actually start them in action" (Z. Moreno 1986–7).
- The director can say, "Look around the room and choose someone to play Dad, Brother, Mom, Partner, and so on," or the director may request that the protagonist provide a sentence or two describing Mom and then ask him to look around the room and invite someone to play her.
  In this case the auxiliary ego will hold the role by taking on the physical, emotional and intellectual attitude of the person he is playing and spontaneously follow the lead of the protagonist, picking up her signals as the scene unfolds.

"Remember that you as director are orchestrating a drama, so try to have the protagonist and auxiliaries face the group as if they were projecting to a group. At times you may want to back off and stand where the audience is so you can get their point of view. The auxiliary ego may play roles, apart from the ordinary parts of the protagonist's body, pets or inanimate objects. It's often an interesting technique to ask the protagonist what in the room is meaningful to him. A picture on the wall may have a lot to say. The auxiliary may also portray a value or an abstract concept" (Z. Moreno 1986–7).

PRESENT, PAST AND FUTURE SCENES

The past is the present, isn't it? It's the future, too. We all tried to lie out of that but life won't let us.

—Eugene O'Neill
Long Day's Journey into Night

Present-Day Scene

Present-day scenes are enactments of situations occurring in the current life of the protagonist. Playing out scenes from the present can bring current circumstances into clear focus. Examining situations in a sort of clinical slow motion can illuminate the dynamics within, so that new, informed and intelligent choices can be made if needed. Perplexing circumstances can be played and replayed in order to understand the best attitudes and choices for attaining more clarity and comfort. When group members take on the role of the double, in order to articulate what may be going unspoken, for example, the inner life of the protagonist can come to the fore. Through role reversal a new point of view may be entertained, and through the interview and the soliloquy, inner worlds can be brought from the background to the foreground.

Time Regression

Time regression is perhaps the most common type of psychodrama. It is used to explore any situation from the past. There is therapeutic advantage to reliving the past in a safe setting, and the time-regression technique allows a protagonist to do just that. Time regression is a process of making the *then and there* the *here and now*. We bring material that may have occurred in the past and reexperience it in the present moment. In the surplus reality of the mind, heart and spirit, the past lives and breathes. When something is painful we may banish it from consciousness, but its effects impel us if it remains in a state of open tension or what we might call unfinished business. Psychodrama allows this past to move from the background into the foreground for exploration in the here and now so it does not continue to insinuate itself into the present life of the protagonist without conscious awareness. It is important that the protagonist and all role-players speak in the present tense at all times. In this way the "as if" falls away and becomes the "as." Both Jay's scene with his mother and Martina's with her father would represent scenes that regress back into time. Martina asked for a corrective moment, a moment where she could ask for and receive the attention from her father that she so deeply yearns for. She had the choice of choosing a new auxiliary to play that father or asking it from Martin, who was already playing him. She asked for the moment from Martin, and took in, on a feeling level, the experience of being held, seen and wanted.

Future Projection

Future projection allows the protagonist to role-play a scene from the future that she may anticipate either with excitement or dread. The scene is structured as normal and the protagonist is able to walk into a rehearsal for her own life and play it out in a variety of ways that may help her make better choices, reduce anxiety, or experience anticipated emotion in a safe manner. If the anticipated scene is loaded with intense emotion, this provides a clinical damage control, if you will, as the potentially harmful effects of a scene that could occur in the future are explored in the present. Another use of the future projection is to play out a scenario, such as quitting a job or separating from a partner, in order to "try it on for size." Sometimes clients are not fully aware of what taking an action might actually imply or feel like in reality. This technique can allow clients to open that window and peer through it in order to gain a better sense of its true reality. Martina wanted to do a future projection in which she chose a man who she thought she would like to be with. She played out a future scene, a lovely dinner scene, of being with the sort of man that she wishes would be with her someday.

Spiraling

Spiraling is a psychodramatic technique that can be used in conjunction with present-day enactments in order to link transference reactions and/or conflicts to their origins in the past. For example, a scene from the present in which the protagonist is experiencing pain or conflict might be put on the stage. As the scene is played out it becomes obvious that the problem is one that repeats itself—it is a reenactment. The director asks, "Where did this dynamic begin for you?" When the protagonist identifies a scene or model scene (Lachman 2002), one that represents the key emotional and psychological elements of a particular concern or conflict, the director helps the protagonist to "spiral back" to that scene from the past. After the regression scene is fully explored, the role-players can spiral back up to the present-day scene and replay it, having gained new insight as to the origins of problematic dynamics, transferences and projections and relieved some of the past pain that may have been projected onto the present. Spiraling can also go from the present to the future if the present-day conflict is caused by anticipated events, then back to the present.

TECHNIQUES AND DEVICES WITHIN THE PSYCHODRAMATIC ENACTMENT

Scene Setting

Scene setting speaks to memory being state dependent; that is, we recall more fully when confronted with the physical, psychological or emotional locus in which a scene initially occurred. Setting the scene, which is done following the protagonist's lead, allows the protagonist to enter the actual memory more fully. Part of protagonist's warm-up is setting the scene in whatever rich variety or lack and poverty feels right to the protagonist. It is part of the show-and-tell of psychodrama, the concretizing of the protagonist's reality. The protagonist should be allowed to set the scene as he or she wishes, elaborating on detail, moving things into just the right place, and even narrating the mentations, the thinking or reasoning as they go.

"At times it's possible not to bother spending any time (to speak of) setting up the physical elements of the scene. . . . i.e., where is the door, where is the seat . . . because the person is warmed up enough to enter the scene without all of that. At other times, it is possible to spend a great deal of time just setting up the scene, for the imaginal involvement is itself therapeutic. Indeed, it's an interesting warm-up to set up the room that you once lived in" (Z. Moreno 1986–7). Adam Blatner, M.D., TEP, at the Menninger Foundation in Topeka, Kansas, used a related technique of diagramming one's house like a map or diagramming one's neighborhood as a form of structured anamnesis.

There are some cautionary notes. Setting the scene for the exploration of traumatic material should be approached carefully. A traumatic scene needn't be set in order to explore traumatic material. Simply talking to those involved, including the self, can be as much as needs to happen. In making the scene real we are also using the mind's state-dependent tendencies to recollect. In the case of trauma, sudden recollection may not be useful or even desirable. It may be better just to chip slowly away at the ancillary issues, such as dispowerment, feelings of rage, hurt or helplessness, for example, surrounding the trauma.

I had a client, for example, whose parents had been through the Holocaust. One of the stories in his family was that his father, at eight years old, watched as his grandmother had her teeth knocked out by a German soldier who then shot her. After this, the boy and his six-year-old brother ran and hid, surviving on the lam for the next four years. During this client's first two and a half years with me, I did not once choose to revisit this scene. Without my knowing, in his search to know himself, he attended a daylong workshop for Holocaust survivors where the scene was reenacted, and he returned to group on Monday quite shattered. We worked very carefully to help him calm down and feel safe again.

Another example is Bob, a therapist in my training group with great recovery and the ego strength to do what he wished to do. We likewise approached his material gingerly. He set an elaborate scene, that of finding his mother stretched out on the kitchen floor looking dead after a beating by his stepfather. Much of the psychodrama was Bob's double who articulated the terror, shame and sadness that he couldn't articulate at the shocking moment of discovering his mother.

Quite in the opposite direction, I remember setting a very important scene in my own training, talking to my father on a sunny day. The scene was our balcony, a place of many happy memories. After I had placed the two chairs where they needed to go and put a table and more chairs at the other end, I had a very strong impulse to move my father's chair ever so slightly. My director, Zerka, encouraged me to "get it right" and *boom*—the scene began with that slight move of the chair. Suddenly the sun came streaming in on our little corner of the world and I took my accustomed perch on the arm of my father's big, red wood chair. As my legs psychodramatically dangled into his lap, words poured forth into the still, light morning, and I felt a part, once again, of a moment in time I thought I had lost forever. And with it I recaptured a sacred connection with that part of my father who was all I could have wished him to be: available, generous, attentive and sober. My beloved father, whom I missed terribly, was with me again on the psychodramatic stage. At this moment I reconnected with the part of myself that was my father: strong, courageous and full of wonder. I connected with the alive and brilliant man he was capable of being, along with one of the sustaining relationships of my life that allowed me to remain resilient even through his own degradation and demise from alcoholism. Had that slight movement of my chair been thwarted or not seen as important, had it not been understood as an act hunger, I might have lost my tenuous connection with that most precious moment of healing and reconnection.

"In exploring the scene with the protagonist, the director may, or the double may, walk in circles; clockwise for reviewing the future and counterclockwise for reviewing the past. Thus time is converted into a special metaphor which partakes of an archetypal sense of direction" (Z. Moreno 1986–7). Here Zerka is talking about what is sometimes referred to as a "walk and talk," or a walk that the director or double can take with the protagonist as the protagonist soliloquizes (see Soliloquy in this chapter) about what is going on inside of himself or describes the scene being entered.

The Double or "Doubling"

The double speaks the inner life of the protagonist, bringing the material that is lodged in the background toward the foreground. The double gives voice to the interior reality of the protagonist. The double should feel ego-syntonic, (in line with the protagonist's natural tendencies,) rather than an ego-dystonic, (discordant with protagonist's natural leanings) and type of voice, as if it is the protagonist's own words struggling to be said. The double helps to bring the protagonist to the threshold of his or her own experience. In her paper the "Double Situation" in psychodrama, Zerka Moreno refers to the double as "the invisible I."

She goes on to say that it is the double's job to "stir up the subject to reach deeper layers of expression by peeling off the outer, socially visible 'I' of the subject and by reaching for those experiences and imageries which a person would reveal in talking to herself, alone, in the privacy of her own room. . . . The more the subject warms up to the double, the more he loses his fear. . . . In psychodrama no moral values are placed on the double, he is neither the better nor worse part of the self; he is merely there, at times the better, at times the worse part. Nor is there in psychodrama any clear-cut division between the subject and the double. They are fuse and separate and fused again. . . . The chief purpose of the psychodramatic double is to stimulate the subject, to help and retrain, not persecute."

If the protagonist experiences the double as out of touch with her inner world, she should be allowed to correct or even ask the double to leave. When the director is the double, the director can encourage this by simply saying "Does that feel right?" or "Put this in your own words." A good double can be very effective in helping the protagonist to feel seen and understood, in acting as a therapeutic ally while confronting painful emotional material and in moving the protagonist's action to a deeper level by giving voice to that level. Protagonists may also double for themselves by taking a step backward into the "double position" and speaking what is not being spoken from their overt role.

Doubles are an optional part of an enactment. In my experience it works well to allow doubles to self-select when they feel warmed up to the protagonist who is playing themselves or in role reversal; at this point they can spontaneously stand behind the protagonist and speak "as the double" and then return to their chairs. This can happen many times and/or with multiple doubles. Returning to their chairs after doubling guards against doubles getting "glued" to the protagonist or falling into doing their own psychodrama instead of the protagonist's.

In the case of revisiting traumatic material, the doubles can play a very sustaining role. As the protagonist revisits scenes in which he may previously have felt helpless and powerless, in which he may have shut down or dissociated, the doubles can help him to stay "in his body." Through speaking what the protagonist dares not say, or perhaps even think, the double helps him to again face a painful situation with what feels like an inner ally who is alive and understands, who speaks the truth of his internal experience and supports him through his presence and understanding. This helps the protagonist to feel and integrate emotions that may have been split out of consciousness because, at the time, they were too overwhelming to entertain. It also helps the protagonist to create new, more mature, sense and meaning of the situation, to see it through two sets of eyes— the eyes of the child and the eyes of the adult, to realize his previous powerlessness and to reframe the dynamic. Perhaps he wasn't bad after all; perhaps he was just in the wrong place at the wrong time, living at the other end of a negative projection or a parent who was not, for whatever reason, up to the job. And having had the opportunity to reverse roles and stand in the shoes of the "other" he may have touched the inner person who lived underneath, also perhaps frail and lost, carrying pain from his own past that got projected into the present.

When a client feels frozen, unable to move either forward or back, one might say resistant, the double does one of two things. First, she can articulate the fears or anxieties she imagines the protagonist might be experiencing, thus bringing the protagonist closer to an awareness of what's going on inside and moving the protagonist along. She can also "double the resistance" by doubling for the part of the client that doesn't trust the situation, doesn't want to explore further, or who simply feels exploration might be compromising, futile, embarrassing or even stupid. Doubles can also double unspoken joy, love, need, empowerment or even laughter.

Role Reversal

Role reversal is what Zerka Moreno refers to as the *sine qua non* of psychodrama, or that without which there is no true psychodrama. Role reversal allows us to temporarily leave the self and experience the position of "the other." The son who is still himself must now warm up to how his mother may be feeling and perceiving him; the mother, now the son, goes through the same process. This concretized changing of roles allows the protagonist to view himself from the role of the other. It promotes both a different vision of the self and a greater understanding of the other. When one is actually able to stand in the shoes of another and see things from the other's perspective, a true role reversal has occurred. It is not exclusively empathy or understanding, though those are indeed the ports of entry. It is psychodramatically trading places, for a moment, with another person, stepping out of one's own skin and into another's, and seeing things through her eyes. We are limited to walking through life with only our set of eyes. A true role reversal allows us to see life through the eyes of the other, if only for a moment. Playing different roles, allowing a situation to be seen from a variety of perspectives, automatically shifts awareness, increases spontaneity and provides relief from our own roles. If a person is not able to role-reverse he may have a fragile self that is not intact enough to be able to leave its usual identifications. This is not typical, however; most people can role-reverse. The person who has trouble may need to have more time playing "themselves" to build a sense of self and ego strength. In addition, group therapy may be appropriate for this person, at this time.

Traumatic bonding is a phenomenon that can occur when there has been a power imbalance and when there was little or no access to other sources of support. Role reversal allows the protagonist to deconstruct that bond, to experience it from both sides and get underneath the situational elements that may have emotionally and psychologically glued the bond in place. This helps to illuminate core beliefs about the self that are being lived out in the present, that may have had their genesis in the past and to separate the past from the present.

Love and empathy, too, can be enhanced through this simple yet profound reversal of roles. Seeing how a marriage partner or your child views you and the world allows for deeper mutual understanding.

One can also be interviewed in the role of the other. If there has been a less-than-satisfactory individuation on the part of the child, standing in the shoes of the mother, for example, and perhaps being interviewed as the mother (or father), can help the protagonist walk into the role of the mother consciously, seeing what parts of himself that may have their locus not within him but elsewhere, and walk out of the role and back into his own more fully. It can help him to individuate and self-define, to see where he leaves off and she begins. The same can be done for sibling dramas and, in the case of couples, employee-employer relationships and so on.

Soliloquy

The soliloquy, or the "walk and talk," enables the protagonist to drop out of the scene for a moment and soliloquize about what is going on in her inner world. It is a chance for her to hear herself think, to remove herself from the heat or even the numbness or lack of emotion of the scene and tune into what is going on within herself without interruption. She may walk alongside the director or alone.

A soliloquy may also be used as the main part of a psychodrama. We remember Bob's scene. He had returned home from school to find his mother lying on the kitchen floor after she had been beaten senseless by his stepfather. Bob, we remember, had feared going home. Most of his second drama consisted of Bob's soliloquy as a boy walking home from school. Bob wanted to revisit the daily walk, complete with the fear that grew in him daily from the moment of his terrible discovery of his mother lying on the kitchen floor. Through the soliloquy, Bob was able to let the frozen boy speak and feel with the support of caring witnesses. Bob's fear was palpable as he narrated his slow walk home. Finally, through a psychodrama, he could give voice to the fear and anxiety he had felt literally every day of his life. It was not only the horror of finding his mother that had been so traumatic for Bob, but having nowhere to go, no one to talk to who could help him understand what had had happened so that he could process it and move beyond it. He had carried it in silence all of his life.

The soliloquy can be a break from a scene or an alternative way of approaching or exploring a scene. Constructing a painful scene and asking the protagonist to walk into it can sometimes be too shocking. If the material is very traumatic, as in this example, the soliloquy can offer the protagonist a way to examine the material from a safe distance.

The soliloquy can allow the protagonist to explore material from any emotional range or an alternate perspective: fear of public speaking, a dreaded interview with a boss, excitement for an upcoming event or a momentary break from a role-played argument with a spouse are all examples of scenes in which introducing the possibility of "soliloquizing" can provide an alternate venue for exploration.

Interview

In the psychodramatic interview, the director asks the protagonist questions in order to clarify and illuminate what might be going on in the upcoming scene or within the mind of the protagonist. The director can interview the protagonist before the drama in order to gain information that will help to focus the work, during the drama to explore what might be going on in the protagonist's mind, or she can interview the protagonist in role reversal. If used before the enactment the director may ask the protagonist questions to gain information about the upcoming scene or those involved in it. If used during the enactment the director may feel a need for more information from the protagonist and may ask, "May I interview you for a moment? What's going on here for you? What do you feel is happening here?" There is a concern that such cognitive queries may pull the protagonist out of her affective reality so this should be used only when there is a good reason to do so. If used while the protagonist is in role reversal the director may ask the protagonist questions while she is "standing in the shoes of the other and the protagonist answers "as" the person they are playing."

Answering questions while in the role of another person can be enlightening and can provide protagonists with more pieces of the puzzle of their own inner lives. The opportunity to spend time in the role of another person and be interviewed in that role can have various beneficial effects:

- It is a source of information about the person being played.
- It offers the protagonist an opportunity to actually experience being that person, to understand her from the inside out rather than the outside in.
- It allows the protagonist the freedom to see what happened or is happening in the relationship from another point of view.

- If the interview is with the parent, much unconscious material comes to the surface: the protagonist learns a great deal more about how she actually experienced the parent than she would by talking about her, for the parent will come to the surface in the heat of action in the way in which he or she was experienced and stored in the psyche of the protagonist.
- It can promote self-definition and individuation through understanding what parts of another person we may be carrying through, having developed our own personalities alongside them.

THE MIRROR TECHNIQUE

The psychodramatic mirror technique allows the protagonist to view herself "as if in a mirror." By choosing a stand-in to play herself, the protagonist can allow a scene to progress and watch it from the outside. With the support of the director, the protagonist can view herself in action, coping, acting and dealing with her life circumstance. When reviewing material that has been painful or traumatic, the mirror can allow for a degree of emotional distance that can be useful to a protagonist who may feel flooded with intense or immobilizing emotion. The mirror technique can also be useful for someone who has become role-bound or glued, as it were, into a psychological or emotional position from which they cannot seem to get loose. Sometimes a protagonist will feel overwhelmed by the intensity of a psychodrama of a painful family dynamic, for example, and will reenact the defenses that she used to cope at the time the situation was occurring, such as shutting down or dissociating. The mirror technique can help illuminate what may be going on and enable the protagonist to see herself with greater clarity and compassion. With assistance, she can come to understand her own defensive structure and how it plays out in life.

On the lighter side, the mirror technique may be employed, for example, in a drama where the protagonist is feeling stuck in a particular dynamic and wishes to view the situation from the outside to gain perspective.

The Encounter

The encounter is a face-to-face exchange between two people in which each person is able to feel his or her way into the reality of the other, to see themselves through the other person's eyes as well as their own. In a group situation, an encounter can be structured by placing two chairs on the stage or work area facing each other. Psychodramatic techniques such as doubling or working with transference figures that may be obstructing the ability to be with each other in the here and now can be used. But the goal is to talk directly to the other person, to encounter him not in a role, but as himself. Encounters allow group members to be in the here and now with each other and work through what might be in the way of their ability to be present.

VIGNETTES, MONODRAMAS AND AUTODRAMAS

We work in the dark—we do what we can—we give what we have. Our doubt is our passion and our passion is our task. The rest is the madness of art.

—Henry James

Vignettes

As with the theatrical form from which it gets its name, a vignette is an abbreviated form of the classical psychodrama much in the way that it is an abbreviated part of a play. Vignettes allow psychodramatic work to be done without mounting a full psychodrama in its classical form. This does not mean, however, that vignettes are small in anything but actual size. They can be as powerful as any psychodramatic exploration, particularly if the protagonist is warmed up and focused. The basic format of warm-up action and sharing are still used. There are several advantages to vignettes. One, they are easily entered into and do not necessarily require the degree of scene-setting, interviewing or selection of multiple protagonists that a larger psychodrama might require, though any of these devises can be appropriately used. Another advantage is that vignettes, because they are smaller in size, can allow more people to do work in one session. Often one person's vignette will act as a warm-up to another group member. If this is the case and if all are in agreement, the group may choose to do a few small vignettes back-to-back and share with two or three protagonists at the end of, say, all three.

Vignettes are perhaps one of the most user-friendly forms of psychodrama. They allow for identification in several sociometric directions and can be catalysts for cohesion. They also mean that a group needn't go through an elaborate process of choosing a protagonist.

Monodramas

Monodrama comes from the Greek root word *monos,* meaning only or one. In a monodrama one person plays all of the roles. A monodrama often uses an empty chair, a technique adopted from psychodrama by Fritz Perls for Gestalt therapy. Protagonists can play out as many auxiliary roles as they need to in order to expand their drama, and they usually do this by using multiple empty chairs.

Monodramas can be used to explore aspects of the inner self, such as "put your anger in a chair" or "put the part of you that's afraid in a chair" or "put the part of you that wants this new adventure or experience in a chair" and so on. Monodramas can also be used to explore the self at varying stages of development. For example, a protagonist may wish to talk to herself at a particular age when something significant occurred. Or in the case of a trauma, before it occurred, so that she can reconnect with the person she was before a traumatic event took her away from herself.

Another use for monodramas can be to put something protagonists want to dialogue with into a chair and talk to it, like a new or old career, or an identity like "the rebel," "the victim," "the hero" or "the overfunctioner," etc. Or, in working with addicts, the bottle, paraphernalia, drugs, sex, living on the edge, cigarettes or whatever it is that has hold of them. In working with trauma, one might put her numbness in a chair, or with grief, her anger, sadness or the light-spirited self she feels out of touch with. Clients may also wish to dialogue with a body part such as a back, a stomach or a part of the body that has been removed.

All of the normal devices of psychodrama, such as role reversal, doubling and interviewing are used in monodramas. Interviewing the protagonist either in his own role or in the role of the person he is dialoging with (in role reversal) can be very helpful in deepening both his understanding of the other person and releasing him from carrying aspects of that other person inside of him. In other words, he becomes more aware of the parts of that person or that person's perceptions about him, which he has been carrying or has introjected. This is one of those rare glimpses beneath the surface that psychodrama can offer.

Autodramas

An autodrama is a drama that does not use a director. In my experience, this technique is not often used in the clinical situation as most clients feel more comfortable having a director to help guide the action. This does not mean, however, that it can't be used. If a client wishes to show something on his own without the interference of a director, an autodrama will allow him to do that. Clients well versed in psychodrama may have internalized enough of the method so they can do a small scene on their own. Teenagers or those with authority issues for whom a director might get in the way can also use autodramas.

Autodramas can also be used as a structured warm-up. The group members can decide to do an autodrama of a moment in their past week or an anticipated future event. They are in charge of using an empty chair or casting an auxiliary, setting the scene, reversing roles and so on. Because autodramas don't have a director, they tend to be short, so this can work well when using them as a warm-up.

A client can also use an autodrama if he wishes to enact a small scene on his own at home. He can accomplish this by using an empty chair, for example, to explore a relationship with another or the self in order to bring relief and resolution or open a new door.

4 The Theoretical Underpinnings of Psychodrama

We cannot give up our unfinished business, but must bring it to fruition and respectability.

—Zerka Moreno

CONCRETIZATION

All action is motivated by some inner impulse. Opening a refrigerator is a simple act motivated by hunger, perhaps boredom or the need to fulfill a role by preparing food for the family. Hugging a loved one may be fueled by a desire to feel close, and slamming a door on that same person may be an action driven by hurt or anger. Behavior is, in a sense, concretized thought and emotion. Some behaviors are more easily acceptable than others, both to the self and the collective. When we have had painful experiences that were banished from consciousness, either because they are socially undesirable, off-limits or shaming, they can wreak much havoc from within. Unfortunately, out of sight does not necessarily mean out of mind. These experiences may still drive our behavior in significant ways, but they may do so without conscious awareness. The rage, for example, that a boy felt toward his abusive father may come out instead when he marries and feels belittled by his wife, or in the workplace when he feels humiliated by his boss. His rage, in other words, will be concretized in a transference reaction. It will come out at the wrong person, in the wrong place and at the wrong time. Far from resolving his historical issue with his father, he will be creating new problems for himself in the here and now because, as far as the psyche is concerned in these matters, there is no past or present. Psychodrama seeks to rectify this situation by offering a therapeutic stage on which to concretize anything and everything that the protagonist needs to explore, in a clinically safe manner. Simply to concretize an emotional or psychological issue, to give it shape and form in the here and now, to talk to it and observe and interact with it in its real rather than imagined form, can bring it out of hiding and into a therapeutic moment where it can be examined as to its genesis, *status* or *locus nascendi,* the place or location from which a conflict or pattern originally took root.

But this concretization is by no means limited to issues stemming from past circumstances, as in regressive dramas. Future scenes are also concretized and explored through psychodrama. Anticipated, feared or wished-for scenes can be concretized and explored through role-play, giving a protagonist an opportunity to peer into her own future and try it on for size or practice it in a dry run. Scenes drawn from the current moment or ones using sociometry to concretize and explore group dynamics in the here and now are central to the triadic system of psychodrama, sociometry and group psychotherapy. In fact, sociometry is the science through which we can study group dynamics in their concrete form. Concretization is a fundamental principle of both psychodrama and sociometry. It is the process of bringing the inner world outside, where it can be observed, explored and reflected upon in its concrete form. So often we don't really know what we're thinking until we do it. Or we don't truly see the self except through our behavior. Psychodrama allows the protagonist and the group to reflect on behavior in its concrete form, *in situ,* where it can be understood in a sort of gestalt.

A picture is worth a thousand words. We understand something when we see it in front of us in a way that we may not when we're searching for words to capture and describe that experience. This metaphor-making is central to all of the creative arts therapies. We are offering alternative forms of self-expression that allow more of the person, or different parts of the person, to become involved in the therapeutic process. This can be very useful in resolving the *alexithymia,* or lack of words, attached to feelings that can accompany trauma. It is also marvelously helpful in training the creative and spontaneous self. Placing one's inner world, mortifications, wishes, dreams and wounds onto the therapeutic stage for expression and observation releases the self in a way that few experiences can. It is, in this way, very integrating for the total being.

CATHARSIS

The concept of catharsis as it is used in psychodrama comes from the ancient Greeks, specifically from Aristotle. He believed that through the dramatic enactment and representation of a real-life situation, "violence within the soul . . . could be purged." Dramatic enactments were used to bring complexes, problems and fears to a conscious level in order to affect a psychic purge. "Catharsis," writes Moreno, "brings about fundamental changes in a situation without affecting any obvious alteration. On the religious plane, a man may undergo profound internal transformation from chaos and panic to the equilibrium of a saint. But all this can take place without the slightest manifest change in his behavior. Everything remains the same: his physical and mental bearing and his status in all social relations. He has not moved from his locus. Nevertheless, his evaluations of the things in him and around him has imperceptibly changed."

Psychodrama embodies both a catharsis of separation and clarification, and a catharsis as unification and completion. A catharsis can happen in three ways: (1) within the protagonist, (2) within the auxiliary who participates in the drama, and (3) in the audience that participates through identification in the experience of the enactment.

Catharsis of Abreaction and Catharsis of Integration

It is also important to understand the difference between a catharsis of *abreaction* and a catharsis of *integration.* Zerka Moreno writes in *The Many Faces of Drama,* "It is somewhat unfortunate that the idea of catharsis as related to psychodrama has become a leftover from the past, because in fact, we have moved beyond that and have become much more supportive of the process of integration, intrapersonally as well as interpersonally or psychometrically. Thinking in terms of the protagonist's social atom, which is frequently revealed only piecemeal in the course of the drama, helps to bring about . . . an integration that is more fundamental than an abreactive catharsis." In other words, we are looking at our client in the context of their relationship network and attempting to help them make changes and gain insights that will help them to ultimately have a healthier, more peaceful social atom. A catharsis of abreaction is a catharsis *against* something, it is an expulsion of feeling, for example, when anger against a parent, partner or boss gets externalized and expressed.

A catharsis of integration occurs as those expressed emotions become witnessed in their concrete form and linked with their early beginnings. This is when their meanings to the self are deconstructed and understood, as in how they impact the personality and drive current thinking, feeling and behavior. A catharsis of integration involves a genuine shift in perception that is often followed by a shift in thinking, feeling and behavior. In psychodrama, catharsis is used in service of healing, for example in the case of anger. We do not promote a mindless expression of emotion just for the sake of getting rid of it; rather, we attempt to create a "safe enough" clinical environment so anger that has been held within the self system can be felt, witnessed and understood. We look not necessarily only for an abreactive catharsis, but a catharsis of integration in which anger that has been split out of consciousness can be felt, comprehended both for what it was about and how it has affected the self system and relationships. The goal is one of reintegration with new insight and understanding.

The therapist who pushes for catharsis, who asks for a particular goal, may arouse in the protagonist the need to be good, and thus, though the feeling may be released, the people-pleasing or codependency within the protagonist may be reinforced. An effective catharsis of integration should return us to a state of equilibrium and move us away from our inability to respond adequately to life situations. According to Moreno, "However relieving [the] analysis of situations may be for the patient, for a final test he must go back onto the stage in a real-life situation. There it may rapidly become clear that the equilibrium he had thought to have gained from the analysis is not adequate. [What seems lacking is a] binder between whatever analysis can give him in the way of equilibrium and in the action and movement of living. This binder is the spontaneity, which the patient must be able to summon with split-second swiftness when a life situation calls for it. Retest after retest must be made in order to assure the patient that the necessary catharsis has been attained within him. It is spontaneity in its various expressions which at last crowns the efforts of the psychodrama."

Psychodrama assumes that a lack of spontaneity in a social setting provokes disturbances, not only in the individual but also in the group. These disturbances increase as the deficit of spontaneity increases. A catharsis that is successful within an individual should have the effect of increasing the spontaneity of the entire group, which should then reduce both the individual and group-dynamic disturbances. Moreno writes, "I discovered the common principle producing catharsis to be: spontaneity. Because of the universality of the act of spontaneity, and its primordial nature, it engulfs all other forms of expression. They flow naturally out of it or can be encouraged to emerge. . . . Therefore my aim has been to define catharsis in such a way that all forms of influence, which have a demonstrable cathartic effect can be shown as positive steps within a single total process of operation."

Spectator Catharsis

In the ancient Greek theater, part of the production of the play in the context of the Dionysian Festival was designed to produce a "spectator catharsis." In other words, through identification, the audience member (like the group member in psychodrama) sees the drama as an extension of the aspects of her inner world. The drama acts to stimulate similar issues from the audience or group members' own lives and bring them to the surface for a second look. Through identification the spectator or witness comes closer to her inner world. "The compelling notion is that this drama is my story; my history's meaning being ritualized before me on the stage. This play is a mirror of my meaning or lack thereof. Catharsis, here, is indeed dramatic clarification and explanation. Psychodrama carries this one step further by providing a situation in which the role-play is a spontaneous enactment of the protagonist's real story" (J. Moreno 1964).

Somatic Catharsis

The body, too, can experience catharsis. Indeed, clients are generally calmed and more regulated after they have experienced a catharsis of strong emotion. "By moving from the present into the past," Moreno writes, "the psychoanalyst had lost sight, not only of the immediate requirements of the individual psyche but also of the immediate requirements of the individual body and, for all practical purposes, postponed and neglected its treatment. Somatic catharsis is defined here as purging or cleansing of any locus of the body; the locus of the body may be the alimentary canal, the urinary tract or the genital organ." Moreno here is referring to the limits of talk therapy as it related to addressing, for example, the residue of trauma that lives in the body. We will discuss this in more depth in our chapter on trauma.

Is All Catharsis Good Catharsis?

In a recent study on catharsis published by the American Psychological Association's *Journal of Personality and Social Psychology* researchers looked for support for their hypothesis that venting anger may increase rather than decrease it. The researchers wanted to test whether or not a media message could encourage people to choose an aggressive behavior, such as hitting a punching bag, when angered. And secondly, they wanted to test whether or not choosing an aggressive activity, such as hitting a punching bag, actually reduced their anger. They set up two control groups. They gave one group a bogus article purporting that catharsis of anger was a good thing and the other an article purporting that it was not a good thing. After the researchers set up anger promoting situations the group who had read the article endorsing catharsis was more likely to resort to an aggressive expression of anger. The group that had read an article debunking catharsis was less likely to become aggressive. In addition the first group displayed more ready aggression on subsequent tests than the second group did. Catharsis needs to have healing, integrative goals to serve therapeutic purposes, i.e. catharsis integration. The goal is not to make anger, for example, desirable, but neither to make it forbidden; to allow it as an emotion that can be explored and understood.

TELE

"Moreno coined the word tele to describe that current of feeling which flows between two persons" (Hale 1981). Tele is a feeling that is projected into distance; the simplest unit of feeling transmitted from one individual towards another. "The socio-gravitational factor, which operates between individuals, drawing them to form more positive or negative pair-relations, triangles, quadrangles, polygons, etc., than on chance, I have called 'tele'—derived from the Greek, the meaning is 'far' or 'distant'" (J. Moreno 1934).

"Tele is always mutual. It has to do with the capacity to feel into the reality of another person. It relates to intuition, perhaps even an extra sensory perception" (Z. Moreno, 1985–1986).

"Moreno defines tele as 'insight into', 'appreciation of' and 'feeling for' the 'actual make-up' of the other person" (Hale 1981). Literally, it has been further defined by Peter Felix Kellermann, author of *Focus on Psychodrama: The Therapeutic Aspects of Psychodrama*, as embracing "not only the attractive but also the repulsive aspects of relations between people and carries with it an authentic meeting or encounter in which people take each other for what and whom they are. 'Tele' conveys the message that people are participants in an interpersonal phenomena whereby they contact and communicate and resonate with one another at a distance and that they send emotional messages projected across space" (1992). Tele describes that unspoken connectedness between and among people and even animals.

From the neurobiological perspective, Alan Shore writes, "Long sequences of interactions between people may be partly determined by nonconscious perceptions and automatic responses on the part of both the sender and receiver. Their conscious understanding of what is going on in the interaction that they can formulate verbally, on the other hand, may be quite independent of this basic level of interaction" (Dimbergard Ohman 1996 and Shore 2004). There is much unspoken information that passes between and among people that remains in the realm of nonconscious affect, that is, we feel it beneath the level of awareness and do not necessarily register it consciously. These nonconscious exchanges can, however, still affect us.

"Affectively charged, facially mediated right brain-to-brain communications, at levels beneath awareness, can instigate the regulation or dysregulation of autonomic function. Despite earlier controversies, it is now well established that the autonomic nervous system reacts to perceptual stimuli that may never enter consciousness" (Lazarus and McCleary 1951) and that it is involved in the generation of nonconscious affect that is triggered by the visual perception of an emotionally expressive face. This unconscious process may initiate early in infancy as the "implicit mere exposure effect" (Gordon and Holyoak 1983) of attachment imprinting (Lickliter and Gottlieb 1986), and may be expressed at later points as "primitive emotional contagion" (Schore 2004).

Tele is not transference. The tele connection enacted within the psychodrama enables protagonists to remain within their own psychic reality by giving it shape, definition and connection. In a group situation, cohesion is in part measured by the strength and number of reciprocal pairs, wherein tele may be experienced as a feeling of nonverbal understanding, a sense of being seen and understood by another person. It is a large factor in determining an individual's position in a group. Tele in action assumes a willingness to play the auxiliary role, combining behavior, thinking and emotions in support of the protagonist's surplus reality, so that the protagonist does not become detached from his own experience. Tele in action opens the door to trust by providing a real surrogate with whom to explore and test connections in reality. Tele allows the bringing of a delusional system into the here and now for examination, making the unconscious material conscious through experience in action so that it can be lived through again and resolved.

Moreno felt that, "A minimum of tele structure and resulting cohesiveness of interaction among the therapists and the patients is an indispensable prerequisite for the ongoing therapeutic psychodrama to succeed. If the auxiliary egos are troubled among themselves because of (1) unresolved problems of their own, (2) protest against the psychodramatic director, (3) poor portrayal of the roles assigned to them, (4) lack of faith and negative attitude toward the method used, or (5) interpersonal conflicts among themselves, they create an atmosphere which reflects upon the therapeutic situation. It is obvious, therefore, that if transference and countertransference phenomena dominate the relationship among the auxiliary therapists and toward the patients, the therapeutic progress will be greatly handicapped. The decisive factor for therapeutic progress is the tele." Because of this, the triadic system provides a concrete method in addition to psychodrama through which transference, countertransference and the other issues described above can be examined and worked through. This is sociometry.

The tele range of a particular individual is considered to be the range of individuals where there is a telic connection. Socio tele is tele that goes from role to role, i.e., the tele between the role of teacher and the role of student, the role of worker to worker, exerciser to exerciser, group member to group member, and so on. Personal tele is the tele that goes from person to person, based not on what each person does, as with socio tele, but on who they are—a feeling of unspoken connection of any sort, good, bad or indifferent.

ACT HUNGER

We are beings of action and the stories of our lives are literally written on our neural systems. We're born with a hunger for certain actions or behaviors. The infant has a hunger for suckling his mother's breast. The hunger for eating, resting, having sex or simply for moving our bodies through space and time are all built into us; they are needs. Act hungers can also build through interaction. If we have a fight we may feel aggressive and hunger for attacking our opponent; if we've been hurt we may have a hunger for revenge or crying or raging in anger. If we have not said what we wished to say to someone we may hunger to finally get it off our chests. The longing to take action toward completion is act hunger. Psychodrama offers a unique opportunity to personalize act hungers through the use of auxiliary egos, who play the roles necessary to bring situations into a concrete form. If the drive and need are sated in the enactment of the psychodrama, the behavior can be diminished. The psyche or brain accepts the auxiliaries as real or "real enough," allowing the protagonist to rework the experience and become reempowered.

Act hunger is not the same as the repetition compulsion but has some things in common with it. The compulsion to repeat the contents of painful or traumatic experiences that are held in the unconscious without awareness may be an unconscious attempt at mastery over the painful experience. But the key word is unconscious. Psychodrama offers a stage on which these compulsions can be made conscious, met in the here and now with the help of other therapeutic allies. Without this conscious light brought into the material in one way or another, we repeat these relationships without consciousness. If they go unresolved, they can preclude pleasure, as the demand for action or the repetition compulsion supersedes the pleasure principle according to psychodynamic theory.

Open Tension Systems

Open tension systems, as the name implies, are inner tensions that have not been brought to adequate closure and are therefore stored inside the self with a sort of jagged edge, one that occasionally tears at our inner world. When we are frightened we tend to freeze. Our brains do not function normally, and we may not come to adequate closure around a set of events. We do not understand or know the experience and integrate it because we are not living through it. Rather we are splitting off important pieces of the puzzle of emotion and thought, banishing it out of consciousness through one or another of our psychological defenses, or through a somewhat more involuntary process of numbing or dissociation. As a result, when the experience is triggered, a fully integrated memory cannot come back. What comes back instead is a sort of unresolved state of frozen needs. Thus, in a psychodrama, it is important that the environment and action be reasonably safe so that when the memories surface, the split-off affect associated with them can be felt or refelt and reintegrated into the self-system. Worthy of exploration are the particular ruminations, fantasies and thoughts that the client had at the time a given situation was taking place. The meaning that we make out of painful (or not painful) circumstances can become an indelible part of our core system of beliefs about the self, life, relationships or the world in which we live. Examining that meaning-making process and the extent to which we continue to live by it is also a part of bringing closure to unfinished business.

Surplus Reality

Surplus reality is that which we carry in our psyche that is particular to us, the sum total of all of our experiences and the sense we have made out of it. It is the contents of the internal "I." Words such as *baggage* and *unfinished business* can certainly fit into this category, but as is so often the case in psychodrama, the term stretches to include much more. It is our joys, sorrows, passions, dreams, drives and wishes, our open tensions, act hungers and private jokes, our unuttered thoughts, our internalized relational patterns, and the way in which we see the world; in fact our entire private world in all of its ramifications is our surplus reality. And it is our surplus reality that we work with on the stage, that we concretize and enact, giving it breath and life so that we can meet the self in all its various forms, so that we can live out loud.

In illustrating how the concept of surplus reality reveals itself on the stage, I offer this example. In my work with dissociative identity disorder (DID) patients, I've found that one of the things many of them love about psychodrama is the chance to be what they term "body out"; to meet with as many of their "personalities" as they wish to bring onto the stage through role-play. This, they report, gives them great relief as they can bring these subpersonalities out onto the stage, introduce them to others, talk to them, *as* them and *about* them, and bring them out of hiding. They find this process to be very honoring, integrating and normalizing. They are also placed, by the method itself, into an organizing role as they are entirely in charge of the who, what, when and where of their dramatic action. They are functioning as the executive by organizing their own personality structure with the support and guidance of the director. It also gives them an opportunity to explore and connect the origins or *locus nascendi*, the beginnings of a particular personality and the vital function that it may have played for them as, say, a protector, aggressor or comforter. In this process of concretizing these parts of self through auxiliary egos, illusion and delusion meet and come closer to reality. Patients often find themselves having spontaneous insights into the emotional and psychological needs that gave birth to these personalities or aspects of self. They didn't come from nowhere, not at all. At some point or another they came into being to meet some vital and important need on the part of the patient. Generally they offered protection, safety and solace when life circumstances proved too much for a young child to meet with no help, or when those she might have gone to for help were themselves the aggressors. The imaginative, concrete child mind came to the rescue, creating inner allies to fight battles she was too young to fight, inner supporters to give love when none was available, and inner friends to play with and feel cared about by when real friends were out of reach. All these things assisted in reducing feelings of helplessness. By exploring these aspects of self through role-play, patients can come to see why they came into being to begin with. They could love them, thank them and eventually, it is hoped, let them go or integrate them in a more aware, developed, grown-up state through a process that honors the survival needs these "little people" had been designed to meet in the first place.

Moreno observed that very disturbed clients seem to have a surplus of reality. For instance, they live with a preponderance of psychodramatic or interior roles and lack grounding in the real world. Playing out these role extremes and excesses on stage has the effect of bringing their inner and outer worlds into better balance.

We all have hidden parts in our surplus reality that yearn to breathe fresh air, to unglue themselves from their *locus nascendi* within us and spring forth into concrete form or dramatic action. And the not-so-hidden are also a part of our surplus reality. Through the process of concretization and the flexibility of the method itself, we all go through a similar process of meeting the self in all of its various aspects through action. We are free not only to cast the roles of others in our lives but also to role-play aspects of self: the fearful, angry, weak or empowered self; the dancer, the poet or creator can all come forward onto the stage. Much has been said about inner-child work over the past couple of decades. Psychodrama creates space for the inner child in its rich variety; the inner baby, two-year-old spunky kid or helpless, terrified four-year-old can be met. Or the inner adolescent, struggling young adult, rebel, lost child, scape-goat, mascot or hero can all be cast and "lived in" for a moment carved out of time. And in this moment we can do our own research, because who is better qualified to find the right information, to pull the why and the wherefore out of our surplus reality than us? We can come to understand who we are through having, in a sense, a concretized internal dialogue with the self. And because part of the self is the incorporated personality or points of view of others, we can extend our drama to bring in whoever else needs to be seen in order to gain further insight into our various aspects of self. All of this is a part of placing our surplus reality onto the psychodramatic stage, the living stage.

Psychodramatic Trance

The psychodramatic trance is the trancelike state entered into by the protagonist or role-players during the enactment or action of the psychodramatic moment. When the *as if* falls and becomes *as* in a psychodrama, the protagonist and even the auxiliaries may enter a psychodramatic trance state in which they experience the psychodrama as the real situation and the auxiliaries as real-life representations of their world. The trance state can also be somewhat dreamlike in its capacity to touch deep states of mind where a sort of psychological and emotional time-traveling takes place; when in a dream, one can experience a sense of zoom focusing, or seeing as if through a wide-angle lens, or viewing with an x-ray or penetrating vision. Or circumstances may appear with a metaphoric meaning as the mind scans itself for associations and fits together pieces of an internal puzzle in new ways. This is another reason why de-roling is necessary, as those playing auxiliary roles may have entered the role in an almost trancelike way.

According to Daniel G. Amen, author of *Change Your Brain, Change Your Life*, "Hypnosis is a natural state, it is an altered state that we enter naturally; many people frequently go in and out of them, like when we go into a trance driving along a highway or watching TV. Self-hypnosis taps into a natural 'basal ganglia' soothing power source that most people do not even know exists. It is found within you, within your ability to focus your concentration. The basal ganglia are involved with integrating feelings and movement, shifting and smoothing motor behavior, setting the body's idle speed or anxiety level, modulating motivation, and driving feelings of pleasure and ecstasy." People who have been through trauma can become dysregulated in the basal ganglia region of the brain. The basal ganglia can become reset to be constantly on the alert. This is not only a phenomenon of war, but also of homes that are characterized by chaos, instability, abuse and/or neglect, all circumstances where those involved learn to be hypervigilant, constantly on the alert for potential trouble. Part of healing from these patterns is to learn to reset the basal ganglia (Dayton 2003).

In the psychodramatic trance state we can postulate that the basal ganglia are active, along with the benefits of focusing, integrating emotion and movement, shifting and smoothing motor behavior and remodulating motivation. This is perhaps a part of psychodrama's seemingly mysterious power to heal survivors of trauma. Great sensitivity needs to be exercised when a protagonist or others are in this state so they can experience it with as little interruption as possible.

Much has been theorized about what goes on in the dream state or waking states of mind when we are producing the types of brain waves associated with deeply contemplative or creative states. The psychodramatic trance, in my experience, has some of the qualities generally associated with deep reflection and even repatterning of mental and emotional patterns. There is a quality of scanning the mind in an accelerated manner, coalescing meaning into metaphor, seeing the self as if from a mountaintop, with a kind of zoom focusing and perspective normally associated with deeply meditative states of mind. As in the Eriksonian state of hypnosis, the subject is free "not to listen . . ." and consequently feels freer to pay attention. Erikson weaves a story relevant to the patient's life in critical ways, allowing the patient to explore his standard responses and see the "absurdity of his own responses." Similarly, in the psychodrama, "Others in the enactment make him feel the way he usually feels, but different, freer to be himself. He is less defended. The role-players and doubles seem capable of frustrating and supporting him at the same time. Frequently he finds himself doing or saying things he had never dared do or say, things he didn't know he had in him. . . . Both hypnotist and psychodramatist provide an experience that by definition is extraordinary and thus has some of the quality of ritual or 'heightened reality.'" Eva Leviton goes on to say, " . . . unlike group and individual psychotherapies that rely mostly on the exchange of verbal information, psychodrama and hypnosis provide an arena where the subject can enter a different world, the world of the past, the world of the future, of heightened intensity. Both often make use of 'Story' to frame the subject's dilemma."

Virtually any psychodrama represents a concretizing of one's surplus reality and can, if the work is deep, include psychodramatic trance. Entering this very private world can have an almost trancelike quality.

5 Spontaneity and Creativity Versus the Cultural Conserve

SPONTANEITY AND CREATIVITY

Spontaneity and creativity are twin principles core to the fundamental theory of psychodrama. So important are they to the psychodramatist's basic thinking that I explore them here in my own words and include enough of Moreno's unedited thoughts on the subject so the reader can get a true flavor of his thinking. Moreno felt that real life and the real world was limited and did not provide for the acting out—action being fundamental to humans—of many aspects of the psyche in service of a constant and evolving resolution of internal conflicts. Psychodrama, he felt, provided a world without those limits, a therapeutically controlled environment or living stage on which the client could meet the self in all its various forms, real and imagined. By so doing, the client could engage in not only a healing of past wounds but also develop an ever-strengthening relationship with the creative, spontaneous self. As Moreno defined the role as the tangible form the self takes, he postulated that the self could be strengthened through role-play.

Moreno felt that our spontaneity warms us up to our creativity. Moreno cautioned that spontaneity is not something that we store up and use as we need it, as we would gasoline in a gas tank. Rather, it is a way of meeting the moment, a way of being in life. According to Moreno, spontaneity means that we are ready to respond as is required by the situation. He defined it as an "adequate response" to a given situation, neither too much nor too little. This ability, he felt, must be natural; we cannot attain spontaneity by an act of will. If it is no longer natural, as it is with children, it must grow by degrees as the result of training in spontaneity, which psychodrama provides. "In the psychodramatic situation," writes Moreno, ". . . the whole world into which the actor enters, the person's plots, the objects in it, in all its dimensions, and its time and space—are novel to him. Every step he makes forward in this world on the stage has to be defined anew. Every word he speaks is defined by the word, which is spoken to him. Every movement he makes is defined, aroused and shaped by the persons and objects he encounters. Every step he makes is determined by the steps of others towards him. But their steps, too, are, at least, in part, determined by his own steps." Spontaneity is defined by Moreno as a new response to an old situation or an adequate response to a new situation.

Psychodrama defines three types of spontaneity:

1. **Pathological Spontaneity:** A novel response without adequacy, or pathological spontaneity, e.g., a toast at a graduation party that is entirely about the person giving the toast without paying any attention to the graduate and essentially tells the story of the toaster's life, not the graduate's. It is novel but not right for the situation.

2. **Stereotyped Spontaneity:** An adequate response without novelty and creativity, or stereotyped spontaneity, e.g., a dull sort of toast, read off a card that is right for the form of the situation but has nothing moving, memorable or especially genuine about it.

3. **True Spontaneity:** An adequate response with novelty and creativity. "In this type there is an adequate response accompanied by the characteristics that are both novel and creative. . . . To be truly spontaneous the results must be in some way new and useful for some purpose" (J. Moreno 1966); this is also referred to as the spontaneity of the genius, e.g., being caught in the moment, unrehearsed, delivering a toast rehearsed or that talks about the graduate in a way that they may need, wish for or feel buoyed up and held by that bonds and entertains the party, in other words, that meets the moment with novelty, creativity and relevant meaning.

It is the constant goal of psychodrama to develop and train spontaneity in its participants, to move toward the spontaneity of the genius and to use the method not only to train spontaneity but to remove all the psychological and emotional blocks in its way. Moreno felt that problems in the psyche were often accompanied by a lack of what we might call today healthy spontaneity, that these situations were met by those with psychological or emotional problems with "a novel response without adequacy" or "pathological spontaneity." In these cases spontaneity training is used to restore a healthy internal state and relationship with the world. In the case of those who meet life with "an adequate response without novelty," spontaneity training is used to restore color, aliveness and passion, to help more of the inner person come alive.

Moreno felt that the restoration of spontaneity in the individual allowed the individual to meet life situations in a manner that allowed them, as Albert Einstein says, "to stay alive while living," to have the trained ability to come up with the sets of ever-evolving "adequate responses with novelty" in order to live life to its fullest. "The individual," writes Moreno, "is not endowed with a reservoir of spontaneity in the sense of a given, stable volume or quantity. Spontaneity is (or is not) available in varying degrees of readiness, from zero to maximum, operating like a psychological catalyzer. Thus he has, when faced with a novel situation, no alternative but to use the 's' factor as a guide or searchlight, prompting him as to which emotions, thoughts and actions are most appropriate. At times he has to invoke more of this spontaneity, and at other times less, in accordance with the requirements of the situation or task. He should be careful not to produce less than the exact amount of spontaneity needed, for if this were to happen he would need a 'reservoir' from which to draw. Likewise, he should be careful not to produce more than the situation calls for because the surplus might tempt him to store it, to establish a reservoir, conserving it for future tasks as if it were energy, thus completing a vicious circle which ends in the deterioration of spontaneity and the development of cultural conserves. Spontaneity functions only in the moment of its emergence just as, metaphorically speaking, light is turned on in a room, and all parts of it become distinct. When the light is turned off in a room the basic structure remains the same, but a fundamental quality had disappeared" (J. Moreno 1964).

Spontaneity is closely linked to creativity. It acts as a catalyst or a companion to the creative process. Our spontaneity warms us up to our creativity. Moreno speaks to this moment of creativity eloquently in this description of the act of creation. "In the spontaneous-creative enactment, emotions, thoughts, processes, sentences, pauses, gestures, movements, etc., seem first to break formlessly and in anarchistic fashion into an ordered environment and settled consciousness. But in the course of their development it becomes clear that they belong together like the tones of a melody; that they are in relation similar to the cells of a new organism. The disorder is only an outer appearance; inwardly there is a consistent driving force, a plastic ability, the urge to assume a definite form; the stratagem of the creative principle which allies itself with the cunning of reason in order to realize an imperative intention. The poet hides no complexes but germs of form, and his goal is an act of birth. Therefore, he is not merely following a pattern: he can alter the world creatively."

Moreno created concrete tests for spontaneity in which individuals were tested to see if their response to a situation was adequate, that is, if it met the needs of the moment appropriately. In the spontaneity test, "The timing of a response to an emerging situation appeared to be a major factor in appropriateness," writes Moreno in *Psychodrama* Volume 1. "The minimum and maximum range of duration permissible in each single warming-up process to a particular act and to the total situation had to be established. . . . If the warming-up process to the idea that the babies are in danger is too slow, the emergent action of carrying them to safety may come too late. On the other hand, if the warming-up process is too fast, each act can not be fully executed, and the result will be a jumbled series of incoherent acts. . . ." Moreno created "near replicas" of real-life situations. "A positive score was given to a subject if he operated within the time range; a negative score was given if the duration of a specific act was below the minimum or beyond the maximum." In this way he felt that one's spontaneous reaction to a situation could be measured as to its adequacy in any given situation.

THE CULTURAL CONSERVE

The "cultural conserve" is a term coined by Moreno to refer to a kind of *idée fixe* or finished form. The film, for example, would be the cultural conserve of a dramatic story; the book, a conserve of the thoughts, musings or work of one or more people. Beethoven's Fifth Symphony would be the cultural conserve of the music spinning around the mind of the creator, Beethoven. The spontaneity and creativity of Beethoven is forever caught and represented by his very famous musical work. Then, each and every musician or conductor brings his or her own spontaneity and creativity into the playing of Beethoven's Fifth, which impacts how it will sound. "The book has been perhaps the most important single factor in the formation of our culture," writes Moreno. "The cultural conserve aims at being the finished product and, as such, has assumed an almost sacred quality. This is the result of a generally accepted theory of values. Processes which have been brought to an end as finished and perfected acts. Works perfected seem to have satisfied our theory of values better than processes and things, which remain unfinished and in an imperfect state. These perfection ideas were associated with the God idea, itself. It is significant to note, in this connection, that many of God's quasi-conserve qualities may have been over-emphasized. His 'works,' His 'universe,' His 'all-might,' His 'righteousness' and His 'wisdom' whereas His function as a spontaneous creator, the most revolutionary concept of a god's function, is nearly always neglected. The cultural conserve became the highest value it was possible to produce; the books of the Bible, the works of Shakespeare, or Beethoven's symphonies. It is a successful mixture of spontaneous and creative material molded into a permanent form. As such it becomes the property of the general public, something that everyone can share. Due to its permanent form it is a rallying point to which one can return to at will and upon which cultural tradition can be based. The cultural conserve is thus a consoling and a reassuring category. It is not surprising, therefore, that the category of the moment has had a poor opportunity to develop in a culture such as ours, saturated as it is with conserves, and relatively satisfied with them" (Moreno 1964).

Moreno recognizes the value of cultural conserves in maintaining stability and order but suggests that the *category of the moment*, the ever-evolving here and now of our minute-by-minute experience not be neglected. The moment, he feels, is a doorway into our own spontaneity and creativity, and an even greater opportunity through which to experience a sense of satisfaction, empowerment and aliveness than the finished product. Mihaly Csikszentmihalyi, Harvard researcher, has done extensive research on something he calls the *flow state,* or a state in which one is so completely engaged in the moment that subjects report losing a sense of self-consciousness; time seems to disappear and they feel a sense of "at-oneness." This is a state of "at-oneness" that artists, athletes, musicians, writers and even mothers talk about entering when they are fully in the here and now. "A creator is like a runner for whom, in the act of running, the part of the road he has already passed and the part before him are qualitatively one."

Talk to many artists and they will tell you that it is the process of creation that calls to them, that sustains, nourishes and challenges them more than the thing they are producing. Once produced, they look to the next project so they can again experience the aliveness of creation. And this aliveness is not static. It is real and contains within it all of the joys and agonies incumbent on reaching beyond our own limits, reaching into the unknown and making it the known. Once known, it is lifted out of the category of the moment and placed into the category of the conserve. The artist longs again to create because it is in the process of creation that the aliveness lives; it is in connection with the creative process that the flow state occurs.

Prophetically, Moreno foresaw a time in which cultural conserves might become so common that we would spend our own energy not as the creator but the imitator; our personal lives would lose some of their spontaneity because we would spend our precious hours trying to get our lives to mirror a cultural conserve or a thing already created and reproduced thousands of times. He felt that this would have the effect of deadening everyone's personal creativity and spontaneity. He explained that the problem in chasing after conserves is that the conserve itself is, in a way, dead. We do not see in the film, for example, the spontaneous moments of creativity that went into making it—the warm-up, what led up to the preserved moment, the mistakes, mishaps and miscalculations that were all a part of the experience of creation. We see, instead, a finished product—produced and reproduced. And then, when we want our lives to resemble these conserves, there is a natural distortion, because life contains all of those moments of frustration and failure: excitement, trial and error, disappointment, and renewal of effort. Though characters out of great art, literature or film can help to give us hope by giving us someone inspiring to identify with, many of the media-driven pop idols can have the opposite effect, making us feel we can never reach an ideal of perfection. When the conserve rules, we might feel like failures for not being able to get our lives to look like something that doesn't really exist, something that is an illusion, that cannot and should not be lived because it is without true reality, humanity, spontaneity and creativity.

Moreno cautioned society against becoming ruled by conserves to such an extent that we lose our own spontaneity and creativity.

THE PERSONAL CULTURAL CONSERVE

In the same way in which a cultural conserve is a set of conserved patterns of thinking, feeling and behaving that drive the outward and inward expression of culture, the personal cultural conserve is an equally conserved set of thinking, feeling and behavior that drives our individual lives. From infancy we begin to develop our sets of patterns that impact how we think, feel and behave throughout life, as well as who we become and how we live out and express who we are. The personal conserve can examine the conserved, internalized patterns that drive us, our sets of beliefs, patterns and inner constructs that move us toward a dynamic expression of our beingness.

Understanding the personal conserve of a client can provide a sort of construction from which to work. For example, is Jim withdrawing from social groups over and over again because behaving in this way has become part of his personal conserve, even though he experiences himself as choosing each and every time to not participate? If it is part of his conserved set of behaviors, can we pull it out and explore it as a repeated pattern that might benefit from reexamination? And in so doing, can we (1) look into where and how this pattern may have begun, (2) understand the relational context in which it got set up in the first place, (3) look at the present day to understand what parallel circumstance triggered the conserved response, i.e., why is he again acting this way in this moment, and (4) look at other possible ways of behaving or responding to these parallel stimuli, i.e., make new, novel and more adequate choices in the here and now?

This model obviously takes in many existing theoretical concepts, such as transference, reenactments, core beliefs and so on. What seems to me to be so useful about it, however, is that is creates a context in which the operational self can be viewed as a coherent whole. It holds a picture of the operational self while providing practical directions to make changes. The other thing I like about this concept is that I yearn for a model of self that is neither pathologically based nor ignores pathological potentialities. So many of our theory bases model our crisis-oriented health-care model. We are well, or we are sick; we are broken, or we are whole. But my experience as a person and as a therapist is that we are always some of both, always works in progress, and that just when we have it all together for one stage of life, one set of role relationships, life spews forward a whole new set of challenges that temporarily throw our settled notions up in the air again. Perhaps we have a child who triggers issues from our own childhood that we thought had been cured, but in the face of this powerful new love and connection, they are warmed up all over again. Or maybe we lose someone we love and find our stable sense of self buffeted and challenged and those complexes we thought we had put to rest return to haunt us, along with new ones. Maybe we get fired, retire or move into a new community. The model of a personal conserve allows us to nonpathologically examine the natural and expected changes of our lives in the context of both our own personalities and the manner in which we operate within our social world or our socio-cultural atom. It coalesces many of Moreno's theories both psychodramatically and sociometrically and allows for a way to look at them in combination theoretically. All of Moreno's method's then come to service in working with the personal conserve. What is a client in need of at this moment in their lives? Will they benefit from social atom repair because their family-of-origin social atom has great gaps in it and they need to resolve conflict in old role-relationships and find surrogates to fill in roles that were evacuated or abandoned? Or due to job loss, location change or retirement? Will this therapeutic process of deconserving or gradually removing clichéd or stereotyped ways of behaving be long and need a significant network of support, or can it be done relatively quickly? Does the deconserving of old patterns and creating new, more flexible ones require years of therapy because the origins of their conserved patterns run very deep and need to be slowly, painstakingly reworked? Or can the necessary shifts be relatively quick and easy because the person's life is basically healthy and well integrated?

The idea of a personal conserve provides a way of working with a personality in a nonpathologizing way; it assumes that we all have patterns, we all have origins of those patterns, we all have strengths and deficits, and we all have relationship structures for better and worse that define our sociocultural world.

THE GOD HEAD

The Cultural Conserve Versus a Changing Society

"Moreno was 'trying to plant the seeds of a diminutive creative revolution' as he engaged others—sick or healthy; not in a social revolution (which it was later called) but a religious revolution. Moreno envisaged a religion based upon acknowledging Godlikeness in each person and the capacity to bring out the creator in every person. The expression of these religious beliefs would be in action, interaction with others according to principles based on the sacredness of creativity and spontaneity in every individual" (Hale 1981).

Moreno felt that we cocreate our lives, that we all have the potential to be Godlike, and that spontaneity and creativity are those qualities that can stream us into our Godlike natures. One recognizes in this, and in Moreno's honoring of the depth and power of the present moment, the ideas of various eastern philosophies that were finding their way to Europe around the turn of the century. Indeed, the preoccupation with states of consciousness by thinkers such as Freud and Moreno can also be traced eastward.

Moreno goes on to say, "The highest value of spontaneity and creativity, the top value on any axiological scale, is a totally spontaneous-creative being, the Godhead. The scale has two opposite poles: the maximum of spontaneity at one pole and zero spontaneity at the other, with many degrees of spontaneity between the two, every degree representing a different quotient of spontaneity. This is an axiological scale: the ideal exponent of one pole is a totally spontaneous creator, and the ideal exponent of the other, the total cultural conserve" (Moreno 1964).

Guidelines for Therapeutic Safety:
First, Do No Harm

Psychodrama is an experiential method that involves action. Because of this, guidelines should be followed in order to reduce the possibility of retraumatization and to keep the work safe and contained.

Listen and follow. The role of the director is to listen and follow. This is one of psychodrama's real safeguards as it allows the protagonist to declare his own readiness to explore particular material and it keeps the director from pushing him where he does not wish to go.

Do not prescript material. Therapists who decide beforehand where they want clients to go run the risk of pushing them beyond their ego strength and emotional capacity in order to get there. The director should follow the lead of the protagonist rather than impose their own ideas of where the work should go, and the direction should be checked out with him along the way, with questions such as "Are we on the right track?" or "Does this feel right?" Also, the therapist must be willing to be made wrong and to adjust his approach in midstream. Prescripting can also inhibit feelings from arising in a spontaneous manner (Siroka 1987).

Do not use psychodramatic shock techniques. If the therapist sets up a potentially powerful or frightening scene without the client's knowledge or input and then suddenly exposes the client to the fully set scene, the client may go into shock or be retraumatized. This can have long-term damaging effects, and it may mobilize deep defenses that keep the client from moving forward (Siroka 1990).

Remain with the protagonist throughout the work. The therapist becomes a therapeutic ally for the protagonist as the protagonist takes the risk of revisiting material that she may feel is threatening. It is important that the therapist understand his responsibility to a protagonist who has momentarily put her psyche in the therapist's hands. This bond of trust that the protagonist forms with the therapist is potentially very healing. It is teaching the protagonist that it is all right to depend, that she doesn't have to face painful, feared or wished-for material alone, and that she can tolerate the intensity of her own inner world. This bond is helpful in remodulating the client's emotional, psychological and physical inner world.

Use caution in structuring trauma scenes. Going directly to a scene where a traumatic event occurred and replaying it can be retraumatizing. It is not necessarily helpful to enact the trauma scene unless the protagonist, for some reason, wishes to, and the director feels it will be useful. There is no hard and fast rule on this, of course, as it would inhibit spontaneity or adequacy, but this has been my experience. There are many ways to approach painful material and the fallout from trauma. Learning to talk about the situation and experience the split-off emotions surrounding events so they can be integrated is oftentimes what protagonists find useful as they confront their psychological and emotional taboos or loss of access to self (Dayton 1994).

Use stand-ins for traumatic scenes. In the psychodramatization of traumatic events there is a risk that the protagonist will be retraumatized. Using stand-ins allows the protagonist to witness himself from a safe distance and to get a clearer picture of the dynamics of painful interactions. He can often gain empathy for himself that might have been missing or feel less frozen in place if he can have some distance from the material being explored. However, any structuring of traumatic material should be approached with great caution. If the protagonist uses a stand-in, either the director or a support person chosen by the protagonist should stay close by to help him to feel contained as they witness their drama (Siroka, Dayton 1994).

Allow plenty of time for sharing. Sharing is extremely important to the emotional safety of the group. Sharing is not feedback; rather, it is the continued expression of vulnerable feelings related to whatever the group process and psychodramatic enactment are bringing up within each person self-referentially. Each member of the group should have the time he needs to share so his pain can be contained and brought to closure. Everyone is working at all times in an experiential group: the enactment is designed to bring up feelings not only for the protagonist but also for everyone in the room. This is how the process works to bring issues and unconscious feelings to awareness through identification. The sharing acts as the safe container for the material so it can be held and witnessed by others in safety, without judgment or analysis at that point (Dayton 1994).

Maintain safe group norms. Any group requires group norms so members can feel reasonably safe. Therapists or institutions may have their own set of norms but common ones are punctuality, respect for privacy, no physical violence directed at another group member, stay through the entire group and regular attendance, to name a few. Group norms are an important part of creating a "safe enough" container.

In Moreno's Own Words

"When the therapist faces his group for the first session, he perceives immediately, with his skilled sense for interpersonal relations, some of the interaction between the members, such as the distribution of love, hate and indifference. It is not just a collection of individuals. He notices one or two sitting all by themselves, physically isolated from the rest; two or three clustered together, smiling and gossiping; one or two engaged in an argument or sitting side by side but giving each other the cold shoulder. In other words, the first contours of a sociogram begin to simmer in his mind.

"Because we cannot reach into the mind and see what the individual perceives and feels, psychodrama tries, with the cooperation of the patient, to transfer the mind 'outside' of the individual and objectify it within a tangible, controllable universe. It may go the whole way in the process of structuring the world of the patient up to the threshold of tolerance, penetrating and surpassing reality ('surplus' reality), and may insist upon the most minute details of episodes, in physical, mental and social space to be explored. Its aim is to make total behavior directly visible, observable and measurable. The protagonist is being prepared for an encounter with himself. After this phase of objectification is completed, the second phase begins; it is to resubjectify, reorganize and reintegrate that which has been objectified. (In practice, however, both phases go hand in hand.)" (Moreno, *Psychodrama*, Vol. 1, 1964)

6 Sociometry

S ociometry deals with the nature, quality and quantity of human connection. We are constantly making choices about what we feel, think and do. Sociometry explores and concretizes this choice-making process. Feeling chosen, unchosen, rejected, invisible, isolated or having star status are issues that emerge naturally in groups and throughout sociometric investigation. What is our sociometric status within a group, and how does that play out? What is our sociometric status in the group to which we were originally born, and how do we carry that status, positive, negative or neutral, into all of our life relationships and settings? How do we alter a less-than-satisfactory status? How do we use the social atom or the sociometric test to reveal and rework sociometric alignments?

Sociometry offers a way to study groups in their concrete form. Through the sociometric test, for example, which studies the group preferences or the social atom and/or one's personal network, sociometry offers a way to explore the nature of the group that can be executed either with paper and pencil or experientially.

As the father of group psychotherapy it is no surprise that Moreno created a vehicle for the systematic study of group interaction. An essential element of the science of sociometry is its overt incorporation of all of these group dynamics and a method of concrete study through which to address them. It takes into account the projection and transference that arise inevitably in a group and provides a vehicle for concretizing or studying it. Moreno felt that the group was "society in miniature" and created concrete methods for examining groups.

Many pressing therapeutic challenges became evident to Moreno after his initial experiments with group psychotherapy. His first attempt at group psychotherapy was to "assemble the new members of the group . . . in a room which was fitted out with a number of couches. Every individual was placed on a couch. The fundamental rule of free association was applied to them." However, Moreno goes on to explain, "the experiment failed; the free association of one began to mingle with the free associations of the other. This confused them and produced a chaotic situation. The reasons for the failure seemed to be twofold. Free association works significantly only along individual tracks; free associations which have significance along the track of individual A, for instance, have no significance on the tracks of B or of C and vice versa. They have no common unconscious; in psychoanalytic theory each individual has his own unconscious. When free association was rigorously applied, a number of individuals were being separately psychoanalyzed. It did not develop into group psychoanalysis but into psychoanalysis of several individuals within a group setting. But my objectives were group therapy and group analysis, not individual analysis. As the psychoanalytic method of free association proved unproductive, I developed a new method which was based on the study of the formation of groups in *statu nascendi* . . ." (J. Moreno 1921).

This "new method" heralded the birth of sociometry. It is the constant problem of the group therapist to create an environment that meets the needs of all members present. Just as in a family with many children, each with different needs and at varying levels of development, each group is filled with power struggles, transferences, projections, and met and unmet needs, alongside laughter, a sense of belonging, a wish for intimacy and a sense of involvement.

"Moreno is not content with insight, nor is this the scientist's goal. The science of action theory is firmly based on the belief that what has been learned in action must also be unlearned in action. And this learning has taken place among others, either as interactors or as audience, the learning has been coproduced. It is for this reason that Moreno developed the branch of the social sciences, sociometry, to provide a framework for exploring the involvement of interactors in the development of one's personal cultural conserve" (Hale 1981).

With sociometry, Moreno attempted to create a science that would be capable of studying, recording and working with the acceptance, rejection and neutral reactions among group members, while studying pairs, clusters, triangles, cleavages and other group formations. The ways in which groups organize themselves naturally is encompassed in the science of sociometry. Who is drawn to whom, or who is repelled by whom, and how do we create a method through which to explore this? Who in the group is regularly chosen, and for what reason or sociometric criteria? The person we choose for a study companion may not be the one we wish to see a movie with, for example. Who in the group is regularly unchosen and why are they in isolated positions? Is there a "group think" in every group or merely in groups that are choosing each other because they share common ground? Or does "group think" spontaneously emerge when the larger part of the group is in a situation where common ground is somehow created, as in a social movement or creation of a mass category? Why do some members develop what Moreno refers to as *aristo tele,* or an excess of positive choices, while others have barely what they need or want? How many positive choices can a person actually use and enjoy, and is there such a thing as too many? What do people with an excess of positive choices do with them, or their aristo status? Does one help to incorporate an isolate, remain in a neutral position, or actively investigate and explore his isolation? Are there cliques forming, and around what criteria—why are they choosing each other? Who do they leave out and who do they pull in? How do those on the periphery feel? What do they think is going on? What is the group leader's sociometry? Who are they choosing or not choosing?

Sociometry encompasses everything from choosing a marriage partner to selecting a president. It is the study of choice making in all of its various ramifications. Why do we make the choices we make, what is our warm-up to choosing, do we choose too quickly or with too much hesitation, how do we experience not being chosen? Under which circumstances does it bother us and in which does it not matter? "Sociometric information is revealed over time, layer by layer. It is cumulative. True understanding of a group's complexities comes from being able to step inside the multilayered universe that is constructed from the sociometric perceptions of individual group members as they reveal their personal and collective social atoms to each other" (Lippman 2003). The emotional and psychological patterns surface in the synthetic group through the ever-changing fabric of group interactions; often through projections and transferences. As Moreno says, "By the group we were wounded and in the group we will heal." Sociometry provides a concrete vehicle through which the wounds and strengths gained sociometrically can resurface and be healed or consolidated.

As Moreno said in his seminal work on the subject, *Who Shall Survive?* "The result of sociometric development has been that the investigation of the smallest social aggregates has become more interesting than that of large ones. For the future development of sociometry it may be desirable to separate it as a special discipline and to consider it as a microscope and microdynamic science underlying all social sciences."

EMOTIONS AND DECISION-MAKING

The process of decision-making requires emotional availability in order to make choices. "Recent research has yielded an explosion of literature that establishes a strong connection between emotional and cognitive processes. Most notably, Antonio Damasio draws an intimate connection between emotion and cognition in practical decision-making. Damasio presents a 'somatic marker' hypothesis, which explains how emotions are biologically indispensable to decisions. His research on patients with frontal lobe damage indicates that feelings normally accompany response options and operate as a biasing device to dictate choice" (Thagard and Barnes 1985). In other words, people who lack access to their emotions are not able to sift through all of the incoming data and options and come up with an emotional urge that gives them a sense of direction or bias. "These neurological studies show that what is damaged in these patients is not memory or intelligence, but the neural connections between the emotional and cognitive centers of the brain. More specifically, the ventromedial frontal region is reported to be responsible for emotional processing and social cognition through connections with the amygdala and hypothalamus. After a series of tests, Saver and Damasio conclude that in the absence of emotional input, the research subject's decision-making process was overwhelmed by trivial information" (Thagard and Barnes 1985). We need our emotions to help perceive and coalesce what is important to us and the degree of importance.

Sociometry allows for this external representation of emotional data to be concretized and explored so we can see where we may have lost access to our emotional component of making choices; so we can heal in action. It is a moving from the concrete toward the abstract so we can better understand how our own personal cultural conserve affects how we make choices. Which choices cause clients to freeze in their tracks and why? Where is the emotional block and how did it get there? How can we do, undo and redo our choice-making process sociometrically so that we can become more fluid in accessing our emotions and aware of how we get blocked and go on automatic, become robotlike or freeze like a deer in the headlights? Sociometry allows for the process of choosing and being chosen to be concretized so it can be explored and examined, so we can integrate emotions into our decision-making process and examine the way in which emotions facilitate or block our ability to choose, be chosen, or make decisions that have an emotional bias or weighting.

THE BASIC DYNAMICS OR TENETS OF SOCIOMETRY

Moreno outlined what he felt to be some basic laws of the sociodynamics within groups, whether they be school, work, social, community or spiritually oriented groups. They are:

The Sociogenetic Law: "The highest forms of group organization have evolved from simple ones" (J. Moreno 1966). This "refers to the tribal element which is inherent in each of us, and which has developed over centuries into rituals, custom, territoriality. It is observable in groups of children who form and reform their groups based on these unlearned but 'assimilated' codes of behavior" (Hale 1981).

The Sociodynamic Law: The choices in any given group are unevenly distributed among members of a collective, regardless of the size of the group or its kind. Groups tend to be stratified with respect to relevant sociometric criteria rather than fairness. This means that there will be those who are highly chosen, those who are underchosen and those who are not chosen.

The Sociodynamic Effect: There is an unequal distribution of choices among people in a group. The chosen get chosen more, and the isolated will be more isolated. The overchosen individuals will accumulate a surplus of choices if the number of permitted choices is increased. "This phenomenon results when the wealth of choices falls to a small number of people and when only a few choices must be spread over a large number of people. Access to roles, including access to role-taking, role-playing and role-creating so important to the emergence of self, is denied by the sociometric selection process and by external reality. The result to the chosen few [may be] rigidity, controlling behavior, overwork and depersonalization. The result to the underchosen [may be] isolation, apathy, competition and reduced activity" (Hale 1981).

Sociostasis: Each person or group has an "observable and measurable sociometric set: a quantity and quality of relationships which he or she must maintain in order to experience social equilibrium. The set varies by individual" (Hale 1981). When a person's sociostasis is upset, say by death, divorce, job loss or moving, this person may have a degree of crisis and may thrash around, seeking out people or situations to fill in the missing parts of their social atom.

The Law of Social Gravitation: People from one community will move toward people of another community in direct proportion to the amount of attraction given and received, and in inverse proportion to the rejection. The process of differentiation draws the groups apart; the process of transmission and communication draws the groups together.

Group Cohesion: The larger the number of individuals involved in positive tele communications, the greater the group cohesion. The larger the number of mutual pairings (this can be based on a variety of criterion and is not static; people can mutually pair with a variety of people), the higher the rate of mutual interaction and probability of high group cohesion.

SOCIOMETRIC METHODS
AND TECHNIQUES OF EXPLORATION

In the following paragraphs I outline some of the basic sociometric vehicles developed by Moreno for group investigations. I have begun with the social atom and the sociometric test because the social atom is fundamental to the client's exploration of self-in-relation and the sociometric test is fundamental to the exploration of the group. I then outline the sociometric test, the spectogram and locogram in a further chapter. The social atom can be used throughout treatment as a guidepost and map. It has the advantage of providing both therapist and client with very significant amounts of information naturally and quickly. It is also feedback for the clients that comes from their own hands. The sociometric test is core to sociometric thinking as it evidences group choices and preferences so they can be examined in their concrete form. It is very evocative and should only be done by individuals well trained to manage the depth of feelings that surround choosing and being chosen or unchosen.

On a practical level spectrograms and locograms are two of the most user friendly and available of the sociometric techniques. Because they do not necessarily involve movement into psychodrama, clinicians are oftentimes more comfortable using them than they might be conducting an actual drama. They are very adaptable, give both therapist and group an instant picture of group leanings and preferences, and can be adjusted to any subject being explored. I have used them as psychoeducational basics throughout the book. In these chapters we describe them in their pure form while throughout the book they have been adapted for exploration of particular issues.

Finally, milling combined with sociometric choosing is included. Milling is a nice way to warm up a group and help them get familiar with the space in which they are working and get in touch with themselves and other group members. As I have adapted it somewhat to include elements from drama therapy, theater and sociometry, I find it works well as a gradual entry into the experiential process.

THE SOCIAL ATOM

The social atom represents the nucleus of the range of individuals with whom we are connected at any given moment of our lives. It is a paper-and-pencil diagram of our relational network. The social atom can be used entirely as a paper-and-pencil exploration and as such more than stands on its own as a therapeutic instrument. Or it may be moved into action as an action sociogram.

The social atom's potential for adaptation to any circumstance or time period in the life of an individual, along with its ability to reflect not only the fact of the relationship but the nature and quality of the connection, make it a flexible cornerstone instrument for virtually any treatment modality, be it one-to-one, group or extended treatment. The social atom can also be used to represent changes made over a span of treatment by doing one at entry and then repeating it at six-to nine-month intervals throughout treatment. The social atom can be done to represent past, present and future, and as such, it is a diagnostic tool, a therapeutic instrument and an instrument to explore desired treatment outcomes. It continued to be adapted into its present form by Robert Siroka, Ph.D., TEP.

The social atom influenced the creation of the genogram and is three generational, as is the genogram. But unlike the genogram it is a fluid, affective representation of one's relational world. It can reveal the nature and type of connectedness of the object relationships in one's life.

The social atom can be used as a paper-and-pencil diagnostic tool in most any treatment setting. It need never be brought to action as it is more than sufficient as a diagnostic and treatment instrument on its own. The social atom does not necessarily require extensive training in psychodrama if used as a paper instrument.

Because the social atom is such an important component of psychodrama and sociometry, I have given it its own chapter following this one.

THE SOCIOMETRIC TEST

The sociometric test is the process that makes the unconscious dynamics of the group conscious and should, therefore, be undertaken carefully and with appropriate caution. It uses specific questions as criteria to facilitate the choice-making process. That is, we choose, at least in part, according to what criteria underlie the actual choice. For example, we may choose one person to climb mountains with but not wish to become intimate with him or her, making a different choice for the role relationship of "intimate" or "close friend." "The primary purpose of a sociometric exploration of a group is to reveal information to the group and its leaders about itself. Moreno developed a number of devices to accomplish this purpose to varying degrees. The sociometric test has been in use since 1934 in many settings and in combination with other research procedures. Consequently the procedure has undergone expansion and refinement" (Hale 1981).

SPECTROGRAM

The spectrogram is an enormously versatile and usable sociometric exercise. I have used it in locales all over the country—in treatment facilities, workshops, staff trainings, therapy groups, nontherapy groups, training groups—and it consistently does its job of reveling sociometric alignments within the group, according to particular criterion questions. Group sizes for this exercise have ranged from eight to over one hundred participants with an ideal range being twelve to about thirty-five. The spectrogram reveals significant information about the group very quickly. Then it provides opportunities for many small encounters and connections within the group.

Think of the spectrogram as a graph on a floor. Rather than using lines or dots to represent placement as one would with paper, the spectrogram asks the criterion question then invites group members to "stand in the location that best represents their self-assessment." This moving from one's seat and committing to a standing, choice-making position encourages a greater engagement in the process. Then, as people share, group members express the thoughts and feelings behind their choices.

This spectrogram can serve as an "action check-in," a warm-up for action or an experiential group process in and of itself after which the group can return to their seats for continued psychodynamic processing. This exercise is useful for getting people involved in group process, for developing group cohesion and bonding as group members open up what is inside of them, as well as creating member-to-member connections. Sociometrically speaking, one's status rises along with sincere self-disclosure.

The Locogram

The locogram, as the name implies, is used to designate locations on the floor to represent particular psychological or emotional positions in response to expressed criterion. The therapist or group designate areas of the floor to represent where the group is at a given moment. For example, areas might represent "I am happy to be here," "I don't want to be here," "I can take it or leave it," and "other." "Other" is an ever-present designation that allows group members to "write in" their own answer, so to speak. Group members are asked to stand in the area that best represents "where they are" and then share as to why they chose to stand in those spots. An extension of the exercise can be to make a second choice as to where to stand or to walk over to someone who shared something "you identified with and tell that person why you choose them."

The locogram can be used as an action check-in, a warm-up to work, or a group process that acts as a springboard to sharing and/or psychodramatic journaling.

7 The Social Atom

The social atom is a diagram or picture that represents the nucleus of all individuals to whom we are emotionally related. The study of these atoms and their interrelation is important in understanding the relationships we have with the significant people in our lives and, therefore, in any attempt to modify relationship issues and/or personality disorders. The social atom can be entirely done as a paper-and-pencil exploration, used much in the way a genogram is used only with the added ability to become more fluid in revealing the nature and quality of connectedness from individual to individual. It can also be used in as wide a variety of explorations as one can imagine; for example, social atoms can be done of the family of origin, present-day family, friends and work, imagined or desired future life circumstances, a moment in one's past, a work or school relationships, or a dream. Or social atoms can be done to compare and contrast the before and after worlds of trauma, or the sober versus the using world of the addict or addicted family. The social atom is one of Moreno's very significant contributions to the mental health field, and it influenced the creation of the genogram from family systems theory. For this reason, I have given the social atom its own chapter in order that those wishing to use it exclusively as a paper-and-pencil exploration can understand how it stands on its own.

And for those who wish to concretize the social atom on stage and move it into psychodramatic exploration, instructions are given later in the chapter. Experiencing one's social network on paper is surprisingly adequate and more than meets the need of the client to understand and explore their personal network. Meeting one's network or, say, family of origin, through role-play has a most unusual effect, like meeting up with characters from the past, present or future in the here and now where they can be dealt with in the present moment. The social atom is an excellent focusing instrument for treatment as it can represent virtually any point along the continuum of one's life, including the social atom one was born into or adoped into. Because it can be done for any time—past, present or future—it helps the client to coalesce a variety of influences and understand them in an organized fashion.

A social atom offers the opportunity for us to see ourselves. "The social atom is the visible constellation of the tele range of an individual. It is the nucleus of individuals to whom a person is emotionally related or who are related to them at the same time. It reaches as far as tele reaches, representing relationships near, far, alive or dead. It is the sum of interpersonal structures resulting from choices and rejections centered about a given individual" (J. Moreno 1934). This self-produced clear, concise and objective feedback provides a concrete map of the client's relationship range, which can include people, pets, institutions or careers. The information on a social atom reveals not only the client's relationship range, but also the quality, number and nature of her relationships and her sociometric experience within a particular group.

The social atom is useful both in individual therapy and in a group context. Clients may take time to do it on their own and may share it either with the large group, in smaller subgroups or with a therapist. The social atom can be used as a paper-and-pencil activity or moved into action as an action sociogram. It can also be a warm-up to vignettes or monodramas. If you wish to use the social atom as a paper-and-pencil activity it can be followed by sharing and/or the exploration of questions though psychodramatic journaling or discussion (see Role Diagram, page 167).

We are all born into a particular social atom, or what Moreno referred to as a "model group." The nature of the connections within that model group are represented by a *family-of-origin* social atom and tend to get carried along throughout life and projected onto the various relationships that we subsequently enter. Following are three examples of categories of social atoms, but the reader should keep in mind that the social atom can be adjusted to meet virtually any need.

The *present-day* social atom reveals to both client and therapist, the relational structure in which the client currently lives. Institutions or interest groups can also be represented. The social atom can offer a starting point for life changes. Questions for exploration after the social atom has been written and shared might be: "Where are the issues that you feel you'd like to work on?" or "What about your atom is working well for you?" and "What might you like to change?"

The *family-of-origin* social atom is diagnostic in that it reveals a client's internalized relational structure, the family of origin, and extended family and friend relationships upon which others may have been built. It has the added advantage of being produced by the client herself, so any resistance she may have in looking at her relational world is tempered by the fact that she is the person committing it to paper, rather than the therapist. Once the present-day atom is completed, clients can use the family-of-origin social atom to begin exploring the impact the family has had on their development, and they can look for how their past may be impacting their present in terms of reenactment dynamics and transferences. The family of origin atom provides an object relations map that can be referred to throughout treatment when understanding transference. For example, if an employer is a particular target for transference the therapist might ask, "Who might your employer represent for you from your family-of-origin social atom?" The family-of-origin social atom provides an enormous amount of information for both the client and the therapist as to the constellation of the family model-group and the client's sociometric alignments, misalignments, relations and status within the system.

A *future-projection* social atom can be used to concretize desired social atom repair or goals for the future. An atom can be drawn that represents how a client may want their life to be at any point in the future. The future atom can reflect desired life changes, dreams or ambitions. It can include wished-for relationships, careers or hobbies. It can also very practically and realistically diagram desired treatment outcomes.

The social atom can be a useful referent for change if done every so often throughout the treatment process. We can use it as a guide toward that change by asking questions like: "What would I like to be different on my social atom?" or "What aspects of this might I choose to change?" and "What are the parts of my social atom that I am bringing from my childhood into the present that might not be helpful today?" and finally, "What transferences from the past are being played out on my present-day atom?"

How to Read the Social Atom

In reading the social atom, the primary source of information will come from the client. This is an efficient way of gathering many insights into the client's personal history, and because it is client-driven and self-interpreted, the insights the client gains for himself can feel very meaningful to him. An average atom used in therapy probably has from fifteen to twenty-five people on it and represents the psychological, individual and emotional levels of a person's social structure most commonly worked with during treatment of the individual. It acts as that person's object relationship map. The social, collective and acquaintance levels may or may not appear on the atom, depending on the instructions given by the therapist.

Here are some things to look for when you read a social atom:

1. **Large and distant images.** These may represent concerns with authority figures. Or they may be the way a child perceived a parent at a given period of time if this is a social atom representing childhood.
2. **Small and distant images.** These may represent negative transferences or competitive sibling figures, particularly if they are very small. Or they may simply be part of one's network but not of primary importance (Siroka 1988).
3. **Overlaps.** These may indicate relationships in need of differentiation, if they are not otherwise explained.
4. **Horizontal or vertical bisections.** If a vertical or horizontal line bisects a symbol, note whether there is a difference between what's on the left and on the right in the eyes of the client. For example, past and present, male and female.

5. **Omission.** Is there anyone who is conspicuous by her omission or absence on the atom? For example, did a client leave her father out and, if so, why?

6. **Erasures, changes or multiple lines.** These may indicate there is some unfinished business or anxiety where more will need to be explored. The client's pencil seems to go round and round while drawing the symbol. (Siroka 1988).

7. **Location of symbols vis a vis the writer of the social atom.** The relative size in comparison to and the distance or closeness of the symbols in relationship to the writer of the atom may reveal the way in which the writer views himself vis à vis those represented on the atom.

8. **Location of symbol representing the self.** The location and relative size of the symbol that the writer of the atom uses to represent herself may indicate how she feels in comparison to others on her atom.

Notational System For Social Atoms*

◯	=	female
△	=	male
▢	=	genderless (to represent institutions, careers, large groupings, etc.)
⟨◌⟩	=	deceased female
△̇	=	deceased male
——	=	mutual attraction
- - - - -	=	mutual rejection
··········	=	mutual indifference

*This is the most basic notational system; many more variations are possible. For more information, see Chapter Notes. *Conducting Clinical Sociometric Explorations: A Manual for Psychodramatists and Sociometrists,* Royal Publishing Co., Roanoke, VA. James Vander May, "A Perceptual Social Atom Sociogram," in Anne E. Hale, ed., vol. 28 (1975), 128–134.

The following are different levels of representation on any given social atom:

1. **The psychological.** The psychological level indicates the people who are most intimately connected with us, with whom we have the strongest tele connection. It visually represents an individual's tele range.

2. **The individual.** This level represents the smallest number of people we require to be in balance. It changes as our level of spontaneity changes.

3. **Emotional expansiveness.** On any given atom, these are the people with whom we have some emotional recognition and connection. Emotional expansiveness measures the emotional energy that enables the individual to "hold" the affection of other individuals for a given period of time.

4. **Social expansiveness.** On any given atom, there are people with whom we are not intimately connected but nevertheless with whom we feel a tele connection; they are more than distant acquaintances.

5. **The collective.** This level represents the smallest number of groups and collectives we require to be in balance. It includes the formal structures that provide us with opportunities to express various sides of ourselves, such as family, social groups, job, school or hobby groups. It can be called the cultural atom or the cultural aspect of the atom.

6. **Acquaintance volume.** This might represent anyone with whom we have come into contact and become acquainted. The acquaintance volume represents the volume of "social" expansion of an individual, the range of his social contacts. The acquaintance volume does not necessarily reflect relationships with deep, emotional connection but the number of people one "is able to interest . . . how many people he can transfer an emotion to and from how many people he can absorb emotion." There is a sociometric "point of saturation" of a specific homogeneous group for a specific contrasting element under given conditions. The point of saturation may change with the organization of the interrelated groups (*Who Shall Survive?* Moreno).

PRESENT-DAY SOCIAL ATOM

GOALS:

1. To make conscious the quality and nature of the patterns that form a person's social network.
2. To provide a map of interrelations that the therapist and/or group members can refer to throughout the treatment process.

STEPS:

1. Have participants get pencil and paper.
2. Invite group members to make an atom of their current lives. Say, "Using circles to represent females, triangles to represent males and squares to represent institutions or groups, first locate yourself on the paper, anywhere that feels right to you."
3. Continue, "Now locate your significant relations as close or distant from yourself as you feel them to be and in the size or proportion that feels right. You may include pets, in-laws, grandparents, friends and so on. Use a broken line to represent anyone who is deceased. Write the name of each person inside or next to his or her symbol."
4. Once all the symbols are on paper and the atoms feel finished, people can begin to share them, either in the large group, with a partner, in small groupings or with the therapist one-to-one. Remind them that these atoms are only a current reflection; they are always subject to change.
5. Sharing the atom may bring up many feelings toward or about those present on the atom. Allow plenty of time for sharing all these potentially strong feelings.
6. After the sharing is complete, you may (a) move the social atoms into action (see Action Scoiogram), or (b) keep them and refer to them as a measurement of growth.

VARIATIONS:

Clients may share their atoms with the therapist or group by holding them up and saying something like, "This is me. I made myself," etc., and then go on to describe others on the atom and who they are in relationship to. Present-day atoms provide a picture of a client's current relational network.

REGRESSIVE OR FAMILY-OF-ORIGIN SOCIAL ATOM

GOALS:

1. To concretize the social atom on paper.
2. To offer an opportunity for interaction with real rather than imagined people.

STEPS:

1. Ask group members to find a pencil and paper.
2. Reflect on your family of origin, either a specific time from your past or a general representation of your early life.
3. Say, "Using circles to represent females and triangles to represent males and squares to represent institutions or groups first locate yourself on the paper, anywhere that feels right to you."
4. Continue, "Now locate your important relationships or significant tele relations as close or distant from yourself as you feel them to be, and in the size or proportion that feels right. You may include pets, in-laws, grandparents, groups, institutions, careers, friends.
5. Next, invite group members to share their social atoms with the group, or, with the therapist if done in one-to-one therapy. Family-of-origin social atoms may be shared in the here and now from the self of today or the client may reverse roles and share from the point of view of the age represented by the social atom; e.g. "This is me, I am ten, my dad is large and distant and my mom is small and very close to me. I have a dog Buster who is with me all the time. My grandparents are really close to me on my atom, my brother is bigger than me and pretty close," etc.
6. Continue to allow any who wishes, to share their atom.
7. At this point the group may A) continue to share, B) move into an action sociogram (move the social atom into action) or C) do psychodramatic journaling.

VARIATIONS:

Family-of-origin atoms can represent any point in time from past till present that includes family-of-origin members. Or the director can give specific instructions such as, "'Do an atom of a time that felt problematic in your upbringing, when you felt especially lost, especially happy, when addiction took hold, where there was a crisis, when the family felt calm and secured," and so on. Virtually any time can be explored through the vehicle of the social atom.

If moving into action, protagonists may wish to warm up by walking around the scene they have set up and soliloquizing about what they are experiencing. They may wish to end the enactment in the same manner or simply back up and talk to the family sculpture at large for closure. For example: "Say the last things you wish to say to or about this group being represented." Or a protagonist may wish to sculpture the scene as they wish it had been in order to have a visual picture of that wish.

FUTURE-PROJECTION SOCIAL ATOM

GOALS:

1. To concretize goals for the future.
2. To function as part of a treatment plan.
3. To function as part of an aftercare plan.

STEPS:

1. Have participants get pencil and paper.
2. Ask group members to imagine their future as they might wish it to be at some point, for example, in six months, one year, three years, five years, etc.
3. Invite group members to make an atom of their lives as they would like them to be. Say, "Using circles to represent females, triangles to represent males and squares to represent institutions or groups, first locate yourself on the paper, anywhere that feels right to you."
4. Continue, "Now locate your important relationships or significant tele relations as close or distant from yourself as you feel them to be, and in the size or proportion that feels right. You may include pets, in-laws, grandparents, groups, institutions, careers or friends. Label them appropriately."
5. Once all the symbols are on paper and the atoms feel finished, people can begin to share them, either in the large group, with a partner, in small groupings or with the therapist one-to-one.
6. These can be moved into action or used exclusively as a psychodramatic journaling exercise.

VARIATIONS:

A future projection social atom can concretize wishes, goals, plans or dreams for the future. Desired life situations, partnerships, friendships, hobbies and career plans, to name a few, can be included on this atom.

An aftercare social atom can be done to reflect the sorts of life and relationships that a client may need or wish to create. This can function as part of a treatment or aftercare plan. Addicts often need to face changing groups of friends as part of staying sober. Concretizing these changes and identifying people who might become part of a group of recovering friends can help them take the first step. Other activities that reflect positive life changes can be included as well, such as twelve-step programs, exercise, meditation and so on.

PSYCHODRAMATIC JOURNALING EXERCISES TO DO WITH A SOCIAL ATOM

First, do any type of social atom that you wish to do. Then do whatever journaling exercise the client feels warmed up to do.

JOURNALING VARIATIONS:

- Write a letter to anyone on your social atom to whom you have something to say.
- Reverse roles with anyone on your social atom and write a letter "as" that person back to yourself that you would like to receive, or write a letter as him or her to someone else.
- Write a journal entry "as" yourself as you are represented on your atom (if you are young, journal as yourself at that age; reverse roles with yourself as an eight-year-old, for example).
- Reverse roles with anyone on your social atom and write a journal entry "as" that person.
- Dialogue with anyone on your social atom, writing "to" them, then "as" them.

ACTION SOCIOGRAM

GOALS:

1. To concretize the social atom or any scene or model scene that is being moved into action.
2. To offer an opportunity for interaction with real rather than imagined people.

STEPS:

1. Ask group members to draw any version of their social atoms.
2. Choose a protagonist through any of the selection processes, than ask the protagonist to choose auxiliaries to represent those on the social atom or any grouping of those represented, including a stand-in to play the self, if desired.
3. If you feel the auxiliaries need to find out more about their roles, you may ask the protagonist to reverse roles and show the group a little of what the person being role-played is like before choosing someone for the role.
4. Set the scene or place the auxiliaries.
5. Ask the protagonist either to go where he is drawn to interact or to mill around the whole picture until he feels drawn to a particular person, at which point he may begin to speak to that person.
6. Allow the protagonist, if he wishes, to step out of the picture and take a full view of the setup and see how that feels. He may reverse roles with himself or double for himself where motivated.
7. Move through the enactment, allowing the protagonist to express his thoughts and feelings freely (within group norms, of course) to any and all characters, using all techniques appropriate, such as role reversal, doubling, interviewing and so on.
8. Ask the protagonist to finish the scene in any way he feels inclined to, including, if he wishes, correcting the scene by structuring it as he wishes it had been. You may offer him the choice of having reformed auxiliaries in order to get what he wishes he had had; he can ask for what he wants and receive it psychodramatically.
9. Leave plenty of time for sharing what came up for group members and what the auxiliaries felt while playing the various roles. Derole all auxiliaries by simply stating, "I'm (name of group member) not (name of role played)," or by symbolically "brushing off" the role and/or by sharing what it felt like to play the role, then making a clear and intentional shift into the role of self and sharing what came up personally from

participating in the drama. Even while playing a role it is common for many personal feelings that will need to be shared to come up.

VARIATIONS:

Any scene put into action can be called an action sociogram. Here it represents social atoms or parts of social atoms that are concretized and enacted. Family-of-origin atoms can represent any point in time from past till present that includes family-of-origin members. Or the director can give specific instructions such as, "Do an atom of a time that felt problematic in your upbringing, when you felt especially lost, especially happy, when addiction took hold, where there was a crisis, when the family felt calm and secure," and so on. Virtually any time can be explored through the vehicle of the social atom.

Protagonists may wish to warm up by walking around the scene they have set up and soliloquizing about what they are experiencing. They may wish to end the enactment in the same manner or simply back up and talk to the family sculpture at large for closure. For example: "Say the last things you wish to say to or about this group being represented." Or a protagonist may wish to sculpture the scene as the wish it had been in order to have a visual picture of that wish.

It may be useful to include intergenerational scenes to gain perspective on the generational chain of dysfunction and to promote understanding that parents, for example, passed on what they got from their own parents, concretizing a chain of dysfunction composed of learned behavior patterns. For example, the protagonist, while in role-reversal as the mother, can break off from the scene, freeze it and momentarily do a scene as the mother, perhaps talking to her mother, in order to explore the generational aspect of behavior patterns. They can then bring this to closure and return to the original scene and continue playing it. This can help clients to feel less singled out for abuse and realize they were victims of intergenerational patterns and that individuals have their own history that is brought to bear on their relationships. It also empowers them to choose to do things differently. They may also come to see the strengths that have been passed through the generations.

Possible Variations on the Social Atom

- **Developmental Atom.** People can make developmental social atoms representing particular times of life—as a child, adolescent, teenager, young adult, householder, elder and so on. When sharing them they can share from the present day, or reverse roles and share as the age represented on the atom.
- **Parent's Atom.** Making a parents atom can be a powerful tool when made

for a time during which the parents' life situations may have complicated the life of the protagonist. For example, Ben, who feels his life went off track at age twenty, makes an atom of his father's or mother's life at that time, as well as his own, in order to investigate how their lives impacted his. It is also useful to make a parents social atom at the time of their marriage, or at the time of the birth of the protagonist. Another very useful social atom might be at the time of the birth of a sibling or a family loss or death. Making generational atoms like these can help people reconstruct their history and illuminate what was passed down through the family system.

- **Parent-Child Atom.** This is an age-correspondence atom. If a client feels his child is having a particularly difficult time, it may be useful for that client to do a social atom of his own life at the current age of his child. Doing so will help him to see if the child's problems are triggering unresolved wounds from the parent's past or if the parent's past is, in some way, being projected onto the child.

- **Sober Versus Nonsober Atom.** (See Two Different Worlds, page 98.) Participants who were raised in addicted families can make atoms showing how their family life was organized while the addict was sober and how it was organized while the addict was using. Family alliances, positioning and object relations can shift according to whether or not the addict is using. This atom reflects that shift and sheds light on one of the reasons that living with addiction is crazy-making.

- *Before and After* **Trauma Atom.** Trauma tends to divide life into two; life before the trauma took place and life after the trauma. Object relations can shift significantly after a traumatic event, along with thinking, feeling, behavior, and perception of life and the world. Doing one's social atom before the trauma and then after can help to reintegrate the life before the trauma, which may feel lost, with life afterward, which may have changed significantly or perhaps in subtle ways.

- **Social Atom of a Dream.** A social atom can be done that represents a dream using all of the symbols to represent dream images or people. It can be concretized as an action sociogram and moved into a psychodrama using role reversal, doubling, interviewing, soliliquizing and so on in order to deconsttruct the meaning of the dream for the protagonist.

- **Substance Atom.** Participants can make atoms that locate themselves in relation to any substance, person, place or thing that might be used compulsively or addictively—work, cocaine, sex, food, exercise, cigarettes and so on—to get a picture of multiple addictions. When doing this atom, ask the client to "locate the substance or behavior as close or distant and in relative size to the self as feels right."

- **Addicted Atom.** An atom can be made to reflect sexual relationships and encounters that are a part of a person's addicted world. Relationships can be based around "using friends" or sexual encounters, for example. These relationships can be concretized on an atom.

Questions for Exploration When Using the Social Atom

The following are possible questions for exploration in one-to-one therapy, group therapy or to use as psychodramatic journaling exercises. This can be part of using the social atom as a self-diagnostic tool. The beauty of it is that it provides an objective form of self-feedback for clients. In other words, they can come to their own insights and conclusions by examining what is in front of them on the paper. This is very esteem building because clients feel empowered in seeing the self. This often has the effect of building trust, an ability to depend on others in healthy ways, as clients feel less infantilized and more like partners in their own healing.

Questions for Exploration When Using the Present-Day Social Atom

1. With whom do you feel you have a good rapport or connection?
2. Whom do you feel disconnected from, rejected by or rejecting of?
3. With whom do you have unhealthy relationship bonds, if any?
4. With whom are you reenacting dysfunctional relationship patterns from past relationships (unfinished business)?
5. With whom do you have unresolved issues (hot buttons) that you need to explore in therapy?
6. Are there any covert alliances in this system?

7. Whom do you go to for support?

8. To whom do you give support?

9. With whom is the give and take of support mutual?

10. Are there groups in your current network that do not serve you well?

11. Are there groups in your current network that do serve you well?

12. What changes would you like to see happen in your network or relationships?

Questions for Exploration When Using the Family-of-Origin Social Atom

1. Where were your close-bonded relationships, and do you continue to draw strength from them today?

2. From whom did you experience acceptance/rejection, and does it still affect you today?

3. Whom do you accept/reject?

4. How did you experience yourself in your family system?

5. How do you think others experienced you in your family system?

6. What would you like to say to yourself at the age represented here, from where you are today?

7. What would you like to say to the family system?

8. What do you see as your role or roles in the family system at any given point; is anyone cut off or disconnected from the system?

9. What are the covert or overt alliances in this system?

10. What patterns from the family-of-origin system are getting played out in your life or your family today (intergenerational patterns)?

Questions for Exploration When Using the Future-Projection Social Atom

1. How do you imagine the relationships represented on this atom might feel to you?

2. What do you imagine the activities on this atom might do for you?

3. What practical steps do you think you need to take in order to actualize the categories in questions one and two?

4. What feelings are brought up when you look at your life as you would like it to be?

5. What would you like to say to yourself as represented on this atom?

Two Different Worlds:

Using the social atom to compare and contrast sober versus nonsober family dynamics or the before and after object relation shifts of the trauma survivor

Survivors of trauma, people from addicted homes and addicts themselves oftentimes live in two different worlds. For the person who has experienced a sudden loss, there is life *before* the trauma and *after* the trauma. After a trauma a person's sense of a predictable and orderly world can feel shattered. His or her inner world can be consumed with thoughts and feelings related to the trauma that might manifest as fears, phobias, anxieties, flashbacks, nightmares or somatic disturbances such as an exaggerated startle response, migraines, stomach or back problems and other stress-related disorders. Life after the trauma can feel different with the disquieting awareness that bad things can and do happen. Suddenly, the world can feel like a potentially threatening place or relationships with people can be anxiety provoking—people are neither perfect nor permanent and life is unpredictable. Object relations can shift after trauma, that is, the nature and quality of relationships can change. Concretizing these shifts on **before** and **after** social atoms can help to clarify the impact trauma had on the client and the ways in which it impacted the client's life.

For the ACOA addict and coaddict, there are two distinct realities: the one while the addict is using, and the one when the addict sobers up. Addicts cycle between using and sober behavior. This forces family members to make sense of two different realities, the sober and the nonsober, each of which has its own code of ethics, morality and rules of engagement. The thinking, feeling, behavior, and emotional atmosphere are different for each world and often nearly impossible to integrate into a coherent whole. The person in this environment never knows where to find firm ground to stand on. He "walks on eggshells," holds his breath and "waits for the other shoe to drop." In short, he becomes *hypervigilant* constantly scanning his environment for signs of danger. The object relations for each reality shift, as do alliances and family behavior. For the person living with other forms of dysfunction such as mental illness, abuse or neglect, there can also be two different worlds—the family that is presented to the outside world and the family's inner world. The two may not match up (Dayton 2000).

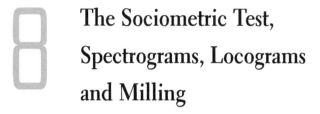

The Sociometric Test, Spectrograms, Locograms and Milling

In this chapter we will explore some basic and frequently used action sociometry techniques and methods. These are cornerstone sociometric exercises in their basic form. Throughout the remaining sections of this book, I have varied these basic sociometric formats and adapted them for use in treating special issues and special populations.

THE SOCIOMETRIC TEST

The sociometric test is a powerful technique and not to be entered into lightly. It is an investigation designed to make the less conscious group dynamics conscious. It requires considerable processing which might need to continue for subsequent sessions. In my experience, this is not appropriate for groups that aren't well bonded and will not be meeting regularly.

These forms of sociometric choosing or the sociometric test should be done by those practitioners who have considerable training in psychodrama and are actively engaged with a primary trainer who can offer supervision and guidance. The feelings that come up through this process can require skilled and practiced processing.

The sociometric test will have a warm-up, an action phase and a sharing phase much in the way a psychodrama does. The warm-up may be group members sharing that they wish to go deeper into group analysis and interaction or that they feel there are some dynamics in the group that would benefit from being brought to the surface and explored through sociometric action. Group members, in this case, are feeling warmed up to each other and in the mood to take a risk. Other warm-ups can involve a group wanting to learn more about a new member or incorporate new members. Groups will need to be told something about the process so they know what to expect. Group members may collectively discuss possible criterion questions they wish to explore. In working with issues of trauma resolution, or with populations that have experienced significant relationship trauma, this process can be too evocative in the early stages of recovery. Being chosen or unchosen can both be fraught with anxiety for the person who feels chosen in ways that put them at risk or not chosen at all. Other, less direct sociometric techniques allow the client to enter in a less threatening way. In the locogram, for example, I add one sociometric choice to many of my locograms. The choice is based on identification only and it doesn't put clients themselves on the spot. I find this works more easily in these populations. Some group situations for using the sociometric test are:

1. When a group is newly formed. Sociometric choosing allows group members to interact in dyads and small groupings, which can promote group cohesion and more relaxed sharing than might occur when the group members sit facing each other in a circle.

2. When incorporating a new member. This process works very effectively at allowing the new group member to make multiple personal connections with more established members and vice versa.

3. When a group is blocked or stuck. It may be used when honesty and spontaneity are low, perhaps out of fear that expression of genuine emotion will compromise self or others. Also, it may be used when there are unspoken thoughts between members either in the here and now of the relationship or for other reasons, perhaps because cliques, dyads or cleavages are causing group disturbances.

4. When transferences within the group need to be acknowledged and worked through in order for group members to feel safe opening up and sharing emotions about which they feel scared or vulnerable.

5. When the group is ready to take risks in furthering intimacy with self and others.

6. When the director and/or group wishes to investigate sociometric alignments or non-alignments within the group in the form of positive, negative or neutral choices or investigations around particular criteria.

7. When a group is terminating as a whole to provide opportunities for closure. In this case, the therapist would take care to allow several weeks to process what might arise.

Action sociometry explores one's role or status within a given group. Following are some of the roles and dynamics that emerge from the group.

Sociometric Positions Within the Group and in Society at Large

The Sociometric Star

The sociometric star is the person or persons who receive the largest number of choices. They can be a star of acceptance or a star of rejection based on the criterion being explored. A highly chosen person in a group who does not reciprocate choices—for example, a popular person who a group cares about but who does not, herself, care about the group in return—can be experienced as a "disruption within the group." She has, so to speak, sociometric weight, but that weight is not in service of the group; she is disconnected.

The phenomenon of "star power" clearly illustrates the power of sociometric stars; they have sociometric weight to throw around at their discretion. Stars can bring attention to a lost cause, raise money for those in need or lend their star energy to an issue they feel needs to come to general attention. On a lesser scale, for example, in the teenage peer group, they can lead their friends down a good and constructive road, or off the deep end. Sociometric stars have a surplus of choices they can assign where they wish. Stars represent the values of the group choosing them, i.e., members of a collective choose someone who best represents the spoken or unspoken values they hold dear.

The sociodynamic effect of how choices get distributed among a group is that the highly chosen continue to get chosen more and the isolated get more isolated. One of the possible benefits of the sociometric test is to continue revolving the criterion for choosing so that the network of possible choice-making gets broken up a bit and expanded. Afterschool programs illustrate this idea of many possible choices nicely. If all that is available for students, for example, is one team and one cheerleading squad, the highly chosen will continue to get more chosen, and cliques versus isolates will be the inevitable outcome. There need to be more available ports of entry into meaningful afterschool activities, more options. Adding cheerleading squads for each sport, having more sports teams available to play on, emphasizing other types of activities, other areas in which to excel such as theater, art, movement, writing, martial arts or chess, are all examples of expanding potential sociometry on both an individual and group basis. They offer more opportunities for choice and thus reduce the potential for isolation.

The same can be true for therapy groups. As criterion questions expand, group members can experience more opportunities to choose and be chosen, they can expand their possibilities for connection. We may choose one person to get advice from, for example, and someone completely different to go to a movie with. Our choices are based on the criterion around which we are choosing.

Isolate and Isolate Dyads

"The true isolate does not choose and is not chosen. He or she may choose others who are not members of the group, preferring to invest choice in persons who are not present. 'They reduce cohesion in a group to a minimum, possibly leading to dissolution and death of the group.' An isolated dyad is a pair who choose only each other, and remain apart from the other members of the group. They are unwilling to join activities within the group and unwilling to share with others. This has an impact of stopping the growth of the identity of the group when it attempts to include the isolates. The isolate's refusal to make choices stymies group members' attention to the task" (Hale 1981).

In the school system, isolates represent a sad, and in recent history potentially dangerous, position. Feeling disenfranchised from the surrounding social world, they cannot seem to find a way to choose in or get chosen and are left to live in a surplus of psychodramatic roles and an impoverishment of roles in their real world. Living in their fantasies because reality feels inaccessible, they may cook up schemes for revenge, schemes they imagine might turn around their constant feelings of powerlessness in order to bring homeostasis to their inner worlds and gain sociometric (albeit negative) power.

Depressed or traumatized people often tend to isolate, retreating into an ever-shrinking world. The more they isolate, the more they remain isolated as choosing in becomes fraught with anxiety, and they may lose the confidence that they are capable of making and sustaining choices. Sociometry can help to counter this isolation through making the dynamics conscious, providing practice in choosing and being chosen and opening doors through which new experiences can come in.

Cliques and Subgroups

"Three or more individuals who mutually choose each other and/or include others in their group (which is less than the total number of the group) comprise a subgroup. The subgroup has the potential for exerting influence over the actions of the group, especially if they have a person in the subgroup who is identified as a star. Subgroups have the capacity to split the group and divert energies from task" (Hale 1981). In my experience, the process of sociometric selection of a protagonist can be impacted by cliques and subgroups who choose each other (members of their subgroups) over and over again to work. This can create frustration on the part of other group members who feel on the outside and can't get in. Theoretically, the person on the outside benefits from eventually being able to articulate his feelings of exclusion and exploring why he is being excluded, as the assumption is that one carries his initial sociometry, or social atom, with him and tends to recreate it in many life situations. While this may well be true, I have found that it is not necessarily true for all group dynamics. One needs to keep in mind while investigating this that that same person who is underchosen by one group may be highly chosen or at least more accepted by another.

One sees this phenomenon ever at play in the school peer group: the proverbial kid who spends all her time and energy trying to be chosen by a "popular" clique that seems bound and determined not to choose her rather than seeking out the less highly chosen classmates whom she might be chosen by. Were she able to seek out a mutuality of choosing, she would gain some sociometric stability; a place to belong, in other words.

Cleavages

Cleavages represent the differences between the overt or stated rules of a group and the unstated or covert ones. Sociometric explorations can help reveal if there are cliques or subgroups that consistently choose each other regardless of the criterion for choosing. Cleavages that remain unexplored or covert (or even those that are in the open) can cause a break or a split in the group structure. Cleavages oftentimes represent the "secret that everyone knows." Generally, groups are only too aware of the covert alliances with a family system or a therapy group and feel mystified, depotentiated and marginalized by them. They may also feel powerless to affect them because challenging them, they fear, will put them even more on the outs. For this and other reasons, sociometric explorations can help expose covert dynamics so they can be aired, discussed and demystified.

Families are also vulnerable to cleavages. In dysfunctional family systems these cleavages can become stratified when, for example, siblings band together for power or parents "claim" one child as their own to the exclusion of other children.

Cleavages in schools or workplaces can also represent a serious challenge to the overall cohesion and comfort of the system. These fixed alignments can create cleavages in the overall system.

Pivotal Persons and Linkages

Pivotal persons are those people who link subgroups or other key persons in the group. They often represent the "Switzerland," or neutral territory of the group. They are very useful to group cohesion because, through their linking of subgroups and key people, they bring together factions of the group and connect them. Oftentimes there are more than one or several linking people who form a chain. When a chain is formed in the sociometric choosing process, the sociometric power of the entire chain gets linked to the person who is linking one person or sociometric star with the chain. Marketers sometimes refer to these people as "connectors" and value them as people who are useful, for example, in creating word-of-mouth publicity for a product.

MUTUALITY AND NONMUTUALITY IN CHOICE-MAKING

Choices can be positive, negative or neutral, reflecting acceptance, rejection or a benign indifference. They can also be mutual or nonmutual. Groups with a high expression of mutuality in their sociometric choices tend to be more cohesive than those without mutuality. Families that have a high instance of mutual pairings in every direction, that is, they get along well in each of their possible dyads, tend to be more cohesive and peaceful than those that don't.

Mutuality of choices on a psychetellic level can provide a sense of comfort and stability in life. Having relationships that are mutual may also provide a person with an actually greater sense of internal security than being highly chosen but not reciprocating those choices (nonmutual). In other words, a less-exalted sociometric status with more mutual pairings may actually feel better and provide a greater sense of belonging than star status if the star does not reciprocate, on a psychetellic level, those choices coming his or her way—the "lonely at the top" phenomenon.

It is generally thought that those people who clearly understand their sociometric status are better off than those who don't. They are reality oriented and in a position to accept themselves. Reality orientation generally puts them in a better position to make changes if they are desired. Those people who imagine themselves to have a different sociometric status from what they actually have may create a sort of internal dissonance between who they think they are and who the world reflects back to them.

THE PROCESS OF SOCIOMETRIC CHOOSING, OR THE SOCIOMETRIC TEST

GOALS:

1. To reveal the nature of member-to-member connectedness or lack of connectedness within the group.
2. To provide a vehicle for processing member-to-member connections that can be shared in a dyad, or in the full eye of the group.
3. To provide an experiential vehicle that involves the whole group.
4. To promote group cohesion.

STEPS:

1. Come up with criterion questions that the group might wish to explore. The entire group can do this before the choosing process begins, or more informally as the process unfolds. The therapist may begin by offering questions to warm up the process as it unfolds, or group members may contribute questions that the group as a whole can informally accept or veto. (See list following this exercise.)
2. Once a question has been suggested the therapist says, "Who in the group would you . . . [see list]? Walk over to the person you have chosen for this question and place your hand on his or her shoulder."
3. Next, allow time for sharing. Group members can either share why they chose a particular member so the whole group can hear, or the group can share simultaneously and quietly with one another. Or these approaches can be alternately used.
4. Repeat this process for as many questions as the group wishes to explore. In addition, the therapist may wish to explore, with the group, how it feels to be chosen, how it feels not to be chosen, how it feels to be a star, and/or how it feels to be an isolate or nonchooser on any given question (see variations).
5. This can be a warm-up to psychodrama or a process in and of itself after which substantial time for sharing should be allowed.

VARIATIONS:

While processing these questions with the group, notice if there are any "isolates" or people not choosing and/or unchosen and ask them if it seems helpful, why they are choosing not to choose or how it feels not to be chosen. Not choosing is a perfectly valid position and can be explored. Not being chosen may be no big deal depending on the question or it may be worth exploring. Use caution here. Notice the sociometric "stars" in the group, or those group members who are being highly chosen for a particular question. Are they stars for a positive or a negative criterion question, and how do they feel about being chosen for either? Notice any "mutual pairs" (group members who are choosing each other equally). Notice if there are "chains" of choices, which lead toward one person giving extra energy to the person at the choice end of the chain. Is the group warmed up to doing a psychodrama with the person who received the most choices—the "star"? Refer to the previous section before this exercise in order to understand and explore possible sociometric configurations.

Some Possible Examples of Criterion Questions for Sociometric Choosing Processes with Positive or Neutral Criteria

- Who in the group would you like to hear more from?
- Who in the group are you drawn to?
- Who in the group are you concerned about?
- Who in the group do you have something to say to?
- Who in the group could you share a secret with?
- Who in the group could you play with?
- Who in the group could understand your dark side?
- Who in the group could understand your spiritual side?
- Who in the group could understand your playful side?
- Who in the group could understand your work side?
- Who in the group could understand your social side?
- Who in the group could understand your intellectual side?
- Who in the group could understand your sense of humor?
- Who in the group could understand your past?
- Who in the group do you feel understood by?
- Who in the group could you go shopping with?
- Who in the group could you play a sport with?
- Who in the group do you feel in sync with?
- Who in the group do you feel chosen by?
- Who in the group would you like to get closer to?
- Who in the group helps you see yourself?

• Who in the group do you have positive tele with?
• Who in the group could you go trick-or-treating with?

Some Possible Examples of Questions for Sociometric Choosing with Negative Criteria: Proceed with Caution

Questions that involve negative criteria can be very threatening and should only be used in a group that is highly cohesive and has ample time to work through the powerful feelings that will get mobilized. Also, only a couple of these questions should be explored at a session, and they should be mixed with positive or neutral criterion questions. Answers to these questions may also reveal transferences within the group, but not always.

• Who in the group do you feel distant from?
• Who in the group do you have transference with?
• Who in the group might play a difficult role in one of your dramas?
• Who in the group do you feel anxious around?
• Who in the group takes up space in a way that makes you uncomfortable?
• Who in the group do you feel misunderstood by?
• Who in the group do you feel hurt by?
• Who in the group are you carrying resentment for?
• Who in the group do you feel might resent you?
• Who in the group do you feel unchosen by?
• Who in the group do you feel defended around?
• Who in the group triggers you?
• Who in the group are you having a hard time with?

Some Possible Examples of Questions for Sociometric Choosing that Can Move Toward Psychodramatic Action

Life Roles
• Who in the group could play your mother?
• Who in the group could play your father?
• Who in the group could play your grandmother?

- Who in the group could play your grandfather?
- Who in the group could play your sister?
- Who in the group could play your brother?
- Who in the group could play your cousin?
- Who in the group could play your childhood playmate?
- Who in the group could play your friend?
- Who in the group could play your girlfriend?
- Who in the group could play your boyfriend?
- Who in the group could play your ex-girlfriend?
- Who in the group could play your ex-boyfriend?
- Who in the group could play you?

Surplus Reality Roles

- Who in the group could play your shadow side?
- Who in the group could play your dark side?
- Who in the group could play your creative side?
- Who in the group could play your crazy side?
- Who in the group could play your sane side?
- Who in the group could play your inner child?
- Who in the group could play your inner adolescent?
- Who in the group could play your inner muse?
- Who in the group could play your inner anxiety?
- Who in the group could play your fear?
- Who in the group could play your anger?
- Who in the group could play your jealousy?
- Who in the group could play your nobility?
- Who in the group could play your talents?
- Who in the group could play your creativity?
- Who in the group could play your genuineness?

THE SPECTROGRAM

The spectrogram is the equivalent of a graph laid out on a floor on which people actually stand to mark their "spot." I have found the spectrogram to be one of the most adaptable and useful exercises in sociometry. It is flexible enough to accommodate a wide variety of group sizes and can be titrated as to intensity by using criterion questions appropriate for a desired level. Use criterion questions that are relevant to anything you wish to explore in the group, for example, "How comfortable do you feel in this group? How comfortable are you beginning this program? How comfortable do you feel about your body? How good do you feel about your recovery? How good do you feel about your work life, personal life, family relationships?" Such questions bring up information for processing and also allow people to discover shared feelings. The group as a whole can arrive at several questions then explore them together. Or the therapist can begin asking the questions and then ask group members to come up with questions that they, as a group, feel like exploring. Or the therapist can come up with all the questions.

THE SPECTROGRAM

GOALS:

1. To provide a floor graph that group members can step onto in order to represent the degree and intensity of a particular issue.
2. To provide a method for exploring issues sociometrically.
3. To create group cohesion and build trust.
4. To give several people in the group a chance to feel involved in experiential work.

STEPS:

1. Invite group members to get out of their chairs.
2. Show participants that each end or wall of the room represents an extreme, for example, 1 to 100 percent, or very much and very little. Next, draw an imaginary line from one end of the room to the other on which people can locate themselves in response to criterion questions—Then draw a line bisecting the room down the middle, representing the midpoint. For example, 50 percent or a medium amount.
3. Next, ask a criterion question and invite participants to locate themselves at whatever

point along the continuum that best describes their response to the question. For example, say that the left side of the room represents one and the right side one hundred, with the midpoint represented by the bisecting line at fifty. Ask the question: "On a scale of one to one hundred, how comfortable are you feeling about your work life?" The person who is recently fired might go to the extreme left, represented by the number one, while the person for whom work is not an issue might stand closer to the midpoint or towards one hundred on the right side.

4. When each person is standing at the point that represents his response to the question, allow people to share briefly, either with one another or with the group at large.

The group may wish to share some questions so the whole group can hear and others in small groupings, dyads, triads and clusters, with those standing around them. This automatically sociometrically aligns them; that is, they are standing next to people who have answered the question similarly to them.

5. After the group has explored as many questions as it wishes to, or because it has reached its saturation point, it can either select a protagonist sociometrically or by asking who feels warmed up to do work. Or they can return to their seats and continue to share.

VARIATIONS:

The spectogram can be adapted for any issue the group wishes to explore. In our section on Special Issues, each subject—for example, grief, trauma, anger, depression, resilience and so on—has a self-test. The questions on the self-test come out of the research appropriate to the particular subject and can be used as criterion questions to explore that issue. Those exercises can be used as part of a psychoeducational program.

THE LOCOGRAM

The locogram can be used in any number of ways to explore any issues with which the group may wish to work. Throughout this book I have adapted the locogram to explore issues such as grief, trauma, resilience, anger and forgiveness. It serves as a cornerstone of my adaptation of sociometry for specific uses in treatment centers or private groups (see "Special Issues" and "Special Populations") and the psychoeducational program component.

The locogram can be laid out on the floor in any shape. For example when working with grief the director can name each of four corners according to Bowlby's stages of grief: corner one—*numbness;* corner two—*yearning and searching;* corner three—*disorganization, anger, despair;* and corner four—*reorganization.* The group can be invited to identify a loss and go to whichever corner best describes "where they are." They can share with just those standing next to them or with the whole group. They may also talk to people at other stages of the process if they feel that would be helpful.

A locogram can also be any designation of spaces that the group wishes to represent for instance, "This area represents," "I feel very warmed up to work" or this area represents, "I feel moderately warmed up to work," and "And this area represents," "I don't feel like working tonight."

A locogram can be used as an experiential check-in or as an aid to focus the group for sharing or discussion, or to focus and warm a group up toward action. It accomplishes something along the lines of check in but goes much deeper and allows for a wide range of expression. What's in the designated locations can change, but the process remains basically the same.

Psychodramatic journaling can be used as an extension as indicated in several locogram exercises in sections two and three.

THE LOCOGRAM

GOALS:

   1. To provide an easy way to concretize answers to a particular set of questions.

   2. To allow group members to announce preferences.

   3. To create group bonding and cohesion.

STEPS:

   1. Identify the issue that the group wishes to explore.

   2. Designate four or so areas on the floor to represent possible responses to the issue, including one area representing "other" so group members aren't limited to only the available choices. For example, if you wish to explore how people are feeling about being in group one evening, the director might say, "This corner of the room or stage will represent 'I really want to be here;' this corner, 'I could go either way;' this corner,

'I feel resistant to being here;' and this corner 'other.' Please stand in the area that best represents how you feel about working this evening."

3. Once group members are standing in the area that best describes what they're feeling, invite them to share a sentence or two about why they are standing where they are. Group members may also want to stand between two areas if they feel ambivalent or between feelings.

4. Repeat this process if desired by asking the group if they wish to make a second choice.

5. Either choose a protagonist or return to seats for further sharing and processing.

VARIATIONS:

Group members may double for each other if this seems useful. Sociometric choosing can be incorporated into the process if desired as an extension. The director can invite the group members to "Walk over to someone who shared something with which you identify, and place your hand on his or her shoulder. Now share with that person why you chose him or her or how you identify." Or the director may ask people to simply return to their seats for further sharing.

CIRCLE LOCOGRAM

GOALS:

1. To create a living graph where clients may experientially graph or concretize their response to criterion questions.

2. To make unconscious psychological and emotional issues conscious.

3. To concretize one's location in the group as it relates to particular issues.

4. To create group cohesion.

STEPS:

1. Invite group members up onto the stage or working area.

2. Create an imaginary circle by locating the center with a paper, pillow or some form of marker, and locate a periphery around the edges of the room or a significant distance from the center.

3. Invite group members to locate themselves on the floor graph by standing the appropriate distance from the center in response to criterion questions (see Variations, below). For instance, if the center represents self, ask, "How close or far do you feel from yourself?" Or if the center is program, ask, "How close or far do you feel from your program at this moment?" or, "How close or far do you feel from relapsing?"

4. As group members mark their spots by standing where it "feels right," ask them to

speak or share a sentence or two "from where they're standing." Why did they locate themselves where they did? Any or all may share in no particular pattern.

5. Allow for group sharing and processing or use this as a warm-up to psychodramatic enactment.

VARIATIONS:

The center of the circle can represent anything the group or therapist wishes to explore, for example, "the self," "a life passion," "my own center," "sobriety," "recovery," "the group" and so on.

LOCOGRAM TO EXPLORE SATISFACTION LEVEL
OF SOCIOMETRY WITHIN A GROUP

GOALS:

1. To provide a nonthreatening way to explore the group members' level of satisfaction with their personal sociometry within a particular group.

2. To provide a format through which these concerns can be shared openly.

STEPS:

1. Designate areas on the floor to represent the following criteria:
    - I feel content with my sociometric status within the group.
    - I do not feel content with my sociometric status within the group.
    - I feel neutral in relation to my sociometric status within the group.
    - Other.

2. Invite group members to stand in the area that best represents their answer to this question. Note: they may be standing between certain categories.

3. Invite group members to share about why they are standing where they are standing.

4. Next ask group members if anything has shifted in the sharing and if they wish to move to a different location.

5. Return to seats for continued sharing and processing.

VARIATIONS:

This exercise should only be done in an ongoing, well-bonded group that has many weeks to process what will come up from bringing these issues out into the open. Criterion can vary. For example, sometimes, especially if there are cliques and subgroups, some group members may often be chosen to work or play roles while others feel underchosen. This can be explored by using criterion like "I feel overchosen in the group," "I feel underchosen in the group," "I feel adequately chosen in the group" and "other." Again, count on much processing.

SILLY SOCIOMETRY

GOALS:

1. To connect group members.
2. To have fun and loosen up the group.

STEPS:

1. Form a circle of chairs as if the group was playing musical chairs, with one less chair than there are group members present.
2. One person steps into the middle to get the ball rolling and says something that is true for her, e.g., "I like to play tennis," "I'm an ACOA" and so on; these statements can vary widely depending upon the group; they can get very "silly."
3. Anyone for whom this statement is true can step quickly into the circle, then everyone rushes to leave their chairs and find an empty one. They cannot return to their old chair.
4. Someone gets left in the middle and then it is his turn to come up with a statement that is true for him.
5. Repeat steps three and four until the group is ready to move onto something else.

VARIATIONS:

This is a friendly and fun warm-up that can be used during a long day or weekend to liven up a tired group or after a meal, when people are getting sleepy. It is generally followed by another warm-up.

MILLING PLUS SOCIOMETRY

Milling is a process that can provide for sociometric connections. Though it is not necessarily sociometry in and of itself, in this exercise I have put it together with sociometric choosing and the spectrogram. I have developed this slowly over the years. It contains elements of theater exercises, drama therapy and sociometry, and it works well with groups. There are more examples in the

Appendix. It is a very workable way to warm up a group and introduce its members to each other and preliminary experiential work.

MILLING/SPECTROGRAM/SOCIOMETRIC CHOOSING: A THREE-TIERED PROCESS

MILLING GOALS:

1. To illustrate how one experiential process can flow easily into another, to combine approaches.
2. To provide for a group to begin to make connections and get to know each other.

STEPS:

1. Ask participants to get up from their seats and begin to mill around the room.
2. As the group mills, say the following things in a clear and audible voice:
   - Feel your body in space. Feel the air around you. Mentally tune in to your body and see if you are holding tension in any part of it. Okay, breathe and let it go.
   - Keep walking.
   - As you mill around the room notice how much of you is present and how much of you is still somewhere else, preoccupied with other things.
   - Okay. Breathe, and bring your attention into the room.
   - Next we're going to explore how being here feels.
   - Feel your body in space, the air on your shoulders.
   - Sense how your body is moving through space. Speed up a little, now become slow and deliberate your movements.
   - Look around the room and make eye contact with someone you can share something with.
   - Walk up to this person and share with him or her how you feel about being here. Take turns sharing.
   - Okay. Say good-bye and continue to mill around the room. Take some deep breaths and relax into the space around you.
   - Next, find another person you can share something with. Make eye contact.
   - Walk over to that person and share with him or her what you'd like to get from being here today. Take turns sharing.
   - Let this go.
   - Next, we will do a . . .

SPECTROGRAM:

(Follow instructions for spectrogram, page 110.)

Criterion questions:

- How comfortable are you right now?
- How much concern or anxiety are you feeling about this process?

SOCIOMETRIC CHOOSING

(Follow instructions for sociometric choosing page 106.)

- Ask group members to identify someone who said something with which they resonate.
- Ask them to walk over to that person and place a hand on his or her shoulder.
- Ask them to share with this person why they choose him or her.

VARIATIONS:

This is an exercise with several sociometric approaches one after another. The idea is to present a format for flowing from one process into another in a seamless manner. This flow can be applied to any other set of criterion questions or issues that the group may wish to explore. If you wish to introduce some fun into the group, you can ask questions like: "Share with someone what you wanted to be when you grew up."

Other examples of milling exercises can be found in the Appendix.

MILLING, PAIRING, SHARING:
EXPLORATION OF DISOWNED PARTS OF SELF

GOALS:

1. To offer clients a way of bringing into the group parts of themselves they may hold back.
2. To act as a warm-up for a psychodramatic vignette encountering the parts of ourselves that we may keep in hiding.

STEPS:

1. Ask participants to get out of their seats. In a clear, audible voice, say:
   - Mill around the room.
   - Go to your breath and BREATHE. Allow yourself to bring your awareness into this room. Feel the air around you. Fill your body with breath and let it go.

- On a scale of one to ten, in terms of the speed you're walking, walk at a two. Now a four, an eight, a ten and a five.
- We're going to lead with parts of our body. Lead with your forehead.
- Now lead with your knees . . . with your chest . . . elbows . . . toes . . . back.
- Okay. Now as you mill, look for someone with whom you feel you could share something personal.
- Okay, connect with him or her and share how you're feeling about doing this exercise. Both people share.
- Okay, mill some more. Again make eye contact with someone. Connect. Share with him or her what is on your mind at the moment, what you brought to group with you.
- Okay, mill. Breath. Let that settle in your mind and your emotions. Return to milling. Make eye contact. Connect. Share about any fears you may have about being here.
- Okay, let it go. Mill a little more.
- Now we're going to go a little deeper. We all have a part of ourselves that we have lost touch with or don't want to be front and center. A part that we may even keep hidden. Let that part of yourself come into your body.
- Walk and move like that part of yourself. Let it come into your feelings, into your thinking. Now let it come out in words. Speak out as that part of yourself. What do you want to say as that part of yourself? Say it; let the words grow freely.
- Now, make eye contact with someone. Pair up and take turns sharing about what that experience felt like, any feelings around letting that part of yourself come out. (Allow plenty of time for sharing if it seems productive).
- Return to milling. Breathe; let it go. Relax.

2. Use this as a warm-up to doing vignettes with the hidden part of self that clients have come in contact with, or return to the seats for further sharing.

VARIATIONS:

This format can be followed with other themes, e.g., parts of the self we want to enhance, resilient parts of self, parts of the self we can't forgive, hidden talents and so on. I have chosen this topic in response to particular presentation needs but it can be adapted in any ethical direction. This is done in *The Process* film, see about the author.

FIRST CAME THE GROUP

The treatment of audiences (groups) has become an important alternative to individual treatment. The relationship of the group to itself in a psychodramatic session, being treated by its own spokesman on the stage, gives us a clue as to the reasons of the cathartic effect of psychodrama. According to historians of the Greek drama the audience was there first, a chorus, musing about a common syndrome. There were "keynoters" among them but they remained within the chorus. Thespis is credited with having put the first actor upon a social space outside of the chorus, the stage, not speaking to them, but portraying the woes of their own hero. Aeschylus is credited with having put the second actor on the stage, thus making possible the dialogue and interaction of roles. We may be credited as having put the psyche itself on the stage. The psyche, which emerges from the group, after a process of reconversion on the stage personified by an actor [role-player] in a psychodrama returns to the group. That which was most startling, new and spectacular to see and to feel on the stage appears to the participants after thorough exposure as a process which is familiar to them and as intimately known as their own selves. The psychodrama confirms their own identity as if in a mirror.

Two thousand years ago mankind underwent, as we do today, a crisis of the first magnitude. To the broad masses catharsis came from Christianity instead of from the philosophical schools of Egypt and Greece due to the universality of the methods and the practicality of its instruments [love and confession, charity and hope]. . . . In our time the social and mental sciences aim at a similar accomplishment as religion once attained. Mankind's masses suffer from social and mental unrest. Catharsis will probably come again from instruments, which combine universality of method with great practicality. One of the most promising methods developed in the last twenty-five years and fulfilling these demands is the psychodramatic method.

—J. L. Moreno
Psychodrama, Volume 1

9 Group Psychotherapy

As the Acorn Becomes the Oak
The Conscious and Unconscious Life of the Group

The mind is like an iceberg—we only see the top while its vastness remains beneath the surface. The group as a whole also has both a surface life and an unconscious life. We may interact with the surface part of ourselves for days, weeks, years or a lifetime, often wholly unconscious of the drives, desires, struggles and conflicts that operate underneath. It is this vast underworld of unspoken truths and unfelt feelings that so strongly impacts our lives and relationships, that we examine through psychotherapy. In the here and now of the group, the self emerges and tells the story of its relationships, from the nature of interactions, both benign and conflictual, that get played out member to member and member to group. The group then provides a window into the unconscious, a mirror in which we see ourselves reflected back to us through the eyes of others. In this privileged world we make an agreement with other members of the group to act in service of our own personal actualization, to embark upon the greatest odyssey—our journey inward, as we become "each therapeutic agents of the other." We create a safety zone, not for blind alliance and support or pointless aggression but for cocreating a safe enough environment so we can allow the self to emerge with relative safety. We hide parts of ourselves consciously or unconsciously. Perhaps we restrain aggression or the open expression of emotions that we feel might compromise us, making us more vulnerable than we care to be or drive people away. This is a conscious operation designed to get along with a larger community of people and occupy a comfortable place within that community. Unconscious self-restraints often have different origins. They tend to stem from those parts of self around which we have built defenses. For example, a man who had an overly critical father may have learned, as a child, to hide his vulnerability so that he would not have repeat experiences of feeling as humiliated as he did when he was a boy. We make sense of a situation with the developmental equipment available to us at a given stage of development. Children on their own reach their own conclusions, and make their own meaning out of their circumstances. "In the absence of adequate assistance in making sense of emotions, the brain organizes a variety of coping strategies and defense mechanisms. These strategies can vary in the degree to which they distort reality in order to achieve their goal of reducing anxiety. This distortion is accomplished in circuits of unconscious memory that control anxiety and fear" (Critchley et al. 2000). "The neural connections that result in defenses shape our lives by selecting what we approach and avoid, where our attention is drawn, and the assumptions we use to organize our experiences. Our cortex then provides us with rationalizations and beliefs about our behaviors that help keep our coping strategies in place, possibly for a lifetime. These neural and psychic structures can lead to psychological and physical health, or symptoms and disability" (Corzolino 2002). In the group he has the opportunity to allow himself to be vulnerable. As he experiences that new feeling, he can articulate the feelings he has about his own vulnerability. In this way the group makes his own defensive structure more conscious.

Other group members may help him take this risk by encouraging him to explore his own blocks or letting him know that he feels remote to them or unavailable for meaningful interaction. They may act as cheerleaders, provocateurs or agents of change.

When internalized patterns of relating emerge and get played out in member-to-member and group interactions, layers of self emerge for reflection.

As we become comfortable with more of who we are and understand what makes us tick, why we do the things we do, resolution of internal conflicts and mastery of self is possible. The neural patterning that nature placed into us to keep us safe (emotionally and physically), to help us sense danger and get ourselves and our children out of harm's way, is largely unconscious. But nature is ever imaginative and adaptive and it has evolved for us, over time, the frontal brain regions such as the cortex, where we can modify these ancient responses. How we modify them is evolving, too. We are ever experimenting with what works best in maintaining a healthy relationship with ourselves and others, trying, discarding, selecting and maintaining what works, or getting stuck in a pattern that doesn't work, inhibiting our own progress.

There is a delicate balance between finding the solution that allows us to stay vibrant and connected to ourselves and others and still maintain a sense of autonomy and emotional safety. Defenses work to keep us safe, and many of them contribute to our ability to remain stable. It is only when they become pathological that they systematically undermine our happiness.

The Self Emerges from the Roles We Play

Group therapy is the container within which we can observe the self in action. How do I feel about myself in the presence of others? Who am I in relationships? How much of my private side emerges into the collective and what parts do I keep hidden? How do I behave when I am scared, feeling left out, chosen, rejected or at home in my own skin? Who am I vis à vis other people, how do others impact me, and how do I impact them? Who do I choose, who do I reject and toward whom am I neutral? Who chooses me, rejects me or is neutral toward me? How do I feel about being chosen, not chosen and anywhere in between? Groups have a life of their own that Moreno felt could be measured and studied. Though nothing pertaining to humans can ever be purely scientific, Moreno developed fluid structures such as the social atom, sociograms (diagrams of group relationships) and sociometric tests (sociometric choosing) with which to better diagram and understand the internal structures of groups.

"Individuals who never met before and who from the first meeting on have to be participants in the same group represent a new problem to the therapist;

we see them when they enter spontaneously into interrelations which lead them to form a group sub species *momenti;* we can study their spontaneous reaction in the initial stage of group formation and the activities developed in the course of such organization . . . we can develop the treatment forward instead of backward; we can begin with the initial attitude one person has for the other and follow up to what fate these interrelations lead, what kind of organizations they develop.

In support of the existence of such an initial common matrix, sociometric research has shown that 'immediate' response between strangers differs significantly from chance. In other words, there is tele already operating between the members of a group from the first meeting. This weak, 'primary' cohesiveness can be utilized by the therapist toward the development and sharing of common therapeutic aims. All the interactions between men, abreactions, soliloquies, dialogues, tele, and transference relations to therapist, auxiliary egos, and each other in the course of therapy will be influenced by this original structure and will in turn, modify it. This is the new operational frame of reference from which one can look at the successive stages of a synthetic group" (J. Moreno 1964).

Moreno felt that the objective view of science, looking at subjects as static, inanimate objects, had no place in the social sciences such as psychology, anthropology and sociology. He also felt that in a group there was a fundamental problem when the analyst held himself as a dispassionate, supposedly objective observer. Moreno recognized the observer effect at work in the therapeutic clinic; that the observers always impact the observed and vice versa no matter how "objective" or "neutral" they were supposedly being. The very neutrality could in itself have an impact that might vary from person to person. He understood that there is always an interaction specific and unique to those involved. In solving this problem Moreno reasoned that one way of eliminating the power disparity between leader and group members might be to make all present subjects members of a group equal in status. But he quickly enough tossed this option out as irresponsible, someone had to mind the store. So he came up with a solution that became a cornerstone of his philosophy of group psychotherapy. This was to "elevate everyone involved to the status of researcher." (J. Moreno Vol. 1). It is from this thinking that psychodrama's point of view that *each person present in a group becomes the therapeutic agent of the other* grew. In psychodramatic terms this is its *status nascendi*. Any group leader, in fact anyone who has participated in a group, well knows that you never know from where in the group healing will come. If the sociometric connection of one group member, for example a mother, is identified with another mother more than with a group leader who may be a man, she may be better able to heal through that connection, at least on issues relevant to that role. Likewise, a man's point of view on being a husband or a father might be better understood by the other men in the group. They are simply more sociometrically aligned on these subjects. In the actual psychodrama itself, much healing comes from auxiliaries who take on roles from a particular protagonist's life and play them out in the manner needed by the protagonist. This is the beauty of group; it multiplies the possibilities for healing by offering more possibilities for identification, conflict, transference both positive and negative, and other types of connection.

Groups go well beyond the leader, and the whole is greater than the sum of its parts; they come to have lives of their own with varied, volatile, nourishing, challenging dynamics that, at times, can be powerful enough to set even the most practiced therapist back on her heels. The intensity of the group process tends to bring forward relationship styles learned and practiced by group members in their own lives.

Self-regulation, the ability to bring one's physical, emotional and psychological self into balance, can be greatly enhanced by group therapy. Fritz Perls used the term "safe emergency" to describe the experience that therapists strive to create in psychotherapy. A safe emergency is a "challenge for growth and integration in the context of guidance and support. Therapists create this emergency by exposing clients to unintegrated and deregulating thoughts and feelings while offering the clients tools and nurturance with which to integrate these experiences. Psychodynamic therapies alternate confrontations and interpretations with a supportive and soothing interpersonal environment" (Weiner 1998; Cozolino 2002). Group therapy creates such an environment. "As in development, the repeated exposure to stress in the supportive interpersonal context of psychotherapy results in the ability to tolerate increasing levels of arousal. The process represents the building and increasing of cortical circuits and their increasing ability to inhibit and regulate subcortical activation.

Flexible and balanced affect regulation enhances continued cortical processing in situations that evoke strong emotions, allowing for flexibility to permit ongoing learning and neural integration" (Corzolino 2002). This harmonizes with Moreno's belief that in order to identify whether or not therapy is truly taking hold we need to return to the stage of life to "test and retest" our spontaneous reaction to situations that might previously have disturbed or baffled us.

If our spontaneous response is changed we may have turned that therapeutic corner where enough new neural rewiring has taken hold so that we're truly different on the inside. Along with our anxious response comes understanding, insight and an increased ability to tolerate the intense state of arousal without avoidance through shutting down, disappearing (inwardly or outwardly) or raging to avoid the experience of sitting with painful emotions. Cozolino goes on to describe how the therapeutic environment plays essentially the same role as parenting as it provides models in the brain for affect regulation, or the regularity functions of the social brain. "As affect is repeatedly brought into the therapeutic relationship and managed through a variety of stabilizing mechanisms, the client gradually internalizes these skills while simultaneously sculpting the neural structures necessary for the autoregulation of emotions" (2002).

This building of tolerance is a process that most good therapists understand intuitively, but recently neuroscience has been able to describe, in detail, the brain and body science behind it. "As in childhood, the repeated cycle of attunement, rupture of attunement, and its reestablishment gradually creates an expectation of reconnection" (Lachmann and Beebe 1996). "The learned experience of relief in the future enhances the ability to tolerate more intense affect in the midst of the stressful moment" (Corzolino 2002).

An important aspect of therapy is to help arouse the client's curiosity about his own therapeutic process. This shift from being triggered, and hence avoiding painful stimuli, to being triggered and becoming willing to explore and interested in processing is a key component of the therapeutic alliance that develops within the group. This is part of how group members become therapeutic agents of each other; they develop a therapeutic climate and help each other stay in this zone of healing exploration together, anchored by a caring professional. The group then acts as a container in which to learn and practice new behaviors.

THE ROLE OF THE GROUP THERAPIST

The role of the therapist in a group is different from the role of a therapist in one-to-one therapy. The group therapist facilitates a connection between each client and the group, both as a whole and individual to individual. Each member of the group will bring his own internalized family and social system to the group room. That system is warmed up and played out in the context of the group. The individuals in the group transfer their inner system—relationships with parents, siblings, friends, relatives, authority figures and so on—onto the group members and therapist, allowing the therapist to observe where the healing work lies for each individual. If, for instance, a group member had a harsh or critical mother, she might transfer that characteristic onto the group leader, the group as a whole or another member of the group. It is the advice of psychoanalysts not to interpret a negative transference. The transference may need to be felt and played out to some extent before it can be seen or understood by the client. A picture is worth a thousand words; seeing oneself in action is, too. Ideally, through the context of the group and the therapeutic bond with the leader, the client will eventually come to see herself. The atmosphere of honest self-reflection should encourage communication that will help a person to eventually see his own patterns. Throughout the group process, transferences will be flying in all directions. Working with and through these intense historical feelings helps people shake loose from their powerful grip and frees their energies to move in more creative and dynamic life directions. It restores spontaneity.

It is incumbent upon the group leader to keep the group what I would call "safe enough." If the group is "too safe," or too highly structured, members may not feel safe on a deeper level in expressing negative or hostile feelings. The group will not be fluid enough to arouse the transference material that will eventually lead to clarity and healing. If the group is too hostile, on the other hand, the participants will also not feel safe in expressing painful feelings because doing so makes them feel vulnerable to attack. Like Goldilock's porridge, the optimum "group temperature" is probably in the midrange, or that space that allows for intense and powerful emotion, along with loving and compassionate feelings, in which both the cognitive and emotional selves are able to remain conscious and awake. The process of making the unconscious conscious is painful. For those people who have used substances or acting-out behaviors to "not feel" or to escape from painful emotions, feeling their pain without anesthetizing it may hurt—but it will also heal. The feeling of community, identification and support that the group can offer in these painful moments goes a long way toward correcting clients' original experiences of emotional isolation—of having nowhere to go where it felt safe to hurt. These healing moments, slowly and over time, help to lower the walls of defense that keep people from being able to experience themselves, others and life more fully and replaces them with a more integrated balanced and secure sense of self.

The Body Comes to Group Therapy

Psychodrama allows the body to come to therapy in a natural and organic fashion. Rather than being asked to reflect upon an incident in the abstract, psychodrama allows for the full situation to emerge in the therapeutic moment, for all of the senses to be involved just as they were when recording it. Power imbalances, closeness or distance, and connectedness or the lack of it are revealed organically as the scene progresses, and the manner in which emotion was stored in the body becomes only too evident. Protagonists may feel their pulses racing, their breath shortening, their teeth chattering or their muscles tightening as they attempt to confront painful material. Conversely, they may experience deep physical release, pleasure and openness as the body feels or remembers what the mind has forgotten and shakes off the stored tension.

How Emotion Travels Through the Body

"The body is the unconscious mind," says Georgetown University research professor, Candice Pert in *Molecules of Emotion*. "Repressed traumas caused by overwhelming emotion can be stored in a body part, thereby affecting our ability to feel that part or even move it. . . . There are infinite pathways for the conscious mind to access—and modify—the unconscious mind and the body. . . . Until recently, emotions have been considered to be location-specific, associated with emotional centers in the brain such as the amygdala, hippocampus and hypothalamus. While these are, in fact, emotional centers, other types of centers are strewn throughout our bodies. Emotions travel through our bodies and bind to small receptors on the outside of cells, much like tiny satellite dishes. There are many locations throughout the body where high concentrations of almost every neuropeptide receptor exist. Nuclei serve as the source of most brain-to-body and body-to-brain hookups. Nuclei are peptide-containing groups of neuronal cell bodies in the brain" (Pert 1997).

Emotional information travels on neuropeptides and is able to bind to its receptor cells through the binding substance of ligands. The information is sorted through the differentiation of receptors. That is, certain information binds to certain receptors. So our emotions are constantly being processed by our bodies. The brain and body are exquisitely intertwined systems that are constantly interacting with the environment. All five senses are connected to this system and feed us information that determines our unique response to anything from petting a soft rabbit to being slapped. The more senses involved in an experience, the more the brain remembers it. The smell and taste of Grandma's cooking—as well as her gentle touch, familiar voice and the sight of her standing at the stove—all engrave themselves onto our memory systems, along with the feelings associated with them, because every sense is involved. The same is true in the case of trauma.

One way to illustrate the commonality of this mind-body connection is in the study of the universality of facial expressions. Emotions seem to have an inborn genetic mechanism for expression. Whether you are observing Hungarians, Indians, Africans or Eskimos, their facial expressions for anger, disgust, sadness, anticipation and joy will be the same. Not only are we a vast mind-body network for the processing of the everyday emotions we feel, we also carry a genetic coding for experiencing basic emotions. So the emotional system is more or less like the endocrine system and moves throughout our mind-body.

To review, emotions travel on neuropeptides, attach to tiny receptors on cells through the binding agent in ligands, and are sorted through as to type and binding site because each receptor is coded to bind to particular emotional messages. Psychodrama has a unique ability to work with this system through the spontaneity of role-play along with its full use of people in the act of being themselves.

Darwin felt this emotional system was highly conserved throughout evolution because emotions were so critical to our survival.

THE ROLE OF THE LIMBIC SYSTEM

Altering deep emotional patterns is slow and painstaking work. Limbic bonds imprint themselves onto our emotional systems. The limbic system "sets the mind's emotional tone, filters external events through internal states (creates emotional coloring), tags events as internally important, stores highly charged emotional memories, modulates motivation, controls appetite and sleep cycles, promotes bonding and directly processes the sense of smell and modulates libido," according to Dr. Daniel Amen, author of *Change Your Brain, Change Your Life*. Our neural networks are not easily altered. "Early emotional experiences knit long-lasting patterns into the very fabric of the brain's neural networks," writes Thomas Lewis, M.D., in *A General Theory of Love*. "Changing that matrix calls for a different kind of medicine altogether." Our emotional life is physical; it imprints itself on our bodies. When we have problems in our deep limbic system they can manifest in "moodiness, irritability, clinical depression, increased negative thinking, negative perceptions of events, decreased motivation, floods of negative emotion, appetite and sleep problems, decreased or increased sexual responsiveness or social isolation," says Amen. Our neural system carries with it our emotional sense-memories from childhood. Familiar smells, sounds or places can send a cascade of memories flooding through us that either wrap us up in their warmth or challenge us to maintain our composure. Along with the memories, comes the cognitive sense we made of what happened at the time (Dayton 2003).

Relationships that allow us to repattern our limbic systems, such as those we experience in psychodrama, sociometry, group psychotherapy, twelve-step programs, spiritual communities, hobby groups and healthy intimacy, are some ways of repatterning our limbic systems. Simply "describing good relatedness to someone, no matter how precisely or how often, does not inscribe it into the neural networks that inspire love or other feelings," says Lewis (2000). "The limbic system is associated with our emotions and the neocortex is associated with critical thinking. Both are operative in processing emotions." While the neocortex can collect facts quickly, the limbic brain does not. Physical mechanisms are what produce our experience of the world, and we need new sets of physical impressions to change or alter those impressions.

"Emotional impressions shrug off insight but yield to a different persuasion: the force of another person's Attractors reaching through the doorway of a limbic connection. Psychotherapy changes people because one mammal can restructure the limbic brain of another. . . . The mind-body clash has disguised the truth that psychotherapy is physiology. When a person starts therapy, she isn't beginning a pale conversation; she is stepping into a somatic state of relatedness. Evolution has sculpted mammals into their present form: they become attuned to one another's evocative signals and alter the structure of one another's nervous systems. Psychotherapy's transformative power comes from engaging and directing these mechanisms. Therapy is a living embodiment of limbic processes as corporeal as digestion and respiration" (Lewis 2000).

One of therapy's ultimate goals is to restore our ability to care and be cared for in reasonably functional ways, to learn to love and be loved. The three neural "manifestations" of this caring human are *limbic resonance, regulation* and *revision*. It is relationship that heals. Most research done on the efficacy of therapy arrives at the same point: Ultimately, it is the quality of the relationship between client and therapist, or between group members, that is core to the healing process. Insight is helpful in understanding and cognitive restructuring, but the relational patterns encoded into the limbic system do not necessarily respond to insight alone. Instead they respond to the slow repatterning or recoding of the complex brain and body systems that hold the story of us, the sum total of our experiences written on them. We take in information through all of our senses; the more senses that are involved in our learning, whether it's the alphabet or emotional learning, the more the brain absorbs and stores it. The more powerfully the memory is encoded in us, the more it takes to alter the patterning.

LIMBIC RESONANCE

We are always giving off emotional signals, or an emotional essence for other people to pick up on. Some people are, of course, more aware of this than others, but aware or not, we vibrate who we are or how we're feeling to those around us. Our brains are designed to pick up on these signals and translate them. We know much about people without exchanging a word. We get a sense about them, what their essence is, and how we relate to them. In psychodrama we call it *tele*, the connection between people that is nonverbal but says everything.

Lewis likens it to listening to a piece of music: "The first part of therapy is to be limbically known—having someone with a keen ear catch your melodic essence. A child with emotionally hazy parents finds trying to know herself like wandering around a museum in the dark. . . . She cannot be sure of what she senses. . . . Those who succeed in revealing themselves to another find the dimness receding from their own visions of self. Like people awakening from a dream, they slough off the accumulated, ill-fitting trappings of unsuitable lives" (ibid). The experience of being seen, of feeling understood and "gotten" by another person or people can be fundamentally altering and healing.

LIMBIC REGULATION

We, as humans, are physiologically patterned to resonate with each other at a deep neural level. Lewis says, "Our neural architecture places relationships at the crux of our lives, where, blazing and warm, they have the power to stabilize. When people are hurting and out of balance, they turn to regulating affiliations: groups, clubs, pets, marriages, friendships, masseuses, chiropractors, the Internet. All carry at least the potential for emotional connection. Together those bonds do more good than all the psychotherapies on the planet. A parent who rejects a child's desire to depend raises a fragile person. Those children, grown into adulthood, are frequently those who come for help. . . . If patient and therapist are to proceed down a curative path, they must allow limbic regulation and its companion moon, dependence, to make their revolutionary magic" (ibid).

Working in the addictions field over the past three decades has taught me endless lessons about limbic regulation. People who have been traumatized by inadequate parenting, who are living with addiction or are addicts themselves, need to put in the time it will take to heal in therapy and twelve-step programs. The ones who do poorly are invariably the ones who, for some reason or another, won't put in their hours. Maybe they go to twelve-step meetings and are bothered by what people say or don't say; maybe the idea of groups annoys or threatens them and makes them feel vulnerable; or perhaps a one-to-one relationship brings up more fear and mistrust than they can get past. But sooner or later they will need to come to terms with their aversion to connection. Lewis describes that "people do not learn emotional modulation as they do geometry or the names of state capitals. They absorb the skill from living in the presence of an adept external modulator, and they learn it implicitly. Knowledge leaps the gap from one mind to the other, but the learner does not experience the transferred information as an explicit strategy. Instead, a spontaneous capacity germinates and becomes a natural part of the self, like knowing how to ride a bike or tie one's shoes. The effortful beginnings fade and disappear from memory" (ibid).

As a client depends, she internalizes this regulation, and it becomes a part of her. Gradually, she feels more whole, capable and confident until, eventually, she is ready for independence and self-regulation.

LIMBIC REVISION

According to Lewis: "When a limbic connection has established a neural pattern, it takes a limbic connection to revise it. . . . Coming close to the patient's limbic world evokes genuine emotional responses in the therapist—he finds himself stirring in response to the particular magnetism of the emotional mind across from him. His mission is neither to deny those responses in himself nor to let them run their course. He waits for the moment to move the relationship in a different direction. . . . And then he does it again, ten thousand times more. Progress in therapy is iterative. Each successive push moves the patient's virtuality a tiny bit further from the native Attractors, and closer to those of the therapist. The patient encodes new neural patterns over their myriad interactions . . . with enough repetition, the fledgling circuits consolidate into novel

Attractors. When that happens, identity has changed. The patient is no longer the person he was" (1964).

Group therapy offers clients the opportunity to revise and repattern their limbic systems. Simply to experience powerful emotions in the presence of others and get from the beginning to the end of them without acting out or triggering a crisis is repatterning. Slowly, over time, it reregulates our emotional response. It helps us learn to listen to someone else while still tuning into our own inner voice, to be in connection with someone else while staying connected to ourselves.

Psychodrama, sociometry and group psychotherapy allow more senses to get involved directly in the therapeutic process, which, we believe, creates more opportunities for healing. To quote Moreno, "The body remembers what the mind forgets" (1964). If it didn't, none of us would breathe, walk or ride a bike. Being around people in ways that model tolerance, patience, acceptance and understanding can, over time, help reregulate a limbic system that may be out of balance.

TRANSFERENCE AND PROJECTION

As therapists, and indeed as people, we all know the frustration of working with people who constantly sabotage the quality of their lives and relationships. Core beliefs about the self and life become unconscious patterns that get played out in the form of reenactment dynamics and transferences. Working with these patterns, resolving them and bringing them to consciousness to be felt and understood is the work of psychodrama, sociometry and group psychotherapy. Because our first relationship was within our families of origin, emotional and psychological patterns particular to these roles often get played out in group (and life) in the form of transferences and projections. Group members transfer the qualities of the earlier relationships onto the present-day relationships in the group. They may also surface as reenactment dynamics, that "here I go again" operation by which we, in spite of our best resolve not to, move like heatseeking missiles toward the very relationship style we wish to shed. Psychodrama offers more ways of dealing with these transferences and reenactment dynamics than the average group. In addition to talking through the transference or recurring pattern, and untangling the past from the present, psychodrama can, for example, begin by putting the conflict between the group members onto the stage as it is. After deciding which person in this particular conflict the group is going to work with, the director can ask, "Where do you remember feeling this way before, or where do you think this pattern began?" The protagonist can spiral back to the original role relationship and work with it psychodramatically, exploring all that is attached to it. After working through and bringing closure to this scene, the protagonist can return to the conflict in the group with new insight and try to understand it in a new light. This process can also be shortened by simply asking a question like "Who might this person represent for you from your social atom, and is that relationship transferring onto this one?" then proceeding with a drama exploring the earlier relationship. In this way the unconscious material that gets projected into the container of the group has both the stage and regular group processes as avenues for resolution. This safety zone allows particularly gnarly material to be explored on the stage rather than exclusively head-to-head among group members although it is important that group members are eventually able to talk directly to each other. After the exploration the protagonist can return to the group for sharing, identification and holding. The support of the group helps heal and integrate the split-off material. I refer to it as split-off because it is generally felt that transference is an unconscious process and that it is resolved when we can "remember" the circumstances, usually cumulative and relationship-oriented, that seared it in place. As we learned in the previous chapter, sociometry also offers concrete ways of working with transference through the social atom and sociometric choosing.

Transference and reenactment dynamics sound a silent bell informing us as to where our pain lies. If, like Theseus, we can follow a golden thread through the labyrinth of our unconscious to the source of the problem, we can find our way out of darkness and into the light where we discover the why and wherefore. The only cautionary note here is to not create an "us versus them" situation in which the family of origin, for example, becomes pathologized or seen as the bad guys, while group members become the good guys. The goal is to separate the past from the present so that past issues aren't constantly lived out in the present, not to create a before and after but an integrated, fluid whole. Though the support of a healing group is critical to safety in exploring, confronting and healing painful material, it should be recognized that it is relatively unencumbered by many of the strains and pressures that our day-to-day relationships naturally carry. A good group, like a good parent, acts as a boat to carry us safely across the river; it does not become the river. It's important for psychodrama groups to maintain many intermittent here-and-now groups or purely psychodynamic groups where group process is alive and completely in the member-to-member interaction. Eventually, group members need to use language to work out their issues directly with each other, to talk things through, as it were. This allows for conflicts or concerns of any sort to surface and provides a "world in miniature" in which to learn and practice adequate ways in which to work them through.

COMBINING PSYCHODRAMA WITH GROUP PSYCHOTHERAPY

Aspects of psychodrama can become naturally integrated into group process as group members become adept and comfortable with its various forms. Spontaneously doubling, for example, as one group member identifies with another during group process, or standing behind one's own chair and doubling for one self, saying what might be hard to get out in the heat of the moment, or letting the group in on what might be going on inside that's not coming out, are ways in which psychodrama and group process can interact.

Role reversal is another of these. If two group members are locked in a problematic embrace, the group leader might ask them to "reverse roles" in order to get a sense of themselves and the other from a different perspective. Or perhaps a group member who cannot hear and take in something good about herself can use role reversal to see how she might be blocking positive feedback. In this method, the person unable to take in good things reverses roles with the one saying them and experiences trying to talk to herself.

In my experience, these are the most common points of intersection between psychodrama and group process, with spontaneously doubling the most common.

Bear in mind, as we said before, that it's beneficial to preserve some group process without any psychodrama so that group members develop the skills of relating that most accurately mirror the outside world. What the intersections do is to help in "thinking outside the box" during psychodynamic group sessions, both in terms of relationships and that of deeper insights both into the self and the other. This quality can potentially benefit any interaction, in or out of the group.

A Brief History of Group Psychotherapy

Moreno explored the beginnings of group therapy in his work with prostitutes early in this century. Prostitutes were not seen as valuable people by turn-of-the-century Vienna. Rather, they were viewed as "unredeemable, as despicable sinners." This made them a population that was ripe for an experimental form of therapy; they were not given what was then considered to be the chosen form of therapy, i.e., one-to-one, as they were not seen as worth saving. Moreno worked with the prostitutes in groups of ten or so women, two or three times a week to "contain" and "to restore to them some dignity." Initially, the prostitutes talked about practical issues such as being arrested, what to do with their children and problems with those they worked for. But over time, their sharing began to take on a more personal and relevant flow. Moreno observed that the simple act of sharing personal information and identifying with the stories of others had, in itself, a curative effect. He came to observe how, in a group, each person becomes a therapeutic agent for the other, that there is a potential for healing through a vast variety of sociometric interconnections among group members. This represented the major turning point from "treating people in isolation to treating them in a group" (Moreno 1964), it represented the birth of group therapy.

After World War II the therapeutic group grew in use and popularity. Due to the significant influx of patients into the Veterans Hospitals (VA) system who had been in some way traumatized by war, the need to provide cost effective care for large groups of people increased.

In this day of managed care, group therapy is emerging as one of the important forces in mental healthcare alternatives. Groups can make therapy available and cost effective on a short or long-term basis. Groups can have a specific focus, such as early sobriety or grief, or they can be nonspecific, open to the needs of the individuals within the group. Deep internal change takes time. It does not happen in four or seventeen sessions. It takes years of committed work to explore the process of healing and recovery. In the addictions field we have the network of twelve-step programs to support this process. Long-term group work coupled with one-to-one work, at least in part, alongside twelve-step recovery can affordably create the structure necessary to contain and guide a person on the path toward healthy, balanced living. Twelve-step groups are fundamentally aligned with psychodramatic philosophy in that there is socio-metric alignment, i.e., ACOAs are with other ACOAs, spouses and codependents are with other spouses and codependents, addicts are with addicts, and subgrouped even further. In addition, each person becomes a therapeutic agent for the other in twelve-step programs, not through advice, as ground rules discourage this, but through support, identification and mutual availability and containment. Twelve-step programs work well in conjunction with psychodrama groups.

Virtually all of the major religions and philosophies, including those espoused by psychoanalysts Carl Jung, Karen Horney and Irwin Yalom, to name but a few, propose that the drive toward self-actualization is built into the psyche, soul and body of each person. Just as an acorn will become an oak tree, human beings have a drive toward self-actualization. Groups of all kinds have the power to help us self-actualize through sociometric identification, mutual support and inspiration. The power of the group can be harnessed for growth or destruction. In therapy we harness it for growth.

10 Sociodrama

Sociodrama deals with the collective role. In a sociodrama, a group member is chosen to represent a collective role on behalf of the group at large—for example, one role-player might represent all mothers and another all fathers. Or one role-player could represent all employers and another role-player all employees; one role-player might represent all bullies, another, all students, and still another role-player could represent all teachers—and the scene is structured and played out. Perhaps the scene is a family, and role-players are chosen to portray the generic roles of son, daughter, mother, father, grandmother, grandfather, uncle, cousin and so forth. "This is the genesis of the drama and of its original aim, that of collective catharsis" (Moreno 1964).

Sociodrama is helpful as a way to use role-play in the classroom, the workplace or law enforcement training programs. Police academy trainees can practice a role-play on arresting a burglar; school administrations can help children learn how to say "no" to drugs by enacting a scene where a student is offered marijuana; customer service employees can role-play to help them deal with irate customers. In treatment facilities it is very common to use sociodrama-type sculptures and role-plays to represent the roles within alcoholic family systems. Sociodrama is perhaps one of the most widely used derivatives of Moreno's methods. While psychodrama explores the personal role, i.e., we play ourselves, sociodrama explores the collective role.

"The difference between psychodrama and sociodrama should be extended to every type of group psychotherapy. A difference should be made between the individual type of group psychotherapy and the collective type of group psychotherapy. The individual type of group psychotherapy is individual-centered. It focuses its attention upon the single individuals in the situation, of which the group consists, and not upon the group in general. The collective type of group psychotherapy is group-centered. There is no difference between spectators and actors; all are protagonists" (J. Moreno 1964).

Moreno may have foreseen the incredible social power of the media and understood its potential role in shaping society. He refers to harnessing this power in *Psychodrama*, Volume 1, as an alive and immediate method of exploring cultural concerns and phenomenons that affect the individual. "It is here that the sociodrama can step in and serve as a check and balance to cultural tensions and hostilities arising from worldwide events and as a means to social catharsis. In the form of the psychodramatic and sociodramatic conserve in film and television, the drama conserve may come back revitalized, opening a new vista for the future of the drama" (J. Moreno 1964).

The media has certainly played a sociodramatic role in America and in our world. Over and over again, role-players on television act out the concerns of the larger group. They do this, however, through a variety of cultural conserves, plays, situation comedies or dramas. The ever-popular talk and more recent "reality" shows have become arenas for individuals to put their conflicts on the stage. In these cases the conflicts are personal and the television audience identifies with the person representing what amounts to a central concern of the audience. The audience then identifies and has what Aristotle referred to as a "spectator catharsis."

Oftentimes the protagonists are self-selected as they have responded to some advertisement on the show to call in if they meet a specific profile. Sometimes these shows are actually helpful and even healing for the participants, and other times they have a freak-show or circus quality and mentality. In any case they reflect an ever-present thirst for people to see themselves represented in some form on some stage. Done consciously and with a professional eye, the media could be used for much good. "Records are made in the course of psychodramatic and sociodramatic procedure as a matter of routine—stenograms, photographs, films, phonograph records, etc., can be made. In this way the conserve returns but in a subordinated function, secondary to the function of spontaneity and creativity" (J. Moreno 1964).

Sociodrama accesses the concerns of the collective and recognizes the audience to be what Moreno referred to as "a thousand unconscious playwrites" in sociodrama's beginnings at the Komoedien-Haus.

A SOCIODRAMATIC PROCESS

The following is a basic process for setting up a situational role-play. I published this in 1994 under the title "In the Classroom" because I feel that sociodrama is uniquely well suited to schools and the psycho-educational component in treatment facilities. I include it here because I have found it to be most useful in the settings in which I commonly work, which are often treatment centers. It is not necessarily the orthodox method, but my step-by-step approach incorporates some theatrical devices like freezing the scene in order to make the process more manageable and offering safe and easy-to-read opportunities for doubling.

Essentially, it allows groups to come up with roles that are relevant to their setting, explore the collective role, and personalize and deconstruct it in terms of the self through doubling and group sharing. The combination of approaching the problem from the collective aspect—that is, the roles commonly involved, for example, in addiction, classroom dynamics or work roles—allows for an identification with the problem from a safer "distance" than psychodrama offers. The role of the double allows group members to go a little deeper into the internal dynamics of the role and the sharing after the sociodrama provides further opportunity for deconstructing the experience in terms of the self, if desired. Alternatively, sharing can be used for discussion and closure.

SOCIODRAMATIC ROLE-PLAY

GOALS:

1. To concretize issues that represent group concerns.
2. To use role-play to explore the central concerns of the group.
3. To deconstruct group issues as to how they relate to the self (if desired).

STEPS:

1. Ask the group members to name the scene or the issue they wish to work with (write on a blackboard if desired.)
2. Ask them to name the people in the scene or the roles in the scene.
3. Ask the group members to think of words that describe characteristics of each person in the scene, and write those down on the blackboard next to the characters.
4. Ask for volunteers to play each role.
5. Ask each role-player to take a position that seems to embody the characteristics the group came up with. Invite group participation for this with ideas.
6. Ask group members to come up with a couple of sentences for each role.
7. Open the scene. Move into action by saying some of what was suggested or whatever the characters come up with.
8. Allow the scene to naturally progress and unfold.
9. At any point you can freeze the action to reflect upon what is going on with the audience or group and then continue the action again.
10. When the action is frozen, ask for doubles, if you choose to, who identify with any role or who feel they might know what is going on inside a role. Ask these doubles to take turns standing behind the role they choose to double for, and speaking the inner life of that character and then sit down again.
11. This freezing and moving back into action can take place as often as seems appropriate. Doubling can also occur without freezing.
12. End the scene by asking characters to say the last thing that needs to be said for the time being, a sort of closing statement.
13. You may choose to enact more than one ending. After one ending, ask the group what other endings or resolutions may be possible, and then role-play them. This can help the group to imagine choices or different ways of handling a situation; it can also introduce playful, humorous solutions. Group members can take turns playing out

different endings as the person who is representing the role stands aside.

14. Allow plenty of time for group sharing. This includes a discussion of what came up for participants as a result of watching the action and how the group members may have identified or understood the scene in terms of themselves and their own lives. Also for de-roling, discuss how it felt to play particular roles and perhaps how it touches on their own lives if the situation permits this type of self-reflection. The de-roling is important because of the somewhat gray zone in which this modality may operate, i.e., not necessarily in therapy alone. Those who take on roles may find that many feelings and issues may get aroused, and this needs to be processed, if they so choose.

VARIATIONS:

If in an addiction facility, you can work with Sharon Wegscheider-Cruse's alcoholic family roles, choosing group members to represent the addict, enabler, family hero, scapegoat (symptom bearer or target child) and lost child. The scene can be set and played out with each person representing the generic or collective role, or it can be sculpted and used as a teaching scene. If this is done, the scene can also be frozen and group members invited to double for the inner life with which they identify. This can then be a springboard for sharing and discussion. It also can be used as a warm-up to vignettes.

In an addiction facility you can set up a sociodrama concretizing a relationship with a drug, alcohol, food, sex, or gambling etc.

In a school setting, sociodramas can center on social issues that students may face, such as bullying or drug pushing. In the first case, group members can volunteer to play the bully, people being bullied and perhaps an adult authority figure, depending on whether or not that's appropriate. In the second, someone can play the drug pusher and someone else the person being approached to buy drugs. In all of these, the scene can be frozen and group members can double for what's going on inside the role. They can also discuss several ways of dealing with the situation and role-play each one them, then check in with role-players and group members to see how the various approaches felt to them. Zany, out-of-the-ordinary solutions can also be role-played to allow humor and imagination to enter the process.

Issues of prejudice can be role-played with group members representing various sexes, races, ethnic groups or socioeconomic sectors of society. It can be useful to double for more than one role in order to gain sensitivity to what it's like to stand in each role. Role reversal can also be used if it works and if the person is trained; otherwise, some of the same "learning" can occur through doubling.

In a workplace session, group members may choose to play out scenes in which they are handling difficult customers. They can play out the scene and practice role-playing different approaches to dealing with them (see Role Training exercise in the chapter 6).

This approach can be good for developing insight, team building, sensitivity training and role training. It also allows the group to bond and provides a safe way to share material. There is the "emotional distance" and protection from taking on a "generic" role rather than revealing the self, both for role-players and doubles.

FOLLOW-UP EXERCISES: PSYCHODRAMATIC JOURNALING

Follow-up exercises allow the group members to both further the healing process and share their feelings and to open up new, creative methods of expression. For example:

- Ask group members to journal "as" any one of the characters they identify with or write a poem about the scene or feelings elicited relating to the scene or any aspect of it.
- Ask group members to mentally reverse roles with any person in the sculpture and write a monologue or soliloquy from that person's point of view.
- Ask group members to make cartoon drawings of each of the characters in the scene and draw above each character two bubbles—a speech bubble for what the character is saying and a thought bubble for what the character might be thinking.
- Ask group members to divide a piece of paper into two columns. Title one column "Outer Person" and the other column "Inner Person." Ask them to mentally reverse roles with any character they choose or with all the characters in the scene. Then have them write in the first column what the outer person seems like or how they present themselves, and in the second column write what they imagine might be going on inside the person.

Note: These journaling exercises can also be used as follow-up exercises for films that are used during treatment, such as *The Process* (see back of the book).

TEACHING SCULPTURES

GOALS:

1. To teach about the family disease of addiction in a way that is involving and engaging.
2. To provide a living picture of the family disease that allows clients to see themselves and their families.
3. To act as a segue between awareness and action or therapy.

STEPS:

1. Let the group know that you're going to do a sculpture on the kinds of family dynamics that are present in alcoholic families.
2. Ask for volunteers to play particular roles. Start with the following roles, which are taken from the research of Sharon Wegscheider-Cruse:

   Get the group involved in placing each member of the family system where they best demonstrate their position within the system. Allow each role-player to take a body position that shows his role. Cast each of the following. If the group wishes to play out a scene, ask them to name a scene that goes along with these roles.

   • Addict
   • Enabler
   • Hero
   • Lost Child
   • Scapegoat
   • Mascot
   • Other

3. Next, ask each role-player to say a couple of words about how it feels to stand in each role or play out the scene. *Note: Standing in these roles can warm up feelings to which the director needs to be sensitive.*

4. Now invite members of the group to come up and stand behind one or more roles that they identify with (for any reason at all) and double for what they imagine to be the inner life of that role. Ask them to make it short, one or two sentences at most, then sit down and give someone else a chance to double.

5. Continue to play out the scene as outlined in sociodramatic role-play, freezing the scene, if desired, then returning to action.

6. When all who care to have had a chance to double, de-role role-players or ask them to de-role themselves, "My name is, _____ . I'm not _____," and return to seats for further sharing and processing with the entire group. Because this is a sociodramatic process and the roles represent collective roles, the group can share about which role or roles they identify with and what that brings up for them. They may also wish to share any other feelings or awareness that came up during the process. Role-players can also share what it was like being in the role.

VARIATIONS:

This sociodramatic sculpturing can be used as a warm-up to psychodrama if desired. It can also be a warm-up for letter writing (see Letter Writing, page 196). Group members can write a letter to anyone they wish to talk to after witnessing the teaching sculpture, including themselves.

Groups may use props, such as a bottle or costume pieces, if this feels useful or appropriate in the program. Groups will often ham it up in one way or another, which lends a little levity to the process and tends to spontaneously bond the group.

If the clinician is uncomfortable doing a family sculpture, try Addicted Family Systems Roles (see page 386), which is a locogram from our chapter on ACOAs and addicts.

ROMANCE WITH ADDICTION

GOALS:

1. To concretize the constellation of fantasies that an addict has about what his addictive substance or behavior might do for him and the reality-bending nature of addiction.

2. To offer a psychoeducational approach or ritual that concretizes the process of saying good-bye to the relationship with an addictive substance or behavior.

3. To provide a way to concretize the process of exchanging dysfunctional roles for more functional, life-enhancing roles.

STEPS:

1. Warm up the group by talking about the "broken promises" of addiction. How we initially think we have found the answer to our problems but find that we have created even more chaos. Discuss how in saying good-bye to an addictive substance or behavior, we're saying good-bye to our relationship to and with it. Often addicts have looked

to an addictive substance or behavior for a sense of intimacy, strength and companion-ship. In recovery, they will need to find new ways to meet these pressing, personal needs. This progression is what we will explore in this exercise.

2. Invite group members to choose role players to concretize the roles associated with their fantasies of what using a substance or behavior will do for them. **Note:** This part of the process can be done as a group by throwing out a lot of possible roles and writing them on a blackboard or by selecting one protagonist or volunteer to decide upon all the roles or a combination of both. As you come up with the roles ask the group to throw out "lines" for each role. Possible suggestions for roles with definitions and lines are:

The Seducer: The irresistible lure of the sirens call. A false sense of good feelings; a filling up that leaves one empty, hungover or regretful. ("I am what you've been looking for, together we will find happiness.")

The Companion: Nonjudgmental, a sense of never being alone again. ("I am always here for you.")

The Seeker: Constantly seeking a state of ecstasy and nirvana wanting an endless high. ("You have found the way to feel good forever and I'm it.")

The Liar: Casts everything in an unrealistic, positive light, a drunken glow, without illumi-nating the negative or dangerous aspects; denial of reality, delusion. ("Don't worry, this is a great idea; don't listen to anything but my voice.")

The Hot Shot: Grandiose, false sense of courage and strength; unrealistic fantasies of supe-riority, liquid courage, beer muscles. ("I know all the answers; I am smarter and better than anyone; I can beat the system; I'm full of courage; I'm fearless.")

The Betrayer: Disillusionment; promises one thing but delivers another, ultimate betrayal. ("Don't listen to anyone but me; I'm your true friend. Put your faith in me; I'll never let you down.")

Genie: The one with all the right answers. The all-wise one who can make everything turn out right. ("I can make all your dreams come true; I'm the one with all the answers.")

The Addict: ("I want to find the answers, I want the pain to go away.") **Note:** Here the pro-tagonist is essentially choosing a stand-in to represent himself.

3. Invite the protagonist to first place himself (represented by the role player "the addict") on stage in whatever location and position that feels right. Allow him to reverse roles with "the addict" and show "the addict" how and where he is standing and what he is saying. He can then add whichever other roles he wants as part of his sculpture, placing them in whatever relationship to him that feels right and reverse roles with each as before.

4. After all role players are in position, invite them to say their lines and concretize the sort of "noise" that is constantly going on inside the addict's mind.

5. Next freeze the sculpture and ask the protagonist, who is standing just outside the sculpture, how it feels to see and hear all of this on stage.

6. While the sculpture is frozen, you may invite members from the group to double for the inner life of any one of the roles represented. Say, "Stand up and say a line or two of what you feel is going on inside the role, that is not being spoken out loud." e.g. doubling for The Seducer: "Maybe this time I'll find what I'm looking for, I want love"; The Hot Shot: "I'm terrified; I'm so tired of feeling small and worthless"; The Seeker: "I want to feel good all the time, no more down times, only highs." The Genie: "I need answers, solutions; I want my problems fixed; I'm scared." The Companion: "I want to fill this emptiness; I don't want to feel lonely or alone." The Addict: "I can't live with it (my substance) but I can't picture life without it. I've got to have it to feel okay, to feel good, I'll collapse without it. What's happening to me, to my life?" The protagonist may also enter the sculpture and double for himself and any of the roles. **Note:** As use and abuse is often a defense against experiencing painful or anxiety provoking emotions; the double is able to stand behind the role and articulate those feelings that are being deadened or medicated by the compulsive use of the substance or behavior. When we remove the substance in recovery the painful feelings return. In recovery we need to come up with new and novel ways to manage those feelings and to grow from and through them toward emotional maturity. We need to restore our spontaneity. Otherwise we risk trading one "ism" for another or one dysfunctional behavior for another.

7. Next, invite the protagonist to say anything he wishes to say to any role in the sculpture, "Who do you want to talk to and what do you want to say?" **Note:** Role reversal can come in play here if the director has sufficient training.

8. Invite the protagonist to talk to himself, "What do you want to say to yourself inside this addictive process?

9. Invite the protagonist to end the scene any way he wishes to for now.

10. Check in with the protagonist to see how they are doing and what new insights they might have from this experience. At this point the protagonist may need to process what they are experiencing for a moment.

11. Next, offer the protagonist the opportunity to choose role players to replace the dysfunctional roles with new, more functional alternatives. For example, the protagonist may exchange "the liar" with "self-respect," "the companion" with "program friends" or "the seeker" with spirituality. The protagonist, for example, can be invited to "say the last things he wishes to say to the role of addict for now," then he can say his goodbyes to "the addict" and choose a more functional alternative such as "the sober person" to come up and take the addict's place on stage. In this same manner, he can exchange all dysfunctional roles in the sculpture for more functional ones.

12. Invite the protagonist to end the scene any way he wants to for now and return to seats for sharing and processing.

11 Role Theory

The self emerges from the roles we play, rather than the roles emerging from a self that has not yet had the opportunity to be formed and integrated. Body, psyche and society are intermediary parts of the entire self.

—J. L. Moreno

Fundamental to psychodrama, sociometry and sociodrama is the concept of role. The role, according to J. L. Moreno is "the tangible form the self takes." Feelings, thoughts and behaviors tend to be role specific; that is, we feel, think and act in ways that grow out of the role we are playing. Moreno felt that "the concept underlying this approach is the recognition that man is fundamentally role-player, that every individual is characterized by a certain range of roles which dominate his behavior, and that every culture is characterized by a certain set of roles which it imposes with a varying degree of success upon its membership" (J. Moreno 1934, 60). "The sociometrist will point out that the playing of roles is not an exclusively human trait, but that roles are also played by animals; they can be observed in the taking of sexual roles, roles of the nest-builder and leader roles, for instance."

Moreno felt that in our modern, western society we each potentially have a very large role repertoire, more than we are likely to use. This access to new and varied roles is a relatively new phenomenon in our mobile culture. "Our task, then, becomes finding the roles that best suit our own uniqueness."

"As a general rule, a role can be: 1, rudimentarily developed, normally developed or overdeveloped; 2, almost or totally absent in a person (indifference); or 3, perverted into a hostile function" (Moreno Vol 1).

Roles have both a public and a private side; that is, we can experience a role in each dimension. We may experience a role differently in each dimension.

How We Develop and Role-Learning

Role-learning begins at or before birth. It insinuates itself into and around thinking, feeling and behavior throughout each stage of development. Therefore, when we examine the contents of a role—the thoughts, emotions, actions, act hungers, open tensions, drives, wishes, needs, pressures and so on— we have a way of tracing the threads of our very self as they weave their way throughout our development. Gradually, roles take shape and increase in complexity as the self emerges from the roles that are played. "The function of the role," says Moreno, "is to enter the unconscious from the social world and bring shape and order into it." Because the development of the role begins at birth or even in utero (in its somatic form), when we explore a role in a psychodrama that exploration can have deep resonance and reverberation; it can reach from the present far back into childhood and infancy. The child is imbedded in the adolescent, both adolescent and child into the adult and so on.

Our neurological wiring is set up not in isolation but in connection. Roles transmit learning on a multisensory level that incorporates the thinking, feeling and behavior of those who came before us into our own self-system where they give "shape and definition" to our unconscious. Then, when the role reverses, when, for example, the daughter becomes the mother, the role learning is passed along to another generation.

When we explore the role, we also explore the thinking, feeling and behavior, along with the act hungers and open tensions, embedded within the role. This is part of what makes role-play such a profound vehicle for growth. In role reversal, for example, as we stand in the role of, say, our mother, we can act out not only the part of her we see with our eyes or perceive with our senses, but the part of her that has become incorporated into our unconscious. Her tears may flow through our eyes but with new awareness as to why we might be carrying not only our own grief but the grief of generations. Or the tender reminiscences that allow a mother and child to touch hearts may emerge spontaneously through the roles we play in our own lives, the laughter that bubbles out of our chests but carries the humor of generations.

"Role is the functioning form the individual assumes in the specific moment he reacts to a specific situation in which other persons or objects are involved. It begins at birth and continues throughout the lifetime of the individual and the socius. It has constructed models within which the role begins to transact from birth on" (J. Moreno 1964).

"A role . . . can also be classified from the point of view of its development in time: (1) it was never present; (2) it is present towards one person but not present towards another; (3) it was once present towards a person but is now extinguished. As the matrix of identity is, at the moment of birth, the entire universe of the infant, there is no differentiation between internal and external, between objects and persons, psyche and environment, it is one total existence" (J. Moreno 1964, Vol IV).

THE BODY-MIND NATURE OF ROLES

Roles develop into a relational context through interaction. They have physical, emotional, psychological, and what Moreno refers to as "psychodramatic" dimensions. . . . "We cannot start with the role process simply at the moment of language development. In order to be consistent and comprehensive we must carry it through the nonverbal phases of living. Therefore, role theory cannot be limited to social roles, it must include the three dimensions. . . . The infant lives before and immediately after birth in an undifferentiated universe which I have called 'matrix of identity.' This matrix is existential but not experienced. It may be considered as the locus from which, in gradual stages, the self and its branches, the roles, emerge. The roles are the embryos, forerunners of the self; the roles strive towards clustering and unification" (J. Moreno 1964).

The three dimensions that Moreno refers to above are: *somatic, psychodramatic* and *social*. The somatic roles represent the physical aspects of self. The first roles that we play are physical or *somatic*, preverbal, and associated with the initial undifferentiated universe in which the infant experiences mother and the surrounding world as one with his own self. Included in the somatic roles that the infant plays are the role of the breather, urinator, defecator, eater and the sleeper. Further somatic roles emerge for the child throughout development, such as the crawler, the walker, the noisemaker and so on.

The next set of co-occurring roles that the developing child plays are *social* roles. Social roles represent the interpersonal roles we play with other people in our families and in society: mother/child, sister/brother. Social roles may have both a private and public dimension.

The *psychodramatic* roles represent the internal dimensions of self, the fantasy roles such as the thinker, the feeler, the dreamer. Exploring psychodramatic roles allows us to give shape and form to internal dimensions of self, concretize them, role reverse with them and work through any issues surrounding them. The blocked writer, the would-be entrepreneur/builder, the Don Juan, the seductress, the stuck victim can all be met and dealt with.

In examining a role, we need to take into account the sociocultural context in which the role developed. What was the cultural context and family environment that influenced, for example, the development of the role of an addict?

IN MORENO'S OWN WORDS

"It may be useful to think of the psychosomatic roles in the course of their transactions as helping the infant to experience what we call the "body"; the psychodramatic roles and their transactions to help the infant to experience what we call the "psyche"; and the social roles to produce what we call "society." Body, psyche and society are then the intermediary parts of the entire self (J. Moreno 1964). In the circle diagram on the next page, "the psychosomatic roles are in the innermost circle, and the next two concentric circles represent the social and psychodramatic roles, with a dotted line to separate them indicating that the threshold between them is thin. A smaller space is assigned to the social roles, since they are less intensively developed than the psychodramatic roles. In terms of development, the psychosomatic roles (role of the eater, eliminator, sleeper, etc.) emerge first. The psychodramatic and social roles develop later, the domain of the psychodramatic roles being far more extensive and dominating than the domain of social roles. After the breach between fantasy and reality is established, the division between psychodramatic and social roles, which have been up to that point merged, begins gradually to become differentiated. The roles of the mother, son, daughter, teacher, etc., are called social roles and are set aside from the personification of imagined things, both real and unreal. The latter are called psychodramatic roles" (J. Moreno 1964).

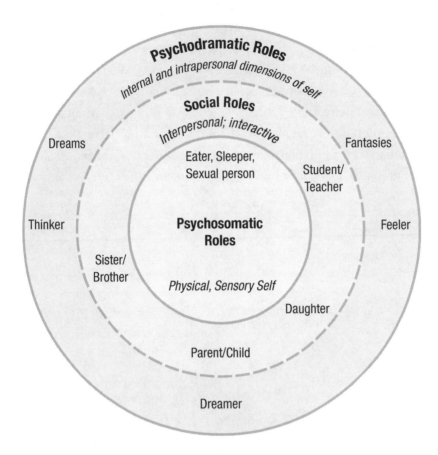

Diagram adapted from *Psychodrama Volume 1*

THE THREE STAGES OF LEARNING A ROLE

Moreno felt that we go through a specific set of stages in learning any role, be it mother, writer, jogger, politician or psychodramatist. He called these three stages role-taking, role-playing and role creation.

Role-Taking—The process of role-taking is most closely related to the concept of modeling. It is the taking in of a role through a modeling process in which we imitate and imbibe what we perceive or experience outside of us. There is generally little awareness of this process as it is happening. It begins in infancy, the way that we are touched, spoken to and held, the way that we are seen or not seen will all go into our brain as our learning on how to be with an infant. When we are confronted with a similar situation, it is this historic knowledge that will be brought to the surface and acted out in role reversal, i.e., the infants, now the parent, will likely treat their infant the way they were treated if there is no conscious intervention in that process. Role-taking forms the brain template that is referred to again and again as a psychological and emotional map. This may be a part of why we play out life scripts for no apparent reason. Role-taking forms the partially unconscious portion of how we behave throughout our lives. The more consciousness we have around this process, the more of ourselves we can bring to playing out roles in our own lives.

Role-Playing—Role-playing is a more conscious level of role experience. We have already learned a role and are playing it out. Naturally, as we play out a role it will be played on our own stages, so to speak. It will come out through us with parts of ourselves insinuating into the role and making it, at least in part, our own. We have some perception of what we are doing and an ability to allow pieces of ourselves to enter the role as we play it.

Role Creation—Role creation can occur when the first two stages have been fully enough integrated so that the most creative part of the self can be brought to bear on restructuring the role in a new and unique fashion. Consider the exquisite early drawings of Picasso, how fine his lines are, how delicate and sensitive his portraits of people, how perfectly he was able to master his technique. Once mastered, he then was in a position to throw away what he learned, to toss it up in the air, into the universe, into the vast expanse of himself, and let fall in a new and highly personal vision of his own uniqueness.

Much in this way we create ourselves and our own lives through the roles that we play. When roles have been fully enough learned and experienced with something new created with the old, something old blended in with the new, when the security of those two stages is internalized, we feel able to take on the ultimate challenge of experiencing our inner dimensions. To enter into our lives with wonder, firmly rooted but with arms open to what might be. After the actor has learned his lines, incorporated the blocking and drawn out the parts of himself that relate to the role and integrated them with the playwright's conception of the role, he is in a position to role-create, to bring to the character that which has never been brought in just this way, to release what is known and walk into what is not known with the confidence that what is available to him (if necessary in milliseconds) will be all the accumulated knowledge of the script, the playwright's conception of the role and his own integrated perception, with the self-assuredness to let it happen spontaneously within the moment.

ROLE PRESCRIPTIONS

One begins to see the advantages of approaching life and clinical work through a role perspective. Treatment plans can have role prescriptions in them that help to bring balance into the outer world of the client, and subsequently balance into her inner world, as the role has the power to "enter the unconscious and bring shape and order to it." In this way it is important not only to explore the inner world of the client but the roles that she is playing in her life. Which roles are in or out of balance, which roles is she overplaying and which is she underplaying? Are there some roles that need to move to the periphery in order to bring balance, and are there others that need to be added or made more central? How much satisfaction and aliveness is she experiencing in a particular role? What are the pressures, tensions or act hungers that are part of the roles?

For example, someone who is addicted has a role that has gotten out of control and is, like weeds, taking over the garden of his life. Roles are alive and growing. The addict will need to cut back certain roles and expand others in order for recovery to take hold. This behavioral emphasis has always been understood intuitively by the addictions field. Addicts need to give up the using role and replace it with other roles in order to continue growing as people. They may need to add the role of the twelve stepper, the group member, the healthy eater, the exerciser, and later, as these refine and bring new balance and order to their inner and outer worlds, and after they are well stabilized and integrated, they can experiment with new roles. We think, feel and behave according to the role we're playing. The addict thinks, feels and behaves like an addict. This is part of why full recovery so often requires a change in friends, the reduction of roles associated with addiction, and the adding of roles associated with health and recovery. The role, remember, enters the unconscious. Being an addict is a powerful role that the unconscious remembers. The addict who remains in the environment that stimulates that role may be constantly tempted, constantly reminded and subtly drawn toward the thinking, feeling and behavior related to addiction.

Role-learning does not always generalize. The man or woman with an over-developed work role and an underdeveloped husband, wife or father role, for example, may succeed in one area admirably and fail miserably in another. The business man who wants to run his family like a corporation has the mistaken notion that the skill set for his business role is the same as that which he needs to succeed within the home. His wife and children are not likely to appreciate bulleted lists of tasks or his conducting a dinner conversation like a staff meeting. Or the doctor who is so used to handing out medical advice that she assumes she has something valuable to say on each and every subject may do well as a doctor but have few intimate friends.

Sara's Story: The Role and Its Subroles

A stunningly beautiful young woman and a recovering addict, Sara announced in group that she was having awful memories of her using days, and some of the things that she did were haunting her. Sara had turned her life around admirably. She has excellent sobriety, a good working understanding of the underlying issues that led her to drink and a deep commitment to living a sober, healthful life. Sara fell in love and became engaged. In the course of becoming a lover to her fiancée, memories from her previous love relationships became warmed up. "Putting roles into action is what brings up the surrounding emotions, thinking, behavior and history attached to the role" (Z. Moreno 2004). Sara was feeling haunted by the sexual encounters that she had had in her drinking days, which were risky and sometimes dangerous. They were her way of feeling powerful. They were also an unconscious reenactment of the confusing and frightening sexual abuse she experienced from her brother, who was ten years her senior. In addition, Sara's jobs while using had always been part of her using world. She was a bartender and a topless dancer.

We decided to do her drama from a role perspective. Sara chose someone to play her addicted self surrounded by auxiliaries representing four subroles she identified of her addicted self, "the seductress," "the professional," "her sadness and shame" and "the substance." As she talked to each role and reversed roles with these various aspects of self, Sara was able to explore the thinking, feeling and behavior attached to each role. Concretizing and talking to the roles she had played as represented by auxiliaries gave her just enough psychic distance and clarity to allow the fuller picture to emerge. This allowed Sara to share the truth of her existence more fully, to self-disclose in service of healing and to gain insight into and compassion for her addicted self.

When Sara felt that she had completed her drama, I asked her to say the last things she needed to say to each role, put a hand on each side of them and put them where she wanted them to be. As Sara put the role-players in their seats, I asked her to choose someone to represent a more positive, functional version of each role in order to do some role-repair. She traded "the seductress" for a seductress who was playful and sexually alive in her marriage, "the professional" for a self-respecting, "ethical professional." "Her sadness and shame" she wanted to keep, honor, comfort and transform into her "feeling self" because it was the part of herself who started to feel bad about her behavior and led her to sobriety. "The substance" she traded for self-esteem. Next Sara dialogued briefly with each new aspect of self. Then I asked her to put these parts of herself into a sculpture that felt right to her now. This was an enormously relieving piece of work for Sara. She felt very exposed, however, and it was through the sharing and identification of the group that her healing became more fully integrated. As the group identified, Sara learned that she was anything but alone in her acting-out behavior. Her willingness to be honest about it allowed other group members to be honest about their own. This allowed Sara to take in caring and support from others, ground her insights and feel less stigmatized, which let her be more comfortable in the group. Through interacting with roles within her own self-system, Sara was able to make changes in her inner and outer worlds.

SPONTANEITY/CREATIVITY AND THE ROLE

"Moreno first began his formal interest in psychology by observing and joining in children's play in the gardens of Vienna," writes Zerka Moreno, "in the first decade of this century." In watching the children he was impressed by the spontaneity with which the children entered the roles and he "became aware that human beings become less spontaneous as they age." He asked himself, why does this occur? What happens to us? The same process struck him when he started to direct children in staged, rehearsed plays. "Initially the children brought considerable spontaneity and creativity to the creation of their roles, but eventually, the more rehearsed they became, the less their spontaneity and creativity. They began to conserve their energy, repeating their best lines, movements and facial expressions because they produced the greatest effect upon the audience. What resulted was a mechanical performance, lacking in reality. Clearly this was the same phenomenon evident in aging and in certain types of emotional disturbances, where one finds repetition without relation to the current situation, a freezing of affect and memory." Moreno recognized these as what he later came to call cultural conserves, or "attempts to freeze spontaneity and creativity." Moreno attempted to correct this or "slow down" the process of losing spontaneity by putting his actors from the Theater of Spontaneity into what Zerka describes as "a variety of situations, taking them by surprise and having them respond to one another. It was a freeing of their ability to act and interact on the spur of the moment. . . . He attempted to tap into the unconservable energy, spontaneity, from within the wellspring of the actor and use it in the developing of interaction, to see if some resolution could be found, either between the actors or within the actors themselves. The bonding which took place between them and which helped them to be more creative due to their cocreation, he called tele."

In encouraging therapeutic actors to throw away their scripts and react spontaneously to new situations he was attempting to train spontaneity. By cutting off the old, scripted route he opened a route toward using the role in a novel way, to develop and train spontaneity.

THE PSYCHODRAMATIC THEORY OF DEVELOPMENT

Moreno puts forward a theory of psychodramatic role development that mirrors the functions of the double, the mirror, the auxiliary ego and role reversal built into the psychodramatic method. A developmental model of treatment is one that has received a much-needed scientific boost in recent years. Studies in neurobiology point to how critical the early environment is in laying down the neural wiring that becomes part of our emotional regulation throughout life. "The emotion-generating limbic system is the most obvious site of developmental changes associated with the ascendence of attachment behaviors. Indeed, the specific period from seven to fifteen months (roughly Bowlby's period for the establishment of attachment patterns) has been shown to be critical for the myelination and therefore the maturation of particular rapidly developing limbic and cortical association areas" (Kinney, Brody, Kloman and Gillens, 1988; Yakovlev and Lecours, 1967; Schore, 1994, 1998a). Here, psychology and neurology meet in seeing early experience and environment as a critical part of a child's emotional and psychological development.

Every role, from birth on, is interactive and develops in a particular context. The environment in which a role develops needs to be taken into account whenever examining a role.

Following are the stages of development that infants go through on their road to maturity.

Stage One: The Double

In the first universe, the roles we play are somatic: the eater, the sleeper and the sensory/sexual being. The social or interpersonal roles develop in concert as the mother, father, siblings and early caregivers respond to and interact with this early universe of oneness. Perhaps the deepest seeds of self-image are planted and germinate here. Moreno refers to this as the "matrix of identity" in which the infant shares a "co-state" with the mother. One in which the universes of the mother and child are experienced by the infant as one; that in which the mother is the first "auxiliary ego" of the child, an auxiliary ego, without which the child cannot survive. Harmony in this dyad seeps into the infant where he experiences it as harmony within himself. Disharmony in this dyad also is experienced by the infant as disharmony within himself. What occurs in this dyad is also a precursor of future relational dyads, "the intrinsic regulators of human brain growth in a child are specifically adapted to be coupled by emotional communicators, to the regulators of adult brains." In these affective interchanges, the mother maximizes positive and minimizes negative affect states in the infant, and they culminate in the development of an attachment system, the function of which is the dyadic regulation of emotion (Sroute 1996). This is how children learn to self-regulate and is experienced by the infant as part of the construction of self. If the parent is an attuned "double" for the child's experience, the child feels a sense of place and belonging. If, on the other hand, she leaves the infant to a world without doubling, the child may feel that he is incomprehensible to others and a sort of fissure may occur within the self due to feeling misunderstood or out of sync with his external representations of self since, from a child's point of view, parents and some siblings are a part his own self. Initially, the child is an entirely sensory being and continues to function primarily from the senses into early development. This is, in part, why holding and touching are so important. We need to speak to our children through our senses as they understand best through their senses. The cooing, oohing and ahhing, the touching, the shared affective world where both mother and child are enveloped in an attuned cohabitation, is where the child begins to feel her own presence in this world. Marsupial mothering, where the child and mother are almost attached and his little physical movement requires a sensitive adjustment on the part of the mother till both are comfortable, is a sort of physical model for an interactional, psycho-social phenomenon. These adjustments happen physically, emotionally and cognitively a thousand times a day. Without the nearness of the mother, there is a very significant loss of connection, as the child's, at this point, connects through her senses and lacks object constancy. When the mother or father is not physically present, the child does not have the mental equipment to conjure them up. They are gone until they return to the child's sensory orbit.

And the senses remain the first port of entry into toddlerhood, at least. Anyone who has raised a toddler knows that his first interaction with any object is to reach out his chubby little hand and touch it, then to bring it straight into his mouth. Sensory integration is every bit as critical to his development as emotional and psychological integration. One is related to the other. One can easily see how deficits at this stage are sensory in nature and may need therapies that allow the senses to participate in new learning. "There needs to be harmony between mother and child in these roles or it causes trouble in that fundamental dyad" (Z. Moreno 2004). The child who is dragged along the street, forced to match the mother's walking speed, or the one whose sleeping, eating or eliminating patterns are treated like annoying intrusions, reflects a lack of attunement in the mother-child or father-child dyad and can have long-term resonance in that child's life in years to come.

Moreno cautions against filling the child's world with too many inanimate playthings and too few real "auxiliary egos" who can, through natural interaction, teach a child the limits of his own psyche and behavior. He refers to dolls as being like "individuals with no spontaneity." This is an especially chilling warning in today's world, which is filled with so many technological playthings. The child gets no human feedback when playing with objects, no matter how animated they may be. The child has no human reaction to base his behavior on, no one falls over, cries, bleeds, hits back, smiles, laughs or loves. The connection with this phenomenon and violent or antisocial behavior is all too easy to make.

Stage Two: The Mirror

The second universe, or the stage of the mirror, heralds a beginning awareness of a separate self. After nine months the infant can engage in "joint attention," or the ability to shift attention between an object and a person. In this form of nonverbal communication the infant coordinates his visual attention with that of the caregiver and is now not only aware of an object but simultaneously aware of the mother's attention to the object. In such an instance of what Trevarthen et. al. (1998) call "secondary intersubjectivity," each member of the dyad co-aligns separable yet related forms of consciousness.

Joint attention occurs with highly affectively charged social referencing transactions, an attachment process that mediates a resonance of positive affect. This dyadic mechanism allows the infant to appreciate that "the other person is a locus of psychological attitudes toward the world, that the other is 'attending' in such a way that shared experiences are possible" (Hobson 1993), a critical advance in the child's adaptive capabilities.

The child begins to perceive her surroundings no longer only "as" the self but also as a variety of reflections "of" the self. The child may still feel that the world exists at her command, that the sun rises and sets not only on but because of her, but there is the dawning of an awareness of self as differentiated from the world outside the self. If the world that is reflected back to the child is friendly and supports her growth and positive self-concept, the child hopefully experiences a growing sense of personal security. You might say ground begins to accumulate underneath the child's feet that can eventually support her weight and be walked on. If, on the other hand, her reflected world is unattuned to her needs, drives and desires, she may experience herself as unmoored to anything constant, as difficult to understand, comfort or be with. This can clearly translate into a discomfort or dissonance within the self.

The transition from the double to the mirror is a constant back and forth and often a place, in my experience, that therapy pulls us back to. The holding function of therapy seems to have great healing power, the unconditional acceptance that slowly gives way to an ability to tolerate less-than-perfect holding so that clients can learn to live in the world without having to overcontrol other people's responses to them in order to feel safe. All of us probably wish to be liked, but tolerating being unliked, rejected occasionally or misunderstood allows us to lead a life in which we can put up with "the slings and arrows the flesh is heir to" and get on with life without collapsing or overcontrolling or becoming enmeshed in order to manage our fears of feeling emotionally abandoned.

Much deep healing work inevitably happens in these first two stages as the holding, therapeutic relationships reach through the role relationship into the unconscious and give it new shape. Twelve-step work, in my experience, also can serve this function of holding and unconditional acceptance.

Stage Three: Auxiliary Ego

This is a stage of separation/individuation of continuing to identify the self in relationship to the other.

It's easier to understand this if we put it into its developmental context. The way we develop is through introjection; we take in the other person, psychologically, emotionally and neurologically. In the doubling stage the child is feeling that his mother's feelings are his feelings, and his feelings are the mother's feelings; this is introjecting. Internal feelings get picked up from the other person, and we're not distinguishing who the feelings belong to; they feel like mutual emotions. Mirroring is the beginning of awareness of the self as separate from the other, but only the beginning. In the stage of the auxiliary ego we are aware of making use of the other person in service of our own needs, but the other person is still not distinct and separate in the child's mind.

Codependency, for example, has some features of an unindividuated state, one in which we cannot fully distinguish between another person's inner world and our own; we're seeing the other person as separate but we think they have the same feelings we do, or that the feelings we imagine they have are their real feelings. The family-of-origin social atom is a concrete representation of this stage of development. Family members appear on the atom, not in their own right, but as extensions of the protagonist's world; they appear as the protagonist experienced them. We work with the protagonist's internalized set of object relations and slowly, work through the emotional or psychological blocks that may have frozen certain aspects of development at points along this stage.

Stage Four: Role Reversal

The stage of role reversal heralds a true sense of separateness, along with an ability to empathize with the other as a separate individual with different feelings and different motivations. It is a stage at which we are able to take our place in the world as an individual among other individuals, accepting ourselves as a person in our own right, with our own motivations, needs and drives, among others who are also separate individuals with their own motivations, needs, drives and histories. We are able to live with the knowledge that another person may not be able to be exactly who we may want them to be, nor should they have to. Others, like us, have a right to be themselves and work with us in what we call a relationship. We can take our rightful place in the larger context of the world without asking the world or our relationships to be what they cannot necessarily be in order to suit us. Having healed enough of our early wounds we are ready to accept the world not as we wish it were but as it is.

Eventually we become capable of a true encounter with another person, one in which there are two subjects, intersubjectivity, when we're aware of the other person's subjectivity at the same time they are aware of ours. And when each person is also aware of herself, it is a true developmental accomplishment.

A Sensitive Moment in Development

Coming to the awareness that life and relationships in the present may not be all that we wish for can be a moment of deep integration that can sometimes lead to a sort of depression, an "is this all there is" feeling. This is sometimes referred to as the "depressive position," when you realize that your parent is separate from you and that she is both the good and the bad mother. The transition is from either/or to both/and; life is no longer black and white but full of ambiguity and paradox. It is a maturation out of the classic borderline position when the parent is seen as either all good or all bad, or the splitting defense. The classic defenses for the borderline position are projection, assigning to another person the parts of yourself that you want to get rid of, or projective identification, where you elicit from the other person an expected feeling or dynamic, perhaps a fear dynamic, e.g., you act as a frightened person so that you elicit retaliatory anger from someone and then they, in fact, become a feared object. Narcissistic wounds often occur in the stages of the double, which can seriously affect a person's ability to tolerate "mirroring" or feedback from the outside. These people have trouble taking it in and may experience it as attacking or dismissing and not seeing them. When someone is stuck somewhere on the continuum of the borderline position, it is considered to be related to the earlier stages of development, while being stuck in the depressive position speaks to a sadness and disappointment at the auxiliary ego transition. The stage of the auxiliary is also a maturation out of the narcissistic position, where others are seen only as extensions of the self and not people in their own right.

The depressive position is considered, in psychodynamic theory, to be a developmental accomplishment. It is also an important stage of therapy in which clients face the reality that they may never get what they yearn for, either from the person from whom they wish it or anyone else, in part because the yearning belongs to another time and place in development. Even if their parents, for example, suddenly became the parents they wish had raised them, they are now adults, less dependent and vulnerable, no longer seeing through the eyes of the child. Getting what they yearned for could feel infantilizing. I see this oftentimes in clients who have mastered an aspect of therapy and come into a workshop, for example, saying, "I'm so disappointed. I've understood my needs, put them out there and still no one is meeting them." They may think they're with the wrong partner or missing something in recovery when actually they may simply be entering the stage of development where all children have to come to terms with the humanity of their parents and realize that all relationships do indeed have limitations. If this stage remains unresolved we may enter our intimate relationships wishing for and expecting in a way that sets us and our partner up for constant frustration and feelings of disappointment. The shame of this is that our intimate relationships with our own partners and children can be among the most healing of our lives. However, if we are marooned in a developmental position that is mired in trauma defenses and are unable to take in the caring and support because it feels ego dystonic (we are not wired for it) and absorb mostly the frustration and anger of the other because it is ego syntonic (we are wired for it), we lose access to one of our best possibilities for healing. We may pass our pain down through yet another generation. Spouses and children, because they stimulate our most primary and intimate roles, can be vehicles for healing the self if we can work through the trauma associated with early role learning and learn to live differently in intimate connection.

ROLE DIAGRAM

GOALS:

1. To familiarize participants with the variety of roles they play and allow for a paper-and-pencil exploration of them.
2. To understand the number and variety of roles played.
3. To observe those roles in relation to one another.
4. To explore content and satisfaction within the roles.

STEPS:

1. Ask participants to get a pencil and paper.
2. Ask them to put a circle somewhere on the paper with their name inside of the circle and extend lines like spokes of a wheel from the outside of the circle for about one and one-half inches.
3. Ask them to write on each spoke the major roles they play in their lives, for example, mother, wife, daughter, daughter-in-law, writer, professor and so on.
4. Ask them to choose one of those roles they would like to explore or one in which they feel some conflict.
5. Ask them to place another circle somewhere on the paper and put the name of that role within the circle, for example, mother. Then, as in the previous diagram, ask them to extend the spokes from the outside of the circle.
6. Ask them to put on each spoke an aspect of the chosen role, for the mother role, for example, chauffeur, doctor, listener, cook, nurturer, playmate, disciplinarian, friend, executive planner, teacher and so on.
7. Next, ask them to write the following words in a column at the side of the page: taste, smell, color, movement, texture and sound. Then, after each word, write the appropriate association with the word that would best describe or relate to the role they are exploring (for example, "the color that feels like the role of mother to me would be burnt orange"). (Adapted from Siroka, 1988)
8. At this point you may allow some time for sharing their adjectives with the group. Ask group members to share why they have chosen them to describe the various roles.
9. If you wish to move into action, the next step is to examine the diagrams to discover in which aspects of the role participants experience conflict or discomfort.

10. Structure whatever scene feels appropriate and ask participants who they wish to speak to about the conflict or issues they are experiencing: that is, where and with whom does the unfinished business lie, what aspects of themselves would they like to address by putting it into an empty chair or selecting an auxiliary ego to represent it?

11. Allow anyone who wishes to stage vignettes in order to further explore the issue or conflict, using doubling, role reversal, interview or soliloquy, or whatever technique might be helpful. The protagonist may wish to use an empty chair, or he may wish to choose someone to represent the person or aspect of self he is addressing.

12. Allow time for sharing after each vignette or for sharing as a group after several vignettes have taken place.

VARIATIONS:

This exercise can be done entirely as a paper-and-pencil exercise ending with group sharing. **Note:** Healthy people tend to be able to move in and out of roles with relative ease, and happy people tend to play more than one or two roles; they have a variety of roles among which they travel easily and naturally. Getting stuck in a role can lead to fatigue, a lack of creativity, and a sense of being bored or even depressed with life. In this case role work can help to gain perspective and a shift in awareness. If someone overplays a role until she feels burned out, she may need to add other roles to her life in order to provide new outlets for nurturing, creativity and growth. Though the answer may seem to lie in leaving the role in which she feels burned out, the solution may lie instead in adding new roles and expanding potential experiences.

ROLE DRAMA: ACTION REFRAMING

GOALS:

1. To concretize a particular role repertoire.
2. To work through the thinking, feeling and behavior attached to a particular role.

STEPS:

1. Invite the protagonist to cast auxiliaries to represent the self and the subroles. Before choosing each subrole auxiliary, it can be helpful to ask the protagonist to reverse roles and "show us the role."
2. Invite the protagonist to shape the self and subroles into an action sociogram or a sculpture.
3. Next ask the protagonist how it feels to look at this sculpture and ask him what is going on. The protagonist can reverse roles into the drama and play the self or double for any of the roles.
4. Whenever the scene seems to be winding down, ask the protagonist to "say the last things he needs to say for now to the self and subroles."
5. Next invite the protagonist to trade each role by deroling the role that may have been problematic and choosing someone to take on a new role (see Sara's Story). For example, the role of "the substance" can be replaced by a new role of "program, exercise and meditation" or "healthy, sober living." This is a form of action reframing.
6. After all of the old roles have been reframed into new ones, ask the protagonist to stand outside the scene and talk to it.
7. Let the scene draw to a close, return to seats and begin sharing.

VARIATIONS:

This drama offers an opportunity to turn the role diagram into an action sociogram and then do action reframing with roles that have become worn out or are dysfunctional, trading them for new, more appropriate roles. The sharing from role-players can be very rich and varied.

ROLE DEVELOPMENT

GOALS:

1. To identify points along the role development continuum where development may have been problematically affected.
2. To focus psychodramatic work on a developmental continuum and place developmental distortions into a context.

STEPS:

1. Familiarize the group with the psychodramatic theory of role development through talking and handouts.
2. Ask group members to quietly reminisce or share in group or subgroups about their development according to the psychodramatic model paying attention to both strengths and weaknesses they felt they experienced along the continuum of the developmental stages.
3. After sharing has occurred, ask if anyone feels warmed up to do work. Ask the protagonist at what point along the continuum she feels her work might lie; "Was there a point during one of these stages when you felt you became blocked or wounded?"
4. Invite the protagonist to choose auxiliaries to represent those people she was surrounded with at that time, primary auxiliary egos.
5. Proceed with a psychodrama. Note the developmental timing of the issue being explored.
6. Bring the scene to closure and allow plenty of time for sharing.

VARIATIONS:

This can also be done along a timeline, in which case the director asks the protagonist to select role-players to represent themselves at various points of development that feel significant from birth to the present. I find it helpful to put numbers along a timeline on the floor representing five-year intervals throughout the protagonist's life. Then auxiliaries representing aspects of self can locate themselves along the timeline in the appropriate period of the protagonist's life.

The timeline can be done as a journaling exercise by the protagonist creating a timeline of her life and then she can write a "doubling" statement or "soliloquy" for herself at each point along her time line. This should then be shared and processed with the group or therapist. This can also be done as a locogram putting each of the four stages of development in a corner and inviting group members to stand in a corner that they feel represents a stage where they may have become wounded or need to work with for any reason.

ROLE TRAINING

GOALS:

1. To gain experience and practice in entering and adapting to a desired role.
2. To explore the nuances of a role as it relates to the self.
3. To explore the impact of the role from the position of the other.
4. To provide practice in underdeveloped roles so the anxiety and newness of a role can be worked through by "trying it on" in a clinical environment and practicing it.

STEPS:

1. Ask group members to come up with a role they need some practice with, wish to explore as a possibility for themselves, wish for a change of behavior in, or are walking into and feeling anxious or insecure about, e.g., career role, intimate role such as spouse, or lover, or a recovery role such as sober person, partner of a sober person, or self-reliant adult. The director may wish to interview the protagonist to gain a deeper understanding about his conflicts, anxieties or dreams.
2. Invite the protagonist to structure an anticipated scene in which he might play his role.
3. Set the scene and choose people to play all roles.
4. Role-play the scene with the protagonist playing themselves in the anticipated role. At any point where it would seem helpful to understand what's going on "inside" the protagonist, the director may ask him to take a step back "behind" himself and "double" for his own inner life, then step forward into the role again and continue the enactment. Group members can also spontaneously double for the protagonist or the protagonist in role-reversal.
5. Use role reversal as you would in any enactment so that the protagonist can (1) gain empathy and understanding of what it feels like to actually be the other person, and (2) to see himself in action from the perspective of the other person.
6. Continue to play the scene out until it resolves itself, then bring it to closure.

7. Invite the group to share identification and personal insight with the protagonist.

VARIATIONS:

1. The protagonist can be pulled out of the scene while a stand-in holds her role. In this way she can watch herself in action and gain insight into how her role plays out in an overall context. If using a stand-in, the protagonist may walk into the scene and double for herself when motivated to do so or simply watch herself "as if in a mirror."

2. While the protagonist is out of the scene other group members can take turns "trying on" the role and experimenting with a variety of approaches or behaviors that might be incorporated into the role. The protagonist may then choose from the group members' suggested options one or two that she may like to "try on," and she can play out the scene using this approach. In this variation, the protagonist can consider various role behaviors demonstrated by other group members from a safe distance. This can also allow for a degree of playfulness to enter the exploration.

3. Group members can take turns as in variation #2, but in this case the protagonist stays in the scene in role-reversal. In this way the protagonist can have the opportunity to experience herself from the other person's perspective.

ROLE RATING

GOALS:

1. To provide a step-by-step exercise to explore a role in a one-to-one therapy, or large or small group.

2. To use as a warm-up to psychodramatic role exploration.

3. To provide a role exercise that can be adapted for journaling.

STEPS:

1. Describe role basics to participants or group members, e.g., thinking, feeling and behavior are role-specific. We think, feel and behave according to and influenced by a role we're playing.

2. Ask group membeers to reflect on some of the major roles they play in their lives and write them on a piece of paper. Answer these questions on paper or out loud.

- Are the roles in your life balanced?
- Which roles dominate?
- Which roles would you like to be bigger?
- Which roles do you feel most alive in?
- Which roles do you feel most shut down in?
- If you could magically add a role to your life, what role would you add?
- If you could magically drop a role, which one would it be?

3. Next, make a circle and place the roles you play into pie-shaped wedges. Draw each wedge to represent the relative amount of time each role takes up in your life as compared with others. How much time do you spend in each role?

4. Using numbers on a scale from one to ten, rate your roles using some of the following criterion:
   - How much satisfaction do you experience?
   - How much fatigue or burnout?
   - How much sense of success?
   - How much sense of failure?
   - How much aliveness?
   - How much conflict?

5. If you wish to move into psychodrama, cast all of the roles with auxiliaries from the group and ask the protagonist to place them in the relationship to herself that she feels best represents her experience (e.g., near, far, large, small) then proceed with a psychodrama.

6. After the drama has been brought to closure, the protagonist may place the roles in the manner in which she would like them to be in her life as a sort of map to work toward, or a wish fulfillment.

7. Examine whether or not this is realistic. Is it a way of moving toward greater satisfaction or setting herself up for failure, and how does it feel to see the roles laid out like this? It may be necessary to modify until the right balance is achieved.

8. Return to seats for sharing.

VARIATIONS:

This can be simply used as a paper-and-pencil exercise. In this case, stop at step five and use the information on the paper as a springboard for continued sharing and exploration. Or make a "role atom" playing roles in relationship to the self on paper. (See social atom).

If you don't want to mount a full psychodrama you may place an empty chair on the stage and proceed with monodramas or vignettes. Invite clients to put one of the roles they feel particularly warmed up to working with in a chair and talk to it. Or this can be done as journaling and dialoguing between the role and the self.

ROLE-RATING SPECTROGRAM

GOALS:

1. To provide a group that shares common roles, a way of rating their satisfaction in those roles.
2. To provide a springboard for group sharing and processing.

STEPS:

1. Set up a spectrogram. (See Spectrogram, page 110).
2. Ask the group members to come up with three to five shared roles they would like to explore as a group, e.g., addict, recovering person, twelve-stepper, intimate friend.
3. Ask the group, "How much satisfaction are you experiencing in the role of recovering person, intimate relator, etc.?"
4. Invite whoever feels warmed up to share a sentence or two about why they're standing where they're standing.
5. Repeat steps three and four for each role the group has chosen.
6. Return to seats for continued sharing and processing, or chose a protagonist and move into a role drama, role reframing or any appropriate psychodrama.

VARIATIONS:

The word "satisfaction" in step three is only a suggestion. You can use any criterion, e.g., satisfaction, conflict, fear, anxiety, stuckness and so on. The criterion question, however, should be consistent so there is a valid comparison from role to role.

This could also be done as a locogram by designating four or five areas on the floor to represent roles and asking group members to stand in the section that represents the role they are experiencing (1) conflict in, (2) satisfaction in, (3) a wish to make more central, or (4) a wish to make more peripheral—or whatever criterion the group wishes to explore. The director may allow doubling in order to explore sociometric identification from role to role.

EXPLORING UNDERDEVELOPED ROLES

GOALS:

1. To explore roles that clients may feel they would like to develop in their lives.
2. To investigate why a particular role is underdeveloped.
3. To work with blocks that may be interfering with developing the desired role.

STEPS:

1. Name a role you would like to develop further and share it in group, along with why you wish to develop that role and what you feel might be standing in your way.
2. Invite anyone who is warmed up to play out the scene that he became warmed up to during this line of questioning.
3. Use any or all of the techniques of doubling, interviewing and role reversal to deepen the exploration.
4. After the protagonist is finished, return to seats for sharing, or permit the group to do a few vignettes and then share with multiple protagonists at the end of everyone's work.

VARIATIONS:

This exercise can also be done for overdeveloped or overplayed roles, roles in which you're experiencing "role fatigue," or roles in which you're experiencing "role hunger" or "role ambivalence." Vary it according to the needs of your clients. Clients from the addictions field may wish to explore the role of the recovering person, the sober person, the person who has a life that's working and so on.

Possible questions that can be explored either through sharing out loud or psychodramatic journaling might be:

What draws you to this role?

What parts of yourself do you feel would be actualized by playing this role?

What strengths do you bring to this role?

What are your weaknesses in this role?

What might you have to give up to play this role?

What might you gain in playing this role?

ROLE SHIFTS

GOALS:

1. To offer a way to examine major life changes from a role perspective.
2. To allow a concrete way of bringing closure (allowing them to be latent) to some roles and ramping up others.

STEPS:

1. Ask group members to take out a pen and paper, or offer them colors to work with.
2. Place a circle on the page. Write the role that is in flux in the center and on spokes jutting out the sides of the circle write all of the subroles associated with the role.
3. Allow the group to share what is on their papers.
4. Invite anyone who feels warmed up to cast role-players to play the role and all of the subroles attached to it.
5. Invite the protagonist to say what he needs to say to any aspects of the role. This might include saying good-bye to some aspects of the role, hello to others, and remodeling still others by allowing them to express themselves in new ways.
6. Invite the protagonist to resculpt his role constellations to meet the role demands reflected in his new stage of life. He may wish to allow some roles to sit down and choose auxiliaries to represent new roles. Some subroles may be kept and given new status, and others may simply represent a vacant space to be filled.
7. Return to seats for continued processing.

VARIATIONS:

Each stage in life has its own constellation of roles. When we move from one stage to the next, we add some roles and modify others. Looking at life changes in terms of role shifts can help us to make the changes with greater optimism and intelligence. For example, the man who has worked all his life within the same profession faces retirement. His major role of worker is in flux; which of his roles will he carry into retirement with him (e.g., husband, athlete, friend, uncle, brother, reader, musician and so on)? Though it may feel like his life is ending, it is actually his role that is changing. Depending upon how he feels about his work life, he will have a variety of responses toward ending it or evolving it into something different. He might make a list of all the aspects of the role that he is letting go of. For example, the worker role might possibly contain teacher, traveler, planner, major earner, friend, listener, lecturer, etc. When he breaks the aspects of his role down, he can take a closer look at his possibilities for carrying on with those aspects of the work role that were most enjoyable for him and letting go of others. He may, in retirement, be able to continue being a listener, a lecturer and a teacher, both in paid and pro bono situations, which can bring him satisfaction, lessen the shock of the role change and give back to the society that has given to him. Equally, he can look at the roles he is moving into and make decisions about how he wants to play them. He may also wish to add roles that are appropriate to this stage in life. For instance, spiritual seeker or elder, or he may deepen the role of grandfather, which could be meaningful for all concerned.

The same basic approach can be used for any change, such as the empty-nest syndrome or midlife crisis. Taking this perspective on our lives gives us that little bit of objectivity that we need so we do not lose ourselves in a role or in a role change (we are not dying—perhaps the role or aspects of the role waning).

12

Psychodramatic Journaling and Near-Psychodramatic Techniques: Letter Writing, Journaling, Working with Photographs and Guided Imagery

R esearch done by James Pennebaker, Ph.D., author of *Opening Up*, clearly demonstrates that journaling about our thoughts and feelings can actually elevate our immune systems. Language and writing are inherently left-brain activities that help us distill, organize and reflect upon our thoughts and emotions. When we write we label what we think and feel, which allows us to categorize and understand what's going on inside of us. Activity in the left hemisphere of the brain is associated with uplifting emotions like cheerfulness and positive behaviors such as choice-making. Emotions and thinking integrate naturally as we journal. Our thoughts and feelings unravel themselves on paper; aspects of a situation we may have forgotten, ignored or repressed oftentimes emerge through writing so we can reflect on them in safety. Hiding what we really feel from ourselves depresses our healthy immune functioning. Sharing our emotions, even with a piece of paper, allows us to confront what we really feel if we write in a reflective manner. Once we open a path inward we are more likely to seek out sharing and support from other people and to take actions to improve our situation. We may initially feel a little anxious, but soon afterward and in the long run, our visits to the doctor for somatic ailments may go down, and we feel better as we integrate all our various points of view. Pennebaker found that writing in ten-minute intervals during workshops was the most beneficial in affecting blood levels in positive ways. Writing at home can follow the schedule and leanings of each individual.

Near-psychodramatic techniques or quasi-psychodramatic techniques are often used as explorations that don't involve, for one reason or another, an enactment. Perhaps the group is not warmed up for full action or the staff is not trained enough in psychodrama to feel comfortable introducing it. Near psychodramatic techniques use the basic concepts of psychodrama, such as talking to rather than about someone, in a way that does not necessarily involve action. Letter writing is an example of a near-psychodramatic technique. Journaling is now so commonly used, everywhere from treatment programs to magazine articles recommending it for some specific reason, that it has been mainstreamed.

A social atom that is not acted out in the form of an action sociogram can be used as a near-psychodramatic technique. Near-psychodramatic techniques can be very helpful in one-to-one sessions during which no auxiliaries are available to role-play in a classical sense. When used in a group, they can be very bonding, as group members use them individually and then share the results with one another. In a large group, the sharing can take place in dyads, triads or small groups, encouraging connection and enhancing group cohesion. Though these techniques do not necessarily lead to enactment, they are powerful in and of themselves and should be used carefully in a highly structured and focused manner, and ample time should be allowed for sharing what comes up. Confronting one's reality on a piece of paper, such as in a social atom, draws much material from the emotional and psychic self.

PSYCHODRAMATIC JOURNALING

I've been developing and using psychodramatic journaling for around fifteen years. In my frustration while training fine and creative clinicians who wish to employ basic theoretical concepts such as role reversal but don't feel comfortable using it in action, I began to adapt psychodrama to the written page. Clinicians can use it on its own or in conjunction with the psychoeducational exercises throughout this book.

As someone who loves to write and has used writing to work out my own issues ever since I can remember, psychodramatic journaling more or less evolved naturally out of my own interests. While concretizing in action is core to the transformational power of psychodrama, I have found that concretizing concepts such as role reversal on paper, is also quite wonderful. In the eight years I spent teaching psychodrama in the drama therapy program at New York University, the students' favorite papers always involved psychodramatic journaling. Students reversed roles with their leg, journaling out their body issues "as," or from the point of view, of the troubled body part, or they reversed roles with themselves in a photograph that was special or significant to them in some way and journaled "as" themselves at that point in time. Another popular technique was to use a photograph and "double" on the written page for whomever they felt warmed up to speak as (including themselves) at the time the photo was taken or to write a letter to someone in the photo with whom they had unfinished business. Another place that I have used psychodramatic journaling is in treatment centers across the United States. It fits nicely into the ebb and flow of in-patient treatment where groups become very bonded, there is time to use it and there is a need for some types of therapeutic activity that are relaxing but still penetrating. Psychodramatic journaling also has the value of being self-directed; the protagonist, in true psychodramatic form, has his own foot on the gas pedal and can go as far as he wishes. Protagonists are exploring their own inner worlds at their own pace in a psychodramatic format and structure. Social atoms, family maps, role analysis, diagrams and sociograms not only warm a person up to further enactment but can be exercises in and of themselves.

BASIC THEORETICAL CONCEPTS
USED IN PSYCHODRAMATIC JOURNALING

Role Reversal. The are two main avenues to consider in this form of psychodramatic journaling. The first is role reversing with the self at any point along the developmental time line of one's life. The second is to reverse roles with another person, again at any point of the time line along the development of one's life, and journaling as the other. For example, it may be very useful to mentally role reverse with one's mother at the time of one's birth and journal as the mother who is about to give birth and giving birth, or to follow the same procedure with the father or sibling.

Journalers can role reverse virtually anywhere they feel moved to do so. The purpose of this is to allow them to see the situation and themselves from another perspective and to begin developing an empathy for that other person and for themselves.

Journaling as the Double: The basic function of the double is to stand behind the protagonist and speak as an inner voice with the goal of bringing the protagonist to the threshold of her own awareness. There are a couple of ways to journal as the double. The first is to double for the self, i.e., to journal from a more deeply internal position within the self, what might be going on underneath what Jung referred to as the "persona." The first layer is, for example, Alice speaking as Alice, as herself. The next would be Alice's double. A second way to double is to double for another person, to write a journal entry as another person's double, to mentally reverse roles and journal "as" the other. Still another way to do this is to reverse roles and double for those represented in a social atom or a photograph. Each of these techniques is more fully described in the sections on working with photographs and the social atom.

Journaling as the Witness: In this technique, we mentally remove ourselves from our position at the center of our own lives and reverse roles with our own, internal witnesses, who views from a safe distance and reflect our lives back to us. One of the primary therapeutic tasks is to develop an observing ego. Journaling as the witness is a way to begin to do that. It encourages journalers to step outside of themselves and see themselves with some dispassionate distance, to disengage from the heat of the moment and get some perspective. Emotional pain tends to have a gravitational force that pulls us toward it and can make it difficult to have a healthy perspective on our lives. Journaling as the witness is designed to train clients to learn the skill of stepping outside of themselves and see themselves with perspective.

The Soliloquy or the Monologue: The monologue, as the word implies, involves one character, one point of view. Journaling the monologue or the soliloquy can allow the journaler to free-write as themselves and unravel all of their thoughts without interruption, or to reverse roles and free-write as that other person.

The Dialogue: The dialogue involves journaling between two people, two points of view. It is a dialogue between two roles. The roles can be two parts of the self, a body part of the self and the personal self, or it can be between two people with the writer playing both roles. The actual dialogue can require changing roles only once or twice, with each entry being long, or it can be a quick and easy back and forth. The dialogue allows for the journaler to practice entertaining two points of view at once, which helps them to develop skills of relational interaction.

Other Exercises: Psychodramatic journaling also includes a variety of other paper and pencil exercises such as the social atom plus journaling, loss chart, and each journaling variation for the exercises in this book where the journaling symbol appears.

Following are a few excerpts from psychodramatic journaling exercises done at NYU and in my own training groups.

The Shadow-Self Dialogue

Liza has reversed roles with her shadow self and begins a dialogue between her shadow self and her persona, or the person she presents in her regular life.

Liza: Shadow? Hi, I know you're never very far from the surface. You are definitely a stubborn and strong shadow. Sometimes I really hate you and your persistent existence; other times I can't imagine life without you.

Shadow: Well, you can't lose me, detach me or even kill me. But you know that; you've thought about this a lot.

Liza: I think you're the biggest part of me, the negative, fearful, closed-off Liza. The almost-always-present depression, negativity and cynicism that I know are ugly emotions and ones other people don't want to hear or deal with. I used to tell myself all the time how boring and depressing I must appear, how distasteful to be with. I'm a little better now, I think . . .

Shadow: Deep down you believe in predetermination. No matter how hard you might want to fight your inner makeup, you won't win. It's there, indelibly imprinted and forever with you. So just accept it and stop the torment.

Liza: Am I better? Have I changed at all? Would I give you up if it were possible?

I know I want to lighten up; I would love to be more trusting and self-affirming. I try not to be so serious all the time, so easily affected and moody, I really do! It scares me that I often feel programmed and conditioned to act and react certain ways. Those ways are too much like my father (and we all know what's happened to him).

Shadow: You're boring me.

Liza: I bore me. I disgust me. I would gladly rip my brain open and vomit up all the dreck and grime. I want out. I want to swim, not just feel as though I'm treading water. I have passion, I have insight, I have a good heart. I know that, and I want to use it all better.

Shadow: You're quite emotional today.

Liza: And you're destructive, scared and egotistical. You get a perverse kick out of being alienated and constantly in a state of flux.

Shadow: Come on, a part of you enjoys your many contradictions. Admit it . . .

Liza: Okay, some of them, yes. They can be quirky and surprising, even exciting. But they can also be harmful and hurtful, sometimes even self-defeating and perpetually setting me up for disappointment, too.

Shadow: And part of you recognizes that a lot of this "dreck" was developed—well developed! It was done in order that you would survive. You are a survivor, and mainly because of me.

Liza: But I don't need you so much now. I gave birth to you and needed you most when I was a teenager. That lost thing, that screwed-up thing that only felt miserable most of the time. I am stronger now. I've dealt with a lot and you have helped there, I must admit. I just don't want to be walled up so much of the time anymore. I'd at least like to give it a go with a little less of you intruding. You'll always be there if I need some more support and protection, right? Take a little time off. You deserve it; you've worked hard for a very long time.

Shadow: Trying to charm me, are you? It's not that easy. Still, I'll do some cognitive processing and get back to you. Try not to be too cheerful, though, sweetie—it doesn't really suit you.

The Somatic Soliloquy

Judith has reversed roles with a body part that she is having concerns with and written a soliloquy as that body part.

I am your leg, and I feel very unwanted. You depend on me so much. You want me to carry you wherever you want to go. You wear cheap shoes that don't help me balance, and yet you despise me so much. Why is that? I work hard for you.

You are ashamed of me. Constantly, I feel you pull at me and punch at me because there are parts of me you don't find attractive. You drag me to aerobics classes, and I am strong for you. I am very powerful, yet you hate me so much. You think of having plastic surgery done to me. How do you think that would make me feel? What is so terrible about me? I am so strong. I work so hard. It hurts me that you hate me so much. I keep trying and trying but you just won't accept me. I am part of you. Why does that have to be so awful? Maybe I am not perfect, but neither are you. What I am is efficient and strong.

What would I have to do to have you accept me? I love you. I want you to be proud of me and accept me as part of your body. No, think of me as beautiful. I think my calves are very beautiful. The muscles are shaped and defined. My thighs are round and strong. Please love me for that. I will work with you. I will not let you down if you take care of me. I like to do aerobics, but I don't want you to hide me anymore. I don't want you to punch me in frustration anymore. I don't want you to even think about plastic surgery. I am a part of you, a valuable part. Please don't buy into some picture of what you think I should be. I am what I am. What I am is strong and beautiful. I love you. Please try to love me, too.

The Letter-Writing Experience

Bob has written a letter to the dad he never met, the dad who died while his mother was pregnant with him. He then mentally reverses roles with his dad and writes a letter to himself, from his dad, that he would wish to receive. He read the first letter aloud in group to an empty chair, then he reversed roles with "Dad" and read the second letter back to himself. He then reversed roles back to himself and we let him end the scene from there (see Letter Writing page 196).

Dear Dad,

My God how I long to know you. Funny, the word "dad" sounds odd. I've never even called anyone "dad" in my life. Dad, Daddy, Father, Pa, Pop, my Old Man—how I long to feel your strength envelop my body. How I wish I could have known you, met you, touched you, kissed you, fought with you and deeply loved you.

I've never, ever heard you speak, yell, tell me to go to bed, do my homework and don't answer my mother back. Don't fight with your brothers and sisters. I've never heard you say, "Let's go up to Maine to visit Grandpa and all your aunts and uncles. We'll have a great time fishing, swimming, canoeing on Moosehead Lake." When I really did go up to Maine to visit Grandpa and all my aunts and uncles, you weren't there, and they treated me like a stranger. I met you once in a psychodrama. A man named Lyle played you in a role. He and I have become good friends. Thanks for speaking to me through him.

Love from your son, Bob

Dear Son,

My heart aches that I had to die and leave your mom with four of my children, and how it grieves me to have missed the golden opportunity to see you come into this world. Bobby, I'm so proud of you for all your accomplishments and for what a fine man you've turned out to be. A good husband, stepfather and a real great grandfather. I'll always be near to you. All you have to do is think of me, and I'll always be close in your imagination to guide you.

With all my love, Dad

Entering a Photograph

Lynette has reversed roles with herself in a photograph that has particular meaning to her and written a journal entry as that self, from the inside of the picture looking out. She then reverses back to herself today and writes from the outside of the picture looking in.

My name is Lynette, and this is a picture of me with my mother and my in-laws. I am an actor and singer, but I am on "vocal silence" during this time. The doctor has ordered me to be quiet for a whole week. This to me does not feel like a punishment, but rather a freedom. I am not required to make any small talk. I am not allowed to find anything witty to say, nor to argue any points with anyone. My only job is to listen and observe, take it all in without anyone knowing what I am thinking or who I am thinking about. They do not even know if I am with them. I could be in Barbados lying naked on a beach, but smiling and nodding in front of them. How strange, then, that I should

READER/CUSTOMER CARE SURVEY

We care about your opinions! Please take a moment to fill out our online Reader Survey at **http://survey.hcibooks.com.** As a **"THANK YOU"** you will receive a **VALUABLE INSTANT COUPON** towards future book purchases as well as a **SPECIAL GIFT** available only online! Or, you may mail this card back to us and we will send you a copy of our exciting catalog with your valuable coupon inside.

(PLEASE PRINT IN ALL CAPS)

First Name _____ MI. _____ Last Name _____

Address _____ City _____

State _____ Zip _____ Email: _____

1. Gender
- ☐ Female   ☐ Male

2. Age
- ☐ 8 or younger
- ☐ 9-12   ☐ 13-16
- ☐ 17-20   ☐ 21-30
- ☐ 31+

3. Did you receive this book as a gift?
- ☐ Yes   ☐ No

4. Annual Household Income
- ☐ under $25,000
- ☐ $25,000 - $34,999
- ☐ $35,000 - $49,999
- ☐ $50,000 - $74,999
- ☐ over $75,000

5. What are the ages of the children living in your house
- ☐ 0 - 14   ☐ 15+

6. Marital Status
- ☐ Single
- ☐ Married
- ☐ Divorced
- ☐ Widowed

7. How did you find out about the book
(please choose one)
- ☐ Recommendation
- ☐ Store Display
- ☐ Online
- ☐ Catalog/Mailing
- ☐ Interview/Review

8. Where do you usually buy books
(please choose one)
- ☐ Bookstore
- ☐ Online
- ☐ Book Club/Mail Order
- ☐ Price Club (Sam's Club, Costco's, etc.)
- ☐ Retail Store (Target, Wal-Mart, etc.)

9. What subject do you enjoy reading about the most
(please choose one)
- ☐ Parenting/Family
- ☐ Relationships
- ☐ Recovery/Addictions
- ☐ Health/Nutrition
- ☐ Christianity
- ☐ Spirituality/Inspiration
- ☐ Business Self-help
- ☐ Women's Issues
- ☐ Sports

10. What attracts you most to a book
(please choose one)
- ☐ Title
- ☐ Cover Design
- ☐ Author
- ☐ Content

TAPE IN MIDDLE; DO NOT STAPLE

BUSINESS REPLY MAIL
FIRST-CLASS MAIL PERMIT NO 45 DEERFIELD BEACH, FL

POSTAGE WILL BE PAID BY ADDRESSEE

Health Communications, Inc.
3201 SW 15th Street
Deerfield Beach FL 33442-9875

FOLD HERE

Comments

look so happy, for I thought I would be a bit nervous to be with my mother during a time of silence because she does not understand rules and usually ignores them.

Yet my smile is genuine when I see her. And I want to show her off to my new family. And I feel safe and secure, protected here in their house, not hers, so she has to be easygoing and let others take the lead more. And she has even let down her hair a bit. She looks somewhat messy, and admits that she is tired and that she cannot go out dancing because she needs to sleep. And she wakes up late and comes out in her bathing suit though her stomach is flabby, and we swim together. And when Jean brings out hummus and pizza, she digs right in. And she does not demand too often that I speak to her, nor does she do anything but giggle when I strongly shake that I cannot. And she plays with Danny, my nephew, in a very neutral way tonight, not like she knows best how to be with kids, and he likes the French chocolate she has brought, a gift appropriate for a spontaneous occasion, not too big. And she seems relaxed, and I am affectionate toward her. It feels nice to be with Mommy. To have a mommy. And even to have this woman be that mommy. I don't feel young or old, just like a daughter with her mom, maybe even looking up to her mom. I do not really feel like telling her any of this because I can't use my voice anyway. I do tell her repeatedly how happy I am that she came, because at first she felt she would be an imposition, but I wish I could find words to better express the depth of my happiness with our comfort.

Lynette, you are sitting a bit higher than your mother in the picture somehow. You are holding her tightly and her arms are simply down, perhaps in her lap, but you do not notice this rather reserved posture from her. You seem almost to be taking care of her here. You look much different from most pictures with her. In this, you are not trying to move away from her, but rather pull yourself in toward her—almost like when you know a pool will be cold but you just take a deep breath and jump in, though in this case perhaps not quite as consciously.

My in-laws' home is a place of warmth and acceptance, of course from my point of view. And perhaps I so wanted to have that relationship with my mother that day that I almost ignored the normal things that bother me and found the warmth and acceptance with her to be like the rest of the gang. But it did work (Dayton 1999).

The above material is excerpted from the last section of *Heartwounds: The Impact of Unresolved Trauma and Grief On Relationships.*

Psychodramatic Journal of a Dream

The vision came in 1954, nine years after the concentration camps were closed down, a year after my brother was born and three years after my own birth.

The term "birth to three" holds that fragile 36 months. A time when life presented its reality to the baby mind that knows no other reality. Traumas are reacted to and defenses created as the baby mind tries to organize chaos into some archetypical notion that life has order and meaning.

The fantasy exists under the black wooden table; a scratchy surface with open lines supporting its weight. Black outlines waiting for feelings to flow into them and fill up the empty spaces. In my memory, the table is next to my bed. A convenient place to have a secret doorway into another world, in what seems like endless hours alone. I can go into that vision and play.

Today the black wood embodies my Steinway piano, slightly scratched, the one I'm trying to sell. There are no empty spaces. They have been filled with truth and with music.

I go underground into the cave. It is cold and damp. The women stand naked, huddled together, nervously talking, barely noticing me walking around. They have dark hair, all of them. Large bodies and darting eyes. They seem to be waiting for something. I can never tell what, exactly, is coming. However, at the moment that I sense it is coming, I escape.

Many, many years later I actually saw this scene in *Schindler's List* when the women await their execution in the gas chamber.

The cave is made of earth, brown and alive. The ground is cold and wet. There is no light and no color except for the red nails, shining through the darkness. The red is deep and feels dangerous. It moves through your body frantically as if searching for something that can never be found. It feels like blood pouring, slow death, red drops of poison.

The body has dried, an echo of itself, never to be restored by water.

And I escape up the ladder, quick to the hidden trap door in the ceiling of the cave, one side dark earth, the other, a new ground.

The earth—the wall of the cave.

I remain the same.

Kathryn went on to reverse roles with all elements of the dream that she felt were significant to her and dialogued between herself and each aspect of her reoccurring dream. The dream dealt with the information that she had absorbed as a very young girl, hearing her parents and their friends recount the horrors of the Holocaust that they had survived. Evidently the adults didn't realize that even at two, three and four years old, this bright, articulate child was absorbing and recording each horrific detail. With no one explaining things to her, she made her own meaning and sense of the terrible images. The dream also dealt with the guilt Kathryn felt at wanting her own life and feeling burdened by parents who psychically remained traumatized by what they had gone through and were, in many very significant ways, very damaged. Kathryn felt that she couldn't ask for anything from parents who had suffered so much, but she carried the horrors of their experience in her own unconscious. At nineteen she had a nervous break-down. At forty-eight, this was the first time she had openly talked about these memories and the stories that had haunted her inner world for her entire life. The connections she was able to make helped her to feel a life-long burden begin to lift, "a small crack of light in the darkness, a tiny shaft" as she described it. Kathryn turned to music as a way to express her pain and confusion. She has used her creativity as a path out of pain; a way to transform it into something meaningful. She has shared her musical gifts with her own children and count-less others through using it therepeutically.

Combining Psychodramatic Journaling and Psycho-educational Exercises

Psychodramatic journaling can be very successfully combined with psycho-educational exercises. Throughout the book I have indicated which exercises include psychodramatic journaling with ✍ . Begin by selecting an exercise from the book that you might like to explore with the group, then follow the steps. The journaling component will either be embedded in the steps or in the variations.

I developed experiential, psychoeducational exercises for two main reasons. One was to provide my students and trainees with experiential exercises that they could feel comfortable doing with clients before they felt ready to direct a full psychodrama, so that they could get their feet wet, so to speak, and intro-duce experiential work into their treatment settings. The second was to provide a way that clients could experientially learn, for example, about the grief pro-cess, symptoms of PTSD or the addicted/traumatized family system. Learning experientially provides a few advantages in my experience. It does double duty in that it teaches clients the theoretical aspects of an issue while engaging them on an emotional level. In addition, it engages clients with each other so they can begin to identify, share and bond.

COMBINING PSYCHODRAMATIC JOURNALING AND PSYCHODRAMA

Combining psychodramatic journaling and psychodrama allows for a natural expansion of the method and adds some variety to action. It has the advantage of allowing more members of a group to personalize their experience and deconstruct it in terms of the self. Psychodramatic journaling can extend the reach of a drama. For example, the group might warm up through sociometry, do a psychodrama and do just enough sharing to reground the protagonist but not so much that the group unwinds all of their feelings. Then allow the group to do some journaling in one of the following ways.

- What came up for you from your own life as a result of witnessing or playing a role in this drama? Journal in the first person.
- Who did you identify with in the drama? Reverse roles with and journal as that person.
- Who did you not identify with in the drama? Reverse roles and journal as that person.
- Who do you feel warmed up to write a soliloquy for?
- With whom do you feel warmed up to dialogue?
- Who can you double for? Write a doubling journal entry.
- Other

After these journal entries have been written they can be shared with the group or with subgroups depending upon group size. In a large group this gives more people an opportunity to explore the psychodramatic work more fully in terms of the self. After sharing has taken place, return to the large group for continued sharing and processing.

In addition, psychodramatic journaling can be a warm-up to psychodramas by either writing then reading letters as described in Letter Writing, page 196, or briefly journaling in between vignettes, and then playing out the scene and sharing.

COMBINING PSYCHODRAMATIC JOURNALING WITH FILM

Any film that is considered appropriate for a treatment population can be combined with psychodramatic journaling. Or you may use a film of an actual psychodrama, like those listed in the About the Author page. Films offer a wide variety of characters that the group can identify with. After the group has viewed the film, follow some of the following suggestions for exercises.

- What came up for you from your own life as a result of watching this film? Journal in the first person.
- Who did you identify with in the film? Reverse roles and journal as that person.
- Who did you not identify with in the film? Reverse roles and journal as that person.
- Who can you double for? Write a doubling journal entry for any or all of those characters.
- Who in the film do you have something to say to? Write a "letter" to that person.
- Who in the film warms you up to an issue you have with someone in your life? Write a "letter" to that person in your life.

After the journaling is finished, participants can share what they have written in dyads, subgroups or the large group. Then continue to share what the group needs or wishes to process.

Using Psychodramatic Journaling in Inpatient Programs

If a group is contained, such as in an inpatient treatment program or an intensive workshop, psychodramatic journaling can be done outside of the group and brought back into the group for sharing and processing. It can offer some welcome program variety. If a facility is low on staffing, for example, and the group prefers to journal together, the group can choose an exercise and do some sharing around the topic as a warm-up or view a film. (Note: therapists may wish to copy ten or so of their favorite exercises from throughout the book and allow the group to choose from them.) Then the room can be set up with dimmed lights, soft ambient sound such as ocean waves or soft music, and group members can journal while staff supervises in a more minimal way. When finished, the staff may allow people to share in small subgroups and read what they have written. The group can then continue to process together with a staff member, and when this is finished the group can be brought to closure, if desired, by putting in a cassette tape and following a deep relaxation or a guided imagery, such as my releasing numbness tape (see About the Author page). This provides the group with meaningful program activity and gives the staff a little breather from intense group work. When doing the imagery or relaxation, it works well to have pillows in the room and invite group members to lie on their backs in a comfortable position if they wish to. Some will prefer to sit, and not all will care about pillows, but this creates a relaxed feeling of community and comfort. The journaling, along with the relaxation tape or exercise, are also training in the vital skills of self-soothing and relaxation.

How to Set Up Psychodramatic Journaling

Pennebaker found that journaling sessions of seven to ten minutes were the most useful length for participants. The instructions for journaling can be as follows: "Find a place in the room where you can feel relaxed and comfortable, in a chair or on the floor. Breathe evenly and deeply and center yourself. As you journal, allow yourself to free-write without editing in your mind; simply put pen to paper and pour your heart out onto the page." Share the journaling in the group, pairs or small groupings.

A Journey into the Many Faces of the Self: Psychodramatic Journaling

- **The Monologue:** Journal in the *first person*, keeping pen to paper and allow your feelings to flow freely and fully onto the page. Try to write with as little break as possible.
- **The Third-Person Monologue:** Write a monologue in the *third person*, describing the situation (e.g., "She was seventeen, her name was Julie and she felt lonely on that hot summer afternoon.")
- **Past-Perspective Journaling:** Mentally *reverse roles* with yourself at any time in your life and journal *from* or *as* that self in the first or third person (e.g., "I am twelve years old. My name is Roger. When I look around I see . . .").
- **Photograph Letter:** Find a photograph of someone to whom you have something to say and write a letter to that person.

- **Photograph Monologue:** Find a picture that speaks to you and write a *soliloquy* or *monologue,* imagining what you're thinking from the point of view of the you in the picture (e.g., "I am Lucy and I love to wear my hair like this. I am holding my mommy's hand. . . .").

- **Photograph Role Reversal:** Find a *picture* of someone else with whom you have strong feelings or unfinished business, *reverse roles* with him or her and journal as that person (what you imagine he or she is feeling).

- **Positive Messages:** Imagine someone you would like to be remembered by, someone who sees you in an especially good light or someone from whom you experience support. Mentally *reverse roles* with him or her. Speaking as that person, describe yourself from his or her point of view (e.g., "My name is Harry and I want to tell you about my daughter, Connie.").

- **Silenced or Hidden-Self Monologue:** In the first person, write a *soliloquy* or a *monologue* from a part of you that you hide or silence. (e.g., "I am Julie and I am small and frightened. Because I'm scared, I act certain ways, and I scare people so they don't want to be with me."). When you have finished, mentally reverse roles back to yourself, and write a response back to yourself.

- **Journaling the Shadow:** Mentally *reverse roles* with the "shadow self" and write a journal entry as the shadow. Carl Jung felt that each of us has a shadow self, or a self that develops in the shadow of what he called our persona or the person we present to the world. Perhaps we insist on experiencing no angry feelings, for example, so our shadow more or less holds them, and perhaps they leak out in ways we are unaware of. Let the shadow speak through psychodramatic journaling.

- **The Somatic Dialogue:** Mentally reverse roles with a body part you are having trouble with, especially love, wish to change or may lose, and write a journal entry as that body part. When that journaling is complete, reverse roles back to the self and write a reply *from* the self, to the body part. Note, this can also be done as a dialogue.

- **Seeking Forgiveness:** Mentally *reverse roles* with someone you have hurt through your own problematic behavior or addiction of some kind, and write a *soliloquy* or *monologue as* that person sharing his or her own hurt.

- **Journaling Internal Blocks:** Name three issues on your path to recovery.

Reverse roles with any or all issues you feel drawn into, and write a *soliloquy* or *monologue as* that block (e.g., "I am anger. I am endless, powerful and overwhelm Rita's life.").

- **The Parent's Perspective:** Mentally *reverse roles* with your mother or father and write a journal entry *as* them describing you (e.g., "I am Betty, and I am describing Daniel. He seems to me to be very. . . ."). Repeat the process with the other parent.

- **Dialoguing with the Disease:** Mentally *reverse roles* with the disease of addiction, depression or a physical ailment, and write a journal entry as the disease, referring to how the disease interacts with the writer (you).When this is finished, reverse roles back to the self and write a reply. Note, this can be done several times if desired.

- **The Wounded-Self Dialogue:** Mentally *reverse roles* with a part of you that felt or feels wounded from any period in your life and has something to say. Write a journal entry as that part of self, freely saying any and all that you need or wish to say. When this is finished, you may reverse roles back to yourself and write back to yourself.

- **The Angry-Self Dialogue:** Mentally *reverse roles* with the part of your self that is angry and write a monologue as that part of self. Write freely and without restriction or reservation, saying all of the angry things and expressing all of the angry feelings that you might normally hold back out of a sense of decorum.

- **The Dream Dialogue:** It is generally considered that all aspects of a dream are in some way representations of the self. For this reason, the dream dialogue can occur between the self and any or all aspects of the dream. Simply *reverse roles* mentally with any aspect or part of the dream where you feel warmed up; it may be a bright blue sky, a rock, an image of a person or God; then write a journal entry as that aspect. You may first reverse roles, and then reverse roles back to the self and respond, or you may dialogue between the self and each aspect of the dream one by one. At the end of the exercise, reverse roles with the self and end the exercise from there, or reverse roles with the "witness" who has been watching all of this and end the exercise with an entry *as* the witness.

- **Engaging the Silence:** *Reverse roles* with the silence that lives between two people, the pregnant silence that lives at the center, the reality that is never spoken or the elephant in the living room and write a journal entry *as* that silence.

- **If These Walls Could Talk:** *Reverse roles* with the walls of a room that held much meaning or many memories for you, and write a journal entry as those walls. You may also reverse roles with other inanimate or nonliving things in the room and write a journal entry as the table, picture, door or whatever you wish to speak *as*.

- **Moments of Empowerment Soliloquy:** Imagine yourself at a moment of your life when you felt particularly empowered or terrific about yourself. Now, mentally *reverse roles* with that part of yourself and write a soliloquy as that part of self, expounding on the moment as almost a sense-memory recall, describing it in detail, then talking about how you felt in that moment, freely and without reservation.

- **Moments of Joy Soliloquy:** Recall a moment in your life when you felt joy, peace and good feeling. Mentally *reverse roles* with yourself at that moment and write a journal entry from that time, *as* you felt it then (e.g., "I am three, sitting on the front steps with my dog, watching the world go by. My Father is coming toward me with a glass of cold water and a cookie."). Let yourself really feel the moment and capture all of its positive feeling.

LETTER WRITING

GOALS:

1. To provide a contained way in which to use letter-writing as an experiential process.

2. To illustrate how to move a letter into a variety of forms or experiential work.

STEPS:

1. After the group warms up through sharing or check-in, ask participants to decide which type of letter to write (see Variations below).

2. Ask them to begin with "Dear So and So," end with an appropriate closing and sign their names.

3. Encourage them to write anything that comes to mind. This letter is not meant to be sent, but to release their feelings. It works best to write quickly, not thinking about how it sounds or imagining that anyone will read it.

4. After letters have been written, group members may elect to do one of the following:
   • Share the letters with the group.
   • Read their letters to an empty chair representing the recipients.
   • Choose a group member to play the person to whom the letter is written and read it to him or her.
   • Form pairs or subgroups and share the letters.
   • Share the letters with a therapist in one-to-one work.
   • Read the letter to an empty chair representing the self.

5. Clients may also write letters they wish they would receive from someone. They may then:
   • Choose a group member to play that person and experience the letter being read by them.
   • Share the letter with the group.
   • Share the letter in pairs or subgroups.
   • Share the letter with a therapist in one-to-one work.
   • Read the letter to an empty chair representing the self.

VARIATIONS:

Letter writing can be useful as a closure technique. If a lot of feelings come up for group members during a session, they can choose people to whom they feel they have something to say and take a few minutes to write letters to them—not to send, but to use as a psychodramatic release.

There should be some sort of warm-up before asking group members to write a letter. The warm-up can be a psychoeducational exercise, psychodrama or any group process.

After they have finished, they can proceed with any of the following examples of possible letters:

- A letter of forgiveness to the self.
- A letter expressing anger toward someone.
- A letter *from* someone expressing sentiments he wishes that person had expressed.
- A letter telling someone about a hurt.
- A letter to someone expressing a desire for reconciliation.
- A letter to someone expressing understanding of what that person went through.
- A letter from someone expressing understanding of what the participant (you) went through.
- A letter to "the disease."
- A letter to an aspect of self or the self at a particular time in life.
- A letter to a substance or behavior to which a person in recovery is saying good-bye.
- Write a letter to a person who you feel you've lost but still have much to say to that has remained unspoken.
- Write a letter of forgiveness, asking forgiveness from someone you feel you have hurt, or a letter you wish you would receive from someone who has hurt you, asking you for your forgiveness.

PSYCHODRAMATIC AUTOBIOGRAPHY

GOALS:

1. To write an autobiography not of how it was but how it felt.
2. To allow for an autobiographical expression of surplus reality.

STEPS:

1. Provide clients with a pencil and paper.

2. Ask clients to write a brief autobiography about themselves in a metaphoric sort of way, or write about a particular moment in their lives, written as surplus reality. In other words, the purpose is not to record accurate details but rather to allow the imagination freedom to record the strange web of associations or idiosyncratic inner experiences. This is not how it was, but how it felt. For example: "My name is Tian, and I grew up on a Greek island located in the middle of Norway, Sweden and Germany. When I married I moved to England." (Actually I'm Greek-American and I grew up in Minnesota.) It is a reflection of the unique way in which we experience our lives. Here is an example of Sara's psychodramatic autobiography of living in her home, with a depressed mother, as a child. "I live in a haunted castle high on a rock above other people. My mother lives in a tower far away from the rest of the family. No matter how high I climb, I can't get to her. She is locked up in her tower where she hums all day and looks out the window. No one can reach her. No one can find her. I scream, Mommy, Mommy, but she doesn't hear me in her tower."

3. Allow as much time as necessary for clients to have a full, spontaneous and creative expression of their experience.

4. If in a group, allow time for group members who so desire to read their stories aloud.

5. Allow plenty of time for sharing.

VARIATIONS:

The psychodramatic autobiography is a concept that can be applied to any person or relationship. Zerka often points out that if we cannot relinquish, for example, our wishes and fantasies for the child, spouse, sibling, etc., that we wish for, we're unable to have a relationship with the child or spouse, for example, that we have, as part of us is engaged in a fantasy relationship in our surplus reality, and we cannot enter the reality we're in. She suggests doing psychodramas with what she refers to as the "psychodramatic spouse," "the psychodramatic child" and so on so that we can experience "having" the imagined object and interacting with it so that we can let it go and live with what we actually have. As a journaling exercise we can write a letter to a psychodramatic spouse, child, parent etc.

Especially wonderful moments or painful episodes can be captured by how we experienced them on the inside, extending the limits of everyday expression to incorporate the complex goings-on of our inner world. The psychodramatic autobiography is part of Moreno's concept of stretching the confines of normal reality to include surplus reality.

THREE PARTS OF PERSONALITY

GOALS:

1. To gain perspective on acting out behavior.
2. To gain insight into our own inner dynamics.

STEPS:

1. Explain to the client or group that we each have three functions of personality, namely:
   - the director who directs our life,
   - the actor who does the action, and
   - the witness or observing ego who watches us from the inside.
2. Invite clients to think of a situation in which they might like to gain insight or experience a shift of some sort.
3. Next, invite clients to mentally reverse roles with each aspect of self, the director, actor and witness, and write a journal entry, as that part of self, about themselves. For example, "I am Al's director, and what he is doing these days really pleases me. He has listened to my voice inside of him, and he is going in a strong direction. I am Al's actor and I'm feeling strong, directed and alive. This is really a direction that feels right, that I am happy doing. I am Al's witness, and I like what I see. I will describe it more fully. . . ." Another example: "I am Eva's director, and I see that she is out of control, banishing my voice. She is all action with no good, orderly direction. I am afraid she will blow her life up if she keeps ignoring me. I am Eva's actor, and I feel a confusion of feelings: gratified, scared, excited, anxious. I want to do what I want to do in the moment, and I don't want to hear about possible consequences. I am Eva's witness, and I am crying inside. What I see frightens and saddens me. I have seen her act this way before; I'm scared."
4. After clients have finished their journaling, invite them to share in a small group or dyads or subgroupings. They don't necessarily need to read everything; if entries are too lengthly, they can choose the most important parts of them.
5. Next, provide plenty of time for group members to share what comes up for them, in the larger group or in subgroupings.

VARIATIONS:

This can be moved into action by casting role-players to play each of the three roles and one more role-player to play the self. The person who is the writer can codirect the scene with the director and move in and out, doubling for any role including the self or reversing roles with any role including the self. After the enactment is finished, return to seats for de-roling, sharing and processing as usual.

LETTER TO GOD

GOALS:

1. To increase your sense of God's presence in your life and to help you have faith that God might help you.
2. To practice surrendering and turning a problem over spiritually and to learn to consciously create positive mental forecasts.

STEPS:

1. Have the clients take out a pencil and a piece of paper.
2. Ask them to pick a current situation in their lives that seems in need of help.
3. Then have them describe how they would like for that circumstance or situation to be. Tell them to describe it as if it were actually happening, as if the experience were real.
4. Next, ask clients to divide a paper into three horizontal sections. On the:
   - **Bottom third of the paper**—Describe the situation as it now exists. For instance, "Recently I met someone who seemed like a very possible life partner, but this person lives many states away. The distance creates a lot of frustration, including some anger at myself for allowing this to happen. I am also aware that I am angry at God because it seems as if I will never be happy in an intimate relationship, and this is just one more example of why it won't happen."
   - **Top third of the paper**—Describe how you wish this circumstance might be. "We are living together happily in a committed relationship. We talk over problems openly as they arise, in a vulnerable, supportive manner. We are in love and feel deeply connected. We have fun together and enjoy the little pleasures of life as a couple."

- **Middle of the paper**—Divine Work, enter here. Leave this section open with the thought toward leaving room for God to work in one's life.

5. Allow group members to share what comes up for them after writing this letter. You may wish to do psychodramas around the fears or doubts that arise when they consider inviting God into their lives as a helpmate, or you can do guided imageries around visualizing their lives as they might wish them to be, or both.

VARIATIONS:

This exercise can be preceded by a guided imagery, where clients image what they would like to see happen in their lives and then release the vision. People who have been traumatized can become negative about the future and create thought patterns that consistently project dark forecasts. This exercise helps to allow some room for positive, or at least neutral forecasts, and encourages trust and faith that life can work out. Other possibilities for a letter to God might be:

- Write a letter to God saying any and all of what you might like to say, including getting angry if you choose. Freely express all of your deepest, hidden feelings to God.
- Open up to God and tell God in a letter what you like best about yourself and what you like least.
- Write a letter to God describing what kind of relationships you would like to have in your life.
- Write a letter describing how you would like your work life to look.

WORKING WITH PHOTOGRAPHS

Working with photographs provides clients concrete material to which they can relate. Many photographs represent a sort of model scene or "picture" for the client to work with. It can be a representation of themselves at a particular stage of life, another person who is important or a family constellation. The photo may also be of a nanny, a pet, or an important relative or friend. The choice of photos that a client brings in is itself diagnostic. The particular meaning they have for the clients becomes the subject of either near-psychodramatic investigation, using psychodramatic techniques such as doubling or talking to the picture or sharing and journaling. Or they can also be moved into psychodramatic enactments such as sculpturing and vignettes. The director might ask, "Can you double for yourself in this photograph?" "Can you double for anyone else in this photograph?" "What do you wish to say to any person in this photograph?" "What do you wish to say to yourself in this photograph?"

A family photo can be used in much the same way as a social atom turned into an action sociogram. The client/protagonist can choose group members to represent everyone in the photograph, including himself. A sculpture can be set up according to the positioning in the photograph. The director can stand outside the sculpture with the protagonist and process what comes up from looking at the sculpture. The client can talk to anyone in the photograph, double for anyone in the photograph or reverse roles with himself or anyone else in the photograph. The director can interview the protagonist while standing in the sculpture to illuminate further the experience the protagonist has internalized. At this point the sculpture can be moved into psychodrama, or it may continue as a sculpture that the protagonist can look at and continue to share about. In either case, when the piece is brought to closure, there can be a moment of reconstructive work. The director can ask the protagonist to reshape the photograph as he wishes it had been and also ask him what he would like to say to the people in this picture or how it feels to look at it this way. This can be a tender moment and often brings up sadness at looking at what might have been as well as hope for carrying a new vision into the future.

WORKING WITH PHOTOGRAPHS

GOALS:

1. To use photographs as a way to focus work.
2. To use photographs as a way to warm up to psychodramatic work and/or psycho-dramatic journaling.

STEPS:

1. Ask clients to bring any photographs that particularly attract them, have special meaning, or illustrate something they feel is telling or important.

2. Reflect on this photograph with your client by asking questions like, "What does this picture evoke for you?" "Who are these people?" "What were you feeling at the time it was taken?" "What does this picture mean to you?"

3. As part of the sharing or warming-up process you may ask questions such as, "What is the voice inside of you saying in this picture?" "What do you imagine the voices inside of others in this picture are saying?" "Can you double for yourself in the picture?" "Can you double for anyone else in the picture?" "Is there anyone in this picture that you want or need to talk to?"

4. As clients share about their photographs they may warm up to psychodramatic activity. At this point you may invite whoever wishes to, or whomever the group chooses, to work and put any or all of her photographs (one is fine) on the stage or bring them up and hold them.

5. Turn the photograph into an action sociogram by asking the protagonist to choose auxiliaries to play the roles of anyone in the picture she may wish to talk to, including someone to play herself if she is in the picture.

6. Arrange the scene as it is represented in the photograph.

7. Invite the protagonist to talk to anyone in the picture she feels warmed up to, including herself, and proceed with a psychodrama as usual, using any and all psychodramatic devices such as doubling and role reversal.

8. After the scene has been brought to closure, invite the protagonist to rearrange this photograph as she might wish to see it.

9. Return to seats for sharing.

VARIATIONS:

This work can also be done as a time line or life review. Clients may bring photographs of themselves or people close to them and place them on the stage along a time line. Arrange numbers at five- or ten-year intervals, or paste the numbers onto long shelf paper. If they are put on stage the protagonist may choose auxiliaries to represent herself or others and place them along the time line as appropriate. She can then talk to or reverse roles with herself at any or all points along the time line. If the photographs are pasted on paper, clients can journal using the exercises below or write responses to some of the suggested questions.

JOURNALING WITH A PHOTOGRAPH OR
QUESTIONS FOR GROUP SHARING

Ask clients or group members to choose a photograph that speaks to them and answer the following questions through journaling or sharing, if desired:

- What feelings come up as you look at this picture?
- What do you imagine the people (including yourself) are thinking?
- What do you imagine they would like to say?
- What would you like to say to yourself or to anyone in this photograph?
- What does this picture mean or symbolize to you?
- What part of yourself in this photo would you like to keep?
- What part of yourself would you like to let go of? If you could be the "inner voice" of yourself or anyone in the picture, what would the voice say?

PSYCHODRAMATIC JOURNALING EXERCISES:

- Reverse roles with yourself in this photograph and write a monologue or soliloquy from yourself at the time of this picture. For example, "I am Catherine. I am eight years old, and I am feeling . . ."
- Write a journal entry as another person in the picture (reverse roles): "I am Gerald (Catherine's father). I am feeling lost at this moment. I am forty-two and have recently lost my job. . . ."
- Write a letter to someone in the picture, e.g., "Dear Dad, . . . Love, Catherine."
- Write a letter you may have wished to receive from someone in the picture, e.g., "Dear Catherine, . . . Love, Dad."
- Write a journal entry as the spirit of the picture or the inner voice of the picture that describes the overall mood of the time, e.g., "I am the voice within the photograph and it is a time of confusion, change, happiness, etc."
- What strengths do you see in yourself in this photograph?
- What strengths did you draw from others in this picture?
- What lessons did you learn from times represented in this picture that affected you negatively?
- What lessons did you learn from times represented in this picture that gave you strength and resolve, that affected you positively?

Write in ten-minute intervals, then share or move into action. Group members may share in the large group, in smaller groupings or in dyads. Reserve plenty of time at the end of group for continued processing and sharing.

WRITING YOUR OWN AFFIRMATION

GOALS:

1. To turn a negative into a positive.
2. To create self-affirming statements.
3. To resolve and integrate emotions through journaling.

STEPS:

1. As a warm-up, have a few affirmation books sitting out. Ask a group member to turn to an affirmation that draws him or her and read it aloud.
2. Invite group members to identify a circumstance in their lives that they wish to work with.
3. Next, read the following to them, or provide them with the written list. After they have listened to or read the objectives, ask the group members to write their own affirmation.

    Affirmation writing is very personal, for the benefit of the person writing and is tailored to the unique needs and wishes of that person. When you write an affirmation, keep the following objectives in mind:

    • **Reframe**. Take a situation that might not be working for you and turn that negative into a positive. For example, if you feel anxious sharing, you may write, "Today I recognize that I do not have to be perfect in order to be okay. I allow myself to share myself with others. Though I have some fear, I need not let this fear take me over. I rest comfortably in the awareness that I can tolerate the feelings that come up around sharing what is going on for me."

    • **Affirm**. Make positive statements about what you believe is possible for you (i.e., "I can, I will, I allow," and so on). An affirmation is set in the positive present. "Today I will," or "Today I recognize," or "I am strong enough . . ."

    • **Confront Your Real Feelings**. Honestly look at what lies beneath whatever may be blocking you from moving forward and attempt to find a path through it. "Though

I may have anxiety in making calls on my own behalf or fears around contacting people for work, today I will allow myself to . . ." And so on.

- **Shape Shift**. Turn something around inside yourself, trusting that a shift in thought and perception, if it is real, has the power to change your life and the way you view the world. Meaningful change begins within and generally involves a shift in perception. Whether the perception is the result of trying a new behavior and seeing that it works, or because we "became willing" to "see" something differently, a shift in perception is usually part of a positive move forward.

4. Next, invite whoever wishes to share their affirmations with the group. This can be done from where group members are sitting or from a special chair on the stage area.

5. After all who care to have read, invite group members to share and process.

VARIATIONS:

If you're writing as a group, you can have a couple of quotation books around to share, or group members can bring a few of their favorite quotations to each meeting and share them. Or, you can have a lot of quotations in a pile and group members can find one that speaks to them and use it as a springboard for writing.

GUIDED IMAGERY

Guided imagery can be used to affect disease, calm the nervous system, and learn to visualize new and desired life situations. Whether we're aware of it or not, we are constantly visualizing. Images are continually running through our minds, forecasting future events, reflecting on past ones and ruminating over the present. The thoughts running through our minds impact our immune systems.

In studies to understand how thoughts may impact our bodies, researchers divided subjects into two control groups. One group was asked to watch films of the work of Mother Teresa and the other of Nazi war crimes. After witnessing the films the viewers' immune levels were tested. The first group had increases in levels of immunity while the second group had declines; but after twenty minutes both were leveled and appeared the same. In order to deepen the study, subjects were again asked to view their respective films, but, in addition, they were asked to think about the films throughout the day. The group thinking about the Mother Teresa films had increased levels of immunity while the group thinking about the Nazi war crimes had decreased levels, and these levels remained constant throughout the day in each group. Our thinking affects our immune systems; what goes through our minds all day matters in terms of our health. Guided visualizations can help to bring awareness to clients' thinking processes and help them work toward positive rather than negative mental forecasting.

Some may worry that guided imagery and guided relaxation are hypnotic states, but self-hypnosis is actually a state that the mind enters naturally. Techniques like visualization can feel almost trancelike, but many people frequently go in and out of them when engaging in activities such as driving a car along the highway at night, watching television or playing video games. As we discussed in our section on the psychodramatic trance state, self-hypnosis and guided imagery can tap into a natural "basal ganglia" soothing power source, which is built into our minds but most of us don't realize we possess. "The basal ganglia are involved with integrating feelings and movement, shifting and smoothing motor behavior, setting the body's idle speed or anxiety level, modulating motivation, and driving feelings of pleasure and ecstasy" (Amen 1998). This may be, in part, why we experience such a sense of calm and integration when we are able to focus on something for extended periods, be it gardening, running, writing or cooking. We enter the *flow* state naturally. "Vegging-out" in front of the television, listening to soft sounds, or going into the basement and working on a private project are all ways that we naturally self-soothe, and we emerge from these activities feeling better somehow, more integrated, settled and calm. Children may self-soothe by "leaning into" their parents, listening to a book read aloud, leaning into pillows the way they would lean into their mothers, curling up in front of cartoons and cuddling their stuffed animals. Other forms of self-soothing, such as thumb-sucking, rocking and twirling hair, are typical, though children grow out of them. Self-soothing is a fundamental task of development. When we have no capacity for it we're in danger of trying to self-soothe in dysfunctional ways, like using drugs, alcohol, sex, or compulsive spending or gambling. Guided imagery can help clients learn some self-soothing skills along with consciously picturing a life that has some good, orderly direction.

People who have been through trauma can become deregulated in the basal ganglia region of the brain. The basal ganglia can become reset to be constantly on the alert. This is not only a phenomenon of war, but also of homes that are characterized by chaos, instability, abuse and/or neglect, all circumstances where those involved often become hypervigilant—constantly on the alert for potential trouble. Part of healing from these patterns is to learn to reset the basal ganglia and consciously self-soothe.

WHEN IMAGERY CAN GET IN THE WAY OF GENUINE EMOTION

There is a distinction, however, between self-soothing and using relaxation techniques to deny genuine feelings of anxiety that need to be processed and understood. Our worried feelings may be trying to tell us something, and using relaxation techniques to get rid of that voice would be counterproductive. What we want to do is learn to modulate the intense feelings that overwhelm us and keep us from hearing our inner voices clearly. We want to develop the ability to self-regulate, or find a reasonable and calm *set point* with ourselves.

Not all anxiety is bad. Some is necessary to prepare us for situations that are in some way dangerous or challenging. And, moreover, there may be a split between our conscious and unconscious mind in how we experience anxiety. Sometimes, though one part of our bodies is clearly relaxing, another part may still be holding onto stress. This is part of the split between the conscious and the unconscious mind.

Blocking our anxiety or fear can put us at risk. Fear can be productive in aiding some part of our minds—conscious or unconscious—to prepare for impending events like childbirth or surgery. Larry Dossey, M.D., in his book *Healing Words,* cites studies that illustrate our need to be aware of feelings like fear so that we can use them to warn us of impending danger or discomfort. In a study done at the University of Cincinnati Medical School, it was discovered that pregnant women who had anxiety-ridden, threatening dream images toward the ends of their pregnancies had shorter, easier labors than those who had only happy thoughts and blocked their fears. "It's as if the threatening dreams are acknowledging the painful event that is to come, while the more pleasant dreams deny that reality, just as perhaps the woman who is dreaming them is denying the pain that will be sure to accompany the birth," surmise Jayne Gackenbach and Jane Bosveld, who conducted the experiment. The women who were unable to block or deny their fears, even if only in their remembered dreams, could better use and integrate them in order to prepare for the pain they were about to experience, and that preparation served them well.

Similarly, British psychologist Anne Manyande of University College in London "examined blood levels of two stress hormones, adrenaline and cortisol, in patients just before surgery and two days following surgery." The patients were divided into two groups. The patients in the first group were taught relaxation techniques and had lower blood pressure, lower heart rate and required less pain medication after surgery than the second group, who received no training. However, their bodies told a story with a significantly differing subplot. The group who had used relaxation techniques had significantly increased levels of the stress chemicals adrenaline and cortisol, while the group that received no training had no increase in the levels of these hormones. In other words, though the "relaxed group" had lower blood pressure, lower heart rates and needed less medication (which is a good thing), their levels of stress, as represented by elevated adrenaline and cortisol, went up (which is not such a good thing). Again, the split between the unconscious and conscious mind manifests in the body. Even though we can seem to be in control of our stress response, another part of us clearly is not. The hypothesis of the researchers was that our bodies seem to need a little worry and fear before surgery so that we can accurately plan for potential pain and immobility. Wipe out the worry and fear, and we wipe out some of our conscious connection with the real experience. Our unconscious, however, seems to be aware of what's coming up and expresses its fear through elevated levels of stress in the body.

So blocking our ability to experience feelings of, let's say, "natural" fear and anxiety—even with something as seemingly helpful as relaxation techniques—if it means we can't integrate and interpret their messages to us, is not *always* the way to go. Again, in Candice Pert's words, "The body is the unconscious mind." We need access to our authentic feelings so we can reconnect the feeling state consciously with words—so that we can ruminate over it and use our thinking to work through our feelings.

IMAGINING LIFE SITUATIONS AS WE MIGHT WISH THEM TO BE

GOALS:

1. To integrate thought and emotion through a slow and deliberate internal review.
2. To learn to self-soothe methodically and deliberately.
3. To provide warm-up for action.

STEPS:

1. Ask clients to find a comfortable place in which they feel they can sink into a nice, relaxing state.
2. Have them go to their relaxation breathing and take even, regular, relaxing breaths without pauses between inhalation and exhalation. Tell them to r-e-l-a-x. They can use the relaxation techniques described in the previous section, or they can imagine themselves going down an escalator, slowly getting to the bottom where they can start their visualizations.
3. Say, "Allow yourself to picture a situation in which you might be experiencing anxiety, fear or frustration. Let it emerge in your mind's eye and feel the emotions surrounding it. As you breathe and relax, experience your feelings and allow your mind to understand them."
4. Next, see the situation in your mind's eye as you might like it to be. Gently modify it so it feels more manageable.
5. Continue by saying, "Now, have it, smell it, taste it, feel it, hear it, touch it and let it touch you. Be in this situation as if it were real and happening just this way in the here and now. Engage with all of your senses through the creative picturing of your imagination."
6. Say, "Now, release your vision and trust the universe to carry it into its vast, eternal manifesting space."
7. Tell them to repeat this process any time they feel inclined to and that it is physically safe to do so. (*Not* in a moving car; *yes,* in an airplane or while sitting at the kitchen table or lying on a couch.) It can take as long as ten seconds or ten minutes. And it should feel relaxing, reviving and reeducating.
8. Say, "After you're finished, slowly begin to move your hands and feet, come back up your escalator or bring your attention back into the room."

VARIATIONS:

People who have experienced some form of trauma, such as disasters, assaults, or being or living with addiction, may have trouble visualizing and taking steps toward creating a positive future. Guided imagery can help to retrain that lost function. It can also help to integrate split-off emotions and bring emotional literacy and understanding. In this case use guided imagery not only to visualize circumstances and process them toward a better outcome, but to retrain the ability to visualize a future.

GENTLY TEACHING ABOUT GUIDED VISUALIZATION

GOALS:

1. To make the natural process of visualization conscious.
2. To introduce the idea and method of consciously changing negative self-messaging for positive self-messaging.

STEPS:

1. Ask group members to find a comfortable place to sit with palms resting on their knees or lie on their backs with palms facing toward the ceiling.
2. Ask group members to relax and breathe in and out easily and completely, releasing any held tension, r-e-l-a-x-i-n-g.
3. Ask them to uncross limbs that may be crossed and to mentally scan their bodies for places where they may be holding tension. Have them release it as they exhale.

   In a clear and easily audible voice, say the following as they relax, breathe and listen:

- Everyone visualizes.
- What's in your mind right now?
- What pictures float through your mind throughout the day?
- We want to get conscious pictures. Creative visualization is the conscious, volitional creation of mental sense impressions for the purpose of changing yourself.
- Receptive visualization is listening to your unconscious. Close your eyes, relax and see what comes into your mind. Is there any resistance or ambivalence about having the life you want? Are there emotions that need to be experienced so they can be understood?
- Programmed visualization is when we create mental pictures of the life we want to be living.
- We're going to do a guided visualization, combining all of these approaches. Breathe in and out easily and completely and r-e-l-a-x.

- Close your eyes. Set a scene in detail as you wish it to exist in your life, and let your subconscious fill in the details.
- Relax and imagine your own life the way you'd like it to be; feel it, think it, be in it. Consciously create and work with your sense impressions; sense the scene; smell it, touch it, feel it with your imagination.
- Now let your sense impressions get clearer and stronger. Add details. Add movement in your mind's eye. Add depth (for example, foreground, middle ground). Add style (for example, visit galleries, watch movies, dress, move around). Increase contrast (see the contrast as you visualize). Switch among different senses (sight, sound, touch, taste, smell, direction of sounds), and make it kinesthetic touching, (hot versus cold, hard versus rough, wet versus dry).
- Include appropriate emotions; react naturally to the content of your visualization as if it were really happening in the here and now.
- Visualize with a positive attitude; see yourself as basically lovable and okay; allow negative thoughts that pop up, "This won't work, this is dumb," to come up as you witness them. Let your thinking mind watch and understand them as your feeling mind brings them forward. Now see them float in and out of consciousness without getting involved in them or giving them undue weight.
- Include positive consequences in the attainment of your goals. See yourself enjoying newfound leisure, friends, comfort, etc. See the universe as a benevolent system where there can be good for all. Suspend judgment; expect the unexpected. As the mind doubts, simply witness as your mental activity jumps around, simply allow it space and listen.
- Explore resistance; what comes up around having a good life? Trauma can create a sense of a foreshortened future. It can become difficult to symbolize, fantasize or play mentally. We may freeze, shut down or foreclose on our mental processes. Can you identify a time when you froze? Go back in your mind to that time and let's unfreeze it a bit. Relax, breathe in and out, and r-e-l-a-x. Tell yourself that you are safe and can breathe and relax as you feel what's coming up.
- Witness what comes up around this picture and let your emotional mind and your thinking mind see it. Let it keep moving through you as you continue to breathe.
- Use affirmation and affirmative statements and reframe any negative images that may arise (e.g., I am a good person; I wish good for the world).
- Assume responsibility; take responsibility for what is in your life; visualize for good not bad. Let yourself believe that good things can happen for you.
- Go back to your breath and center yourself by breathing in and out easily and

completely, taking deep breaths. Release any tension you may be feeling on the exhalation and breathe in light and relaxation; exhale tension, breathe in relaxation and inner peace and calm.

- Now slowly begin to move your hands and feet, and whenever you feel ready bring your consciousness back into the room and open your eyes.

VARIATIONS:

Remind your group that as life begins to improve, or when good things start to manifest, we may doubt it or not connect it with conscious visualization and changing our mental picturing. We may sabotage it with statements such as, "It won't last. I better not get to like this because I'll be disappointed when it's over." We may not use the synchronistic activities that offer themselves up to more forward life. This may require conscious training to change our mental picturing from negative to positive. Nothing in life is permanent, good or bad. The idea is to accept the good, enjoy it and believe it is possible, and accept the ups and downs as part of life.

Part II:

Special Issues

13

Scared Stiff:
Trauma and the Suspended Self

Trauma is an overwhelming emotional experience or shock that does not get processed normally and has a lasting psychic effect. According to Bessel van der Kolk, director of the VA hospital in Boston, "Sudden, terrifying experiences which explode one's sense of predictability can have profound short-term and long-term effects on one's subsequent ways of dealing with emotions. . . . The helplessness and rage which usually accompany these experiences may radically change a person's self-concept and interfere with the view that life is basically safe and predictable, a precondition for normal functioning. People seem to be psychologically incapable of accepting random, meaningless destruction and will search for any explanation to make meaning out of a catastrophe, including blaming themselves, or their loved ones: helplessness asks for a culprit. This may be either turned against the self, for having been unable to prevent the inevitable, or against others" (Van der Kolk 1987). The definition of trauma, however, extends well beyond a one-time, shocking event. As the studies progressed, it became evident that a syndrome similar to that experienced by soldiers was also experienced by survivors of other types of shocking experiences, such as sexual or physical abuse, living with addiction and/or relationship trauma.

Psychiatrist Mardi Horowitz (1997) has postulated a "completion principle" that "summarizes the human mind's intrinsic ability to process new information in order to bring up to date the inner schemata of the self and the world." Trauma, by definition, shatters, freezes or interrupts these inner schemata. The unassimilated traumatic experiences are stored in the body/mind in what Horowitz calls active memory (i.e. act hungers, open tensions), which has an "intrinsic tendency to repeat the representation of contents." The trauma is resolved only when the survivor develops a new mental schema for understanding what has happened. Trauma can be disintegrating. That is, emotions that are too overwhelming to feel can be split out of consciousness or frozen so we lose access to them. They remain a part of us, but we are unaware of their presence. Still they drive and control our behavior. The reenactment dynamic, or "repeating the representations of contents," sends up a red flag marking the spot of previous pain. By paying attention to problematic life experiences that we repeat over and over, even if we wish not to, we have a map to follow into the psyche. The reenactment dynamic tends to be linked to experiences too painful to feel at some point in development. Because it hurt too much to feel it, we banished it out of consciousness. But ignorance is definitely not bliss when it comes to trauma. The pain we cannot feel may get acted out in dysfunctional ways through our parenting, intimate relationships and our ability to live comfortably in our own skins. In working with traumatic memories clinically, we create a safe-enough environment so the contents of those memories can be refelt, reunderstood and reintegrated with new awareness and understanding.

When we are traumatized, we may have one or more of the following responses: fight, flight or freeze. "In any life-threatening situation a person will first be on high alert as the signs of potential danger are perceived. This is termed the 'startle' (Simons 1996) and is the familiar 'deer in the headlights' reaction. Following that is the attempt to fight or flee. If escape is possible, the experience of the near-trauma will be upsetting and temporarily stressful, but the person is unlikely to develop PTSD (post-traumatic stress disorder). If, however, one of these actions is not possible the person experiences a blocking of his or her escape. This results in the 'thwarted intention.' This, in turn, gives rise to the 'freeze.'" (Tinnin & Gantt, 2000; 2003.) When we freeze and cannot process what's happening, we are at higher risk for developing symptoms of PTSD. When we're triggered by a current-life circumstance, previous histories of traumatization can make us feel that we're reliving a painful or frightening situation. "People with PTSD may organize their lives around dealing with the aftermath of trauma in one or both of two seemingly contradictory ways," says van der Kolk (1987), "[Their lives] are dominated by recurrent intrusive, overwhelming memories related to the trauma in the shape of . . . nightmares, flashbacks or anxiety attacks, and/or they show extreme avoidance of involvement in life, fearing that any intense feelings may trigger a re-experience of trauma."

Trauma in childhood can seriously impact development throughout life and can have pervasive and long lasting effects. The amygdala, which is a brain center for the fight/flight/freeze response, is fully functional at birth. This means that a baby is capable of a full-blown trauma response. The hippocampus, which is where we assess stimuli as to whether or not it is threatening, is not fully functional until the age of four to five (Aram 2004). In addition, the prefrontal cortex is not fully mature until around age eleven.

This means that when children are frightened, they have no way of understanding what is going on around them. They do not have the developmental capability of assessing frightening stimuli as to its level of threat, nor do they have the cognitive capability to understand what's happening. They need an external modulator, namely a parent, to help them to regulate themselves and calm down. Without this help, the painful stimuli may become locked in a sensory memory that lives within the self-system without insight, understanding or regulation. The content of the memory has a significant unconscious component because reason has not elevated it to the thinking level. And when it gets triggered, it feels as if it is about the situation that triggered it.

Traumatic memory is an emotional mind/body accident waiting to happen, waiting to be triggered and felt in the here and now, waiting to emerge, not only from the mind, but from the body. Trauma is a body/mind phenomenon. This is also why, when in therapy we search for the memory, it doesn't necessarily come. What comes instead is a sensorial content (shakes, shivers, heart pounding, etc) and a pervasive sense of danger, because this is how the memory was locked in.

This is why a mind/body approach to trauma is critical to full healing.

Children make meaning out of situations using the psychological and emotional equipment available to them at their particular stage of development. For the small child, the parent is all-powerful and of vital importance to her very survival. In their need to stay connected at all costs, coupled with their innocent belief that their parents knows everything, children may make sense of a painful home situation by blaming themselves: "If only I were better, Daddy wouldn't shout at me. . . . Mommy wouldn't feel depressed. . . . They would stop fighting. . . ." They may contort their personalities in a variety of ways to maintain a sense of connection and create some semblance of stability with those they depend upon. Families in trouble may produce a "symptom bearer" or a "target child" who they focus on as "the problem." This diverts the family's anxiety, be it conscious or unconscious, onto a vulnerable child who takes on that identity. Such a child's personality may be affected, and his developing identity may wrap itself around certain negative self-concepts. It is difficult for a child trapped in this system to get help if the adults do not seek it first. If the adults get help, the child may improve on his own. The older the child gets, the more imbedded his personality issues become, and the more these problematic concepts about the self, relationships and the world impact the overall organization of his personality and identity.

Traumatized infants and children may suffer a decreased attachment to their primary caregiver. This can lead to denial of need, erosion of trust and emptiness (Taylor 1984). They, and other victims of trauma, may engage in a process of selective perception: they begin to focus on what they need to survive to the exclusion of what they need for personal development, and they tend to elaborate and condense early memories, losing a sense of context and time. Undoing this in adult patients is a process sometimes compared to peeling back the layers of an onion—undoing distortions of thinking, feeling and behavior one layer at a time and allowing them to heal. It also involves examining the meaning that adults made out of painful situations when they were children that they may still be living out today, their core beliefs about themselves. This is a process of linking reenactment dynamics, or the living out of problematic self-identities in the present, with their origins from the past.

Trauma survivors may experience a sense of a foreshortened future. They have trouble envisioning and, as a result, difficulty taking steps toward a future they wish to create. It is a cruel reality that children from traumatizing families are robbed of not only a part of their childhood but also of significant pieces of their young adulthood. The energy they need to "get their lives together" has been partially spent, and their youthful dreams and hopes have undergone disillusionment. It is sad that because of the developmental timing of the family problems there can be significant life complications during young adult years. Oftentimes, clients arrive at my office in their midthirties, quite discouraged, wondering why their relationships aren't working or why they cannot seem to organize themselves into a productive work life. The traumatic memories are often restimulated when clients again attempt to enter intimate relationships and the very attempt at deep connection brings up the pain, anxiety and confusion that previously surrounded it. The personal meaning they have about themselves, life and relationships can be informed by negative mentations and beliefs from the past.

The manner in which those around the developing person handle traumatic experiences may have as much to do with whether or not symptoms of PTSD develop. Accessing support from caring individuals who help the child to reregulate their state of arousal goes a long way in allowing them to feel safe enough to integrate the painful experience rather than split-off out of consciousness. Even though some degree of painful recollection may still be there, the child may be less preoccupied with developing strategies for staying safe.

Adults who were traumatized as children don't remember things well or necessarily in order. They simply lacked the developmental capability to understand what was happening. So when, in therapy, we ask them to recite their experiences, they may not be able to fully do that. The body has to lead the mind to the truth. Then, as the truth emerges through action, the adult mind, i.e., the observing ego, can witness what is emerging through the eyes of an adult and make new meaning out of the events. It can understand and regulate the memories as to threat. Once healing has taken place, the person, when stimulated, can have his or her own rating as to level of threat. Spilling the milk is not a red alert, as may have been the case in childhood. It can be recategorized to yellow or even green. It is no big deal.

PSYCHODRAMA: A MULTISENSORY APPROACH

The more senses that are involved in a traumatic experience, the more the brain remembers it. The first responder on a scene, the one who hears, sees, touches, smells and possibly tastes a traumatic moment, whether that be a fireman, a medic, or a child witnessing or experiencing abuse, will likely be more deeply affected than the person who only hears the story. Through role-play, more of the self and senses are activated and spontaneously emerge: tears, angry words never spoken or pent-up frustration can be expressed in words and action, released from a self that may have been holding onto them in frozen silence.

Engaging in the therapeutic moment with all senses does not ask us to restrain the self or the intense emotions attached to traumatic memories in unnatural ways. Allowing the senses to participate in healing has the effect, in my own clinical research, of relieving the self in a manner that talking does not always allow for. Talk may leave the traumatized person feeling trapped in a recitation of a trauma story or disengaged from the emotional and sensorial content of the traumatic experience. When trauma survivors begin to contact the real story, they may want to retreat into their heads rather than experience the disquieting body sensations or painful emotions associated with their traumas. The talking may stimulate an urge to do something or take an action that becomes thwarted because talking does not include body and sensorial involvement. When they cannot do anything to relieve themselves of these emotions and body sensations, they may feel frustrated and helpless all over again. Role play allows the helpless victim to stand at the center of his own experience and alter it internally by saying what he couldn't say or doing what he couldn't do, to integrate split-off effect and sensorial moments or sensations into the therapeutic moment. The containing presence and identification of the group further allow the protagonist to learn to absorb caring and support from others and gives group members the opportunity to heal through identification. Opportunities for further reparative experiences with a surrogate and experiencing one's self in novel ways through role-play, in a relational context that allows her to *do, undo* and *redo* a particular dynamic, allow the protagonist to repair traumatic scenes and develop new schema for understanding them. In this way role training becomes a natural part of the psychodramatic process. Psychodrama:

- Puts the locus of control inside of the protagonist.
- Wakes up the body so the protagonist can begin to think and feel about what she is experiencing physically.
- Allows the brain/body to do what it wants to do, such as stomp or shake, in order to release the residue of the stored trauma.
- Integrates thinking, feeling and behavior into a coherent whole.
- Helps the protagonist to get out of her head and get in touch with the split-off affect accompanying the real experience so it can be worked through, understood and reintegrated; new schema can be developed for understanding the truauma.
- Allows the senses, which play such a pivotal role in how trauma is experienced and stored in the brain and body, to participate in healing.
- Restores a sense of being alive in the here and now—restores spontaneity.

WHEN WORDS ARE NOT ENOUGH

"Fundamentally, words can't integrate the disorganized sensations and action patterns that form the core imprint of the trauma" (Van der Kolk in Wylie 2004). This is in part, I think, why psychodrama can be so useful in resolving trauma issues—if it is done slowly and carefully, following the lead of the protagonist. It involves the body, as well as the mind and emotions, and it allows for a picture of what occurred to emerge in a concrete form first, before it is reflected on in the abstract. "The imprint of trauma doesn't 'sit' in the verbal, understanding part of the brain, but in much deeper regions—amygdala, hippocampus, hypothalamus, brain stem—which are only marginally affected by thinking and cognition" (Vander Kolk in Wylie 2004). Van der Kolk feels that, "If clinicians can help people not become so aroused that they shut down physiologically, they'll be able to process the trauma themselves." The idea is to get the client to think about what she is feeling, to become curious about and engaged in what is going on inside of her so that she can process it herself. Less is more. The goal is engagement rather than any specific agenda or expectations of intense emotions. They may well emerge, but should not be forced. The level of arousal can move naturally through the ebb and flow as the enactment unfolds and feeling, thought and word engage and are moved through toward integration.

WHAT DOES THE BODY WANT TO SAY?
LETTING THE BODY HAVE A VOICE

When protagonists experience their bodies during a psychodrama, whether it be a shutting down, queasy stomach, tightness in the chest or unsteady legs, the therapist can slowly explore what is happening within them. "What is going on inside of you right now; what's getting triggered; what's happening in your body?" Taking the time to ask these questions, whether in group or in a psychodrama, can help the client learn to integrate the material being triggered rather than getting stuck in a defensive position to get away from it. The group also may become triggered as the process moves ahead. As the director checks in with the protagonist as to what's going on in the body, the group members learn to check in with themselves in a similar fashion. They become educated as to how to process their own trauma if they witness what is happening with the protagonist. It is important that plenty of time be preserved for sharing so that all members of the group can process what is going on for them. The knowledge that they are, and will continue to be, in a group healing process helps group members stay with what's happening inside of them and use the protagonist's drama to better understand their own inner worlds. As they witness and identify, their minds make a thousand small connections. Their inner world moves through cycles of being fuzzy and then clear, as the veils of illusion lift and their truth emerges.

The material that is getting triggered is largely unconscious, stuck in the body, as it were. Even asking trauma survivors to answer questions like, "What's going on with you?" can baffle them and put them straight into their heads. They may go into a sort of "speed think" and try to come up with the answer they think you might want. In psychodrama I find it much more useful to say, "What's going on in your body? Where is it going on? Can you put your hand there? If that part of your body had a voice, what would it say?" Once the body starts talking through the mouth, the head can quiet down. Once the client knows that it's okay for the body to open up and tell its story, the cortex can take a break and work at normal speed, where it can make sense of what's being said. What we want to do is help the traumatized person calm down enough so that she can tune in to what's going inside of her and begin to become curious about it and articulate it. In this way she can be an agent in her own healing and come to understand both what is happening to her and the process of healing it so that when she gets triggered outside of therapy, she can use it as a healing moment rather than becoming blindly retraumatized. This process helps to integrate fragments of memory and modulate the intensity of the whole response system.

The other question that I find is useful to ask clients is, "What does your body want to do?" When these states are triggered the body often wants to do something, to take some action related to the thwarted intent associated with its trauma responses. Often this is to yell, kick, scream, hit, or run and hide. Psychodrama allows for that action to be taken in a clinically safe manner. If this is done mindfully, if the act hunger is understood by the client and seen in its therapeutic context, it can produce a deep sense of relief and help unblock emotions that have been stored in the body. As these feelings come forward, the thinking that was frozen starts to come forward, too. The body moves, and the mind and heart follow. Oftentimes this takes the form of the kind of reasoning of a confused child trying to make sense of what to him made no sense. Sentences such as, "Am I bad? Stop yelling at me! I hate you! Why can't you see how much I love you?" and so on sputter out as he gains his footing on the new soil that is rapidly accumulating beneath his feet. This is psychodrama in slow motion. Following the lead of the protagonist very slowly and carefully helps the trauma survivor to feel that he is at the locus of control in his psychodrama, that he will not be pushed beyond his capacity and coerced into areas he does not feel ready or willing to explore. The trauma survivor initially may come forward tentatively, frightened of retaliation for even thinking subversive thoughts. Contrary to what many might think, this material, in psychodrama, does not necessarily come pouring forth; it is slow and painstaking work. The tentacles of trauma stretch far beyond a one-time, shocking event. The Chinese have a saying, "The deepest pain has no words." In working with trauma we are working with this sort of pain, and it comes out of hiding like a disembodied spirit that has not seen the light of day, as if back from the world of the dead, or at least the emotionally dead.

WOMEN'S UNIQUE RESPONSE TO STRESS

According to a recent UCLA study, women have a range of response to stress that is not only *fight, flight* or *freeze*. Much of the research on trauma has been done on men. Women may vary in their responses, exhibiting what researchers are calling an urge to *tend and befriend*. In stressful situations most men and women produce the hormone oxytocin also known as the "touch chemical," the one that makes both people and animals "calmer, more social and less anxious," says the study's main researcher, Shelley E. Taylor. But that's where the similarity ends. The testosterone in men counteracts the calming effects of oxytocin while estrogen enhances it. Oxytocin can also lead to maternal behaviors, making women want to grab the children, gather with other women and cluster for safety.

This research may extend our ideas about how stress affects men and women. Oxytocin is a calming chemical that leads women to gather, talk and support each other through stress while men tend to isolate in order to calm down from their unmitigated release of "stand and fight" stress hormones such as adrenaline. All of this was evolution's way of parceling out roles to maintain a tight "family of man" survival system when encountering the proverbial saber-toothed tiger, but may be troublesome if applied to a "one-size-fits-all" treat-ment modality today. In other words, women not only stand and fight, flee or freeze, they also bond and run *together* for emotional shelter. Is this codepen-dency or in this case, nature's way of insuring the survival of the species—or does one impact the other, that is, is becoming codependent part of a woman's maladaptive coping system when trauma is cumulative? Is it a natural response subverted to an unnatural adaptation? I suggest that it may be appropriate to see an overall trauma response as fight/flight/freeze/fuse in accomodating research on women which yields new and different information than research done on men primarily. In any case, it is necessary to be mindful of these gen-der differences in treating trauma so as not to overly pathologize woman's built-in need for connection.

All trauma does not necessarily require treatment. Sometimes the best tonics are the support of concerned friends and relatives and a return to normalizing activities and routines. And treating trauma goes well beyond the clinic. Classes in yoga, breathing techniques, engaging clients in activities that help them to feel restored to the world in which they live and give them a sense of meaningful activity, may be as important as what will go on in the clinic.

How a Traumatized Person Copes and Its Effect on the Personality

Because of the way our brains store traumatic memories, they do not get "thought about," reflected upon and put into a coherent context. The defenses that get engaged during situations of threat—fight, flight and freeze—are associated with the "old" part of the brain. The cortex, which is where thinking, reasoning and long-range planning take place, was developed later in human evolution. That's why when we're "scared stiff" or "struck dumb" the content of the experience that would normally get thought through and placed into memory storage instead gets more or less flash frozen or thrown out of consciousness. Though fear is generally associated with the emotional centers of the brain, the cortex is also involved in processing memories of fear and can modify our response to a frightening situation as we "figure out" whether there is or is not something to be afraid of (Ledoux 1996). The cortex can be overwhelmed if previously mentioned parts of the old brain are on high alert or flooded with intense feeling, as in the rage state. Consequently, the memory is stored as a "sense memory;" i.e., the body/mind holds it in the brain and body. It has not been modulated by the thinking or reasoning part of the brain. This is part of why it remains in the unconscious: because reason hasn't brought it to a conscious, thinking level. Not surprisingly, there can be considerable memory loss surrounding traumatic material, which can make therapy or psychodrama feel threatening as painful memories emerge. We defend against feeling too much emotional or psychological pain. Some of our ability to defend allows us to go about our lives with relative calm and focus. Too much of it can lead to the sort of pathological defenses that mean painful experiences never get processed and put into a healthy perspective. These unintegrated memories may resurface in the form of somatic disturbances such as headaches, back problems, muscle stiffness or queasiness, or as psychological and emotional symptoms such as flashbacks, anxiety, sudden outbursts of anger, rage or intrusive memories, as well as the reenactment dynamics we spoke of earlier. The person experiencing these swings in her physiological, emotional and psychological inner world may find herself in an intense bind in which traumatic memory stimulates disturbing physiological sensations—*and* disturbing body sensations stimulate traumatic memory. This can create an internal combustion, a psychological, emotional and physical "black hole" that can send a client into an ever-intensifying downward spiral. Clients may experience this as panic, frustration, anxiety or feeling "stuck."

In her article entitled "Art Therapy and Trauma," Linda Gantt writes, "It is fundamental to the instinctual nature of this reaction that it occurs without conscious choice. During the freeze, the person experiences an altered state of consciousness (ASC) during which time is slowed down or experienced as being fragmented. This is the point at which the verbal mind ceases to function in a normal fashion. It is also quite disturbing to the individual because aspects of the ASC are substantially different from ordinary consciousness. For example, one's perceptions may be drastically altered and the location of consciousness may be outside the body or in a phantom body. Body sensations occurring during the altered state of consciousness are often not remembered. The person can become unable to willfully function and will automatically obey another person (perpetrator or rescuer) who takes charge. (Once the danger has dissipated, a period of self-repair ensues which may involve rocking, sleeping or sucking one's thumb.)" If there is sufficient repair, the trauma effects may become integrated. However, if a person goes into the instinctual trauma response (which is in effect peritraumatic dissociation), then the likelihood of developing PTSD symptoms is great (Birmes et al. 2003). Often PTSD takes some months or years to become full-blown. A core difficulty of dissociation is that one forgets that one has forgotten. Triggers are unrecognized and the person may go into a panic attack without any recognition of the antecedent conditions. Key fragments of the original traumatic event become inaccessible to ordinary remembering." This is why a safe, therapeutic container that allows for remembering and reintegration can be so helpful and healing for the traumatized person.

Brain imaging has demonstrated that trauma can affect the body and brain much more than had previously been understood (Van der Kolk 1987; Herman 1992). For example, in depression, which is a symptom of PTSD, the amygdala, which is a center of negative emotions in the brain and informs the brain of threat, runs unchecked—in other words, everything feels threatening. In addition, the center of memory, the hippocampus, may lose nerve-to-nerve links. "Brain imaging research shows that both of these centers of the brain are altered in size and shape in victims of trauma such as sexual abuse or the experiences of being a prisoner of war. Research both in animals and in people shows that stress or trauma early in life permanently sensitizes neurons and receptors throughout the central nervous system so that they perpetually over-respond to stress" (Dayton 2000).

The body can't tell the difference between danger and emotional distress. Fearful thoughts can produce the same physiological changes as evidenced in an actual frightening situation. Central to the trauma response is this alternating between feeling overwhelmed and the freezing or numbing response, black and white, no shades of grey. This reflects problems with moderation of affect. Fear leads to biological changes induced by adrenaline. Adrenaline prepares the skeletal muscles for strain as may occur in: running for escape (flight) and protecting self or property (fight). In order to respond quickly to a threat, to flee or fight, for example, the body tries to divert blood flow from the digestive areas and the face, head and neck so that it can be used elsewhere. This has the effect of elevating heart rate and blood pressure and increasing respiration. If diversion of blood from the cortex is too fast, a person can faint, go numb or freeze. If the individual does not engage in vigorous physical activity following arousal, uncomfortable physiological changes may occur, such as: trembling in the arms and legs, general weakness or a heightened awareness of breathing and heart rate. This is part of the body's way of shaking off the physiological residue of the trauma response. It is very important that this occur, if it needs to, so that the sensorial aspects of the trauma memory don't become frozen and block emotions from being felt and moved through.

Various types of trauma can produce fear responses. Over time our body can become sensitized and wired for overreactions so we become more easily frightened. This can send us into a vicious cycle where the physiological changes make us more afraid, which then leads to more fearful thoughts and more physiological changes. As an attempt to protect ourselves or avoid these uncomfortable feelings we may start to live small; to avoid situations that we may fear will stimulate anxious or painful feeling states.

Fear is at the base of the trauma response. Fear is what signals the fight/flight/freeze survival defenses to engage. Feeling overwhelmed by fear, can lead to feelings of helplessness and terror at being confronted with circumstances that feel out of our control, and this sense of desperation can kick in the trauma response. Consequently, we need to remember that when we get triggered, our fear is getting triggered along with our frozenness. Oftentimes, when we do psychodramas, clients freeze when confronted with even a surrogate of someone who has frightened them in the past. This response needs to be recognized as the way they may have coped early in their lives when something frightened them. As they "thaw out" they can describe what's going on with them in mind and body, what they wanted to say, do or even think that was thwarted because of their own fear. And they can make many choices as to how to proceed in their dramas. In this way they can learn to modulate this fear response.

Choice can alter this process and elevate immune functioning. Moving through frozenness and breaking situations down into manageable components and incorporating choice as to, for example, how, when and where, can help to turn this cycle in a more positive direction. Psychodrama incorporates both the possibility of physical movement and choice for the protagonist, which can help to strengthen the client.

MOVING PAST YOUR PAST: THOSE WITH PREVIOUS HISTORIES OF TRAUMATIZATION

Laura's Story: From Nicaragua to Lower Manhattan

September 11, 2001, was an example of how a current trauma can restimulate the symptoms from a previous trauma. Laura, who had come from Nicaragua and had a previous history of both familial and war trauma, was becoming symptomatic, very anxious and irritable, having problems at work, physically tense, not sleeping, and having nightmares after 9/11. The more anxious, tense and tired she became, the more disturbing memories from her previous history got stimulated, and the more memories emerged, the more anxious she got. Her body and mind were playing off of each other, and she felt as if she were descending further and further into a sort of black hole that she couldn't get out of. She wanted help to calm down and feel less frightened. Laura had fled her war-ridden country ten years previously to make a safe place for herself, which she thought she had accomplished. Now all of this safety felt gone in an instant and she was terrified. Laura always found experiential work very effective in releasing held emotion, which allowed her to think more clearly and reorder her psychological and emotional world. She wanted to work this current problem through experientially.

In her psychodrama, we focused on helping her to slowly process what was happening inside of her. By interviewing her and allowing her to do her own soliloquy it became clear that, in her mind, she was in Nicaragua again, and her unconscious was seeing marauding gangs of killers and looting in the streets, and she was cowering for safety in doorways or under tables. Unconsciously, she was reexperiencing her previous situation in the here and now, her past was getting mixed up with her present, and she felt as if it were happening all over again. Her life today and her previous life were co-occurring inside of her, and she was feeling constantly overwhelmed. Through concretizing model scenes of each world, she viewed them on the stage, and was able to move them apart and separate them in her mind. Seeing the two worlds in front of her allowed her to re-enter her body and stop living in the past. Once she could slow down, experience and talk about what was going on inside of her, she could emerge from it. She could separate the past, which was intruding into her present through flashbacks, disturbing images and somatic disturbances, from her present life. She could straighten out her clouded thinking. Over the next few weeks, she was able to hold on to that healing.

Trauma travels—through social systems, family systems and generations. Though its basic symptoms are fairly consistent, the way in which those symptoms manifest may vary. And trauma wears many faces. In order to resolve symptoms, we need to work with the traumatized person and travel with him through the twists and turns of his own psyche, his own personal history, in order to understand how it affects him. We need to follow his lead.

Through the events of September 11, Americans became aware of what professionals have found to be true for some time: that the avoidant, intrusive and arousal symptoms that are characteristic of PTSD can be developed in many ways, and once developed they come to have a life of their own.

It is not uncommon for those who carry unresolved PTSD issues to feel what we in the addictions field call "terminally unique." They imagine that their pain and suffering is different from those around them, that no one can really understand what they are going through. They feel different from other people. This also speaks to their loss of ability to take support from others. "No one can understand my pain. I am different from everyone I know, and no one can ever really understand me or help me—so I won't bother; it will only lead to more frustration and disappointment." These kind of attitudes further isolate them and make reaching out feel threatening.

RELATIONSHIP TRAUMA

These types of trauma are primarily the cumulative trauma that results from relationship fissures, ruptures and abusive power dynamics. The kind of trauma that may occur during childhood affects development and fuels reenactment patterns. Relationship trauma, whether beginning in childhood or later in life, develops a strong grip on the personality for a few reasons:

- It occurs at a time in life when a person is vulnerable and dependent on his parents for his survival.
- It occurs at the hands of those who were meant to provide comfort and solace, and this presents a double threat or a double bind.
- There is a power imbalance.
- There is limited access to outside sources of support; going outside the family is disloyal, or primary caretakers block access.
- It occurs *during* a child's development so the relationship trauma becomes *wrapped around* personality development.
- The child has to contort her personality to stay connected to those she both

loves and is being hurt by, which affects her developing sense of self and self in relationship.

- If beginning in adulthood, there may be a perceived power imbalance, manipulation, or abuse or isolation and lack of outside support. The adult may also be vulnerable due to childhood trauma, setting the stage for reenactment dynamics. If there is access to outside support and not too much previous traumatization the person may not necessarily develop full-blown PTSD, depending on the duration and severity of the trauma.

All relationships have some inherent injury and trauma. What seems to sear the trauma in place and keep it from resolving is if:

- It cannot be talked about in any way.
- There is no recognition or attempt at repair on the part of the wounding person.
- There is a power imbalance in the relationship.
- There is little or no access to other sources of support or other people to validate a person's reality.
- There is no way to get away from the traumatizing situation.

EMOTIONAL TRACKING

I find that educating the group as to what to look for so they can track their own responses, mine them for information, and use them to heal rather than shut down, act out or withdraw is very helpful. It's not difficult to do this with the protagonist, as she is the focus, and tuning into her inner states is the purpose of the enactment, but it is more difficult to track group members. Because of this I teach clients to do something I call "emotional tracking," which is essentially to track their internal responses when they get triggered, to ask themselves:

- What's going on in my body?
- What am I feeling?
- What am I thinking?

• Where am I going inside of myself when triggered?

• What do I want to do?

Because it is impossible to track each and every person at all times in a group, I help clients learn to track themselves. In this way they feel safer, and the container is more secure. A few evenings ago John reported going to a movie that triggered him very badly, but said, "Because of what I learned to do in here, I tracked myself; I asked, 'Where am I going inside? What's going on?' and I realized that it put me right back to getting 'beat on' every day, and it made me so sad what people do to each other." This is the kind of emotional awareness that can allow John to live a more aware and less-triggered life. He learned it while watching psychodrama and using the safety of the emotional distance to track himself, and then he made it portable. He carries it with him in his day-to-day life.

But therapists aren't the only source of help and healing. Group members can reach out to share with and support each other. Teaching group members what to look for in themselves and each other helps to put them at the center of their own healing and empowers them to make meaningful connections with others. This is a skill that translates into their lives as well so that when triggered they know what to look for. It is also a way to do social atom repair as group members learn to identify and tolerate intense feeling states, talk them out rather than act them out, reach out for support, and give support. This is a concrete lesson on what kinds of relating are possible.

Often times, the warm-up of one who has been traumatized can be very subtle. Recently, Virginia, after doing a role diagram indicated that she was feeling "so weird." She was able to track her self and recognize that her response to our exercise felt uncomfortable and out of sync and she was able to reach out.

Virginia: I just can't do this. I think I just don't get it. I'm missing something; I want to bolt out of the room.

Tian: What's going on; can you describe it?

Virginia: I'm feeling nauseous. I'm confused. I can't remember anything. I can't even come up with any adjectives to describe my experience.

Tian: What else is going on in your body?

Virginia: My legs are shaking. You must all think I sound so stupid; I'm taking up so much time.

Group: No, it's fine. We've all felt like this. We want you to take the time. No problem.

Tian: Is there anything you want to do?

Virginia: Run out of the room, I guess.

In working with trauma it is important to remember that less is often more. The warm-up of the trauma survivor may feel intense and blocked, all at the same time. Sometimes it is a relatively smooth path from thought into action, particularly if the person is used to group process and/or therapy, while at other times the person may be confused by the intensity of her body and inner world and her lack of clear memories. This can leave her feeling stupid, frustrated and as if she's not getting something, as if she is talking but making no sense. Clearly something was getting triggered for Virginia, a state of frozenness, confusion and somatic sensation. As we moved forward with Virginia's work, we first set up the scene with who she wished to talk to. Still she felt "out of touch, confused" so I asked her to walk around the stage and floor and "do her soliloquy." Through the soliloquy, Virginia was able to warm up to her scene slowly and in a way that suited her. As she talked to her first husband, who died after a prolonged illness during which she supported the family, layers upon layers of grief emerged. She worked primarily with her first husband, their son and marginally with her current husband. The grief process, with all of its stages, became concretized as Virginia expressed her yearning for what she had lost and the role she had been thrust into, got angry, shed tears and moved toward integration of this split-off affect. Had she not been able to articulate her intense, somatic response to our warm-up, she may have been left feeling alienated or isolated. The body was remembering what the mind had forgotten.

Attention also needs to be paid to the warmed-up person who is very ready to work but cannot work on what she is warmed up to. The sociometric process known as group selection can sometimes warm several people up but only one gets to work. When using sociometric choice it is important for those involved to clearly understand that they may not be chosen. Sociometric choice has the advantage of reflecting the group's choices and the disadvantage of warming people up who are not able to work. One way to deal with this, if there is time, is to allow those who choose to share briefly with the person they chose, why they chose him or her. In this way that person can get some support for putting himself in a vulnerable position, can take in some caring from others and then proceed to work the most highly chosen person. The group leader can check in with anyone who is not chosen in order to make sure they are comfortable.

Working with the person who is self-selecting, letting you know that they are warmed up and wish to work, is a smooth entry into trauma work, in my experience, that simplifies the resolution. Virginia's warm-up could move straight into exploration without too many steps in-between. To use the vernacular, "It's all right there, wanting to come out." The protagonist is on board, and if the group is willing to go with it, what emerges tends to come forward smoothly. The protagonist, at this point, is generally in touch with what's going on inside of her and wanting to move somewhere with it, to examine what's going on in some way. Director selection can also work well, in my experience, because the therapist can feel when the client is ready to work and can offer them the opportunity so that their readiness can be acted upon.

TRAUMATIC BONDS

Traumatic bonds formed in childhood tend to have psychic traction, creating emotional grooves within which the personality flows. Traumatic bonds are salient; they have a flavor all their own that tastes the same wherever it attaches. Through projective identification or because of choosing people who have a corresponding psychoemotional setup, these bonds find new homes in willing hosts. They get revived, repeated and relived over and over and over again.

Recently, I did a psychodrama with Roger, who was presenting a second marriage by which he felt trapped but could not free himself. Roger felt convinced that his wife would do something dangerous if he left her, and he could not bear the guilt of causing this to happen by leaving her. He identified himself as feeling warmed up to work. I asked him where he wanted to start. We began with this scene with his wife. Roger kept trying to convince her not to do anything rash. This dynamic seemed seared in place. No matter what his wife did or didn't do, he felt responsible for her action. And he was welded to the idea that if he left her she would do something horrible to herself, and he would be entirely at fault—that it was within his capability to control her actions—and nothing anyone could say really altered that pattern of thinking.

It became evident that this sense of overresponsibility and pervasive guilt didn't come from nowhere, so I asked Roger where he might have felt this way before. He said that he wanted to talk to his mother—a relationship that had caused him a lot of heartache. We froze the present-day scene and spiraled back to a model scene where he stood rooted to the spot facing his mother. He stood in this scene, trying to talk but paralyzed, locked in a pain-filled embrace that barely allowed him to breathe in her presence. His body was stiff remembering what his mind had forgotten, and he couldn't put words on what was going on inside of him.

Tian: What are you feeling right now? What's going on in your body?

Roger: I just feel horribly tense. I can barely breathe. (His hand moved to his throat.) I can't take a full breath. (His hand unconsciously moved to a part of his body that was tight, emotionally constricted.)

Tian: If that part of your body had a voice, what would it like to say?

Roger: I hate this. I hate the way I feel. I'm so scared standing here. (His hand unconsciously moved more toward his lower midsection, his "gut.")

Tian: What else?

Roger: You told me you didn't want me, didn't want children. I try to be good so you will love me but nothing works. You're only happy when you're running your groups at church. You're important there; you're important nationally. When someone is looking you act like a caring mother, but when we're alone you don't want to be with me.

Further investigation revealed that he was worried that his mother might "do something dangerous" as she had many times insinuated she had "had enough." He felt desperate for her approval, which never came, terrified that if he wasn't good, she might reject him even further, that she might take her own life, leaving him feeling unbearable guilt and "all alone in the world." And perhaps he turned his own intolerable wish to get rid of her into a fear that she would do something to herself, and he would be left feeling responsible. This trauma bond seared itself into his body, mind and heart and repeated itself with each wife. Bewildered, he felt that he kept choosing the wrong people to love. Though this may be true, until he identified and moved past this bond within himself, until he examined it and broke its power, he would likely be powerless to stop repeating the pattern.

In his drama Roger was able to see the intensity and origin of the traumatic bond that was gluing him to an emotional time and place that he continually played out in his adulthood, a relationship dynamic that had the power to rule from within. But no matter what we did in the drama by way of role-reversing and doubling, Roger couldn't shake loose the idea that his mother would try to kill herself, and it would all be his fault. The trauma he had experienced as a child at the terrifying thought that his mother might kill herself and that it would be his fault had literally branded itself onto his unconscious. No matter in which direction he moved, he was haunted by unspeakable images of what could happen if he didn't do what was being asked of him.

Tian: What does your body want to do here?

Roger: Run.

Tian: Then run.

Roger: (After returning from a stage run) That felt good.

Tian: What else?

Roger: I still feel like I can't get through.

Tian: Do we need to see the whole picture?

Roger: Yes, that might help. (Roger brought both his current wife and his previous wife onto the stage where they stood behind his mother. Just the sight of all of them made him feel, as he described, "frozen.")

Tian: What do you want to say to them?

Roger: I'm still so scared you'll do something to yourselves, and it will all be my fault. I'll be all alone in the world. I'm so scared you'll drop dead. (At this point I exaggerated or maximized the scene to concretize the fear and asked the group of role-players to drop to the floor.)

Roger: (Suddenly taking a step backward, putting his hand up, as if pushing something away, the dawning of a new realization flooding into his face) I didn't do that. I didn't do that. (Next, looking at me, surprised, with a sense of realization and conviction.) I didn't do that.

Tian: No, you didn't. You feel like you have that kind of power, but that doesn't mean you actually have it.

Roger: Right, I see that; I'm done here.

Tian: Okay, right, end the scene any way you want to for now.

Roger: That was your stuff. I never had the power over life and death with you. I'm getting out of here. I always loved you, Mom, but that wasn't fair. You go back with Dad and figure your relationship out, figure your own life out. I know you had a painful past, but that wasn't my fault. You shouldn't have held me hostage to your past. I've been stuck with it all these years. I think that's it for now.

Tian: Great, should we spiral back up to the present and end the scene with your wife?

Roger: Okay. (We did this and reset the scene with his wife.) I can't save you, I couldn't save her, and I can't keep making it my fault if you do something to yourself. You have a life, too, and I can't live it for you. I think that's it for now. (We returned to the group for sharing and identification.)

A month later when I checked with Roger to see how things were sitting inside of him he said, "While my mother never overtly threatened suicide, I always sensed that she was extremely depressive, and perhaps I unconsciously feared her suicide. My current wife has hinted at thoughts of suicide (such as, 'No one wants me! What's the use?') during bouts with depression, implying that I am the cause, (i.e., 'I am somebody, I don't want her, what's the use?')." Roger went on to say that, "Since my psychodrama, I've experienced a new freedom from family-related guilt and anxiety. Instead of feeling my gut tightening and souring, I feel a momentary sense of relief, as though they are really gone and none of it was my fault. I am doing fine without them. Feelings of guilt and a sense of duty and obligation still quickly rush in, but now I see their destruction, and I have a self-affirming alternative. Though I want to stay connected, I don't want to feel like they own my insides, and I am a reactor rather than a proactive force in organizing and living my own life." Roger continues to feel a greater sense of individuation and his body is visibly more relaxed.

Characteristics of Adult Children of Trauma and Addiction

The following is a list of characteristics of adult children of trauma and addiction that I first published in *Trauma and Addiction* in 2000.

Learned Helplessness. A person loses the feeling that he or she can affect or change what's going on; this can become a quality of personality or an operating style in general, or specific to certain roles.

Depression. Unexpressed and unfelt emotion may lead to a flat internal world or agitated/anxious depression. Anger, rage and sadness remain unfelt or unexpressed in a way that leads to no resolution.

Psychic Numbing/Emotional Constriction. Numbness and shut down as a defense against overwhelming pain and threat. Restricted range of affect or authentic expression of emotion.

Distorted Reasoning. Convoluted attempts to make sense and meaning out of chaotic, confusing, frightening or painful experiences that feel senseless. Cognitive distortions that can grow out of distorted perception in the moment of traumatization and/or distorted reasoning.

Loss of Trust and Faith. Due to deep ruptures in primary dependency relationships and breakdown of an orderly world.

Hypervigilance. Anxiety, waiting for the other shoe to drop—constantly scanning environment and relationships for signs of potential danger or repeated rupture.

Traumatic Bonding. Unhealthy bonding style resulting from power imbalance in relationships and lack of other sources of support.

Loss of Ability to Take In Caring and Support. This is due to fear of trusting or depending upon relationships and trauma's inherent numbness and shutdown.

Loss of Ability to Regulate or Modulate Emotion. Going from 0–10 and 10–0 without intermediate stages, or exhibit black-and-white thinking, feeling and behavior with no shades of gray as a result of trauma's alternating cycles of numbing versus intense affect.

Hyperactivity/Easily Triggered. Stimuli reminiscent of trauma, e.g., yelling, loud noises, criticism, or gunfire, trigger the person into shutting down, acting out or intense emotional states. Or subtle stimuli such as changes in eye expression or feeling humiliated, for example. A tendency to be hyper-reactive to any type of perceived slight rejection or damage.

High-Risk Behaviors. Speeding, sexual acting out, spending, fighting or other behaviors may be done in a way that puts one at risk. Misguided attempts to jump-start numb inner world or act out pain from an intense pain-filled inner world.

Disorganized Inner World. Disorganized object constancy and/or sense of relatedness, along with internal emotional disconnects or fused and confused affect and thinking.

Survival Guilt. Due to witnessing abuse and trauma and surviving, from "getting out" of an unhealthy system.

Development of Rigid Psychological Defenses. Dissociation, denial, splitting, repression, minimization, intellectualization and projection, are some examples, or developing rather impenetrable "character armor."

Cycles of Reenactment. Unconscious repetition of pain-filled dynamics, the continual recreation of dysfunctional dynamics from the past.

Relationship Issues. Problems with staying present in intimate connection with others, trouble tolerating intense emotion without acting out, withdrawing or shutting down.

Desire to Self-Medicate. There may be attempts to quiet and control a turbulent, troubled inner world through the use of drugs and alcohol or behavioral addictions.

How Psychodrama Works in Resolving the Symptoms of Adult Children of Trauma and Addiction

A critical feature in trauma resolution, in my experience, is to follow the lead of the protagonist, to allow the protagonist to be at the locus of control and impose no agendas on him. Another is to recognize that the goal is not to necessarily to create a grand catharsis or interesting psychodrama, but rather to help the survivor of trauma engage with his own particular internal process and tolerate the overwhelming feelings that seem intolerable to him. This can be a quiet or a noisy thing depending on the client and his particular needs. The goal is to have integrative catharsis. Abreactive catharsis should facilitate a catharsis of integration. If it simply trains a client to release emotion with no further insight and integration it may not facilitate the desired overall healing.

As we mentioned earlier, people with developmental arrests can be concrete thinkers. Psychodrama allows the protagonist to view the contents of her inner world in concrete form before she is asked to reflect on it in the abstract, which models the developmental moment from concrete to abstract thought. This can enhance the ability to self-reflect, which can be difficult for trauma survivors who are removed from their internal experiences through psychological and emotional defenses, or glued to model scenes from their past that never seem to resolve themselves.

Hypervigilance, or constantly scanning one's environment for signs of danger, lessens as clients experience both a catharsis of abreaction and expression of strong feeling, followed by a catharsis of integration that brings new awareness, insight and thus a greater sense of mastery. *Feelings* that have been *fused* (Van der Kolk 1987) such as sex and aggression, love and supplication, or need and fear, begin to separate themselves and be understood in the light of today. The *learned helplessness* that may have developed from feeling that one could do nothing to make a difference, or change a painful situation for the better, begins to lessen as the client is placed at the center of her own experience and empowered to show and tell her story through action and word.

Through the *abreactive catharsis* the protagonist is allowed complete latitude in releasing pain and in giving full expression to feelings of hurt, anger, alienation, love, need, etc. She can express previously taboo feelings, thoughts and words, so that which was repressed or denied can emerge and find voice and expression, thus giving an infected wound a chance to drain and get air. A *catharsis of integration* occurs when split off or repressed memory is felt in the here and now so that it can be integrated into the self system along with new meaning and insight. This allows clients to view the "same landscape through different eyes." This is fundamentally reempowering, because it allows clients to come to terms with a painful past rather than amputate the parts of themselves that have gone into hiding. The nature of traumatic memories is that they are split off from normal memory storage. They often enter partial consciousness through flashbacks and somatic disturbances (I know I must be feeling something because my stomach hurts) or body memories. Psychodrama allows for bits of memory of the traumatic event(s) to emerge and be recontextualized and reintegrated into the memory system of the protagonist.

Defenses such as *numbing* and *dissociation* get engaged when people feel traumatized. This, coupled with the fact that traumatic memory may be stored without the involvement of the cortex, which could label, order and place experience into a comprehensible context, means that a certain emotional illiteracy can accompany trauma. In psychodrama, words can be attached to internal experiences and feelings that have previously gone unlabeled. As emotional literacy enters and begins to describe experiences, new meaning can be made of them and new insight and understanding derived. The *cognitive distortions* that may have grown out of an experience of a distorted sense of reality or represented a child's or adult's best attempt at making sense of a senseless situation begin to clear up. The *loss of trust and faith* in relationships and in life's ability to repair and renew itself, gets slowly rebuilt through a supportive, *healing relational experience.*

The *loss of ability to fantasize* that can be involved with trauma, may be carried into adulthood. This may create fear of the future or even an inability to visualize and take steps toward actualizing a future. In psychodrama, clients can revisit those fears in clinical safety and with therapeutic allies. In addition, they can visit their futures through role-play and face anticipated, feared or wished-for scenes through rehearsal and role-training.

The emotional and physical *constriction* and *numbing* response can lead to a restricted range of feeling and expression. Psychodrama restores *spontaneity* into the self-system. Indeed, it is a central goal of psychodrama to consciously remove blocks to spontaneity so that the authentic personality can be allowed to emerge. It frees up the personality and removes blocks to spontaneity so a person is able to react more fully and appropriately in the here and now.

As the trauma story is shared and moved through in body, mind and heart, the client can begin to let the walls of defense down and *take in support* (Van der Kolk 1987) from others. During the sharing phase the protagonist simply listens and takes in the understanding, identification and support of other group members. Concurrently she can learn to reconnect with herself and others in the same moment.

HOW THE SPECIFIC TECHNIQUES OF PSYCHODRAMA WORK IN TRAUMA RESOLUTION

Doubling: Doubling gives protagonists a sense of being supported as they face threatening personal material or as they revisit their own traumatic past through role-play. When once they may have felt alone and helpless, they now have a therapeutic ally in the face of a painful situation. A sense of "feeling doubled" and seen from the inside can be very healing to people who felt alone, unseen or suffered a loss of attachment that left them feeling empty and detached from others.

Spiraling: Spiraling is particularly useful in the resolution of reenactment dynamics. By linking present-day problems with their origins, clients are able to choose between blindly (unconsciously) reenacting past pain and making new choices as to how to behave. Their transferences and projections that stem from trauma can begin to be clarified as they trace them back to their roots through spiraling. (See Spiraling, page 259.)

Stand-ins or the Mirror Technique: These can provide some therapeutic distance so the protagonists feel less threatened approaching painful scenes. Viewing a conflict from the outside may allow protagonists the emotional and psychological distance to "unhook" from their knee-jerk responses and gain insight that might be unavailable to them in the heat of the moment. It can also allow them to "talk to themselves" from the perspective of today and gain some empathy for themselves. Or they can move in and out of the scene in a more controlled fashion through doubling or role reversal.

Interview: The initial interview is used to gather material that is relevant to the situation being explored. This can occur before the enactment. Or the protagonist can be interviewed in role. The protagonist can also be interviewed in role reversal, i.e., the daughter can reverse roles with her mother and be questioned "as the mother," deepening, through her spontaneous response, her understanding of her mother's role and giving voice to the introjected mother in order to gain awareness of how the mother may have been internalized into the self-system.

Role Reversal: Often survivors of trauma feel at fault, as if bad things happened to them because they are in some way bad themselves. Role reversal enables them to experience the complexities, needs, drives and motivations of another person, perhaps the person who hurt them. This helps the protagonist depersonalize the abuse and understand that the abuser may have abused anyone who was in the protagonist's position, and it opens the door to understanding the humanity of the other person.

RECONSTRUCTIVE EXPERIENCES BUILT INTO THE METHOD OF PSYCHODRAMA

The Reformed Auxiliary: The reformed auxiliary offers a representation through role-play of the relationship as it is wished for (reformed) by the protagonist. For example, protagonists can choose the father they would have liked to have and interact with that person. Some people need to experience being engaged in a particular way or even physically held. While it may be inappropriate for the therapist to be this person, an auxiliary ego can be chosen to give this experience to a protagonist.

The Reconstructive Scene: Protagonists can role-play a scene and experience it, first as it was and then reconstruct it as they wish it had been, thus taking in on an experiential, feeling level how they wish a situation might have occurred in their lives. From this they can form a new vision from which to operate.

Group Sharing and Identification: This both allows the protagonist to break the isolation of their pain and teaches her how to take in support from others. It also allows group members to heal through sharing and identification, or experience a "spectator catharsis."

IMPLICATIONS FOR TREATMENT

Because the types of trauma that occur in homes often constitute ruptures in relationships and often are at the hands of primary caretakers upon whom a child depends for nurturance and survival, the implications for treatment are complicated. That is, the very vehicle that will lead them eventually back to health (i.e., connection with others, relationships in therapeutic situations such as one-to-one or group therapy, or twelve-step programs) are those situations that have become fraught with pain and anxiety.

PTSD symptoms in children who grew up in traumatizing situations can lie dormant for many years. Fears of disloyalty to the family or of being ostracized for "telling the truth" can keep children not only telling a lie to the outside world but living a lie within themselves well into adulthood. This absence of talking through painful circumstances may keep traumas from being understood and placed into a healthy operational framework. Traumatic memories are often somatized, repressed, disassociated or lost to consciousness through some form of defensive exclusion (Bowlby 1973). As we've previously discussed, traumatic memory storage is at least partially associated with the parts of the brain that were formed early in man's evolution as fight, flight and freeze responses designed to preserve survival. The cortex, or the part of the brain where we think about and reflect upon what we do, was developed later in human evolution. Because of this we may have difficulty in reflecting upon, remembering or placing into a context memories related to trauma. This may manifest in therapy as resistance. Because the cortex was not fully involved in the storage of traumatic memories, those experiences may not have been thought about and put into a logical context and sequence. Consequently, they can be difficult to access through reflective talking alone.

Children learn through their senses. Their brain/body sensorial apparatus develops far before their thinking apparatus. As adults, we need to relate to children on a sensorial level. Most adults do this intuitively through holding, cooing, touching and playing. In treatment we oftentimes work with the "inner child." When the child within the adult gets triggered, it may want to again have a sensorial, reparative experience. Psychodrama can allow for a holding experience to occur that doesn't compromise the therapeutic patient/therapist relationship. For example, if a client is doing early childhood work and gets triggered into a trauma sense memory, it may take him a bit of time to come out of the locked position so that he can begin to describe what is going on inside of himself. The fluidity of a healing process that does not deny physical movement as a part of the process can actually allow the client to literally move toward a fuller expression of his inner world. He can be guided by his senses, act upon his act hungers and reveal himself to himself and to the group, layer by layer.

If working with actual children, treatment should be age-related and use mediums that are appropriate to their developmental capabilities. Painting, drawing, dance, music and drama can be ways of expressing the trauma that are useful and natural to children as well as for the child within the adult. We never really outgrow our need for vibrant, sensorial experience. Our adult organism continues to need and get soothed and regulated through experiences of movement, touch, art and music. This makes the creative arts therapies ideally suited for the treatment of trauma if appropriately used.

TREATING TRAUMA ON A CONTINUUM

There is no singular approach to treating trauma and the way that any five people experience even the same trauma can differ. The symptoms of trauma need to be seen on a continuum.

Over the past few decades much has been learned about trauma that has affected the mental-health field significantly. As the symptoms of trauma became known and understood, mental-health professionals in the United States and abroad recognized these symptoms in their own treatment populations. In the addictions field we cannot help but recognize the symptoms of trauma in our own population. But though we generalize the symptoms of war trauma to other mental-health populations, we cannot generalize the severity and intensity. The PTSD symptoms developed by living in a war zone for years, along with all that implies in terms of personal and family disorganization and loss, will not be the same, for example, as those in the person who grew up in an addicted home but was surrounded by a stable, caring society.

Symptoms, as well as treatment, need to be seen on a continuum. As we apply this research to our own populations we need to recognize that the severity of the symptoms may vary considerably, along with a client's ability to tolerate different forms of treatment. A previous history of traumatization is a key factor in assessing trauma's impact, along with the severity of the stressor and each individual's biological makeup and support network and the stage or stages of development at the time the trauma occurred (Krystal 1968).

In addition, the type of treatment for one phase of recovery may differ from what can be tolerated at another stage. We see this every day in addiction treatment. The type of treatment an addict can tolerate in the first few weeks after putting down his substance is very different from what he can tolerate six months, a year or even two years later. To put an addict who has just come off cocaine into group therapy that is intense and highly arousing may be too stimulating and can lead to relapse. In early recovery he may need the equivalent of a recovery room after surgery; where things are calm, highly regulated and supportive. Slowly, as he develops the ability to tolerate strong feelings and his limbic system becomes more regulated, his needs evolve. That same addict a year or two into sobriety may find that early sobriety group not stimulating or challenging enough. He may need the intensity of another kind of group that is less rigidly structured, more challenging, and deals with issues that extend beyond sobriety into family of origin and interpersonal dynamics. It can be advisable for addicts to wait until they are established well enough in their sobriety so that revisiting intensely painful material can be tolerated without self-medication.

In the case of serious trauma and/or abuse, it is important that therapists be aware of what might overly stimulate their clients, causing them to shut down, comply and be helpful, or act out as a way of removing themselves from the heat of the moment. These dynamics are often present in group work, but an awareness on the part of the therapist is important so she helps clients learn to track their own responses as they occur.

DEVELOPING A SAFE-ENOUGH CONTAINER

My own clients who fare the best have several components to their therapy life. They are:

- Group psychotherapy
- One-to-one psychotherapy
- Twelve-step programs
- Treatment programs where indicated

These elements comprise the basic container that I request my clients create.

Clients who use all of these forms of help generally fare better than those who don't. This container, in my own practice, has the highest cure rate in maintaining sobriety and reducing symptoms of PTSD. The extensions of this container that I also try to encourage are:

- Involvement in meaningful outside activities that can provide a sense of passion and purpose.
- Activities that bring pleasure and connection with others.
- Exercise and meditation or centering-type activities.
- Body work and massage.
- Good nutrition.
- Abstention from acting out with substances and/or behaviors.
- Spirituality in whatever form works for the client. (This can help clients make positive meaning out of pain.)

The kinds of traumas we work with in the mental health field can vary dramatically. If issues of PTSD are being addressed in group it is generally important that the client is also in one-to-one so they can further process and integrate the material that is being aroused. Without this one-to-one relationship, the material that gets stimulated may not have the opportunity to get the attention it deserves for processing and integration. It is simply impossible to track all the subtle responses that a trauma survivor may experience in the course of participating in a group. The group, in general, is very useful in breaking patterns of isolation, learning to take in support from others and learning from others. However, the group is also stimulating, and therein lies the rub: how to have enough stimulation so the body can wake up and enter the here and now but not so much that it wants to shut down again. When I have asked clients to tell me why they find psychodrama especially useful to them, they have offered a range of responses: "I have trouble getting to what's inside me; when I can see it, I'm far enough away so I feel safe and I don't have to run; then I can work with what it brings up." "I know it's not real, so I feel safe enough to sit through anger here, but I can't at work, for example; I wanna run." "I can process all the weird sensations I feel in my body when I get 'freaked,'" "I can get a picture of somebody else's life and I can identify." "It helps me to say stuff and do stuff I'd never say and do otherwise." "It helps me put the pieces together, to understand what happened." Somehow reviewing painful, even traumatic material on a clinical stage, with therapeutic surrogates, a therapist/director and a world that has been designated as apart from reality, allows clients to view reality from a safer distance, one in which they can learn to see it differently.

The combination of group and one-to-one therapy covers broad territory that mirrors development. The group mirrors the family dynamic, and the one-to-one relationship mirrors the parent-child relationship. When people attempt to resolve deep trauma-related issues only in group it can mirror their experience of never getting enough in their family of origin, of needing and not getting, or disappearing and complying in order to gain acceptance and a sense of belonging. It is important to have a place to go that is all theirs where they have access to the kind of support and help with working through the issues of transference that inevitably arise with a caring adult or parent figure. On the other hand, one-to-one therapy can be frustrating if it never stimulates enough of the somatic memory associated with trauma. If this never becomes aroused and processed, it's as if the body never wakes up, and the client simply learns to tell a story about her experiences but remains detached. Also, one-to-one therapy cannot always fully address the types of relational and narcissistic issues that become mobilized and evident in groups.

Twelve-step programs can provide a "holding environment" that is available throughout the week and on weekends that is a very important part of an overall healing container and mirrors connection with a broader community. A combination of one-to-one and group therapy, along with other extensions of treatment such as twelve-step work, body work, exercise, nutrition and peaceful activities, seems to provide a framework for recovery that has the best chance of working. However, it is an approach that can easily be built into the recovery life of a client, in or outside of a treatment facility, by encouraging the recovering client to incorporate activities such as yoga, body work, massage, twelve-step programs, exercise, hobbies and connecting with an activity, work-related or otherwise, in which they experience pleasure, purpose and passion.

What Constitutes a Traumatic Event?

According to the American Psychiatric Association's *Diagnostic and Statistical Manual of Mental Disorders, IV*, a traumatic event involves "direct personal experience of an event that involved actual or threatened death or serious injury, or other threat to one's physical integrity; or witnessing an event that involved actual or threatened death or serious injury, or other threat to one's physical integrity; or witnessing an event that involves death, injury or threat to the physical integrity of another person; or learning about unexpected or violent death, serious harm or threat of death or injury experienced by a family member or other close associate. . . . The person's response to the event must involve intense fear, helplessness, or horror (or in children, the response must involve disorganized or agitated behavior.)" I would include extreme numbing here. I would also emphasize that the types of trauma that occur within the home when there is a power imbalance and children are dependent upon parents with little access to outside support and a vulnerable developmental level can also be traumatic and lead to PTSD and the tendency to engage in and repeat traumatic bonds.

This can occur as a result of any of the following:

- car accident
- natural disaster (earthquake, flood, hurricane, fire, storm, etc.)
- home or workplace fire
- workplace accident/violence
- hospitalization
- childhood abuse
- robbery or assault
- being held hostage
- rape
- military combat
- airline crash
- injury to self or a loved one
- loss of a loved one
- domestic violence
- relationship trauma (my addition)

Common Reactions to Traumatic Stress

Although the actual cluster of symptoms experienced by any individual will vary, the following two lists include common reactions experienced following exposure to a traumatic event. Gradually, a traumatized person will alternate between two distinct phases of hyperarousal and avoidance.

The hyperarousal can be expressed through symptoms of:

- nightmares
- recurrent and intrusive thoughts about the event
- intense psychological distress and/or physiological hyperreactivity when exposed to stimuli either internal or external that symbolize or resemble an aspect of the traumatic event
- flashbacks
- unusual muscle tension or tightness
- suddenly acting or feeling as though the event were happening in the present
- difficulty concentrating
- a free-floating sense of anxiety
- sleep problems—difficulty falling or staying asleep
- hypervigilance—waiting for the other shoe to drop
- problems with anger—irritability, outbursts of anger
- exaggerated startle response—overreacting to sudden noises in the environment or cues that were previously not bothersome

Avoidance may be manifested by:
- attempts made to avoid thoughts or feelings associated with the trauma
- attempts made to avoid activity or situations that arouse recollections of the trauma
- inability to recall an important aspect of the event
- restricted range of feelings (e.g., feeling numb, spaced out, unable to have love feelings)
- feeling detached or estranged from others
- sleep problems—difficulty falling or staying asleep (to avoid nightmares associated with the event)
- markedly decreased interest in pleasurable activities
- a sense of a foreshortened future (e.g., do not expect to have a career, marriage, children or a long life)

For most people these symptoms will significantly subside within a period of thirty days with complete disappearance of nearly all symptoms in a few months. For others, these reactions will persist, and the resulting disruption of day-to-day functioning can become chronic. At this point, if the person experiencing the symptoms has enough to constitute a diagnosis, they may be given the diagnosis of PTSD. Some people with PTSD are greatly impaired in their functioning while others seem to function reasonably well as long as they avoid stimuli that trigger the emotions and thinking that relates to the trauma and impairs their functioning.

In resolving trauma we need to understand the full impact of the event or events on our lives. This may have involved losing a sense of safety or having the world feel like a safe place, having ruptured relationships, or a loss of trust and faith. Emotions surrounding and associated with events are activated in recovery, and language is developed to both label the emotions and describe the meaning they have had within the self. It can be difficult to know whether memories are accurate representations of past traumas.

Memories may be stored as:

- fragments of dreams that were symbolic of emotional conflicts
- screen memories/memories that defend or cover up the more distressing details of the event
- memories that are distorted by a desire to see the situation or individual in a different light; sometimes this manifests as idealization
- memories of trauma witnessed that actually happened to someone else
- memories that are vague or distorted through dissociative defenses used to cope during the trauma

FACTORS AFFECTING THE DURATION AND SEVERITY OF THE TRAUMA RESPONSE

1. *The severity and duration of the stressor*
   How intense and how long was the stressful situation?
2. *Genetic predisposition*
   Central nervous system (CNS) reacts differently in different people.
3. *Developmental phase*
   An adult with a firm sense of identity and a good support system is infinitely better protected than a child with less-advanced cognitive skills.

4. *A person's social support system*

Disruption or loss of social support is intimately associated with inability to overcome the effects of psychological trauma. Children are particularly vulnerable to this when the very people on whom they depend for safety and nurturance physically, emotionally or sexually abuse them.

5. *Prior traumatization*

People with a prior history of traumatization are more likely to develop long-term symptomatology in response to later trauma.

6. *Preexisting personality*

People with preexisting, untreated phobias and maladaptions to stressful life circumstances are seven to eight times more likely to have psychiatric reactions to trauma (Krystal 1987).

7. *Ability to flee*

The ability to get away from the stressor is critical in whether or not PTSD develops (van der Kolk 2004).

The response to psychological trauma can be biphasic reliving and denial with alternating numbing responses (van der Kolk 1987). In other words, the traumatized person cycles between reliving aspects of the trauma, then denying its impact and shutting down or numbing out. Some further reactions to trauma are:

Warning Signs of Unresolved Trauma

- Risk-taking behavior
- Desire to self-medicate with alcohol or drugs
- Chronic or recurring depression or feelings of despair
- Emotional constriction/lack of affect and spontaneity
- Drive to recreate painful emotional relationship or life dynamics
- Loss of ability to modulate emotion
- Inability to take in support
- Psychosomatic symptoms
- Hypervigilance
- Black-and-white thinking/feeling/behavior

- Sudden bouts of anger and rage
- Reenactment dynamics: Seemingly voluntary reenactment of situations reminiscent of the original trauma, or repetition compulsion as an attempt to gain mastery over the original trauma and feel powerful rather than helpless or restore a compromised sense of self.

SELF-TEST FOR TRAUMA RESOLUTION

TRAUMA SELF-TEST

Rate each item from 1–10, with 1 meaning the item never applies to you and 10 meaning the item is highly applicable.

1. Do you have a hard time envisioning your future?
2. Do you experience flashbacks or nightmares that are reminiscent of your trauma or are otherwise upsetting?
3. Do you experience intrusive thoughts related to your trauma(s)?
4. Do you feel emotionally constricted; is it hard for you to feel freely?
5. Do you have bouts of depression and despair that do not resolve themselves within a reasonable length of time?
6. Are you constantly waiting for the bottom to fall out; do you mistrust calm and orderly living?
7. Do you have trouble trusting in intimate relationships?
8. Do you tend to go from 1 to 10 in your emotional life and have trouble staying on middle ground?
9. Do you feel you recreate the same problems over and over again, getting stuck in the same place?
10. Do you have trouble identifying what you really feel?
11. Do your feeings evidence themselves as body sensations, such as headaches, stomachaches or backaches instead of as conscious feelings?
12. Do you have larger-than-appropriate emotional reactions when some sort of situation or interaction triggers you?
13. Do you have trouble taking in help and support from others?

14. Do you isolate and have trouble being in community?

15. Do you feel guilty when your life improves?

16. Do you self-medicate your feelings or try to alter your mood with drugs, alcohol, food, sex, spending or other "ism's"?

17. Do you engage in high-risk behaviors in order to "feel alive"?

18. Do you experience more anxiety than you feel is normal?

19. Do you find yourself avoiding situations that are reminiscent of your trauma(s)?

©2004 *Tian Dayton,* The Living Stage

THE TRAUMA TIME LINE

GOALS:

1. To bring to consciousness how trauma breeds trauma.

2. To connect related traumas so that one can see the full impact not just of one traumatic event, but of a string of related traumas.

3. To put life experience back into context and place traumatic experiences into real time.

STEPS:

1. Ask participants to draw a time line of their lives.

2. Draw bisecting lines to represent five-year intervals.

3. Ask group members to recall events, situations or behaviors from their families that have felt traumatic to them. Have them locate these events in the appropriate place along the time line.

4. Share the time lines and invite clients to make observations as to what they see in their own time lines.

5. Continue with sharing and processing. The Trauma Time Line, followed by sharing, is complete in and of itself, since the real goal is to see the interrelatedness, context and patterns of the traumas. However, you can choose to continue, using one of the variations listed below.

VARIATIONS:

The Trauma Time Line can be used as a warm-up to psychodrama. In this case, ask participants which part of themselves they may wish to talk to, and do a vignette between the self today and the self represented in the time line. The time line can also be used as a full intrapsychic drama. Participants can choose role-players to represent the self at all of the ages presented and then talk to whichever auxiliaries they feel warmed up to, reversing roles and then reversing back to the self today and continuing to move along the time line into the present. If this is done, place cards on the floor with numbers on them representing five-year intervals and place the role-players accordingly. (See *tiandayton.com* for download of time line or consult Dayton 2000).

The Trauma Time Line tends to reveal some of the following: How traumas actually occurred in real time; did many occur in a short time period or were they spread out over time; how those traumas may have fueled repetitive dysfunctional behavior patterns or reenactment patterns; and how a client's life may have changed after a trauma occurred. This is a self-diagnostic tool that clients do as a paper-and-pencil exercise and then share or move into action. It allows both client and therapist to gain much information and insight as to how trauma may have affected a client.

SPECTROGRAM FOR ASSESSING PTSD ISSUES

GOALS:

1. To allow group members to become aware of the PTSD issues they may carry.

2. To create group cohesion and build trust.

STEPS:

1. Designate one side of the room as representing "very much" or 100 percent and the other as "very little" or 0 percent.

2. Ask group members to locate themselves on a spectrogram at the point that best describes where they are in relationship to any or all of these characteristics—where they are on the continuum of their own trauma response or resolution, e.g., "How much depression do you feel in relationship to this issue or in general?" Choose the characteristics that the group wishes to explore or that the therapist feels are most relevant to the group's current needs:

- Learned helplessness
- Depression
- Emotional constriction
- Traumatic bonding
- Easily triggered
- High-risk behaviors

- Distorted reasoning
- Loss of ability to modulate emotion
- Loss of trust and faith
- Hypervigilance
- Loss of ability to take in caring and support
- Disorganized inner world
- Survival guilt
- Development of rigid psychological defenses
- Desire to self-medicate
- Other _____

3. Invite group members to share a sentence or two about why they are standing where they are standing.
4. Repeat this process for as many times as it feels useful to the group.
5. Ask group members to walk over to someone who said something that resonated with them, place a hand on their shoulder and share with him or her what it was.
6. After all questions have been explored that the group wishes to explore, the group can move into psychodramatic work or return to their seats for further sharing and processing.

VARIATIONS:

The purpose of this exercise is to place the locus of control within group members in terms of identifying where they are on the continuum in relationship to symptoms and to educate them as to what those symptom might be. In addition, because trauma is on a continuum, individuals will vary considerably in how they experience even the same symptom, depending on previously identified factors. The spectrogram allows clients to assess themselves. They may move around if they change their minds as to where they belong as sharing progresses.

It is up to the clinician to ascertain whether or not this exercise is useful for their particular group. The concern is that clients in early recovery may become overwhelmed with the feeling that there is too much wrong with them to fix. The advantage is they may receive support and identification around the idea that they are not alone and that many people from painful family backgrounds carry unresolved issues that caused them to self-medicate. It is a psycho-educational approach in which clients can learn about symptoms of trauma and addiction and process what comes up as they do.

To add journaling to this spectrogram, ask participants to identify an area in which they feel they have unfinished business and write a journal entry from that place within themselves, unraveling their thinking, and emotion.

SPIRALING: A PSYCHODRAMATIC APPROACH
TO TRAUMA RESOLUTION

GOALS:

1. To provide an experiential vehicle for resolution of past issues that may be impinging on life in the here and now.
2. To experientially separate the past from the present.
3. To link conflicts in the present day to their origins in the past.
4. To provide an experiential vehicle for confronting and working through fears or anxieties attached to anticipated future events.

STEPS:

1. Invite the group to share about conflicts they may be experiencing in their current lives. When an appropriate issue presents itself in group and use this technique to work with it.
2. When the issue has presented itself, ask who would like to move the work toward psychodramatic enactment.
3. Set the scene and proceed with the enactment of the present-day conflict. When transferential material becomes clear (what is being projected onto present-day relationships, creating a conflictual set of feelings within the protagonist that repeats itself in his life) ask, "When have you felt this way before? And with whom?"
4. When the protagonist answers that question, freeze the present-day scene then spiral back to the origin or root scene (what Moreno would call the *status nascendi*). Choose role-players to represent the people with whom the protagonist previously felt this way.
5. Work through the issues concretized in the root scene or *status nascendi* psychodramatically. Allow adequate time and space for the protagonist to experience a sense of resolution and new insight to bring closure to the root issue. This will likely be the longest enactment.
6. Spiral back to the present-day scene. Revisit the scene again psychodramatically and role-play the scene. The protagonist will naturally bring new insight and awareness that will likely alter the dynamic or his perception of it in some ways.
7. When this scene is finished, return to the group for sharing.

VARIATIONS:

Spiraling allows a client to begin to separate the past from the present and identify sources of transferences that may be affecting current life situations.

At any point a scene may be stilled so the protagonist can process the subtle goings on of their inner world or somatic reactions and the director can check in with them. This need not be formalized. The group will naturally adjust to the slowing down as it witnesses the director taking the time to tune in on the protagonist and see how that allows the protagonist to move through his own frozen spaces and come to awareness of what emotion, thought and action is coming alive. A stand-in may be used to represent the protagonist if desired, and the protagonist can codirect with the director, double for himself or reverse roles in and out of the scene.

PSYCHODRAMATIC JOURNALING WITH THE SPIRAL

If you are not sufficiently trained in psychodrama to feel comfortable and competent carrying out a spiral, you can employ a variation of this exercise using journaling.

STEPS:

1. Invite the group to warm up by sharing as outlined in step one of the previous exercise, Spiraling.
2. Instead of choosing a protagonist, give group members ten minutes or so to journal about the present-day life situation that repeats itself (see Journaling, chapter 12).
3. Have group members gather in small clusters or subgroups to share what has been written. Allow people to group naturally or sociometrically rather than forcing them, in any way, into a group.
4. Invite group members to visualize a situation from the past where they have experienced these types of dynamics or feelings before.
5. Allow seven to ten minutes for the whole group to journal about that scene.
6. Have clients return to subgroups and share their journaling.
7. After sharing is finished, invite group members to journal once again, but this time focus the journaling on what they learned from exploring the past root scene. Ask them, "What do you understand today that you didn't understand then?" "What choices are

you aware of now that you were unaware of before?" and, "What new behaviors might you try beginning now that could affect or alter your situation?" "What could you say to yourself then from where you stand today?"

VARIATIONS:

Groups may also spiral from present day to future scenes then back to present day again.

The Resonance of Traum

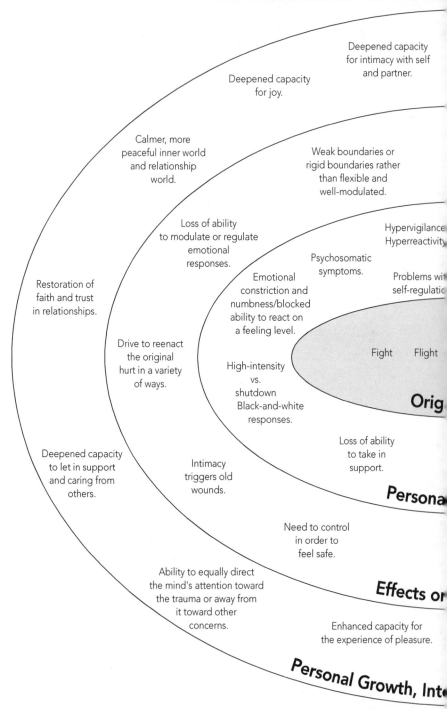

Deepened capacity
for intimacy with self
and partner.

Deepened capacity
for joy.

Calmer, more
peaceful inner world
and relationship
world.

Weak boundaries or
rigid boundaries rather
than flexible and
well-modulated.

Loss of ability
to modulate or regulate
emotional
responses.

Hypervigilance
Hyperreactivity

Psychosomatic
symptoms.

Restoration of
faith and trust
in relationships.

Emotional
constriction and
numbness/blocked
ability to react on
a feeling level.

Problems wit
self-regulatic

Drive to reenact
the original
hurt in a variety
of ways.

High-intensity
vs.
shutdown
Black-and-white
responses.

Fight   Flight

Orig

Deepened capacity
to let in support
and caring from
others.

Intimacy
triggers old
wounds.

Loss of ability
to take in
support.

Persona

Need to control
in order to
feel safe.

Ability to equally direct
the mind's attention toward
the trauma or away from
it toward other
concerns.

Effects or

Enhanced capacity for
the experience of pleasure.

Personal Growth, Int

om Hurt to Healing

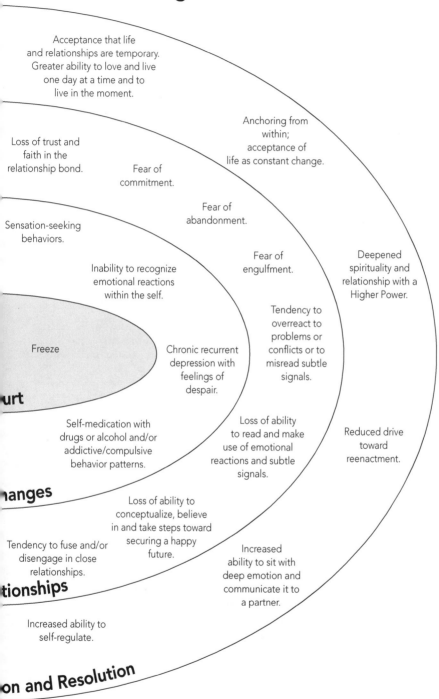

Acceptance that life and relationships are temporary. Greater ability to love and live one day at a time and to live in the moment.

Anchoring from within; acceptance of life as constant change.

Loss of trust and faith in the relationship bond.

Fear of commitment.

Fear of abandonment.

Sensation-seeking behaviors.

Fear of engulfment.

Deepened spirituality and relationship with a Higher Power.

Inability to recognize emotional reactions within the self.

Tendency to overreact to problems or conflicts or to misread subtle signals.

Freeze

Chronic recurrent depression with feelings of despair.

urt

Self-medication with drugs or alcohol and/or addictive/compulsive behavior patterns.

Loss of ability to read and make use of emotional reactions and subtle signals.

Reduced drive toward reenactment.

anges

Loss of ability to conceptualize, believe in and take steps toward securing a happy future.

Tendency to fuse and/or disengage in close relationships.

Increased ability to sit with deep emotion and communicate it to a partner.

tionships

Increased ability to self-regulate.

on and Resolution

artwounds 1997

14 Getting the Self Back: Grief, Mourning and Moving Through Loss

Loss is a natural part of life, and there is nothing to do, oftentimes, but process it, accept it, experience and integrate the often painful emotions surrounding it and move on. There is a growing body of research suggesting that intervention is not necessarily beneficial in all situations of loss. Feeling grief is a natural occurrence when we lose someone we care about; it is a testimony to our ability to become meaningfully attached and is not pathological or unnatural. A major new study entitled "Report on Bereavement and Grief Research," prepared by the Center for the Advancement of Health concluded:

"A growing body of evidence indicates that interventions with adults who are not experiencing complicated grief cannot be regarded as beneficial in terms of diminishing grief-related symptoms. . . . In fact, the studies indicate, grief counseling may sometimes make matters worse for those who lost people they loved, regardless of whether the death was traumatic or occurred after a long illness, according to Dr. John Jordan, director of the Family Loss Project in the Boston area. Such people may include the only man in a group of women, a young person in a group of older people, or someone recently bereaved in a group that includes a person still suffering intensely a year or more after the loved one's death.

Further, the research suggests, bereavement counseling is least needed in the immediate aftermath of a loss. Yet it is then that most grieving people are invited to take part in the offered services. A more appropriate time is six to eighteen months later, if the person is still suffering intensely (Brody 2004). The researchers found that the care and comfort offered by friends and relatives proved to be the most beneficial and helpful to those who were going through a loss. Unless the loss is complicated, most people can work through their loss, even though it is painful and difficult. And men and women tend to grieve differently, which can also influence how they experience grief counseling. Women, for example, prefer to focus on emotional issues, while men like to focus on their process of thinking. In my own clinical work I find that over time men also like to process emotionally and women focus on thinking. Their emphasis and point of departure may be different but eventually both groups often want to address their full inner picture.

Clients who experience loss while in treatment, in my experience, benefit from having their feelings of loss recognized and understood but vary after that point as to how much attention they wish to devote to the loss or benefit from working with it.

COMPLICATED LOSS

Complicated loss is different from normal grieving. Those with painful histories, for example, may find the loss of a loved one or a job very hard to tolerate. They may sink into feelings of hopelessness that are more pervasive and persistent than the hopeless feelings that are considered a part of a normal grieving process.

When the loss begins to evidence symptoms of complication, that is, when a current loss triggers painful emotional states from previous losses that have gone ungrieved or are overwhelming in nature, mourning may be complicated and need attention. People in recovery from addiction and codependency, or those who have experienced previous traumatization, may be especially vulnerable to becoming symptomatic over current life losses because of the cumulative effect of their painful histories. Unresolved grief can fuel addiction.

Warning Signs of Unresolved Grief

- Excessive guilt
- Excessive anger/sudden angry outbursts
- Recurring or long-lasting depression
- Caretaking behavior
- Self-mutilation
- Emotional numbness or constriction
- Chronic relationship issues

Disenfranchised Loss

Some losses are more socially acceptable than others. In the case of socially acceptable losses there is a natural support from the surrounding community, and the person experiencing the loss tends to feel entitled to her feelings of pain and grief. But what about the losses that are less obvious, that we bring upon ourselves such as with divorcing a spouse, getting sober, moving or sending children off to college? These losses also contain emotions that may be painful to feel and process. In addition, we may experience conflicting feelings such as sadness *and* joy, excitement *and* fear, or pain *and* relief. This can create an emotional dissonance or ambivalence that makes the loss difficult to process. A surprisingly large number of life events go ungrieved and thus they become disenfranchised. Some examples of these losses are:

- The effects of divorce on spouses, children and the family as a unit.
- Dysfunction in the home, loss of family life or parental attention.
- Addiction, loss of periods of one's life to using and abusing.
- Loss of the addictive substance or behavior.
- Loss of job, health, youth, children in the home, retirement, life transitions

Disenfranchised losses often do not get grieved. Unlike a loss to death, there is no funeral to acknowledge and honor the loss, no grave to visit, no covered dishes dropped at the door, nor sitting in the company of fellow mourners and supporting each other through the tears. These losses live in unmarked graves within the unconscious of individuals and family systems who often avoid discussing them for fear of causing eruptions. This can lead to a loss of authentic connection with the self and within intimate relationships. Pain becomes covert rather than overt. It vibrates beneath the thin membrane separating the conscious from the unconscious at moments of connection, celebration or stress.

If we cannot mourn these types of losses, we may:

• Stay stuck in unresolved anger and pain which can fuel addiction, depression etc.
• Lose access to important parts of our inner, feeling world.
• Have trouble engaging in new relationships because we are still actively in a relationship with a person or situation no longer present.
• Project unfelt, unresolved grief onto any situation, placing those feelings where they do not belong.
• Lose personal history along with the unmourned person or situation; a part of us dies, too.
• Carry deep fears of subsequent loss or abandonment.

ADDICTION AND GRIEF

Addiction can be a form of pathological mourning. Addicts, ACOAs, codependents and those who have lived with trauma experience issues of disenfranchised loss related to living with addiction that need to be examined. One of the pervading symptoms of PTSD both in soldiers and those who have experienced some form of physical, sexual or emotional abuse, neglect or living with addiction, is the desire to self-medicate with drugs or alcohol (van der Kolk 1987).

Addiction itself, along with codependency, leaves much grief and loss in its wake. People abusing substances have been able to medicate pain associated with grief, often for many years. Many have experienced emotional damage and have relied on a substance to deaden their pain. When they put down their medicators and live sober lives, that pain often reasserts itself. Initially the addict may feel renewed hope and self-esteem from becoming sober, what psychoanalysts refer to as a "flight into health." But as reality sets in, issues that have been pushed aside in addiction may emerge, and this can be discouraging and lead to feelings of helplessness and hopelessness. Furthermore, the emotions they arouse may be confusing because they may reach back years, even decades, in the life of the addict or recovering person. Without the coping strategy of self-medication, sober addicts will need to summon the strength to live through the pain that previously felt like too much to tolerate. To make matters tougher still, they will be grieving these issues with a weakened set of psychological and emotional tools. For these and other reasons, grief is widely accepted as an issue that needs to be addressed during recovery. Clients may need to grieve the lives they have lost through addiction, lost time or lost years that they could have devoted to getting their lives in order. Along with this is grieving the pain those they love have experienced in their relationships. The instillation of hope, and engaging the client with a recovery zeal and network, therefore become very important. The client needs a solid support environment to sustain himself through this period. Learning about the grief process and doing some initial work with it can be informative and relieving. Psychodrama can offer a way to work with these overwhelming emotions when they surface. Oftentimes, treatment programs get legitimately concerned that addressing powerful issues of grief could undermine sobriety. However, not addressing them opens the door to relapse when they eventually do emerge. Some teaching on the grief process can actually normalize grief for clients, so that when it does come up it is somewhat less derailing. It is generally recommended that sobriety be established before these feelings are worked with experientially but exceptions can be made according to the needs of the client.

How Can Psychodrama and Sociometry Help in Resolving Grief?

Psychodrama and sociometry provide an alternative form of ritual for the kinds of losses that all too often go unrecognized and unacknowledged. They are extraordinarily helpful in processing grief. For example, psychodrama's ability to concretize what has been lost gives it a unique advantage over other forms of therapy. The psyche wants to see and touch loss with all the senses in order to process and integrate it. But as with so many losses in life, there is nobody, no specific person, to point to. Millions of dollars are often spent trying to locate the bodies of lost loved ones so we can mourn them. This yearning to concretize the object of loss on a sensorial level appears to be a deep, psychic need, without which the minds and hearts search without settling. When we cannot locate or deal directly with an object of grief, we all too often create one, projecting our feelings of loss and pain where they do not belong. Clients may feel they have no right, for example, to mourn the loss of a problematic relationship, be it a parent, spouse, addict or abusive person, because they are "better off without him." They may have conflicting feelings of love *and* hate, guilt *and* relief that they don't know what to do with or may feel conflicted about. But painful and complicated relationships can be hard to let go of because there is so much unfinished business connected with them. Psychodrama fills this emotional vacuum by giving the mourner the possibility of connecting and dealing with that which has been lost, sensorially and in the here and now. If an addict has lost a period of his own life he can choose someone to role-play himself and talk directly to, and as, that lost part of self. If a child of divorce feels that he has lost the security, love and comfort of a family that is no longer united, he can concretize that lost family on the stage and process those feelings. Or if a client cannot seem to let go of a stage of life, she can concretize the parts of that stage she yearns for, encounter them in their concrete form, and explore the hold they have on her. Misery seeks an object. Psychodrama allows for the concretization of an object, person or place to deal with. When a loved one is lost, people are sometimes haunted by what they never got a chance to say. In psychodrama they can say it; then they can reverse roles and speak back to themselves and hear the words they need to heal their hearts. Even if the words they long to hear would not have been said in reality, their power to mend a broken heart cannot be denied. Allowing clients to have what their souls yearns for, to actually experience hearing what they long to hear, even from a surrogate, can break through emotional barriers erected to ward off pain and open the door for healing. It can create a new template for accepting love and caring from others that they may otherwise block.

CREATING LIVING RITUALS: STAGES OF THE GRIEF PROCESS

Grief rituals are themselves inherently psychodramatic. Psychodrama allows us to construct living rituals to address all forms of loss so that those carrying the complicated feelings associated with losses of all kinds can process them and move toward resolution. Psychodrama and sociometry are useful in resolving grief in some of the following ways. They:

- Provide concrete closure.
- Give voice to words that went unspoken.
- Allow for catharsis of abreaction to express emotion and engage in the grief process, and a catharsis of integration of split-off or unfelt emotion.
- Facilitate the experience of grief so that a loss can be integrated and new meaning can be made about the loss and new insight arrived at.

Jonathon Bowlby, in his seminal research on attachment and loss, outlined four stages that humans go through during loss. I have added a fifth stage.

Numbness: Psychodrama and sociometry can help clients to get in touch with their inner worlds. Numbness and shock are a very natural stage of loss that should be respected and not pushed. It is unwise to force anyone into premature grief. However, eventually, a person will need to experience blocked emotion to regain connection to self.

Yearning and searching: Psychodrama and sociometry can concretize what one is unconsciously yearning and searching for by bringing it from the semiconscious state onto the stage in concrete form. Words that were not spoken can be spoken. Clients can deal with real rather than imagined representations of what they yearn for.

Disorganization, anger, despair: Withheld anger or rage is hard on the body and can fuel depression. Through role-play, psychodrama and sociometry allow anger to surface in a clinical environment where it can be experienced, expressed, and then processed and understood. Feelings of despair and unfelt sadness can surface and be felt, then integrated back into the self-system.

Reorganization, integration: Psychodrama and sociometry allow for the safe experiencing of split-off emotion so it can be reintegrated into the self-system. Thus, the loss is processed and the self becomes reorganized to include it. New awareness grows out of processing rather than numbing, medicating or dissociating from strong feelings.

Reinvestment: Psychological and emotional energy, having been freed up, can be reinvested in life and relationships. Psychodrama and sociometry, through group process, provide countless opportunities to learn to relate to people differently and search for new, adequate responses to previously baffling situations. They also allow for role-training new behaviors within the group, which can then be used later in life experiences.

Though these stages appear in order, they do not occur in order, nor should they necessarily. Working with these stages both sociometrically and psychodramatically (see Locogram on Stages of Grief, page 112) gives fluidity to the stages. Group members can hover between stages, skip some and zig-zag between others. In addition, there is the ever-present category of "other" in the grief locogram, allowing group members to tailor their particular responses to their own needs rather than try to fit their experiences of grieving into a prescribed category.

Inadequate Attempts at Dealing with Grief

The following are some attempts to deal with or manage grief that do not necessarily lead to satisfactory resolution and integration:

Premature resolution: This is when people try to force themselves to resolve grief without allowing themselves to move through the full cycle of mourning. In these cases, the unresolved feelings tend to come out sideways in the form of projections, transferences, bursts of anger, simmering resentments, excessive criticism, excessive caretaking, bouts of depression and so on.

Pseudo-resolution: Pseudo-resolution is a false resolution that occurs when a person fools himself or herself into feeling that grief has been resolved, when it actually has not run its course.

Replacement: This is when we replace the lost person or circumstance without mourning the previous loss first. For example, the divorced person who immediately marries again may feel he or she has solved the pain of loss when, in fact, the loss has not been processed and learned from. In the case of divorce, the same issues that led to one loss tend to reappear in the next relationship.

Displacement: This occurs when mourners cannot connect their pain to what is actually causing it and instead displace the grief, upset, anger and sadness onto something or someone else—*displacing* the pain, or putting it where it does not belong. It becomes difficult to resolve the grief because it is projected onto and experienced around the wrong subject. It needs to be consciously linked back to what is actually causing it.

Possible Signs, Symptoms and Manifestations of Unresolved Grief

Note: Many of these symptoms have a range within which they are natural responses to grief. They are only a problem if they persist or interfere with a person's ability to function after a normal grieving period.

Caretaking: Displacing emotional pain, anxiety and worry onto another person rather than owning it in the self.

Sudden Angry Outbursts: Outbursts of anger and/or rage that seem inappropriate given the situation; they seem to carry the intensity of previous unresolved grief issues.

Emotional Numbness: Emotional shutdown, loss of access to feeling.

Survival Guilt: Feelings of guilt over being a survivor when someone else did not survive also can be experienced as feelings of guilt for getting out of a situation that others were unable to extricate themselves from.

Memorialization: Conscious memorialization of grief allows for closure and integration, such as a funeral, fund or gift in someone's name, or a plaque in honor of a person. This allows the griever to consciously locate the lost person. Unconcious memorialization can occur through reenactment dynamics.

Mummification: The excessive preservation of objects or a room that exactly belonged to a lost person, exactly as they were at the time of the loss.

Self-Mutilation: When a griever feels internally fragmented and disintegrated they may self-mutilate in order to manage their sense of fragmentation and despair. The sight of blood can bring the cutter back from a dissociated state.

Ghosting: Imagining one is continually seeing a lost person. Visual signals get perceived as the person for whom the griever is yearning.

Anticipatory Grief: This is grief at anticipating a coming loss. This is natural and is only considered a problem if it seriously interferes with life functioning.

GOOD-BYE, GRAM

Four weeks ago, Leonard arrived in group feeling very out of sorts. In one week his favorite grandmother had died and his assistant's wife needed surgery for a sudden accident. Just the week when he needed extra support, his workload doubled. He immediately became symptomatic. He began to smoke again after having stopped a year earlier. He was constantly finding fault with, and experiencing deep disappointment in, the same partner who had brought light and love into his life only two months before. He was having intense fantasies of acting out sexually, a self-medicating behavior that he had used for years but had been sober from for his entire relationship. He had no drink fantasies.

Leonard had not wished to do a psychodrama saying good-bye to his grandmother, which I respected. Working with the loss of a person is tricky. If you force it too soon, you may lose the person, and if you never address it, you may also lose the person. Timing seems to be everything, and there is no magic formula; it depends on the nature of the relationship, how close it is and how much life disruption surrounds the loss as well as other factors. Leonard's life was well-established in another country, the United States. He saw his grandmother perhaps once or twice a year, but his day-to-day life was lived without her. However, she was of deep symbolic importance to him. Leonard was a child of poverty who grew up with daily physical abuse. This grandmother was the one person who was kind to him. I was aware that this loss could have a kind of resonance for him that could become complicated.

The dilemma I was facing was how to give him the space he seemed to need while encouraging him to express feelings associated with the grief process, such as sadness and anger, that I felt were fueling his symptoms. After weeks of waiting, in which he talked guardedly about it but did no psychodramatic work, I felt that his symptoms were not clearing up—in fact they were worsening, approaching a danger point. I asked him if he needed anything from the group.

Leonard: No, I am fine with just checking in.

Tian: Can we help you to talk to your grandmother so you can process some of your feelings psychodramatically?

Leonard: No, I don't think so. This is fine.

Tian: Can we give you a little more help with this. After all, you have a lot on your plate.

Leonard: Well, I guess I could try something small.

Tian: Who would you like to choose to play your grandmother? (Leonard pointed at a female member of the group.)

Tian: What did you call her?

Leonard: Gram, we called her Gram.

I didn't structure a drama initially. I simply let Leonard talk from his chair, just in case he didn't wish to go further. He warmed up slowly and eventually indicated that he would like to move the scene onto the "stage."

Leonard: You are my safe house; we have a special relationship; you used to run your fingers down my back when I was a little boy, and I would spend the night at your house. I would come to you when I couldn't take my home any more. [Leonard grew up a poor boy in Brazil with only a mother who was often absent and a different grandmother who beat him daily.] You are my place to go. We are friends. I love you. [He continued to say what was on his heart, so that feelings could follow. He needed to bring her alive on the stage so that he could feel in her presence.] I miss you. I'm so scared to miss you. I don't know what I'm going to do without you; you have always been there. I can't picture the world without you in it; I don't want to. I'm so angry that you're gone. I'm so angry, I just feel so mad all the time, I don't know what to do with this feeling [he clenched his fists in a gesture of holding anger].

At this point I brought a tackle dummy for Leonard to hit to give him an opportunity to release some of the anger and rage that he kept talking about now and over the past weeks.

Leonard: No, I can't.

Tian: Okay.

Leonard: Maybe a little. [Leonard began to let something come out of him that he seemed to have been storing in his bones. Clearly deep anger was emerging, the kind that was not only about the loss of his beloved grandmother, but many other losses in his life. With little necessary encouragement, he spilled out what seemed like a ton of anger. I kept gently prodding him to add sound and words, which he did whenever possible. Eventually, when his anger was played out, he straightened up and smiled from deep inside.]

Look at me, what I have become. Look at the good and successful man your little boy became against all odds. Look at me. Be proud. Thank you, thank you, and thank you. I love you. That felt great. [The expression of anger allowed his sadness to surface and he was able to begin to attach words to previous losses, such as his loss of safety as a boy.] I was so lonely, so scared. [This turned out to be work that he gained a tremendous sense of relief from. Leonard went on to dialogue with his grandmother and ended the scene as follows.]

Tian: Say the last things you want to say for now.

Leonard: I love you, I love you, you'll always be with me, inside here [pointing to his heart]. I love you.

This was all he wished to do and all he seemed to need to do. In the following month, Leonard made a quantum leap. He reported "loving" being alone for the first time in his life. Leonard's symptoms cleared up.

GRIEF TRIGGERS

Below are some life circumstances that can trigger grief reactions. A substantial part of the reaction may be beneath the level of conscious awareness. Bringing it into consciousness helps us understand where our free-floating sense of anxiety, irritation or depressive thoughts might be coming from so that they don't emerge in problematic, unconscious ways.

Anniversary reactions: Anniversary reactions are common on or around the anniversary of a loss or death. One may feel a vague or significant sense of pain related to a loss that feels as if it is coming out of nowhere. This reaction may also be experienced around previous significant dates such as hospitalization, sickness, sobriety, death or divorce.

Holiday reactions: Holidays often stimulate pain from previous losses. Because they are traditional ritual gatherings, they heighten our awareness about what is missing or what has changed.

Age-correspondence reactions: This reaction occurs when, for example, a person reaches the age at which there was a loss by someone he or she identified with. A daughter whose mother divorced around age forty-five, for example, may find herself thinking about or even considering divorce when she reaches that approximate age. Or a parent may assume a child of twelve is having a hard time when, in truth, they were in pain around age twelve and are unconsciously projecting that pain on their twelve-year-old child.

Seasonal reactions: Change of seasons can stimulate grief or be unconsciously associated with a loss, thus causing a type of depression during a particular season.

Music-stimulated grief: Music can act as a doorway to the unconscious. It activates the right brain, which is associated with emotion, drawing out associations and feelings that get stimulated by a particular song or piece of music, or even a reminiscent sound.

Ritual-stimulated grief: Important, shared rituals can stimulate grief when there has been a loss. For example, family dinners or Sunday brunch can be a sad time for family members who have experienced divorce. Or simple rituals like reading the Sunday paper or walking around the block.

Smells: Smell is associated with the oldest part of the brain and stimulates memories.

GRIEF-RELATED EXERCISES

The following are experiential approaches to grief resolution. First are four basic techniques to use where appropriate and following are locograms, spectrograms and paper-and-pencil exercises adapted for grief resolution.

EMPTY-CHAIR EXERCISE

Ask group members to allow the person, job, aspect of self, etc., to be represented by an empty chair (or a role-player). Invite the person to freely say all that was left unsaid, to bring a feeling of closure to the relationship and to say his or her good-byes (see Saying Good-bye/Empty Chair later in this chapter).

LETTER-WRITING

Ask group members to write a letter to the person or thing they feel they have lost. Invite them to fully share any and all emotions and move toward closure. Their loss issue may require a letter to a part of themselves, a period in their own lives that they feel loss around, or a substance or behavior that they are saying good-bye to. They may also wish to write a letter that they would have wished to receive from the person, part of self, substance or behavior. See Letter Writing page 196 for complete process.

PHOTOGRAPHS

Photographs are a powerful tool for healing grief. They may be brought to group or one-to-one and used as a "near-psychodramatic" technique, "talking to," "doubling for" or "speaking as" the person in the picture. This can be done out loud or through writing next to the picture. (see Working with Photographs, page 201). A client may also wish to make a scrapbook of a stage of life that has passed, or a child who is going off to college as a way of working through letting go. In the latter case, the scrapbook can also be a gift to the departing young person, consolidating her youth and holding it in her own hands.

TRANSITIONAL OBJECTS

Transitional objects hold a sense of the presence of a person who has moved on through death, divorce or departure. Clients may wish to do a vignette or monodrama talking to a special object associated with a person, any object that holds their presence. Or clients may simply wish to bring these objects into therapy and talk about what they are feeling.

GRIEF SELF-TEST

GOALS:

This questionnaire is designed to give a person more information about his current loss and heighten his awareness of the role that unresolved grief might be playing in his life.

STEPS:

First, have the client determine the issue that is his current concern. Then ask him to answer these questions by placing a check in the box that most closely represents his experience.

Note: These questions can also be adapted to a spectrogram (see following exercise).

1. How much unresolved emotion do you feel surrounding this loss?

   ❑ Almost none   ❑ Very little   ❑ Quite a bit   ❑ Very much

2. How blocked are you from getting in touch with your genuine feelings involved in this issue?

   ❑ Almost none   ❑ Very little   ❑ Quite a bit   ❑ Very much

3. How much disruption in your daily routines do you feel?

   ❑ Almost none   ❑ Very little   ❑ Quite a bit   ❑ Very much

4. How much depression do you feel?

   ❑ Almost none   ❑ Very little   ❑ Quite a bit   ❑ Very much

5. How much yearning do you feel?

   ❑ Almost none   ❑ Very little   ❑ Quite a bit   ❑ Very much

6. How much sadness do you feel?

   ❑ Almost none   ❑ Very little   ❑ Quite a bit   ❑ Very much

7. How much anger do you feel?

   ❑ Almost none   ❑ Very little   ❑ Quite a bit   ❑ Very much

8. How much ghosting (continued psychic presence) of the lost person, situation or part of self do you feel?

❑ Almost none   ❑ Very little   ❑ Quite a bit   ❑ Very much

9. How much fear of the future do you feel?

❑ Almost none   ❑ Very little   ❑ Quite a bit   ❑ Very much

10. How much trouble are you having organizing yourself?

❑ Almost none   ❑ Very little   ❑ Quite a bit   ❑ Very much

11. How uninterested in your life do you feel?

❑ Almost none   ❑ Very little   ❑ Quite a bit   ❑ Very much

12. How much old, unresolved grief is being activated as a result of this current issue?

❑ Almost none   ❑ Very little   ❑ Quite a bit   ❑ Very much

13. How tired do you feel?

❑ Almost none   ❑ Very little   ❑ Quite a bit   ❑ Very much

14. How much shame or embarrassment do you feel?

❑ Almost none   ❑ Very little   ❑ Quite a bit   ❑ Very much

15. How much regret do you feel?

❑ Almost none   ❑ Very little   ❑ Quite a bit   ❑ Very much

16. How much self-recrimination do you feel?

❑ Almost none   ❑ Very little   ❑ Quite a bit   ❑ Very much

17. How much hope do you feel about your life and the future?

❑ Almost none   ❑ Very little   ❑ Quite a bit   ❑ Very much

GRIEF SPECTROGRAM

GOALS:

1. To make unconscious material conscious.
2. To provide a method of action sociometry (see chapter 6, Sociometry, for working with grief).

STEPS:

1. Draw an imaginary line dividing the room down the middle, showing group members where it is as you do so.
2. Explain to the participants that each end of the room represents an extreme: for example 100%, 1%, very much/very little.
3. Now ask one question at a time (see Grief Self-Test for criterion questions) and ask participants to locate themselves at whatever point along the continuum that feels right for them in response to the question.
4. Allow people to share a sentence of two about why they are standing where they are standing, either with one another or with the group at large.
5. Repeat this process for as many questions as can be absorbed or is helpful.
6. Next, the director may extend the exercise by inviting group members to think of someone who shared something with which they resonated and walk over to that person and share why they are choosing him or her.
7. Or return to seats for further sharing and processing.

VARIATIONS:

This exercise can be used as a warm-up to empty-chair work or vignettes. In grief work, one side of the room can represent very much and one side very little. You can use some of the questions from the Grief Self-Test, or ask some of the following questions: "How much grief is in your life right now?" "What is your level of loss?" "How angry do you feel?" "How tired?" "How disrupted?" "How much fear do you feel about your future?" "How much excitement do you feel about your future?"

If you want to adapt this for journaling, ask participants to choose an area in which they feel warmed up and do one of the following:

• Write a letter to someone they have unfinished business with and feel a need for closure.

- Write a journal entry around one of the areas in which they feel warmed up.
- Reverse roles mentally with a part of themselves that is hurting and write a soliloquy as that part of themselves.
- Write a letter to God, spilling out all of their conflicted emotions.

GRIEF LOCOGRAM

GOALS:

1. To allow group members to identify which stage or stages of the grief process they might be in.
2. To allow group members to identify with and learn from each other.

STEPS:

1. Assign one stage of the grief process, as outlined by Bowlby, to each of the four corners of the room. For example, one corner of the room represents the stage of numbness, the next yearning and searching, the next corner disorganization, anger, despair. The next corner reorganization, reinvestment, etc. Designate a space somewhere on the floor to represent "other" so that anyone who feels they are experiencing something outside of what is mentioned can stand on that and later share about their specific experience.
2. Invite group members to go to the corner of the room that best represents where they feel they are in their grieving process for the issue they are working with. (Note: Some may stand between stages).
3. Ask whoever wishes to share why they chose to stand where they are standing. Group members can share one at a time, in the group at large, or in subgroups with those who are standing next to them. They will be standing in sociometric alignment, e.g., those in anger will be standing next to those in anger and so on.
4. Next, ask group members if they feel a need to stand anywhere else and, if so, repeat steps two and three.
5. After all who wish to have shared, the group can move into psychodramas with whomever feels warmed up to work, or they can return to their chairs for further sharing.

VARIATION I:

Doubling or sociometric choosing can also be part of the process, e.g., "Who can you double for?" "Who said something with which you identify?" Group members choosing to stand on "other" can share about why they are standing there.

VARIATION II:

This can be used as a warm-up for psychodramatic journaling or letter writing. Clients may journal whatever is warmed up, or they can write the four stages of grieving in four boxes on one page, or use four pages and journal their feelings in each stage in the first person. For example, "I am eight years old. I'm feeling . . ." or "I am forty-four and I . . ."

VARIATION III: WARNING SIGNS OF UNRESOLVED GRIEF:

Do the locogram as instructed above but put the following on the floor either by designating areas to represent them or by writing them on large sheets of paper and placing them around the floor so that people can stand near the ones they identify with. Ask "Which of these manifestations of grief, if any, do you identify with?"

- Excessive guilt
- Excessive anger/sudden angry outbursts
- Recurring or long-lasting depression
- Caretaking behavior
- Self-mutilation
- Emotional numbness or constriction
- Chronic relationship issues
- Other

LOSS CHART

One loss can trigger unresolved (or resolved) emotion from another loss. Below is an exercise to investigate this. In the empty box in the center of the page, instruct clients to write a loss on which they are currently focusing (i.e., loss of a friend, a break up, death of a loved one, parents' divorce, a substance, etc.). On the lines jutting out from the box, write words or phrases that describe what other losses they, in some way, associate with this one, what comes up around this loss.

LOSS CHART

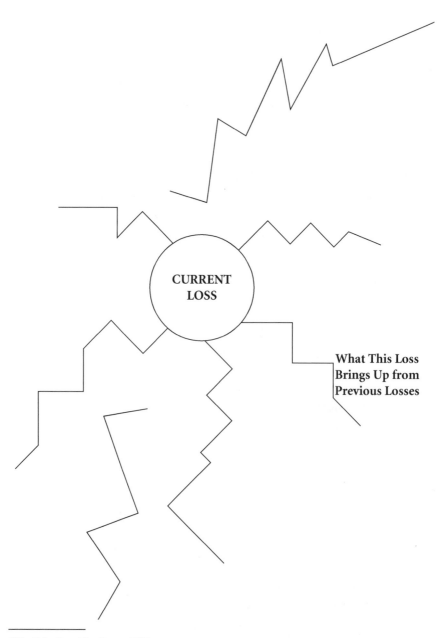

CURRENT LOSS

What This Loss Brings Up from Previous Losses

GUIDED IMAGERY FOR LOSS

GOALS:

1. To trace past issues, investigate what messages were received and explore how one was taught to handle loss.
2. To see how past losses may be affecting current losses.

STEPS:

1. Say, "Find a comfortable position and allow yourself to relax. Leave behind whatever outside concerns you may be carrying, and bring your attention into the room. Go to your breathing. Breathe in and out easily and completely, and allow yourself to relax. Sit up straight. Uncross your legs and arms. Place your hands on your lap with palms facing upward, or, if you are lying on the floor, facing the ceiling. Take a deep breath, hold it and blow it out slowly, as if you were blowing out through a straw. Notice areas of tension and breathe into them, allowing them to release."

2. Continue with, "Allow yourself to remember a loss, perhaps the first one you can remember: when it was, where you were, what happened, what you were told to do, what you learned about grief and loss. What are your thoughts? Observe yourself in your mind's eye. How do you look? What is your expression? Body posture? What are you expecting to be true about yourself or life around the loss? What meaning are you making out of this situation?"

3. Continue, "What has this experience and other experiences taught you about loss, and how are the lessons you learned being played out today? Whenever you feel ready, open your eyes." Slowly return to your breathing. Now, whenever you feel ready, move your hands and feet and gradually bring your attention back into the room and open your eyes. Slowly return to your breathing. Now, whenever you feel ready, move your hands and feet gradually and bring your attention back into the room and open your eyes.

4. Have clients share what came up, in dyads and/or within the group.

VARIATIONS:

This is designed to help clients to understand how they may have been taught, or learned by example, to deal with loss. It can be folllowed up by journaling about what comes up in addition to sharing or by doing vignettes about any losses that people may have gotten in touch with.

The guided imagery for loss is developed by Ronny Halpren, M.S.W., bereavement coordinator for the Cabrini Hospice in New York City.

SAYING GOOD-BYE/EMPTY CHAIR

GOALS:

1. To say good-bye fully to someone who has left one's life.
2. To release that person and move on in one's life.

STEPS:

1. Allow the protagonist to share about the person she wishes to say good-bye to.
2. Allow her to choose a person or use an empty chair to represent the person.
3. Ask her to set the scene.
4. Encourage the protagonist to be specific, saying good-bye, in detail, to all that she will miss.
5. If it seems appropriate or helpful, allow her to say what she will *not* miss.
6. The protagonist can reverse roles with the person whenever appropriate.
7. The protagonist can ask for something that she may wish to have from the person in the form of a word, gesture or object. She may receive it from the role-player, or reverse roles and give it to herself from their role, or both.
8. The protagonist may wish to give something to the person as well.
9. Ask the protagonist to finish the good-bye in any way she wishes.
10. Allow plenty of time for sharing in the group.

VARIATION:

Setting the scene can be very personal. The protagonist may wish to be in any type of setting, either real or imagined. The setting can be a funeral, a deathbed, a park scene, a field of flowers or anywhere the protagonist may choose. The idea is to say good-bye fully wherever it works best. If life did not offer an opportunity for the protagonist to say good-bye and put closure on the relationship, psychodrama can allow that to happen (Dayton 1994).

This can also be a letter-writing exercise, writing a letter to the person she is losing. The letter can then be read to an empty chair, if desired, and processed with the therapist or group if necessary.

The entire group can also write goodbye letters and read them either to a role player or an empty chair and follow with group sharing.

15

A World Without Windows: Depression

A complex body-mind disorder, depression affects ten to twelve millon Americans. Research over the last few decades has found that "abnormally low levels of neurotransmitters" in the brain contribute to depressed states in which "messages cannot easily get across synaptic gaps" (Driesen 2003). This slows communication within the brain. It appears that depression occurs if there aren't enough neurotransmitters circulating in the brain, or if the neurotransmitters cannot connect well with the receptors for one reason or another. "While there are as many as one hundred different kinds of neurotransmitters, norepinephrine, dopamine and serotonin seem to be particularly important in depression. The pathways for all of these neurotransmitters (the catecholamines) reach deep into many parts of the brain (e.g., hypothalamus) responsible for functions that are disturbed in depression—sleep, appetite, mood, and sexual interest" (Driesen 2003). The hypothalamus has long been associated with the processing and storage of painful or traumatic memories such as sadness, fear and anger (Ledoux 2002).

Cortisol, which contributes to everything from thinning hair to fat storage (Northrup 2001), has emerged as a major culprit in depression. "One of the most consistent biological findings about depression is that the adrenal cortex secretes more of the stress-related hormone cortisol in depressed people. This simple fact, which can be determined from a cotton swab containing saliva, links depression to the biology of stress," says Antonio Damasio, author of *The Feeling of What Happens*. When we're stressed, the concentration of cortisol in our bloodstream goes up. "In the short run, stress responses are useful in mobilizing bodily resources to cope with danger. But if stress is severe and continuous, the consequences can be serious. Your cardiovascular system can be compromised, your muscles can weaken, and you can develop ulcers and become more susceptible to developing certain kinds of infections" (Goleman 1998). Too much cortisol contributes to problems with short-term memory; it's elevated in elderly people, especially those with memory problems and depression.

"People who have low self-esteem, who consistently view themselves and the world with pessimism or who are readily overwhelmed by stress, are prone to depression. Whether this represents a psychological predisposition or an early form of the illness is not clear" (Driesen 2003).

GENDER DIFFERENCES AND DEPRESSION

Depression in Women

Due in part to hormonal factors such as menstrual-cycle changes, pregnancy, miscarriage, the postpartum period, perimenopause and menopause, women experience depression about twice as often as men. Many women also face additional stresses such as responsibilities both at work and at home, single parenthood, and caring for children and aging parents.

"A recent study by the National Institute of Mental Health (NIMH) showed that in the case of severe premenstrual syndrome (PMS), women with a preexisting vulnerability to PMS experienced relief from mood swings and physical symptoms when their sex hormones were suppressed. Shortly after the hormones were re-introduced, they again developed symptoms of PMS. Women without a history of PMS reported no effects of the hormonal manipulation" (Driesen 2003).

Depression in Men

Though men are generally less likely to suffer from depression than women, three to four million men in the United States are affected by the illness. "Men are less likely to admit to depression, and doctors are less likely to suspect it. The rate of suicide in men is four times that of women, though more women attempt it. In fact, after age seventy, the rate of men's suicide rises, reaching a peak after age eighty-five.

"Depression can also affect the physical health in men differently from women. A new study shows that, although depression is associated with an increased risk of coronary heart disease in both men and women, only men suffer a high death rate.

"Men's depression is often masked by alcohol or drugs, or by the socially acceptable habit of working excessively long hours. Depression typically shows up in men not as feeling hopeless and helpless, but as being irritable, angry and discouraged; hence, depression may be difficult to recognize as such in men. Even if a man realizes that he is depressed, he may be less willing than a woman to seek help" (Driesen 2003).

PLACEBO EFFECTS AND TALK VERSUS MEDICATION

A recent study conducted by UCLA Neuropsychiatric Institute used brain imaging to track the placebo effect versus antidepressants to treat depression. In the group receiving antidepressants there was depressed activity in the cortex, the area of the brain responsible for critical thinking, while in the group receiving a placebo there was increased activity in the prefrontal cortex. This changes how we think about placebos. They are not a nontreatment; rather they seem to stimulate activity in the areas of rational thinking. In other words, the thought of being helped produces changes in the brain that are real. "Over nine weeks, the researchers found that 52 percent of the antidepressant group and 38 percent of the placebo group responded to treatment, defined on a Hamilton depression scale score of ten or less. However, the two groups' brain responses were very different. Patients who responded to placebo showed increased activity in the brain's prefrontal cortex, while those who responded to medication showed suppressed activity in the area. . . . People have known for years that if you give placebos to patients with depression or other illnesses, many of them will get better," says Leuchter, director of adult psychiatry and a professor at the UCLA Neuropsychiatric Institute and Hospital. "Participants' decision to seek treatment, hopefulness for the treatment's effectiveness and positive interactions with health-service providers could all contribute to the placebo effect," says Leuchter. And while the findings do not explain why people respond to placebo treatment, "it does change the way we think about the placebo effect," according to Leuchter. "What this study shows, for the first time, is that people who get better on placebo have a change in brain function, just as surely as people who get better on medication."

Another study funded by the Rotman Research Institute, the University of Toronto and the Canadian Institute for Health Research found that antidepressants reduce activity in the brain's emotional centers, or the limbic system. Their findings were that talk therapy had a better cure rate than the antidepressants. Those who used talk therapy had a relapse rate of 25 percent in the year after treatment, while those using antidepressants relapsed at a rate of 80 percent. The study's other finding was that talk therapy quieted activity in the cortex.

Each of these findings varied in terms of the role of the cortex in modulating depression, but both claim to work.

EXERCISE AND DEPRESSION

According to Dr. Robert Goldman, president of the National Academy of Sports Medicine and author of *Brain Fitness,* a study of forty women with a depressive disorder at the University of Rochester Sports Center found that an aerobic activity—running or walking—or working out on weight machines almost completely erased signs of depression. The women exercised about three times a week. Each workout consisted of a five- to ten-minute warm-up, a main session of either progressing through a ten-station weight circuit, or walking or jogging around an indoor track, and ten minutes of cool down. A control group of women with similar signs of depression did no exercise. After eight weeks, the active women's scores on standard depression tests had improved dramatically, while their sedentary peers registered no improvement in their mental health.

Moreover, the women were again tested for signs of depression a year later, and the exercising group maintained their rosier outlook."

Exercise kicks in the body's natural opioid system. Exercising three times a week or more, along with thirty minutes of sunlight a day, is a very effective antidepressant. When we exercise and get outdoors, we tend to feel motivated and good about ourselves and our habits, while we're simultaneously getting our recommended thirty minutes of sunlight to further stave off depression.

The soothing body chemicals that nature meant us to experience don't get a chance to work their daily magic if we don't stimulate them through exercise of some sort. This affects our moods, our motivation and our pleasure in living. We need dopamine, serotonin and norepinephrine to be released into our bodies in order to feel good. This prescription, according to research, is as effective as any drug is for healing depression. In a recent study at Duke University, researchers Michael Babyak, Ph.D., and James Blumenthal, Ph.D., found that depressed patients who exercised had declines in depression equal to those who received antidepressants. In addition, those who continued to exercise after treatment were 50 percent less likely to become depressed again.

A ten-minute walk gives us more energy in the long run than a candy bar. These researchers have found that exercising in whatever way is most convenient works best. Whether it's a brief walk during a lunch break, walking the dog or biking to work, exercise seems to work well when it's combined with purposeful activity or works naturally into our lives. Research also reveals that exercising with other people helps us make it a more regular part of our lives.

Addicts have often damaged their natural supplies of feel-good chemicals through drug and alcohol use, and those in recovery for other forms of addiction or codependency may be prone to bouts of depression.

When we try to get recovery to work on a strictly psychological level, we ignore the fact that we live in a body, and that that body has significant power over our moods. This is one of the easiest places for clients to start turning their lives around or getting out of an emotional slump. A daily, brisk, thirty-minute walk outdoors is free and one of the best habits clients can cultivate for their bodies, minds and spirits. It can elevate moods, maintain or control weight, relieve depression, and give them time with friends.

Walking outdoors can be a component of treatment that can be taken into life and continued. There is plenty of good material on the Internet on the benefits of walking that can be downloaded and handed out to clients to motivate them to really adopt this life-enhancing habit.

Massage is another common adjunct that helps clients learn to relax and get in touch with their bodies. Massage supports the body's immune system and introduces soothing touch. It helps decrease tension and physical holding and increases relaxation and a sense of overall well-being.

Find out what clients' exercise habits are and make a treatment plan that includes regular exercise in order to maintain levels of "feel good" body chemicals. As addicts remove the substances that they use to obtain synthetic "feel good" states, it is important for them to find what are alternative ways to achieve that "feel good" state. Exercise can be one of them if not done to excess.

The first questions to ask a depressed client may not only be psychological and emotional but also biological, because biology becomes emotion, which, in turn, becomes psychology. Ask clients what their exercise and eating habits are. If clients are eating excessive amounts of sugar and white flour and drinking significant amounts of caffeine or diet soda, ask them to refrain from these things if they wish to get over their depression. Ask clients to refrain from the use of mood-altering alcohol and drugs and cigarettes. Simple carbohydrates, such as sugar or white flour, that the body converts into sugar create unnatural spikes in energy, which lead to dips in energy or feelings of listlessness that can make one feel down. Caffeine can have a similar cycle. Mood-altering drugs can mask feelings of depression that get medicated rather than worked with. Moderation is the key if abstension is not indicated or necessary, that is, if the person is not using the above mentioned to excess.

In addition, a therapist might ask:

• How do you sleep at night?
• Is your sleep fitful or sound?
• Are you working too much or too little?
• What are the relationships in your life, and how do you live in them?
• What are the stressors in your personal world?

• How is your support system?

• Describe your diet.

• What kind of exercise do you do?

• How much caffeine do you drink? (Caffeine triggers the release of cortisol.)

So connected is the body to the mind that to ignore its impact and hope to get better without addressing these issues may be like expecting to lose weight without adjusting our food intake or exercise program. If we want to get past depression we may need to address all of it.

DEPRESSION AND ISOLATION

Social isolation is a significant factor that both contributes to depression and causes it to persist longer than it otherwise might if the depressed person could get out of his narrow orbit. In a study conducted in Alameda, California, by Dr. George Kaplan, isolation was a key factor in earlier death. People with secure relationships and social support live longer—even if they smoke. Social contact with pets is also life enhancing.

A Duke University study conducted in the late 1970s by Redford Williams, M.D., et al., (1993) studied 1,300 patients. Among those who said they had no one to confide in and were unmarried, 50 percent were dead within five years, compared to 17 percent who were married, had a confidante or both. Depressed people are often isolators. If depressed individuals cope by withdrawing they tend to prolong and deepen their depression. Consequently their coping strategy makes them their own worst enemy. Isolation can feed on itself; that is, the more we isolate, the more anxious we become about connecting and the less likely we are to try.

On the flip side, not all connection is productive. In expanding social networks, one needs to be aware of entering support systems that are unhealthy, rigid, repressive or that demand conformity. These can have just as damaging an effect as having no connections (MayoClinic.com 2003).

How Can Psychodrama and
Sociometry Help in Treating Depression?

Psychodrama allows the self to emerge and strengthen through role-play. If the role is the tangible form the self takes, then psychodrama provides a way in which the roles associated with depression can be examined and worked with toward resolution. The psychodynamic view of depression is that it is, at least in part, fueled by anger turned inward. Psychodrama allows for meeting all aspects of the self on the stage and working with aspects of depression as they emerge through specific role-play. Anger can be creatively discharged, and anger toward the self can be concretized and examined. The grief or trauma symptoms that may also be contributing to depression can be worked with in ways discussed earlier in this section.

Sociometry also provides an excellent vehicle for working with depression. Give and take are healthy types of connection. Sociometry provides experience and training in give-and-take connecting. Sociometry provides concrete experiences in connecting with others repeatedly and in a variety of ways, that strengthens the individual's ability to connect. Sociometry puts clients in situations where they have several small connections with others in a contained, clinical environment. This works directly against the tendency to isolate and provides role-training in interacting with others.

Evelyn's Story

Evelyn was born in Germany and raised in Ireland. She was four when her mother first began to leave her at the orphanage. Eventually, the sisters who cared for her asked her mother to stop visiting because Evelyn became so inconsolable when she left her again. When Evelyn became old enough to be left on her own for part of the day, she was allowed, by her mother, to return home. Today, Evelyn "cannot bear the comings and goings of a relationship." Evelyn announced her desire to work on this and was overwhelmingly chosen by the group as the protagonist.

> **Evelyn:** I cannot let somebody get close to me because I get so scared that they will leave.

Tian: So you want to talk to your mother?

Evelyn: Yes, but I need support to talk to her. Can I choose someone to support me?

Tian: Sure.

Evelyn: Can I choose two people? (Evelyn chooses two people to support her and they stand next to her) This isn't enough. Can I choose someone else?

Tian: Sure.

Evelyn: (chooses someone else) This still isn't enough. Can I have more?

Tian: Choose as much support as you'd like.

Evelyn: (Evelyn goes on a choosing spree, and by the end of it has half of the group, at least twelve people, surrounding her) That's good.

Tian: Is that enough?

Evelyn: It's enough for now.

Tian: Fine, you can always add. What do you want to do with your support?

Evelyn: I want to lean into it.

Tian: Lean into it and talk to your mother.

Evelyn: How could you have left me? I was four years old. I never knew what was going on; no one explained anything to me; no one told me anything. I didn't know if you were coming back, if I would ever s-e-e you again. The sisters told you not to come to see me because I used to get impossible to console. I was so lonely. I m-i-s-s-e-d you, I missed you, I missed you. I hate you for leaving me. I h-a-t-e you. How could you do that to me? I can't get close to anyone now because I can't stand the coming and going. I get so depressed; I feel desperate.

At this point Evelyn doubled over and tears came up from down deep. I asked her to put a sound on her feelings, and she came forward with a low moan alternating with whimpers.

Tian: Lean into your support.

Evelyn: That feels so good.

Tian: Okay, more sound, more words.

Evelyn: I'm so angry that I'm like this. I feel so handicapped. (she utters a sort of scream alternating with a low moan.)

Tian: Lean into your support.

At this point Evelyn introduced that even though her mother was far away and left her—she still expected Evelyn to move back to Ireland to care for her. Evelyn felt very guilty for not wanting to do this.

Evelyn: I like the way this feels. Mom, I have my own life. I have my own support. I need my own life. I've got to have a self. I want a life. I can't only take care of you. (Evelyn reverses roles into the role of her mother.)

Mother: But what am I going to do? I'm lonely. I need you. (Evelyn reverses back to herself.)

Evelyn: I know you need me, but I need a life.

Mother: But I want you here.

Evelyn: I love you but I can't take care of only you. I have to have myself. It's not enough to have you; I need a self.

Mother: What will I do? I want to cling to you; I need you here.

Evelyn: I need a life, too.

Mother: I need you. I feel terrible. I need you to fill my life.

Evelyn: I can't do that for you.

Tian: Choose some friends for your Mother.

Evelyn: (Chooses two friends and asks them to stand next to her mother.) This is what I long to see. I want to see you happy. This is what I need to see, Mom, that you can be happy.

Tian: End the scene with Mom any way you wish to.

Evelyn: I love you, Mom; I do, but I can't cross the ocean to take care of you. It's hard enough for me to take care of myself. I know you need me, but *I* need me. *I* need me. I love you, Mom. I want you to be happy. I want us both to be happy.

DEPRESSION SELF-TEST

GOAL:

This questionnaire is designed to provide more information about the way depression might be manifesting and affecting one's life.

Note: These questions can also be adapted to a spectrogram (see the following exercise).

1. How much depression do you feel?
   ❏ Almost none ❏ Very little ❏ Quite a bit ❏ Very much

2. How much anxiety do you feel?
   ❏ Almost none ❏ Very little ❏ Quite a bit ❏ Very much

3. How much emptiness do you feel?
   ❏ Almost none ❏ Very little ❏ Quite a bit ❏ Very much

4. How much hopelessness/helplessness do you feel?
   ❏ Almost none ❏ Very little ❏ Quite a bit ❏ Very much

5. How pessimistic or negative in your thinking are you?
   ❏ Almost none ❏ Very little ❏ Quite a bit ❏ Very much

6. How much sadness do you feel?
   ❏ Almost none ❏ Very little ❏ Quite a bit ❏ Very much

7. How much anger do you feel?
   ❏ Almost none ❏ Very little ❏ Quite a bit ❏ Very much

8. How much guilt do you feel?
   ❏ Almost none ❏ Very little ❏ Quite a bit ❏ Very much

9. How much loss of interest in life do you feel?
   ❏ Almost none ❏ Very little ❏ Quite a bit ❏ Very much

10. How much fatigue or lethargy do you feel?
    ❏ Almost none ❏ Very little ❏ Quite a bit ❏ Very much

11. How much is your sleep affected?
    ❏ Almost none ❏ Very little ❏ Quite a bit ❏ Very much

12. How much is your weight affected?
❏ Almost none   ❏ Very little   ❏ Quite a bit   ❏ Very much

13. How irritable do you feel?
❏ Almost none   ❏ Very little   ❏ Quite a bit   ❏ Very much

14. How much trouble are you having concentrating?
❏ Almost none   ❏ Very little   ❏ Quite a bit   ❏ Very much

15. How much loss of interest in life, hobbies or sex do you feel?
❏ Almost none   ❏ Very little   ❏ Quite a bit   ❏ Very much

16. How much somatic disturbance, e.g., headaches, body aches, digestive disorders, chronic body pain that does not respond to treatment, do you feel?
❏ Almost none   ❏ Very little   ❏ Quite a bit   ❏ Very much

VARIATION:

This self-test can be turned into a springboard for psychodramatic journaling by returning to seats and journaling about the feelings and thoughts that are coming up.

DEPRESSION SPECTROGRAM

GOALS:

1. To make unconscious material conscious.
2. To provide a method-of-action sociometry to work with depression.

STEPS:

1. Explain to the participants that each end of the room represents an extreme: for example, in depression work, one side of the room can represent very much and one side very little.
2. Draw an imaginary line from one end of the room to the other, connecting 1 with 100, for example. Then draw another line bisecting it, showing group members where it is as you do so.

3. Now ask a series of questions that apply to your particular clients (see Depression Self-Test above) and ask participants to locate themselves at whatever point along the continuum feels right for them. Note: use only a few questions that apply particularly well to your group in order to avoid flooding the group.

4. Allow people to spontaneously share feelings that come up for them each time they respond to a question.

5. This process may be repeated a few times until the group seems to have reached a saturation point.

6. This can lead into a sociometric choice by asking group members to think of someone who said something that moved them and asking them to walk over to that person to share what it was.

7. Move into psychodramas, or if this is the entire experiential process being used, return to seats for continued sharing and processing.

VARIATION:

Journaling can also follow the questions. You might ask participants to journal "as" their depression or to dialogue with their depression, e.g. self to depression and back and forth.

LOCOGRAM FOR DEPRESSION

GOALS:

1. To get people talking about their depression.
2. To identify how a person's depression manifests.
3. To break down depression into its possible components or manifestations so it can begin to move and be explored.

STEPS:

1. Designate areas of the floor to represent anger, sadness, anxiety, numbness/ withdrawal and other.

2. Ask group members to walk to the area that best describes how their depression is currently manifesting and stand in that place.

3. Invite group members to share why they are standing where they are standing.

4. Next, ask group members if anything has changed since they began sharing; are they aware of some facet of their depression that they were not in touch with? Invite them to walk over to another area that might represent that new awareness, if they have one. If not, they can stay where they are.

5. Invite group members to share about why they are standing where they are standing.

6. Next, invite group members to think of someone who shared something they identified with and walk over to that person and place their hand on the person's shoulder.

7. Invite group members to share with the person they chose why they chose him or her.

8. Move into action or return to seats for continued sharing and processing.

VARIATIONS:

The criterion for the sociometric choice in step six can vary depending on what the group wishes to explore, e.g., did anyone say something that you want to hear more of, that you understand and can empathize with, or that concerns you? Who did you identify with the most? Who did you identify with the least? Who could you double for? Who feels like a double to you?

If you wish to return to seats for further sharing, you may explore some of the following: What open tensions are you aware of after doing this work? What act hungers are you aware of after doing this work?

This can be done as a psychodramatic journaling exercise by designating parts of a piece of paper to represent each area in step one and writing a soliquoy for or "as" whatever aspect of depression the group member identifies with.

FLOOR CLOCK

GOALS:

1. To concretize times of the day that one is likely to get depressed

2. To allow those prone to depression sociometric opportunities to identify their own depressive patterns and make positive connections with others.

3. To break patterns of isolation.

STEPS:

1. Write the numbers from the face of a clock on pieces of paper, or come to group with prepared numbers.
2. Lay the numbers on the floor in the shape of a clock, i.e., twelve on the top and six about ten feet below with other numbers placed appropriately.
3. Invite group members to "stand on or near" the time of day they are most likely to feel down.
4. Invite group members to share about why they are standing where they are standing; what goes on for them?
5. Repeat steps three and four if they want to explore another time of day in which they get depressed, or move into one of the variations, or both.
6. When all who care to have shared, allow group members to return to their seats and continue to share or move into enactments.

VARIATIONS:

Participants can double for each other throughout the process. They may continue to share by forming small subgroups with those standing next to them, where they will be sociometrically aligned with the people who tend to get depressed at the same time they do. Or allow sociometric choice to be a part of the process if appropriate. For example, ask: "Did anyone say something that particularly resonated for you? If so walk over to that person, place your hand on the person's shoulder and share with the person why you choose him or her." This will provide more possibilities for connection.

This can be used as a psychodramatic journaling exercise by drawing the clock on a piece of paper or tag board and writing in the times of day they feel most down and writing a journal entry from that point of view, e.g., "It's seven A.M. and I . . ."

WEEKLY REVIEW

GOALS:

1. To concretize times of the day or days of the week that one is most at risk for becoming depressed.
2. To offer a sociometric way of processing depression.

STEPS:

1. Write the days of the week on large sheets of paper or come to group with prepared sheets.
2. Lay the papers with the days on them on the floor in a straight line.
3. Invite group members to "stand on or near" the day of the week when they most likely feel depressed.
4. Invite group members to share about why they are standing where they are standing and what goes on for them either with the group at large or with those standing next to them.
5. Ask group members if there is another day that is especially hard for them, and invite them to stand on that day.
6. Invite group members to share about why they find that day difficult.
7. Repeat process if necessary, allow doubling where identification is strong, or invite group members to think of someone who said something with which they identify and walk over to that person, place a hand on his or her shoulder, and share with the person why they identify.
8. When all who care to have shared, allow the group members to return to their seats and continue to share.

VARIATIONS:

The group can double for each other throughout the process in order to deepen their sense of connectedness with themselves and others.

This may be adapted as a psychodramatic journaling exercise by writing the time line on paper and writing a journal entry for the days of the week they are likely to feel most down. Or reverse roles with "the spirit of the day" and write a journal entry as the day. "I am Sunday and I . . ."

FLOOR CALENDAR YEAR

GOALS:

1. To physicalize times of the year that one is likely to get depressed.
2. To allow those prone to depression sociometric opportunities to identify their own depressive patterns and make positive connections with others.
3. To break patterns of isolation.

STEPS:

1. Write the months of the year on pieces of paper or come to group with them already prepared.
2. Lay the months on the floor in a time line representing the calendar year.
3. Invite group members to "stand on or near" the time of year they are most likely to feel depressed.
4. Invite group members to share about why they are standing where they are standing, and what goes on for them. Repeat steps three and four if desired.
5. Group members may share with those standing next to them who are sociometrically aligned with them. They will all be feeling depression at a similar time of year. Or skip this step and go directly to step six, depending upon the needs and size of the group.
6. Invite group members to identify someone who said something that made them curious so they want to hear more about or with whom they identify and walk over and place their hand on that person's shoulder.
7. Invite them to share with that person why they chose him or her.
8. When all who care to have shared, allow the group members to return to their seats and continue to share.

VARIATIONS:

Group members can double for each other if desired.

This may be adapted as a psychodramatic journaling exercise by writing the time line on paper and writing a journal entry for the times of the year they are likely to feel most down. Or group members may reverse roles with "the spirit of the season" and write a journal entry *as* the spirit. For example, "I am spring and I bring with me. . . ."

The Wound That Never Heals: Unresolved Anger

Anger is an emotional state that can range from mild irritation to rage. The biological changes that accompany anger are increased heartrate and blood pressure and increased levels of the "energy" hormones adrenaline and noradrenaline, which are associated with the "stress" chemicals. Anger also leads to increased levels of cortisol, which can do anything from weakening our bones to locking in fat storage as it triggers the body's fight/flight response in order to ensure survival in threatening situations.

Anger can be functional or dysfunctional and is related to self regulation. Functional anger generally moves a situation forward in some way; we recognize we're angry about something, and that motivates us to reassess. Maybe we make a change in the way we're handling a situation or shift our expectations so we're not setting ourselves up for disappointment, and subsequently, anger. Or we process our angry feelings with someone we trust and make choices about what to do with them.

Dysfunctional anger, on the other hand, can be a place we get swept into, where our anger seems to multiply and feed on itself until it has a life of its own. Though there is not a diagnostic category called anger, problems with anger and its dark companion, rage, can lead to many problems, both in intimate relationships and the workplace. Because anger is a somewhat denied emotion, we have not developed ways of working with it as a society that allows it to be functional rather than dysfunctional. It simmers, boils up, explodes, hides, lies in wait or freezes up like a gas tank in winter. Anger is also often used as a defense against deeper feelings of fear and sadness or, as discussed earlier, it can contribute to depression.

Three common things people do with their anger are *expressing, suppressing* and *calming.* In *expressing,* we find some way to articulate our anger; we're assertive, and we use it to propel us to make some shift, however minor or major. In *suppressing,* we do not express it; we repress, deny, dissociate, minimize or in some way hide from ourselves what we're really feeling. *Calming* means we take active measures to calm down, like using breathing techniques, attitude adjustments, counting slowly to ten or taking a time out.

THE MANY FACES OF ANGER

Anger can express itself in many forms and through many faces. Stonewalling, criticism, withdrawal, whining, sulking, irritability, control, grumpiness, cutting others off or a preoccupation with negative subjects can all be manifestations of unacknowledged or unprocessed anger.

ANGER AND EARLY WOUNDS

Anger can also be a secondary reaction to early narcissistic wounds or relationship wounds. These wounds occur for everyone; they are a part of growing up and developing a separate sense of self that is no longer just an extension of our parents. But if we're separate, we can get hurt. Maybe the birth of a younger sibling with whom we had to share our mother was an early wound. Others could include a childhood illness, moving too often, persistent parental absence or any combination of such occurrences that built up over time. When we're separate and young, we're especially vulnerable to those we love and need because they have such power over our lives. Many of these early wounds resolve themselves naturally as we become secure in our sense of self and feel increasingly capable and autonomous or find other ways of getting our needs for love, attention and security met. Some wounds, however, persist.

THE SADNESS/ANGER CONNECTION

Some people find it easier to express sadness because, perhaps, their own anger frightens them. Others find it easier to express anger because their sadness may make them feel vulnerable, as if they're falling apart. Anger can feel like an organizing emotion, while sadness can feel like a disorganizing one. Anger can also be used as a defense to ward off powerful feelings of sadness, loneliness, fear or vulnerability that feel overwhelming. Expressing anger can open the door to grief. When clients can begin to engage in the grief process, of which anger is a part, they often report the experience of a burden being lifted as their feelings emerge and they experience and understand them in the here and now.

A more dysfunctional expression of anger might be when clients continue, in a sense, to retraumatize themselves with their own anger cycle. They get angry, in a state of high stress, and the old anger gets triggered to such an intensity that it makes the current situation very complicated to work through. The current situation and the past form a sort of amalgam and become a self-fulfilling prophecy; past hurts get recreated in the present with new names and faces, and rather than moving past anger and the sadness that is often beneath it toward resolution, the anger comes to have a life of its own. When this occurs, other emotions associated with the grief process, like sadness, hurt and a feeling of "falling apart," never emerge.

TRIGGERS AND TRANSFERENCE

When emotional and psychological pain remain unresolved, they lie in wait, often unconscious of their power and content, until some stimulus in the here and now *triggers* them and they jettison to the surface for quick expulsion. One might react to a perceived threat (this can be as subtle as a change in vocal tone or the look in an eye) with a response that is far greater than the situation merits. If we were repeatedly humiliated, experiencing humiliation in the present can trigger an intense reaction that appears to be about the present, but actually has its origins in past pain that's getting *transferred* onto the present-day situation.

For clients who have experienced chronic emotional and psychological damage, the body can get damaged as well; it gets deregulated. When these clients get scared and triggered, they may experience some of the following: trembling, voice changes, breathlessness, palpitations and flushing. These are not under conscious control and may be out of proportion to the current emotional stimuli. It is the arousal state of the autonomic nervous system. Learning to sit with this state or explore it through role-play and *talk from it,* put it into words, can help clients to make sense of what's going on inside of them so the past does not continue to pollute the present.

The Rage State

The rage state can take us over, obliterating reason and blowing past ordinary boundaries like a tornado leaving devastation in its wake. "During rage attacks those parts of the brain that are central to feeling and expressing anger, such as the amygdala and the hypothalamus, commandeer the rest of the brain. In this wholesale takeover, the cerebral cortex is overwhelmed and restraint and reasoning are impossible. . . . Although rage—by which I mean anger that is extreme, immoderate or unrestrained—may be adaptive as a response to severe threat, in most situations it destroys much more than it accomplishes," says Dr. Norman Rosenthal in *The Emotional Revolution.* Chronic rage might also be an indicator of depression. It's been estimated that 40 percent of those suffering from rage attacks also suffer from clinical depression. Rage attacks can also be a part of the PTSD syndrome. Rosenthal continues, "Dr. Martin Teicher and colleagues at Harvard have found that adults who were abused as children, whether verbally, physically or sexually, show brain wave changes over the temporal lobe of the cerebral cortex. These changes resemble those seen in people with documented seizures in the temporal lobe, which surrounds the limbic structures. . . . Teicher suggests that early traumatic experiences might kindle seizure-type activity in this area, resulting in a storm of electrical activity in the emotional part of the cerebral cortex. . . . The end result could be a brain that is cocked and all too ready to fire off a limbic storm."

Anger and Relationships

Persons with high levels of hostility (HO) were found to have a four-times-higher death rate and similar patterns with cancer when compared with a population with normal HO scores. Timothy Smith, a University of Utah researcher, found that students with high HO scores reported more hassles and negative life events and had less social support than those with lower scores. In the same study, married couples with high HO scores had more "dominating, acrimonious interchanges" than those with low HO scores.

David Masci, founder of Associated Couples for Marriage Enrichment (ACME) cites anger as one of the key issues in faltering marriages: a failure to manage anger issues reasonably well, which results in too many or too few disagreements. According to Masci, couples who cannot deal well with anger tend to withdraw from intimacy and lose passion.

In a further study of hostile workers at a financial management firm, seventy-five men and women, with the average age of forty, reported experiencing:

- greater stress in interpersonal aspects of work
- less job satisfaction
- negative view of work relationships

Anger creates problems in the work environment. A study at the University of Kansas at Lawrence comparing women of low and high HO scores found that the middle-aged women with high levels of hostility experienced:

- more stressful job experiences
- more daily stresses and tensions
- more role conflict
- feelings that skills were being underutilized

ANGER'S CUMULATIVE EFFECT

People with high HO ratings suffer more than those with low HO ratings when they get angry; their anger has a cumulative effect. A high HO (hostility) person gets more stressed out when they are angry than a low HO person and has greater health effects, much in the way that salt makes a person with high blood pressure experience a dangerous increase, while salt for a person with normal blood pressure causes no increase in blood pressure. Hence, anger-prone persons get triggered faster than nonanger-prone people—blood pressure goes up, heart rate increases and stress chemicals get pumped into the body. If cumulated anger is trauma related, the anger may have an historical component that fuels an overreaction to present-day triggers. They may perceive danger that isn't really there. Traumatized people may regress to their early defenses when they perceive danger. Thus, the reactions they get from others further isolate them, which confirms their core beliefs that the world is a hostile, unfriendly place and they need to always be on guard. This may also increase their primary loss of trust in people.

How Can Psychodrama and Sociometry Help in Resolving Anger?

Psychodrama, sociometry and group psychotherapy offer a support system in which clients can learn to express their anger in more functional ways, explore possible historical roots of anger and make new connections. Anger can be very isolating. Handling anger through blowing up, numbing, withdrawing or becoming depressed leads to further isolation. Using sociometry as we do in the Anger Floor Check for example, exercise provides new avenues of connection for that isolation.

Making sociometric connections around the subject of anger does a few important things:

- It breaks the shame and isolation around anger.
- It respects gender differences around anger, i.e., people pair and cluster according to sociometric identification.
- It provides support and connections around the particular forms that anger takes, for example, ragers can choose each other, passive-aggressive types find other passive-aggressive types and so on.
- It allows group members to share their emotions around anger and take in some support around the emotions the anger may be covering up.

In the case of anger that is cumulative or results from trauma, sociometric connection helps clients break through the fear that may have them frozen in a particular behavioral dynamic. They can reach out their arms and make a sociometric choice or be chosen (literally reach out and touch someone), thus breaking through isolation and shame. Traumatized people tend to get too angry too fast or express no anger. This mirrors the high intensity/shutdown emotional world of the trauma victim with its black-and-white thinking. The trauma victim has learned to, in a sense, burn hot with intense feeling—get overwhelmed—then control it by shutting down or numbing, or the reverse scenario, start out numb then burst open like a hot water pipe. They may have used chemical numbing agents, such as alcohol and drugs, substance numbing agents like food, or behavioral numbing activities like a preoccupation with sex, gambling, excessive work, etc. to manage their anger. Psychodrama offers a clinical situation in which the client can express anger and rage in clinical safety and observe anger behaviors in their concrete form. Healing is thought to have occurred when the client's spontaneous reaction to life circumstances changes —in the case of anger, when he is less easily triggered.

Harry's Story

Harry's wife complained of Harry's bouts of rage. When he wasn't having them he was sometimes depressed for several days at a time. As a child, his parents' constant raging and his father's subsequent departure had traumatized Harry. He had no role model for a relatively healthy relationship, and thus he never witnessed the working out of sticky issues. Consequently, he came to mistrust intimacy, wishing either for more than a normal relationship generally offers and getting hurt, disappointed or rageful when confronted with conflict. Intimate relationships, for him, became fraught with feelings of frustration, anxiety and fears of abandonment. And the feelings of vulnerability and dependency that were brought up through intimacy, or his wife's rejecting statements, acted as triggers of old pain.

Harry had an experience with his couples therapist that deeply upset him. The therapist had suggested that Harry and his wife consider a trial separation. Harry's unconscious heard divorce, finality and enduring pain. We used his couples session as the warm-up, then he asked himself where he may have gone "inside" when hearing the word *separation*. He came up with a scene, from when he was sixteen years old, in which he was watching his parents (whose marriage ended in divorce) throw things at each other, both objects and verbal abuse.

Tian: What scene comes to mind?

Harry: I guess just a scene that happened over and over again, but I remember the one when I was sixteen the best. (He set the scene, choosing a stand-in in case he needed one—but ultimately deciding he wanted to play out the scene himself—and role-players to play his parents. His instructions to the role-players: "You're just fighting, as usual, really taking each other out.")

Mom: You're always running off with your women.

Dad: That's none of your business. I'm young. I have to have a life.

Mom: You have a life, a wife and two children.

Dad: I support you, don't I? Leave me alone.

Mom: (Hysterical) I don't know what to do. I've had it. Get out of here.

Dad: I'm not leaving; this is my family.

Tian: What's going on inside of you? Can you take a step back and double for what you couldn't say then?

Harry: You're both crazy. What about me? I'm here; I'm here; don't I matter? (As he stood frozen in place, he recognized where the *status nascendi* of his current dilemma might, at least in part, reside. He reported feeling immobilized, unable to move or even think, rooted to the spot, frozen in fear.)

Tian: What are you thinking?

Harry: It's like I'm invisible. I must not be worth loving or staying for. No one even knows I'm here; I don't matter to them.

Tian: What would you like to say?

Harry: STOP IT! This is HORRIBLE! I can't bear to listen to you. You're both crazy. I can't stand you! It's not only about you; you have children. Don't you get it? This is our life, too; you're tearing us apart!

Tian: Is there anything you'd like to do?

Harry: Well, I was just out of there. I left home at fifteen and got my own apartment. But I think I'd like to just get really angry at them.

Tian: Okay, get really angry, then.

Harry: (Picking up a bat and hitting a tackle dummy, Harry became furious at his parents, expressing the pent-up rage that he had to shut down at the time but kept emerging as an act hunger in his current situations.) I'm so angry at both of you. You made home a crazy place, all about your issues, not about us. We were children; we needed to feel like we could count on you, but you were just lost in your own stuff. Dad, you were a drunk and a womanizer. You didn't think that would affect us? You're a Neanderthal! Don't you know anything? Mom, you just couldn't stand up to him. You tried, but you couldn't. You guys are too young to be parents. You're hopeless. (Harry then felt a new surge of anger and fought through his own feelings of helplessness and hopelessness.) It wasn't fair! If you couldn't take care of us, you shouldn't have had us.

Tian: Anything else?

Harry: No, that's good for now.

Tian: Would you like to resculpt the scene as you wish it had been, or say anything else?

Harry: I just want to say that you guys just couldn't be parents, you were just too wrapped up in being cool and leading the hip life. But that doesn't mean we didn't need parents. We were kids; we needed parents. I'm going to do it differently with my kids and my family. I *am* doing it differently. There's a lot of help out there, and I'm seeking it out. That's it.

Harry's core beliefs about himself and relationships, the ones that had been largely unconscious, undermined his ability to live in an intimate partnership or tolerate natural ups and downs. And the sense and meaning he made of his family at the time of childhood, which was that he must not be worth loving. His unresolved pain and anger manifested as bouts of rage and depression.

After the scene came to closure, we entered the sharing phase in which he was surprised and gratified to find that others understood what he had gone through and had had similar experiences themselves. This made him feel much more normal in his reactions. He could even let in some of the support others were offering rather than block the good and trusting feelings as he had previously when he viewed them as insincere or inauthentic. Over the subsequent week he reported feeling "lots of emotions running through me. I see the scene again in my mind's eye but this time with emotion attached to it." He also reported feeling less likely to pop off in a rage because when he got triggered by some slight or feeling of humiliation in his relationship with his wife, he was more aware of what was getting set off inside of him. Slowly, his trauma response was getting modulated. This process is slow and uneven and it takes a long time but Harry is making very steady progress and showing constant improvement in this area. Today his relationship looks dramatically different. He feels sane, stable and empowered. As he comes clean about his side of the problem it is clearer to him what his wife is bringing. He is calmer and more confident.

By revisiting the *status* and *locus nascendi,* an unconscious response with no words or emotion attached can be reprocessed and have feeling and literacy brought to bear. Emotions that were thwarted become felt in the here and now and have words attached to them so they can be shared and processed.

ANGER SELF-TEST

Have clients answer the following questions.

1. How comfortable are you with your own anger?
   ❏ Almost none   ❏ Very little   ❏ Quite a bit   ❏ Very much

2. How comfortable are you with other people's anger?
   ❏ Almost none   ❏ Very little   ❏ Quite a bit   ❏ Very much

3. How much anger do you feel?
   ❏ Almost none   ❏ Very little   ❏ Quite a bit   ❏ Very much

4. How much hurt do you feel?
   ❏ Almost none   ❏ Very little   ❏ Quite a bit   ❏ Very much

5. How flooded with feeling are you?
   ❏ Almost none   ❏ Very little   ❏ Quite a bit   ❏ Very much

6. How angry are you about the fact that you're angry?
   ❏ Almost none   ❏ Very little   ❏ Quite a bit   ❏ Very much

7. How depressed do you feel around your anger?
   ❏ Almost none   ❏ Very little   ❏ Quite a bit   ❏ Very much

8. How overtly aggressive do you become?

    ❏ Almost none   ❏ Very little   ❏ Quite a bit   ❏ Very much

9. How passive aggressive do you become?

    ❏ Almost none   ❏ Very little   ❏ Quite a bit   ❏ Very much

10. How much does your anger affect your intimate relationships?

    ❏ Almost none   ❏ Very little   ❏ Quite a bit   ❏ Very much

11. How much does your anger affect your career?

    ❏ Almost none   ❏ Very little   ❏ Quite a bit   ❏ Very much

12. How good are you at dealing with your anger in healthy ways?

    ❏ Almost none   ❏ Very little   ❏ Quite a bit   ❏ Very much

13. How much fear do you feel around your anger?

    ❏ Almost none   ❏ Very little   ❏ Quite a bit   ❏ Very much

14. How much physical/body reaction do you experience when angry?

    ❏ Almost none   ❏ Very little   ❏ Quite a bit   ❏ Very much

15. How much does anger disrupt your life?

    ❏ Almost none   ❏ Very little   ❏ Quite a bit   ❏ Very much

VARIATIONS:

The questions in the self-test can serve as criterion questions on a spectrogram (see Spectrogram, page 110), along with others the group might add.

If you adopt this for use as a spectrogram, invite group members to share, on each criterion question, why they chose to stand where they did. They may double for each other if the director wishes to incorporate this. In this case, choose only a few at a time to work with. After several have been shared, invite clients to walk over to someone who has shared something with which they identify and place their hand on the shoulder of that person. At any point the director deems appropriate the group may move into psychodrama through one of the processes of choosing a protagonist (see page 26) or return to seats for continued sharing and processing.

ANGER FLOOR CHECK

GOALS:

1. To allow group members to broaden their concept of the many ways in which anger may manifest.
2. To provide a sociometric exercise for the exploration of anger.

STEPS:

1. On large pieces of paper write or have the group write the many manifestations of anger, including: cynicism, passive aggression, whining, rage, acting-out behaviors, irritability, violence, stonewalling, withdrawal, cut off, coldness, avoidance and so on. Always leave a blank piece of paper for any spontaneous write-ins the group may wish to do.
2. Scatter the words around the floor and invite group members to stand on or near the manifestation of anger they identify most as their own.
3. Invite group members to share why they are standing where they are standing.
4. Invite group members to make another choice and repeat the sharing. Most of us have more than one way that we manifest anger. Repeat this process if desired.
5. Next, invite group members to walk over to someone whose sharing they identified with and place their hand on that person's shoulder. Then ask them to share with that person why they chose him or her or what they identified with.
6. At this point the group may be ready to simply return to their seats and continue sharing, or they may wish to chose a protagonist and move into psychodrama. In either case, always allow plenty of time for sharing.

VARIATIONS:

This exercise can also be done from the point of view of the types of anger group members have the hardest time dealing with or fear the most. In this case the instruction would be, "Walk over and stand on or near the type of anger that you have the hardest time with or fear the most." Continue the process from that point. Anger can be experienced differently by men and women. Step five can allow for sociometric identification with a particular gender which can feel very supportive to each gender.

If used as a warm-up to psychodramatic journaling, return to seats and ask group members to choose one expression of anger they would like to work with, reverse roles with it and journal "as" that type. "I am rage and I . . . " Share journaling in group or subgroups.

To download this exercise, log onto *tiandayton.com*.

ANGER MAP

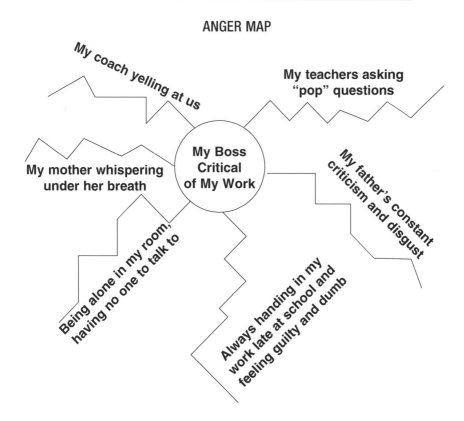

In the center of the circle, ask clients to write a word or phrase describing a current situation or a type of situation that often makes them angry. Next, on the jutting lines, have them write any association they have that comes to mind or gets triggered by the central circumstance. Have them share the Anger Map with the group or in one-to-one. This exercise can provide significant insight as to how one situation triggers emotions underneath it, such as fear, sadness, resentment, rage and loneliness, and links it to the situation from which these emotions stem. This may be used as a warm-up to psychodramatic vignettes or a paper-and-pencil exercise followed by sharing and discussion.

SPIRALING

GOALS:

1. To trace possible sources of anger.
2. To add insight and understanding to irrational anger.

STEPS:

1. Ask group members to identify an anger or conflict issue from their current lives that they wish to work with. You can say, "Think of a situation that often makes you angry or that is presenting a problem for you in your current life." You can also use the Spectrogram or Anger Floor Check as a warm-up.
2. Invite the protagonist to choose auxiliaries to represent the roles in her drama and set the scene.
3. Play the scene out until the historical connection becomes evident. You may ask the protagonist where she might have felt this way before or allow her to identify the connection in her own manner.
4. Freeze the present-day scene and choose new auxiliaries to play the scene or model scene from the past that may be a source of transference onto the present or may be fueling present-day anger.
5. Play the scene out to its closure with all psychodramatic devices.
6. Spiral back up to the present-day scene, unfreeze it and play it out again. The quality of the playing out should be different and informed by new understanding gained from getting some relief and insight from exploring the *status nascendi.*
7. Return to seats for sharing.

VARIATIONS:

Spiraling is a technique in which we begin with the current conflict, spiral backward to the original wound and process related feelings, thoughts, distortions and personal meaning; then we spiral back to the present day to resolve the conflict in new ways.

This may be adapted as a psychodramatic journaling exercise by Journaling the Spiral (see page 260).

17

Thriving in Spite of the Odds: Psychodrama and Resilience

U nusual upbringings can and often do create unusual strengths—which we need to pay attention to during the therapeutic process *along with* identifying pathological dynamics. Studies of those who thrive in spite of conditions that would put many under reveal that there are several factors that go into creating resilience. While it is critical to go back and rework significant issues as we've discussed throughout this book, focusing exclusively on the negative qualities of others and the damage others wreak can have the adverse effect of weakening the self rather than strengthening it. It can create the illusion that if we can get everything right on the outside, choose "functional, available" people, find our passion and get into great shape, happiness will inevitably follow. Or that if we can identify our needs and state them clearly, they will always be met. But this is not always the case. The world is busy and sometimes doesn't seem to notice us even when we're in our best emotional outfits. The truth is probably more like happiness comes to those who see beauty in things as they are, without requiring life to meet them on their terms but living, as we say in program, "life on life's terms." Happiness seems to follow those who have "an inborn sense that life will work out," who look around them and see not only what is missing but what is there.

Peter's Story

The following letter is excerpted from Peter Yelton's upcoming book *Infinite Hope*. Peter's story represents a lifelong struggle and a real and lasting victory.

As a child of adoption searching for the missing pieces of his life, Peter received this rather mind numbing missive from the New York Foundling Society:

Dear Mr. Yelton,

According to our records you were found in the bathroom of a theater on 42nd Street, September 26, 1946, and taken to Polyclinic Hospital. You were described as a newborn, white. The medical report stated that upon admission you were scratched, cold and cyanotic. You were placed in a heated crib and given oxygen. Within a half hour you were active, pink and warm, and the oxygen was discontinued. You took your feedings well and continued to gain weight. You appeared to develop normally in all respects. You remained at the Polyclinic Hospital until your transfer to the New York Foundling Hospital on November 8, 1946.

The city of New York, Department of Welfare, gave you the name of Eugene Lane, assigned your religion as Protestant, in turn, and your birthdate, as September 26, 1946. The city also referred you to Spence-Chapin for adoptive study. You were baptized in the Protestant religion on January 28, 1947. You were transferred to Spence Chapin on March 12, 1947, for adoptive placement.

A social worker from Polyclinic Hospital had visited you while you were at the Foundling. The record states that she was very fond of you while you were under the care of the Polyclinic. You were described as a very attractive little youngster with gray eyes, light brown hair and a ready smile. You were extremely friendly and well-developed for your age.

There is no mention in the record of your birth parents or any relatives.

May the Lord's peace be with you on your search.

Sincerely,
Sister Agnes

Peter was born in a movie theater in Times Square, the son of a girl who, alone in the ladies room of the theater, delivered her son and then abandoned him. The ticket attendant noticed blood on the floor, then a baby, and she called the police. All Peter knows is that a police officer named Rizzo tied his umbilical cord and carried him through the streets of Manhattan during a summer blackout that had the city in chaos. Peter has carried the consoling image of being held in Officer Rizzo's arms in his own heart ever since.

Peter was able to uncover social service records that showed he had spent the first six weeks of his life in a hospital, became sick with pneumonia and was then transferred to another hospital for a time before being transferred back to the first one. He knows that between the ages of six to ten months old he was taken care of by a loving foster family who were not allowed, by law, to adopt him. He then described himself as "yanked away" when a family he never really felt part of adopted him. When Peter uncovered the information about the foster family seven years ago, he had the somatic symptom of getting sick with what felt like pneumonia for about twenty minutes during massage appointments, then the body memory would "just go away." This happened repeatedly over a period of six or seven months.

Peter did not come to our training group intending to work with this, though he had always indicated a desire to when the time was right. Like so many resilient clients, he was willing, and he had that look in his eye that said, "I'll give it a shot. Why not?" We did a warm-up in group around the Addicted Family Model (see page 374). I asked if there was anyone warmed up to do work. I had talked with this group about being aware of their bodies and letting the group know when they become somatically triggered. Peter self-identified, "Something's going on, [looking uncomfortable, quizzical]. I guess something must be getting warmed-up [hand on his gut, head angling forward]. I feel sick in my stomach; I'm obviously experiencing something." Note that this is often how this material comes forward, first with awareness that something is going on in the body, then the client infers they are experiencing some sort of inner discomfort. Peter has the advantage of years of work as a therapist and in recovery and he understands trauma; he knew what he was signing on for.

Tian: Would you like to work with this?

Peter: Yes, I guess so. Yes, I do, definitely.

Tian: What would you like to do?

Peter: Ah . . . let me think . . . I'd like to talk to myself at nine, when we were having a party for my cousin who was getting married. Yes, that's what I'd like to do.

Tian: Who could play your cousin for you?

Peter: Martie could. Could you, Martie?

(At this point, Martie came onstage and enrolled as cousin Mary and reversed roles with Peter so we could get a sense of Mary. Peter also chose someone to play himself at nine, and we went through the same procedure. Peter began to freeze up much in the way that he had when in this situation, at the party. When he spoke with his cousin, he tried to tell her how much he would miss her and then began dropping clues as to why.)

Peter: I'm going to miss you so much. It's going to be awful when you go, they all hate me.

Tian: Can you double for yourself?

Peter: Why is this a party? Why is everybody celebrating? You're going away; you're leaving me. You're the only one who gets me, who thinks I'm a cute kid. The rest of them hate me; they talk about me, criticize me constantly.

(This part of the psychodrama was slow, quiet and not overtly emotional. At moments Peter's chest would heave and emotion would try to come out and he would tear up, but most of his emotion was still in his body, though it was beginning to come out in short fits. After allowing him to go back and forth with his cousin I felt we could move in the direction that he was leading us. There was clearly more that Peter wanted to say.)

Tian: Is there anyone else you want to talk to?

Peter: Well, yeah, my mom. (Same choice procedure.)

Tian: What would you like to say to Mom?

Peter: Why can't you think I'm okay?

Tian: Reverse roles.

Peter : (As his mother) I don't know what you're talking about. Be quiet. Stop saying these things. Get dressed for dinner; we're going to the club.

(Peter's feelings about his mother became more evident as he played her and showed us how he experienced her. Eventually, after a few such statements I asked him to reverse roles and double for himself, what was he saying on the inside that he couldn't articulate from his nine-year-old self. The verbal and physical action that he wished to take, namely telling his mother off, had been thwarted so may times that he couldn't say it even in role-play. Doubling for himself allowed him to move both physically, by taking a step back, and emotionally, by receiving permission to speak in a sort of stage whisper that is not really "talking out loud.")

Peter: (Suddenly) I hate you! I hate you! I hate you! You're so cruel to me; all you do is find things wrong with me. I'm maybe not what you want, but I'm a fun little guy. I'm not nobody. I was a cute kid. I was funny and goofy; why couldn't you see that?"

(Variations on this theme went on for a while as Peter, through what he said, revealed that his adoptive mother was an alcoholic who he encountered as falling-down drunk sometimes, slurred while coherent at other times, was invasive of his personal boundaries, etc.)

Peter: You wanted me to be your little partner, someone to talk to when you were drunk, someone to fall all over. You disgust me; ugh, you disgust me.

(At this point Peter was still speaking through a clenched jaw, his chest very constricted and his gut clearly experiencing something. He kept on in this vein for a while and then, rather abruptly:)

Peter: You're dead. I never want to see you again. You're dead, you're dead, you're gone.

Tian: She's dead? Do you want to bury her? *(I would not have asked this had Peter not been so vocal about killing her off in his life. I wanted to see if he could make any sort of connection with her, if he could move from here to some other, less amputating place. Amputation doesn't really work in my experience. Clients develop "phantom limb" syndrome.)*

Peter: Yes. (He put pillows on top of her.) There, you're buried. Go away.

(Knowing that nothing in life is this easy, that people don't just disappear even though we think we might wish it, I wanted to find some creative ways to continue to release the anger and disgust he clearly wanted to express. I also wanted to find some way to help him move himself from a catharsis of abreaction to a catharsis of integration though the abreaction was clearly satisfying and met an act hunger.)

Tian: Do you want to continue to express your anger? (Stage-glancing over to a tackle dummy a few feet away that we keep for this purpose)

Peter: Yes.

Tian: (Handing over a bat with which to hit the tackle dummy) Would you like to write her an epitaph: Here lies . . . ?

(This clearly appealed to him. Resilient clients, in my experience, want to get the feelings that are bothering them out of them.)

Peter: (As he was hitting the tackle dummy) Here lies a disgusting drunk, a negative, absent hole of a mother.

(Clearly, he was continuing to express his anger toward his mother at every juncture, in a variety of ways. I invited him to continue hitting it while letting sound or words come out

with his actions. Sound came out, words came out and he continued to hit the dummy but in a somewhat spasmodic manner, which is very often how blocked emotion emerges as the mind struggles to give voice to the somatized emotions.

Consciousness slowly dawned as Peter witnessed himself in action, as he felt a growing freedom to get this out of him in a way that he never felt before. His body began to remember the thousand injuries that his mind had forgotten. His mind began to unfreeze as his body took the lead. Like watching the soundtrack of a movie that had been "off" slowly become synchronized with the action, Peter began to exhibit thought, emotion and action as a coherent whole. Eventually, he started to behave differently, to look different, to feel different. His movements became more fluid, his speech flowed more freely, and his emotions attached themselves to what he was actually saying. His body began to change, and some color flowed into his face. He was accessing this part of himself and bringing it into the rest of his generally relaxed, intelligent and fun-loving self. The disintegrated part was being integrated into his self-system.

Still, there seemed to be more that wanted to come out. Here I took a calculated risk, ready to accept his last word on the subject.)

Tian: This is just a thought, take it or leave it, do you have any wish to talk to your biological mother? *(An unqualified yes let me know that Peter had wanted to do this; he indicated that it was going through his mind, too.)* Who can play your biological mother for you?

Peter: Calixte can. *(Calixte arrived into the psychodramatic moment with a kind of angelic spontaneity. Her face was all-welcoming as she greeted her long-lost child into her arms and spoke tender words of recognition.)* I knew you'd come. I knew you'd come for me. (Tucking himself into her.) I knew you'd come.

(This was the most that Peter had cried during his psychodrama. Calixte lowered to the floor, let Peter rest his head on her lap while she stroked it. In a moment of healing a wish came true a gratifying wish that Peter's heart had held but had never been able to act on. Calixte kept talking in a mother's voice, saying the soothing, calming and loving things that mothers say to their children, which their hearts soak up like little sponges. Peter's face looked like that of a newborn: awake, alive and full of love.

In order to ground the experience and give some more time to integrate it into real time, I asked Calixte to take Peter around the room and introduce him to various group members. As group members greeted him they made comments: "We've heard so much about you." "Aren't you a big, strong boy!" "Your mother talks about you all the time." At this point I asked him if he wanted to end the psychodrama, and he said he felt ready to do that.)

Tian: Are there any last things you want to say to your mother?

Calixte: May I say something to him? (*Sometimes the role-players are the ones who spontaneously know what needs to happen next, as Moreno said, "In a group, each person becomes the therapeutic agent of the other."*)

Peter: Yes.

Calixte: (Speaking to Peter's adopted mother) I know things weren't great at home but thank you for taking care of my son. I'm so sorry that I didn't have what was needed to do this job, you did it instead of me, maybe not always so well, but you did it in my stead, and I thank you. He's grown up to be a wonderful man, so something good happened.

Peter: "May I do something else?" (Reclosing his epitaph) "Here lies a woman who was not all bad. It was tough, but there were good things, too. I got hurt a lot, but I got some of what I needed, too. She died, but before she died we had healing with each other. We told each other we loved each other."

(Once again, we see qualities of resilience in being willing to see the glass as half full, being willing to see the other side, and letting go of some of the pain, enough to move on and get on with life.

Peter ended the scene by coming back to his cousin, back to his bonded relationship, talking about how much it meant to him to reconnect with her in his real life and talking about when he planned to get together with her next. He returned to his chair, and the group shared with him for about forty-five minutes, which further allowed him to integrate his experience, come back into the group in real time, and also allowed the group to continue its own processing, integration and healing.)

After all sharing had ended, Peter reported feeling very relieved and "just really good." He said that something that had always been in his midsection felt gone. He said that reconnecting with his birth mother was something that he had always wanted to do and this felt wonderful and very healing to him to do psychodramatically.

Peter later told me that his father's life completely fell apart when he was forty-one to forty-two years old. That is when Peter, himself an alcoholic, got sober. His age correspondence reaction motivated him toward recovery rather than self-destruction. He feels a powerful drive to live. He sees his birth mother as having the strength to deliver him alone and Officer Rizzo as an angel of mercy who carried him to safety. This is typical of resilient children who soak up love and support wherever they can find it. One salient feature of Peter's resilience is the positive meaning he gives to circumstances that were painful, saying things like: "Rizzo carried me," and "I must have gotten a lot of strength from my mother; she had me all alone at nineteen." Also typical of resilient children, Peter found a person to bond with, "who saw that I was a cute kid," namely his cousin, and he drew strength from that relationship. Peter has experienced plenty of trauma, but he still sees life as basically beautiful; he lets people in slowly, but still he opens his heart and wants to build trust and friendship. He has an inborn feeling that life will work out. Furthermore, he has made it his life's work to help others bring these qualities into their lives.

Over the next few months Peter reported forging a new and close relationship with his cousin. The two of them experienced unexpected and cherished healing as she let go of life. Peter read the eulogy at her funeral.

Helping clients identify and claim their resilient qualities is very important in building a stronger, more-integrated self. Clients need reasons to feel good about themselves, and identifying qualities of resilience helps them build on what's positive within them, to claim what was good in their families and have the courage to move forward. Resilience, which is so important in marshalling and mobilizing inner strength that has already been developed or the qualities that need to be developed throughout treatment, is beginning to get noticed. Helping clients identify their own resilient qualities can give them a chance to feel good about their more positive sides and motivate them to develop other strengths.

Those who have lived with or grown up with some form of psychological or emotional trauma, such as ACOAs, and survivors of childhood abuse or neglect, can develop qualities that researchers S. J. Wolin and S. Wolin (1993) identify as associated with resilient children or adults. Resilient adults may display some of the following qualities that the Wolins, in their research, found that resilient people tend to possess. They can be wonderfully *creative*, as for many creativity was a way to meet needs, make sense of or even escape from what was going on around them. The arts are full of trauma survivors and ACOAs who have developed their creative spirits through deep yearning, who have sublimated their grief into an artistic form. Graveyard *humor*, as any ACOA or addict can show you, often gets honed to a fine art as a coping skill. Thus, this can be a very funny population. Often children from troubled homes become very *independent* from a young age because they learn they cannot necessarily depend upon their parents. The ones who thrive often do so because they have exercised *initiative* and have taken the reins into their own hands, recognizing that if they didn't no one would or perhaps could. Problems, if they don't sink us, deepen us. We develop *insight* and *wisdom* from tackling problems and overcoming them. Oftentimes *morality* grows as much from seeing what should not be done as what should. Those who have been wounded can have clear life lessons on what hurts and may feel determined not to hurt others in the same way. They may even dedicate parts of their own lives to helping others.

QUALITIES OF RESILIENCE

S. J. Wolin and S. Wolin, authors of *The Resilient Self,* have created what they call a resilience mandala, or a circle representing those qualities that enhance resilience. They are:

- Independence
- Creativity
- Relationships
- Insight
- Humor
- Morality
- Initiative

Note: I often add spirituality to this list because in my experience it is a very significant factor in resilience or in developing resilience. It helps restore trust, faith and hope in the future and give meaning to suffering.

RISK FACTORS THAT UNDERMINE CHILDREN AND QUALITIES OF RESILIENT CHILDREN

Some of the risk factors for children that can lead to psychological and emotional problems later in life are:

- Poverty
- Overcrowding
- Neighborhood and school violence
- Parental absence
- Unemployment or instability

These can be the children who are likely to wind up in the social services or penal system. However, some children are raised in the middle of all this still grow up to have productive lives and relationships. Emily Werner, author of *The Children of The Garden Island*, who conducted the longest research study ever done, studied these children in Kauai, Hawaii, through the social service system in order to identify the qualities that resilient children seemed to possess and what factors might have contributed to building them. Werner discovered the following about resilient children:

- They tended to have likable personalities from birth that attracted parents, surrogates and mentors to want to care for them. They were naturally adept at recruiting support and interest from others and drank up attention, care and support from wherever they could get it.
- They tended to be of at least average intelligence, reading on or above grade level.
- Few had another sibling born within two years of their birth.
- Virtually all of the children had at least one person with whom they had developed a strong relationship, often from the extended family or a close community member.
- Often they report having an inborn feeling that their lives were going to work out.

In studying resilient adults, Wolin and Wolin found that they exhibited these characteristics:

- They can identify illness in their family and are able to find ways to distance themselves from it; they don't let the family dysfunction destroy them.
- They work through their problems but don't tend to make that a lifestyle.
- They take active responsibility for deliberately creating their own successful lives.
- They tend to have constructive attitudes toward themselves and their lives.
- They tend not to fall into self-destructive lives.

They discovered that resilient adults had:

• Found and built on their own strengths.
• Improved deliberately and methodically on their parents' lifestyles.
• Consciously married into happy, healthy and/or strong families.
• Fought off memories of horrible family get-togethers in order to reestablish family rituals.
• Tended to locate themselves two hundred miles or more away from the epicenter of dysfunction. Wolin and Wolin refer to this as the "magic two-hundred-mile radius" between them and their families of origin, enabling them to be separate and somewhat out of the daily fray of potential family dysfunction but still connected.

Wolin and Wolin found that the price these persons tended to pay were:

• Stress-related illnesses.
• A certain degree of aloofness in their interpersonal relationships.

HOW THE TRIADIC SYSTEM SUPPORTS AND DEVELOPS QUALITIES OF RESILIENCE

Psychodrama places protagonists at the center of their own experience, empowering them to take charge of the material they wish to explore and the manner in which it is to be explored. As the group examines and explores life and relationships, and teases out the drives, motivations and consequences of thinking, feeling and behavior, *insight* continues to grow, along with a coherent context for *moral* structure. Moreno wished to be remembered as one who helped to restore *humor* to the field of psychiatry through the cooperative and spontaneous process of role-play and group interaction.

One of the common traits that resilient children share, according to Emily Werner (1989), is a *strong, bonded relationship* with at least one other person, usually within the extended family network, often a grandmother, aunt or uncle. Psychodrama can allow clients to reconnect with people from their past through role-plays with those who have played an important and helpful role in their development, and to consolidate those gains. A vignette recognizing a loving grandmother, or a sustaining aunt or uncle or teacher, helps clients claim the strength and direction they gained from those relationships.

The interactive emphasis of psychodrama, sociometry and group psycho- therapy strengthens relationship skills and works through blocks in intimacy. This is because group is a very intimate experience, and problems in connect- ing tend to surface over time in the sociometry of group process. *Creativity* and psychodrama go hand in hand; the artist can be nourished and challenged through the highly inventive process of role-play. The triadic system encourages *initiative*; group members have to put themselves forward or get lost in the shuffle. *Insight* deepens daily as clients come to see how the pieces of their lives actually fit together and as parts of themselves emerge from the shadows to be processed and understood. And *humor* is ever present. The catharsis of group laughter can be just as healing and bonding as the catharsis of tears.

CLAIMING RESILIENT, POSITIVE QUALITIES

GOALS:

1. To claim and use positive qualities.
2. To explore blocks to claiming positive qualities.

STEPS:

1. Ask group members to think of and share about positive qualities they have identified with from the qualities of resilience or feel they value in themselves.
2. Invite whoever wishes to choose a role-player to represent that quality, or a person from whom they feel they got that quality, or use an empty chair to represent it.
3. Invite group members to self-select and do a monodrama or a vignette with that inner quality or that person.
4. Use any or all techniques such as doubling, role reversal or interviewing to deepen the exploration.
5. Bring the scene to closure at whatever point feels natural.
6. Invite any and all who wish to repeat steps two through five.
7. Reserve ample time for sharing what came up for all concerned during these vignettes.

VARIATIONS:

Another variation is to write the qualities of resilience on large pieces of paper and place them on the floor, then proceed as with any locogram or floor check. This can be used as a warm up to this exercise.

Group members may also choose to role-play a scene with a representation of their block or blocks in the process of claiming and feeling good about their positive qualities, or with a person who lives in their minds who feels in the way.

The idea here is to help clients identify and claim their resilient qualities so they can continue to build on them and enhance their good feelings about themselves.

This may be adapted for psychodramatic journaling by "dialoguing" between the client and the resilient quality, then sharing it in group.

SAYING THANK-YOU

GOALS:

1. To acknowledge and show appreciation for someone who reached out to help in time of need.
2. To consolidate gains from a positive relationship.

STEPS:

1. Ask the group members to think of and share about a significant relationship from the past, one that helped them feel they belonged somewhere, who gave them the feeling that they were worthwhile in some way.
2. Allow anyone who feels warmed up to self-select to do a vignette or a monodrama.
3. Invite the protagonist to set the scene by choosing someone to play the person to whom she feels bonded and grateful, or use an empty chair to represent the person.
4. Proceed with the scene as usual, incorporating role reversal, doubling, interviewing and so on.
5. When the scene seems to be drawing to closure, say "Say the last things you wish to say for now," and end the scene.
6. Return to seats for sharing.

VARIATIONS:

Group members may wish to vary this by putting a part of themselves into the chair to thank, or selecting someone to play that role.

This may be adapted for psychodramatic journaling by writing a letter to the person the client is wishing to say thank-you to, then sharing or reading it to a role player or an empty chair.

INTRODUCING THE SELF TO THE GROUP FROM THE ROLE
OF A SIGNIFICANT OTHER

GOALS:

1. To strengthen the memory of and connection with a significant bonded relationship.
2. To consolidate and build on the strength gained from that relationship.

STEPS:

1. Invite group members to think of a person who was significant in their childhood, someone who liked them or saw their struggling and reached out to help them, someone who saw them in a generous light.
2. Invite whoever wishes to self-select to work.
3. Set up an empty chair on the stage to represent the protagonist. Have him reverse roles with the other person and introduce himself (represented by the empty chair) to the group, e.g., "I am Jack's grandfather, and I want to tell you about my grandson Jack."
4. Allow the monodrama to proceed as usual. You may include role reversal, interviewing the protagonist in role reversal, asking him questions about his relationship with himself, or doubling.
5. End the scene whenever it draws to natural closure.
6. Invite other group members to repeat steps two through five until all who wish to have done a monodrama or vignette, or time runs out.
7. Reserve plenty of time for sharing in the group about what came up and where identifications of any kind might be.

VARIATIONS:

This can allow many people to do a piece of work that is meaningful, and the sharing can be done after all who wish to have worked. This may be adapted for psychodramatic journaling by asking the client to think of a person he would like to have introduce or talk about him, mentally reverse roles with that person, and write a letter of introduction as that person about the client, e.g., "My name is Jackson and I am introducing my nephew, Tyrol. I have always found Tyrol to be. . . ."

18

A Leap of Faith:
Amends, Forgiveness
and Letting Go

In a way, forgiving is only for the brave. It is for those people who are willing to confront their pain, accept themselves as permanently changed, and make difficult choices. Countless individuals are satisfied to go on resenting and hating people who wrong them. They stew in their own inner poisons and even contaminate those around them. Forgivers, on the other hand, are not content to be stuck in a quagmire. They reject the possibility that the rest of their lives will be determined by the unjust and injurious acts of another person.

—Beverly Flanigan

Forgiveness both of self and others is not an issue that is typically named in therapeutic journals and coursework. Perhaps because it has been seen as the province of religion or because it feels too prescriptive or forced, it is not often directly addressed. Letting go is seen as a part of most therapeutic paths, though it is seldom called forgiveness. Whatever we choose to call it, this phenomenon implies a recognition that some things don't change on the outside so we need to come up with a way to change them on the inside. We need to reframe them and view them in such a way that our faith in life and relationships can be restored and we can move forward.

The twelve steps have also long recognized the need for addicts to make amends to those they hurt except when to do so could cause further harm. This is considered a part of the process of recovering from drugs and alcohol, a preventative from relapse—and a part of attempting to restore both inner peace and relationship equanimity. And forgiving the self has to take place at some point in recovery in order to continue to grow in our ability to embrace life and love.

In order to fully heal, it is important to consolidate the "good," so to speak, to work through what pain is blocking our ability to experience, and, in a sense, lay claim to our own positive inner and outer experiences and incorporate them as a living, breathing part of self. Without this consolidation, we may keep living in the wound. We can revisit the wound, embrace and understand it, but we do need to live in the "good" as well to integrate it and accept all of it, good, bad and indifferent, as being a part of our experience. Because we are more than our woundedness; we are life itself, with all of its richness and potential.

Forgiveness is a process, not an event, and it is generally motivated by some kind of recognition that what we're holding on to is causing us damage and holding on to it just isn't worth it anymore. If it's ourselves we're forgiving we may have come to the realization that no one is benefiting from our holding a grudge against ourselves. Instead we're keeping ourselves glued to pain from the past, and we acknowledge that we want to find some way of letting go of it. We may benefit from just considering forgiveness, even if we only entertain the idea. After all, there may be no magic moment when all is forgiven; we may always carry some residual feelings of hurt or resentment toward ourselves or another.

Considering forgiveness is simply a way to lighten the load a day at a time, to live toward a solution even if we never fully get there. Forgiveness gives us a positive goal, so that in working with anger and sadness we remember that the goal is not to live in anger and sadness but to eventually get beyond them, to let them go and move on. It is an organizing emotion as opposed to a fragmenting one, much in the way anger can feel organizing and mobilizing.

Clients may need to consider forgiveness toward themselves so that they can have the motivation to stay with recovery, and toward others so that they can get free of a past that may be keeping them locked in a cycle of self-destructive behavior. Forgiving, in my experience, is not necessarily a one-time act but a way of looking at a circumstance with a greater sense of compassion.

BLOCKS TO FORGIVENESS

There are a few stumbling blocks when clients consider forgiveness. One is the feeling that if they forgive they are in some way condoning wrong actions. Another is the finality of it and releasing the hope of ever righting the wrong or getting retribution. Another is letting go of the wish of finally getting what they always wanted. Still another is the implication that forgiving means that they wish to continue having a relationship with the person they're forgiving. But forgiving someone who has hurt us doesn't necessarily mean we want to continue a relationship with him or her. Forgiveness is not a one-time event, and it doesn't mean we relinquish our right to continued feelings about an issue. Some clients feel that if they forgive they have to eradicate any residual feelings of hurt and anger or they haven't really forgiven, but in my experience this is not realistic.

Forgiveness in my experience plays out as a recognition within the self of a wish or a need to place a particular issue into a different internal context—moving something from the foreground to the background. Clients who consider forgiveness as part of their healing process are coming to terms with all of these issues and recognizing that they want inner peace more than a grudge to nurse. They are forgiving to free themselves and to restore their own equilibrium and sense of joy. It is a statement about where they are in their own healing process.

The twelve steps have built an amends process into the steps, which they encourage all addicts to work. Addicts have often hurt those who love them throughout their addiction. They can carry a deep sense of self-loathing for their actions. They need to do what they can to make it right, if the situation permits, so that they take responsibility for their own actions. Otherwise they risk feeling very bad about themselves, plagued with guilt, shame and other negative feelings that can make them want to self-medicate to make the pain go away—to relapse, in other words.

MAKING AMENDS

Addictive behaviors are often attempts at running from our own inner turbulence, misguided attempts at quieting an inner storm. The storm is often about feeling hurt by others or hurting others through our own behavior. The two are intertwined, feeding off of and fueling each other. Asking for or granting forgiveness offers a way out, a way to make an attempt at restitution, to restore peace and serenity. We've done our part to right a wrong from both sides.

Dr. Ken Hart of the Leeds Forgiveness for Addiction Treatment Study (FATS) says, "Controversy often arises because people fail to understand that forgiveness is always desirable, but attempts at reconciliation may sometimes be ill-advised." Dr. Hart's study is testing two different approaches to forgiveness: *secular* and *spiritual*.

The secular approach aims to speed up the growth of empathy and compassion so that addicts can better understand the imperfections and flaws of those who have hurt them. In psychodrama, we do this through role reversal by giving clients the opportunity to stand in the shoes of another person. Usually, they come to realize that the sense of "badness" they carry around from having interpreted their abuse to mean "something must be wrong with me, or I wouldn't be treated this way," isn't, and probably never was true. They were in the wrong place at the wrong time; they got hurt because another person was projecting his own unhealed pain on them. This awareness can be a great burden lifted and allows the hurt person to see her hurt differently and to take it less personally. It can also develop some empathy, as the next question is, "Well, if it wasn't about me in the first place, then what was it about? What was inside the person who hurt me?" This is a step toward real understanding.

The second type of forgiveness tested is spiritually based twelve-step-oriented forgiveness used by Project MATCH in the United States. In this approach, addicts who have harmed others are encouraged to apologize for their wrongdoing, thereby making attempts at restitution. According to Hart, "Seeking forgiveness through the amends process requires incredible humility; the assistance of a Higher Power (God) helps people to transcend their ego, which normally balks when asked to admit mistakes." He goes on to say, "We think the two treatments can help people in addiction recovery drop the burden of carrying around pain from the past."

These two approaches to forgiveness—gaining empathy if we're the hurt party, and making amends if we're the offending party—are useful cornerstones in our own practical approach to forgiveness.

But forgiveness cannot and should not be pushed, rushed or arrived at prematurely. Clients who have been deeply wounded need to take ample time to process all of their feelings of anger, resentment and sadness, to mourn the losses they have experienced and come to terms with them. Generally this process itself will bring them closer to letting go, but it can often take many years. People develop PTSD symptoms because something has terrified them, whether they are a prisoner of war, a rape victim or a child who has been sexually, physically or emotionally abused by a parent. Someone in a position of power has forced the victim to submit to his or her will. That makes him vulnerable and when he shares his stories that vulnerability surfaces, along with fear, mistrust and other feelings such as anger and sadness. It can be retraumatizing if he feels coerced into forgiving either before he is ready or by sharing material he would rather not share. He needs to feel safe, supported and to go at his own pace with encouragement that is gentle. Generally forgiveness isn't an idea introduced by me; it arises spontaneously from someone in a group and then we talk about it or work with what might be in its way, as is the case in our next case study.

Anne's Story

Anne came to group wanting to do a very particular psychodrama; she wanted to forgive her first husband, to finally get past her hurt and anger toward him so that he would "stop living inside me."

Anne: I just want to let this thing go, to let him go, to get past this somehow. I just feel so stuck here and I'm not sure why.

Tian: What's the scene?

Anne: I need to talk to Bill. Andy, could you play Bill? Sorry, I know it's a lot to ask.

Andy: Sure, I'll do it.

Tian: Reverse roles with Bill and show us a bit about him.

Anne: (As Bill) Anne, you ruined my life; you ruined our children's lives. I don't want you near our granddaughter, and I have custody of her, so I'm going to do everything to make it impossible.

Tian: (to Andy) Have you got that?

Andy: (nods, yes, then talks to Anne as Bill) You can't see our granddaughter.

Anne: (in tears) Why are you like this? We both messed up; we both made a mess of things. I had a horrible time with your drinking when the kids were small; it was so hard. Then you sobered up, and I thought it would be better but you never got recovery. You were just awful, a dry drunk, no program, no inner growth. Then I got into drugs, and I left you and lived in a situation with the kids that was bad for them. I know that. But we both messed up. Can't you see that? Can't you understand that it was both of us?

Tian: Reverse roles.

Anne: (as Bill) It was you, your fault; I didn't want you to leave. You ruined my life.

Tian: Can you take a step back and double for what you imagine is going on inside of Bill?"

Anne: (as Bill) I'll never let you have her. I can never tell you how much you hurt me. I loved you, and I hated you for leaving me. I won't budge. I don't want to hear that I did anything; I loved you and you left me.

Tian: Reverse roles.

Anne: (screaming with anger) I'm so angry with you. How could you be so petty; don't you get it? Our grandchildren aren't pawns; they're innocent. How can you be so evil? I can't believe I ever loved you. What happened to us? We loved each other once. That's what's so hard. I was so in love with you. You were drunk and hard to live with, but I loved you. (Anne breaks into sobs) It's just so sad. I loved you, I loved you, I loved you.

Tian: Would you like to have Bill as a reformed auxiliary?

Anne: Yes, it would never happen, but I'd really like it. Jerry, can you play the Bill I wish was there?

Jerry: Yes.

Anne: (putting her arms around Jerry's neck and her head on his chest) We love each other. I love you. I love you. It feels so good to say it. I want us to get along. We had these wonderful children together. We created two people; it's a miracle. Our beautiful children. Oh, I love you.

Jerry: I love you, I love our children. You're a wonderful grandmother. I love to watch you with our grandchildren.

Anne: This feels so good. I don't want to hate you. I loved you so much. We're a part of each other. I carried your children inside me; I carried you inside me; I carried us inside me. I'm so tired of hating you. That's good. I'm done.

Anne ended the scene with both "Bills" and sat down for sharing. In the weeks that followed, Anne reported feeling freer than she had felt for years around this issue. She said that she'd been sharing it with a friend who wondered how it could work, as it hadn't really happened. Anne replied, "But it did happen; it happened in me. That's where I needed it to happen, inside of me, and I just feel so much better and free of something that was hanging over me and taking away my peace of mind."

THE STAGES OF FORGIVENESS

Clients seem to pass through a predictable set of stages before forgiveness occurs much as in the grief process. I have attempted to name those stages and have created exercises to address the process of forgiveness. I would remind the reader that there is no one-size-fits-all approach to anything, including forgiveness. These stages are meant only to suggest a process and make it a workable one, to provide a framework. They may be experienced in a different order, leapfrogged or some skipped entirely depending upon the severity of the issue and the person involved. Also, the goal is not to get rid of feelings like anger or sadness but to experience them and integrate them into the self-system with greater understanding and insight and through doing so moderate them and reframe the issue. Once people understand that they are hurting *themselves* by nursing resentments and undermining their *own* happiness, reframing has begun.

1. **Waking Up.** We realize we're holding onto something that's hurting us maybe even more than the other person, or that we need to forgive ourselves for something and stop beating ourselves up on the inside.
2. **Anger and Resentment.** We're hurt and angry. We resent the other person because we see him or her as being the cause of our pain.
3. **Sadness and Hurt.** We're in pain. We feel wronged or wounded, and we're probably also worrying that we did something wrong that we don't quite understand.

4. **Integration, Reorganization.** We feel and experience split-off emotions associated with internal blocks and place them into a new context. We reintegrate them into ourselves with new awareness and insight.

5. **Reinvestment.** The process of forgiving and working through blocked emotion frees up energy that can be reinvested into improving relationships with self, others and life.

EXAMINING MYTHS ABOUT FORGIVENESS

GOALS:
1. To provide an action format for working with issues of forgiveness or letting go.
2. To provide a way of bringing forgiveness into the recovery process that isn't overly prescriptive.

STEPS:
1. Using a locogram format (see page 346) write each myth on a separate sheet of paper and scatter them on the floor:
   - If I forgive, my relationship with the person I'm forgiving will definitely improve.
   - If I forgive, I'll no longer feel angry at that person for what happened.
   - If I forgive, I forgo my right to hurt feelings.
   - If I forgive, it means I want to continue to have a relationship with the person I'm forgiving.
   - If I forgive, it means I'm condoning the behavior of the person I'm forgiving.
   - If I haven't forgotten, I haven't really forgiven.
   - I only need to forgive once.
   - I forgive for the sake of the other person.
   - Other.
2. Invite group members to stand near the myth they most identify with.
3. Ask group members to share about why they chose that particular myth.
4. Repeat this process for a few of the myths that people most identify with.
5. Next, invite group members to walk over to someone who said something that they particularly identify with and place their hand on that person's shoulder.
6. Invite group members to share with the person they chose why they chose him or her. Allow time for the sharing of the subgroupings that will have naturally formed.
7. Move into psychodramas or return to seats for sharing.

VARIATIONS:
The director may allow group members to double for each other throughout the process if they feel warmed-up to do so. These myths can also be talked about by writing them on a chalkboard and asking participants which myth they identify with.

Psychodramatic journaling can be added by journaling about the myth most identified with and sharing what is written in the group or subgroups. (See *tiandayton.com* for download of myths.)

STAGES OF FORGIVENESS: LOCOGRAM

GOALS:

1. To provide an experiential format for dividing the process of forgiveness into stages.
2. To allow for a supportive setting in which to confront issues related to the forgiveness process.

STEPS:

1. Designate areas of the floor to represent each of the following stages of forgiveness:
   - Waking up
   - Acceptance, integration and letting go
   - Anger and resentment
   - Reinvestment
   - Sadness and hurt
   - Other
2. Invite group members to identify a forgiveness issue that they are dealing with and to walk over and stand in the area that best represents where they feel they are in their forgiveness process.
3. Invite group members to share about why they are standing where they are standing.
4. Repeat this process if group members feel that they identify with more than one stage.
5. Next, invite group members to either share with those who are standing near them and are at the same stage in their process or find someone who they feel they can get help from in moving along in their process or someone who has said something with which they identify and place their hand on that person's shoulder.
6. Invite group members to share with the person they chose, why they chose him or her.
7. Next, either move into psychodramas around issues of forgiveness or return to seats for further sharing and processing.

VARIATIONS:

Doubling can be a part of this exercise. This exercise can also be followed by journaling what comes up or writing a letter to someone with whom you have an unresolved issue. If you use letter-writing refer to the Letter-Writing Exercise (page 196) for ways of sharing the letter psychodramatically.

FORGIVING ANOTHER PERSON OR FORGIVING THE SELF

GOALS:

1. To concretize a relationship that involves forgiveness issues.
2. To work through issues that may be blocking forgiveness.

STEPS:

1. Ask group members to think of and share about someone who they are having trouble forgiving, including themselves if that is what is most present.
2. Invite whoever feels warmed-up to self-select and choose someone to play that person or herself, or use an empty chair to represent one or the other.
3. Allow the scene to unfold and work with it using any and all techniques that might be appropriate, including role reversal.
4. Bring the scene to closure whenever it seems to be coming toward resolution by saying, "Say the last things you need to say for now."
5. Return to seats for sharing.

VARIATIONS:

More than one vignette or monodrama can be done one right after the other, and the sharing can happen after several are finished. In this case group members can share with whomever they identified with and role-players can de-role.

Psychodramatic journaling can be an extension by writing a letter to the self or to another person and then sharing the letter (see Letter Writing 196). If this is added, continue sharing and processing after all letters have been shared.

ASKING FOR ANOTHER PERSON'S FORGIVENESS

GOALS:

1. To get square with the self so clients can stop carrying unspoken shame and guilt.
2. To concretize a forgiveness issue and work through the blocks within the self that may be keeping a client from making amends.

STEPS:

1. Ask group members to think of someone from whom they want forgiveness or someone they feel a need to make an amends to.
2. Ask them to share about this person.
3. Invite whoever feels warmed-up to self-select and choose someone to represent this person, or use an empty chair.
4. Allow the protagonist to begin the scene in which he is asking for someone's forgiveness. Let the scene progress and use role reversal and whatever other techniques feel appropriate.
5. When the scene seems to be coming to natural closure say, "Say the last things you'd like to say for now."
6. Allow others to follow with more vignettes, and then share after several, or return to seats for sharing.

VARIATIONS:

This scene can be done asking forgiveness from more than one person, if necessary. Psychodramatic journaling can be added by writing a letter to someone asking for their forgiveness. Letters can be read in groups or subgroups and then continue sharing and processing. (See Letter Writing page 196.)

Part III:

Special Populations: Adapting Sociometry and Psychodrama for Focused Use in Addiction and Co-occurring Issues

A House Divided Against Itself: Working with Addicts, ACOAs and Codependents

Children of alcoholic parents are conservatively numbered at twenty-two million people (Deutsch 1982). Children of alcoholics are at an over-five times-higher risk for becoming addicts themselves and frequently marry addicts or ACOAs (adult children of alcoholics). Because of the unpredictable, uncontrollable and inherently traumatic nature of substance abuse and addiction, people who are chemically dependent, or those in an addict's family system such as spouses, children and siblings, usually experience some form of psychological damage; in other words, they are traumatized by the experience. "Family members as well as many addicts present disorders that extend across a range of clinical syndromes, such as anxiety disorders, reactive and endogenous depression, psychosomatic symptoms, psychotic episodes, eating disorders and substance abuse, as well as developmental deficits, distortions in self-image, confused inner worlds with disorganized internal dynamics, and codependency" (Dayton 2000). After all, they have grown up in family systems that managed emotional, psychological and spiritual pain with a drug. The patterns of behavior they have learned have been sinisterly designed to keep its use and abuse uninterrupted and intact. And their own grasp on normal has been seriously compromised. Along with genetic factors that may be present, it is no wonder that alcoholic family systems are self-perpetuating if intervention and rigorous treatment don't halt the progress of the disease. But during the recovery those intense emotions, such as sadness, that are an inevitable part of grieving our losses, can make them feel like they're "falling apart" all over again, and consequently they may resist the grief process so necessary for healing. The rupturing of deep limbic or emotional bonds that have imprinted themselves on our neural systems can leave one feeling "shattered" or "fragmented," making it difficult to pull the lost pieces of self together into a coherent whole. This can make entering recovery feel even more threatening.

Trauma and Addiction as an Intergenerational Disease Process

Because living with addiction creates trauma symptoms and trauma symptoms can lead one to self medicate with drugs and alcohol, trauma and addiction can become an intergenerational disease process. Children who grow up in addicted systems have been traumatized and they have all too often been taught, by example, to deal with painful emotions by acting out, withdrawing, numbing or self medicating with drugs, alcohol, food, sex or hyperactivity. Because pain is not openly addressed and because of the family's problems with regulation, children may not learn to manage their emotional lives in healthy ways. In addition, as these children grow into adulthood and pressures to get their lives together increase, they live under greater amounts of emotional stress. As they form families of their own, the intimate relationships that they inevitably engage in with partners and children can create more stress as they trigger unresolved pain, and the ACOA may lack the tools to handle it well. As this occurs, the ACOA may do what they learned to do: they may attempt to self medicate. Another common pattern is to adopt another medicator or partner with someone who self medicates. In this manner, both trauma and addiction may become self-perpetuating. Children of addiction are four times more likely to become addicts themselves, and these statistics don't include multiple addictions such as food, sex, gambling, work addiction etc. Nor do they include those who marry addicts. Many feel that there is a genetic predisposition to addiction and there is certainly evidence that this may be the case. However, even putting genetics aside, the patterns that emerge generation after generation put each generation at risk for addiction if rigorous treatment doesn't intervene. Even if the generation beneath the addict doesn't evidence drug or alcohol addiction, they may well be passing on the types of dysfunctional relationship dynamics that put the next generation at risk. In this way, addiction becomes a family illness that is intergenerational. This is why, in addictive family systems, each person in the family needs to undergo a rigorous recovery effort in order to arrest the disease progression in its path and learn and adopt new, healthy patterns of relating.

THE DRY-DRUNK SYNDROME

This commonly known syndrome occurs when the addict sobers up from the drug but does not do the recovery work necessary to become what Bill W. referred to as "emotionally sober." This attempt to stay sober without recovery supports in place is often referred to as "white knuckling it." Without the medicator taking the edge off, the addict is left with the symptoms that hurt to begin with and no way to deaden their effect. Hyperreactivity, grouchiness, bouts of rage, tendency toward depression and problems with intimacy are all part and parcel of the dry-drunk syndrome, where the addict still exhibits many problematic behaviors but is not abusing a substance. If there is a duel diagnosis, which is so often the case in addiction, the diagnosis of addiction is properly dealt with by removing the substance, but the underlying diagnosis, say of depression, anxiety, PTSD or whatever it is, is not dealt with. Recovery is about more than recovering from substance abuse. It is also and very importantly about recovering from the other diagnosis reflecting the symptoms that may have been self medicated in the first place. And even if there is no duel diagnosis, the addict will still need to engage in a full recovery process in order to deal with the emotional and psychological complications that stemmed from the addiction. If they do not do this, they are asking both themselves and their family members to live with emotional and psychological burdens that can keep the family and the individuals within it mired in dysfunctional patterns of relating that get passed along through the generations, commonly referred to as "passing on the pain."

Part of what addicts, ACOAs and codependents are doing in recovery is rewiring their body/mind systems to be able to tolerate increasing amounts of emotional and psychological pain without blowing up, shutting down or self medicating. This limbic reregulation happens slowly and over time. A week or a month or even a year is not enough time to accomplish this intricate mind/body task. It takes years for clients, in my experience, to accomplish these deep changes and it requires that they are vigilant and responsible about staying on the recovery path, i.e. "walking the walk" not just "talking the talk."

It includes:

- limbic rewiring
- creating a new support network or revitalizing aspects of existing ones
- doing body work, exercising and adopting good nutritional habits
- learning healthy ways of self soothing
- doing the family-of-origin, present-day family and trauma work in order to work with issues that contributed to using and dysfunction
- finding alternative ways to attain a "feel good" state, such as exercise, meditation/relaxation/breath work, finding meaningful activities and hobbies.

For all concerned, recovery is a must, in my opinion. All too often, family members want to cordon the problem off somewhere outside of themselves because the trauma that they have experienced simply makes deep reflection feel too risky. Unconsciously they may feel that if they let it hurt again, if they allow themselves to know how much pain they carry, they won't come out the other end whole and intact. And they have developed lifelong patterns designed to avoid feeling pain. But avoiding large pockets of the self means that we have to avoid large pockets of others as well; we have to avoid deep connection because it triggers old fear and pain. I am not suggesting that we make therapy a lifestyle and feel that each and every hurt needs to be dug up and dealt with, but the major blocks need to be faced in order for those who have been wounded to heal. If healing doesn't occur, the likelihood of passing on the pain to another generation is high. And all too often, the parents themselves aren't modeling good recovery. They may even behave as if they feel they have little to do with how their own lives look, constantly pointing the finger toward someone else and not pausing to reflect on their piece in each situation; as if someone else were in the driver's seat of their lives and they simply came along for the ride.

Clients who grew up in an alcoholic family system may have struggled through childhood and adolescence trying to paste together some sense of "normal" while daily warding off a variety of assaults on their self-esteem, peace of mind, and sense of comfort and safety. They may also have found themselves moving into adult roles carrying huge burdens from the past that they don't know exactly what to do with and may get them into trouble in their current relationships and/or work lives. In a family where addiction is present, one virtually never hears the addicted parent say, "I have a real drinking problem. I must be wounding you deeply with my erratic behavior, causing hurt and confusion by what I say, what I don't say, the plans I mess up and the promises I break." Nor is it likely the addict's partner will have the presence of mind or lack of guilt, hurt and rage to say to the children involved, "I know how tough this is for you, but don't worry. You are our top priority, and you can count on us to do our level best on a daily basis to provide a comfortable, nurturing and safe environment for you to grow up in." It is equally unlikely that we would hear the siblings open up and say to each other, "Do you feel as crazy as I feel? Do you spend your days feeling anxious about our parents, our family and our future?" And to make matters worse, parents often blame their own problems on the children, who then feel bad and guilty. About at this point children set about the impossible task of trying to make their parents feel better, helping them to heal. Out of this, stratified roles may emerge: the family hero striving to restore dignity; the scapegoat and the mascot both busy distracting the family from the real problems; and the lost child, the one "no one needs to think about." The top of the authority structure is occupied by the addict who uses and the enabler who is also, oftentimes, subsumed by the disease.

When ACOAs attempt to have families and relationships in adulthood, they may overreact to the vicissitudes of daily living, not so much because they feel strongly about a given situation, but because they are afraid of the potential strength of their own feelings. They may fuse with partners or children in an unconscious attempt to ward off feelings of abandonment, withdraw into an emotional coolness to keep them at bay or get easily triggered into historical emotions that current intimacy is stirring up. They can have trouble sustaining a sense of self while in the presence of their partners, a challenge for the most normal among us, but for ACOAs this can be unusually difficult. Parenthood and intimacy act as triggers, and the feelings of dependency and vulnerability that are a part of them can put ACOAs into a state of fear in which they see chaos, out-of-control behavior and abuse looming around every corner because this was their early childhood experience. They may unconsciously be so convinced that distress is at hand that they may experience mistrust and suspicion if problems are solved smoothly. Often they will push a situation in a misguided self-protective attempt to ferret out potential danger until, through their relentless efforts to avoid it, they actually create it. And so the pattern of strong feelings leading to chaos, rage and tears is once again reinforced and passed along.

THE BRAIN: TRYING TO MAKE SENSE OF THE SENSELESS

An additional reason that triggered unconscious pain can be so confusing for the ACOA to decode is that emotional responses to trauma are processed primarily by the parts of the brain that were developed early in our evolution, often referred to as the "reptilian" or "old" brain. These are the parts of the brain associated with the fight-flight-freeze response and where fear, anger and sadness are, at least in part, processed. The cortex, which is where we do much of our critical thinking and meaning making, where we think about what we're feeling and make sense of it, was an evolutionary add-on. Consequently, while being deeply frightened and hurt as children, ACOAs may have been too frozen in fear to process what was happening around them. The cortex did not get a chance to modulate the memory, or reflect upon, think about, quantify and categorize particular painful events so they could be worked through and integrated with a rational read on the situation. Marooned in a full-blown trauma response, they may have been left unable to regulate it or to make sense of it on their own with only the powers of reason and the emotional maturity and capability for insight available to them at the time. The adults in the situation may have been too preoccupied with their own problems to take time out to help children understand what was happening around them. As a result, when these fragments of unprocessed memory get triggered in their adult present, they have no context; they're all out of order and can get mindlessly blasted onto the surface of their current relationships. They feel like they felt when the original events happened: defenseless and vulnerable, perceiving whomever they feel hurt by, be it a boss or a partner, as having all the power. All this intense feeling seems, in their minds, to relate only to the current situation but, in truth, it has its origins in the past. When it gets interpreted as if it belongs exclusively to the present, they may try to make sense of an adult situation through the traumatized mind of the child living inside of them. So they do what they did: they dig in, rely on their old defenses and ride out the supposed storm.

And to make matters even more challenging, the parents who hurt them may have improved through recovery, therapy, or just grown somehow nicer as their lives became less stressed and more manageable. This can make the ACOA feel as if they've made something up. "How could the relatively benign or recovered person sitting in front of me have ever been as damaging and hurtful as the child in me feels he was. I must be the crazy one." They may struggle with issues of forgiveness, wanting to let go of a past that's dogging their trail and undermining their lives.

THE CONNECTION BETWEEN TRAUMA AND ADDICTION

A significant symptom of PTSD is to "self-medicate with drugs and alcohol"(Van der Kolk 1987). "As the psychiatric diagnostic system became more sophisticated (American Psychiatric Association, 1980; 1984; 1994), researchers and clinicians realized that many people with substance disorders qualified for other Axis I diagnoses (Deas-Nesmith, Campbell, & Brady, 1998). Major depression in its several manifestations (mild, moderate, severe, or severe with psychotic symptoms) is a common condition that is frequently co-morbid with substance abuse. Substance abuse is often an attempt to self-medicate for depression and other distressing symptoms. Current research such as the Adverse Childhood Events (ACE) study from the Center for Disease Control (Edwards et al., 2003; Felitti et al., 1998) reveals another correlation—that of adverse events in childhood (such as sexual and physical abuse and "witnessing maternal battering") with negative outcomes in adult physical and mental health. In addition, just as traumatic events can lead to substance abuse, substance abuse can lead to traumatic events" (Vik and Brown 1998, cited by Linda Gant 2003).

Trauma, because it is stored in the body, gives rise to somatic disturbances and upsetting body sensations such as heart-pounding, queasiness, sweating, tightness of muscles and shortness of breath. The rise in disturbing body sensations can trigger the disturbing trauma imagery that is stored in the mind such as nightmares and flashbacks (Van der Kolk 1987). This can become a vicious circle in which the body and mind play off of each other, causing a negative synergy in which the disturbing imagery triggers disturbing body sensations and visa versa, putting trauma survivors into a emotional crisis. Drugs and alcohol, for trauma survivors, can provide a way to quiet the mind and the body they can have control over, a sort of self-administered medication. But sooner or later, the medication becomes a primary problem of its own. As the body builds tolerance, and both body and mind become addicted, greater amounts of the drug are needed to feel "okay." Thus the addiction takes hold, the PTSD symptoms become worse not better, and lives become unmanageable for all concerned. This is why counselors in treatment centers across the United States find themselves working with complex dual-diagnosis cases. As the addict sobers up, the depression, anxiety and/or PTSD symptoms begin to emerge. The following diagram illustrates the connection between trauma and addiction.

The Wheel of Trauma and Addiction
(Dayton 2000)

Life complications get deeper, more overwhelming, and harder to solve as drugs and other addictions take over, invading all aspects of one's life.

Emotional and psychological pain, shame, helplessness, rage and turbulent inner world related to trauma.

Greater need for larger amounts of drugs, alcohol, food, sex, nicotine or combinations of several of these due to increased physical tolerance and persistent and pervasive emotional and psychological problems.

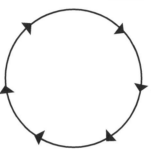

Self-medication through drugs, alcohol, food, sex, spending, hyperactivity, etc.

More emotional and psychological pain, shame, and turbulent inner world, and weakened personal resources to deal with them due to drug dependence.

Life complications—trouble with relationships, work, loss of true play and enjoyment as a result of unresolved trauma and drug use pervading and controlling inner world. Somatic symptoms.

©*Tian Dayton, Ph.D. Trauma and Addiction, HCI, 2000*

A Holistic Approach to Treatment: Treating the Whole Person/ Treating the Whole Family

MULTIPLE ADDICTIONS

One of the problems often faced in recovery from drug and alcohol addiction is that when the primary medicator is removed, the recovering person may reach for another to take its place. Having relied on a synthetic substance to regulate moods and "feel good" (or feel normal) the recovering person reaches for something else that will produce that "feel good" experience associated with serotonin and dopamine. Food, sex, overspending/gambling and overworking are some of the places clients go when they remove their substance. Drugs can play with brain chemistry by flooding the brain with excessive amounts of feel-good chemicals that produce a high. When the substance is removed the brain is not always able to produce needed quantities of the mood-elevating chemicals that nature meant it to do.

Many addicts who have been self-medicating emotional pain have also been looking for alternative ways to produce "feel-good" states. It is important to actively retrain alternative methods for producing feel-good chemicals in the body and soothing the limbic system and the basil ganglia, both of which play a central role in regulating moods. Treatment programs need to provide training in alternative methods of mood management that can be incorporated into daily life in order to help clients to remain sober not only from their primary addiction but other or multiple addictions they may engage in.

"The attempt to regulate affect—to minimize unpleasant feelings and to maximize pleasant ones—is the driving force in human motivation" (Schore 2004). For this reason, it is critical when doing therapy with addicts to create new, powerful motivators that are pleasurable for the recovering addict, or family members who may be depressed or deregulated. Such motivators may be in-house treatment programs; twelve-step meetings; new sober friendships; pleasurable activities such as working out, jogging, biking, hiking and so on; and hobbies such as gardening, reading, writing, painting, drama, woodworking, crafts or body work such as massage, yoga or other forms of gentle exercises. Play and leisure activities also become very important so that addicts, ACOAs and those in recovery can learn new skills of interpersonal relating in a sober, lighthearted manner and absorb new skills of self-regulation. All of these activities can also open the doors to new ways of self-soothing as the activities tend to stimulate the body's opioid system.

THE OPIATES OF ATTACHMENT

Recent research has revealed that the mother/child attachment bond works on the pleasure-reward centers of the brain known as the opiate centers, much like a drug. Evolution has seen to it that both mothers and children "feel good" through their mutual connection. The circulation of naturally occurring opiates like endorphins helps us experience relief and comfort. Messenger chemicals like dopamine help reinforce the sensation of being rewarded. We are being rewarded by the body's natural "feel good" system, the system that calms, soothes and regulates when we experience a close, nurturing bond. Oxytocin, known as the "touch" chemical, releases as we touch and make us want to touch more. Attachment is an all-over experience; it's in the body and the mind.

One may theorize from this that children who grow up with "good-enough" parents have the advantage of knowing "naturally" how to draw comfort and pleasure from a normal range of relationships and activities. Addicts may be seeking a way to self-medicate or create or recreate a state of pleasure and well-being through chemical means: to create for the first time or replace a lost or desired emotional experience—that sense of calm and oneness experienced in the early holding relationship with the parent. Whether or not this is the case, however, recovery needs to create a soothing, regulating "holding environment" that can create a sense of pleasure if it is to motivate addicts to stay sober, or ACOAs or codependents to stay with recovery.

The convivial joking feeling (including even graveyard humor) that one so often finds in treatment programs, twelve-step rooms and successful clinical groups actually heals and motivates. It is the recovering person's intuitive attempt to reregulate the limbic system through laughter and connection. Most plants grow toward the sun. So do people.

In addition, there will likely be a period of intense neediness as clients regress into early stages of development. They may want to attach intensely to therapists, group members and the program in order to rework early attachment bonds. This can be a very intense period for the therapist as well as the client. Indeed, how therapists respond at critical junctures such as these can be important moments of creating a strong attachment bond with clients or contributing to a repeated feeling of rupture. Therapists need to be aware of the intense sense of vulnerability the client may be experiencing as they reach out to see if anyone will be there, if they can experience a sense of holding and pleasure. But as clients experienced disappointment, their cries for help may be experienced as panicky demands. It's hard enough to tolerate this from a child let alone an adult who is able to come at you with the all the force of a tall, experienced and verbal (or acting-out) person. Creating a solid recovery holding environment is helpful here so the client can have many possible recovery resources from which to seek "first responders" when in need.

Early Versus Late-Stage Recovery

When Can You Safely Use Experiential Approaches and Work with Dually Diagnosed Clients?

In the first stage of recovery, clients need to stabilize their addictive patterns so they can live without picking up. Oftentimes addicts demonstrate that if they become too stirred up emotionally they desperately want to reach for their medicator, be it alcohol, sex, a drug, etc. Doing intensive family-of-origin work at this point, for example, whether it be through psychodrama or any other modality, can overwhelm the addict and make him want to use. This is because the symptoms that the addict was self-medicating—the emotional and psychological pain that he has been drinking or drugging to numb—may begin to surface when the medicator is removed. (see Characteristics of Adult Children of Trauma and Addiction, pages 240–1). His symptoms may be too intense to allow him to tolerate forms of therapy that overwhelm and make him want to self-medicate. However, as recovery progresses, not addressing these issues can become a problem that can also lead to relapse. Dr. Joseph Kern, director of treatment for the Nassau County Department of Drug Addiction, puts it this way, "We've been treating addicts as if they didn't have a childhood, meaning ignoring the childhood trauma. Addiction treatment generally is here and now, how to stay clean and sober one day at a time, teaching skills to discharge feelings using some healthy discharge like sharing, human contact, centering, exercise, etc. This is a very important first step, because until the recovering person develops the ability to tolerate strong emotions without resorting to chemicals, working with early loss and trauma issues may contribute to relapse. The addict needs to get new hard wiring so he can learn to tolerate the powerful emotions that will inevitably surface. However if he doesn't process his unresolved pain at some point, it will continue to be the pain pump that fuels relapse." Dr. Kern continues, "In the beginning stage of recovery, if you talk about how mad you are at your father you may pick up, while in the next stage the reverse is true, if you don't talk about how mad you are at your father, you may pick up."

The pressure from unresolved childhood wounds doesn't disappear. Quite the contrary, the healthier you get and the more risks you take toward intimacy and connection, the more the unresolved pain gets warmed up. Many treatment centers have added trauma tracks to address just these issues. Having said all this, each treatment center finds its own balance, which is to say, sometimes it can be more retraumatizing to be told not to talk about something that is coming up early in recovery than finding ways of sharing it that are not too disequilibrating. In this case, adhering to strict rules about avoiding certain subjects may be less than helpful. There is no cookie-cutter approach; as with motherhood, the therapist's intuition is often the best guide if he or she is well attuned to his or her client population.

GETTING HELP FOR THE ENTIRE FAMILY SYSTEM

The effects of living with addiction for years don't go away in a "family week," though it is an excellent intervention. Family members need their own form of help or treatment, as well as addicts, in order to:

- allow the family system that has supported addiction to change enough to support sobriety;
- allow family members to heal from their own PTSD issues from spending years living with addiction or heal from the pain they brought into their partnership or family that may have contributed to family dysfunction or both.

The family problems faced by clinicians attempting to address issues of addiction are so significant and numerous that no sooner is one set of problems solved than another emerges. The addict becoming, as Bill W. put it, "emotionally sober" requires treating the PTSD or family-of-origin issues that were being medicated in the first place, which can be even more challenging than getting sober was. Becoming emotionally sober for the spouse, codependent or ACOA means treating the issues either brought into the partnership or those developed through living with addiction.

The trauma that this population experiences may be keeping them from getting the help they need. Remember, the defenses associated with trauma are often designed around warding off or minimizing the resultant pain, confusion and sense of helplessness that is virtually always a part of living with addiction. And people who have been traumatized often don't want to go near the emotional and psychological material that left them feeling wounded, vulnerable and helpless. The psychological defenses that surround trauma, such as numbing and dissociation, may make traumatic material either unavailable or feel threatening and confusing when approached. Consequently, people who need help may not wish to "go there," and the more wounded they are, the stronger their defenses can be.

The Addicted, Traumatized Family System Model

THE BLACK-AND-WHITE WORLD OF THE ADDICTED FAMILY

No family is well enough fortified to maintain a healthy, nourishing structure in the midst of the spreading decay of addiction and the damage it wreaks on all who surround it. Substance abuse decreases the ability of a family to provide an environment for its individual members in which healthy bonding, growth and development can occur. Deep defenses designed to ward off feelings of humiliation, fear and helplessness get seared into place, affecting emotional and cognitive development. The healthy development of the family as a whole, along with each individual, is seriously compromised by living with addiction and the dysfunctional patterns of relating that surround it.

Addiction also makes it virtually impossible for the user themselves to heal his own pain; instead he is anesthetizing it and living on borrowed time. Initially, addicts may feel they have found a way to manage a pain-filled inner world. Unfortunately, in the long run, they create one. Their partners, too, become involved in the disease process to such an extent that they lose their sense of normal family and life functioning. Their life becomes about hiding the truth from themselves, their children and their relational world. As they do this they come to live a secret life, one in which their secure hold on the so-called normal world starts to slip. Because the disease is progressive, family members seamlessly slip into patterns of relating that become increasingly dysfunctional. They may adopt elaborate defenses designed to "look good" or seem normal; withdraw into their own private world or compete for the little love and attention that is available; they yell, withdraw, cajole, harangue, criticize, understand or get fed up—you name it. In the absence of reliable adults, siblings may become parentified and try to provide the care and comfort that is missing for each other. Or they may become co-opted by one parent as a surrogate partner, filling in the gaping holes and massaging the sore spots of a family in a constant low level of crisis; on-the-job training for codependency. Such families become characterized by a kind of emotional and psychological constriction, where members do not feel free to express their authentic selves for fear of triggering disaster; their genuine feelings are often hidden under strategies for keeping safe, like pleasing or withdrawing. The family becomes organized around trying to manage the unmanageable disease of addiction. In their desperate attempts to maintain family equilibrium they invent a novel strategy at each new turn of the disease progression. Some members overfunction, filling in ever-widening gaps to restore order and dignity, while others underfunction, providing an alternative focus for their ever-growing problems or defending against their deep fear of ultimate disappointment and failure. These families become remarkably inventive in trying everything they can come up with to contain the problem and keep the family from blowing up. The alarm bells in this system are constantly on a low hum, causing everyone to feel hypervigilant, ready to run for emotional (or physical) shelter, or to erect their defenses at the first sign of trouble.

Because family members avoid sharing subjects that might lead to more pain, they often wind up avoiding genuine connection with each other. Then when painful feelings build up they may rise to the surface in emotional eruptions or get acted out through impulsive behaviors shut down or withdrawal. These families become systems for manufacturing and perpetuating trauma. Trauma affects the internal world of each person, their relationships, and their ability to communicate and band together in a balanced, relaxed and trusting manner.

Individuals in these systems may behave in ways consistent with the behaviors of victims of other psychological traumas, in other words, they are traumatized by the experience.

The tendency to cycle back and forth between black-and-white thinking, feeling and behavior reflects the family's problems with regulation. All or nothing tends to characterize the family that has contained trauma and/or addiction. This constant back and forth is dizzying for family members who can't figure out "which end is up." They may lose their grasp on normal (Woititz 1980) functioning and their trust in a reliable, predictable order (Van der Kolk 1987). The inner world and the outer world don't match up properly; they are out of sync with each other, which can make them feel "crazy" inside. The family as a whole and each of its members can lose their ability to "right" themselves when thrown off balance.

Members who act out the underlying emotional climate in dysfunctional behaviors may become scapegoats who provide the family with a distraction, giving parents and other siblings something to be anxious about other than what's really going on. Children are sitting ducks for absorbing unprocessed emotional pain. Feeling crazy because of alternating patterns or emotional pain, they may eventually explode—at which point they are labeled the problem. They become what family systems theorists call the "symptom bearer"; they become symptomatic on behalf of the whole family. This can also have the effect of getting warring parents to pull together in order to address what's going on for the child, thus the family buys some more time, the focus is diverted and homeostasis, albeit a sick one, is again achieved. Those in the system who have the courage to act as whistle blowers, who attempt to reveal the truth of the family pathology, are often turned against and perceived by the family, who is steeped in denial, as the problem. Naming the dysfunctional behavior becomes the sin, not doing it.

However, the future need not be bleak for families who seek recovery. Much is understood about the disease process today that was not understood before. Those who embrace recovery often report that they "do not regret the past nor wish to close the door on it." This is because they have learned to find meaning in their struggle and transform it into wisdom and a deepened capacity to experience the mystery, beauty and passion of the human experience.

All families are systems in that they have their own sets of rules and behaviors, interrelated substructures, and predictable patterns of behavior. Family systems theorists have outlined some basic ideas to describe some of the fundamentals of the family system:

Families have interrelated elements and structures. The elements of the system are its family members. Each element or family member has it own set of characteristics. There are relationships between the elements that function in a relatively independent manner, and all of these create a structure.

Families interact in patterns. There are predictable modes or patterns of interaction that emerge in a family system. These patterns help maintain a family's equilibrium and provide clues to how one functions in this system.

Families have boundaries that tend to be open or closed. They have ways of defining who is on the inside or the outside of the system. Open boundary systems allow other elements to influence them and may even welcome external influences. A closed system isolates its members in a self-contained world. No family system is entirely one way or the other.

The whole is more than the sum of its parts. Families function by this composition law. Though families are made up of individual elements, the elements combine to create a whole which is greater than the sum of its parts.

There are messages and rules that shape the relationships. These messages, rules and agreements prescribe and limit a family member's behavior over time. They tend to be repetitive and redundant and are rarely, if ever, explicit or written down. They may give power, induce guilt and control or limit behavior, and they tend to perpetuate and reproduce themselves. Most messages can be stated in just a few words: be responsible, look good, keep family business private, succeed, etc.

Families have subsystems. These subsystems contain a number of small groups, usually made up of two to three people. The relationships between the people in these subsystems are known as alliances or coalitions. Each subsystem has its own boundaries and unique characteristics, and membership in the subsystems can change over time.

Families maintain a homeostasis or equilibrium (Steinglass 1987). Families tend to make many small and large adjustments to maintain what family theorists refer to as homeostasis or an overall equilibrium. This is much like a mobile, which when acted upon, will adjust to rebalance itself. (Satir 1988) A family system, too, will seek to rebalance itself in order to maintain its equilibrium when the winds of the world act upon it.

Some of the therapeutic tasks for this population are to help clients to develop the ability to tolerate strong emotions without acting out, along with enough emotional literacy so that problems can be talked out rather than explode or implode. The cerebral cortex "has more inputs from the limbic system than the limbic system has coming from the cortex" (Shore 2004). Consequently our emotions highly impact our thinking and choice-making process. Integrating these emotional messages with our reason is part of how we come to better understand ourselves and develop emotional literacy.

The Model for the Addicted/Traumatized Family System is designed to illustrate the dynamics that are present in a family that is containing both trauma and addiction in order to help clients gain a sense of the dynamics they may have internalized as children and that may be continuing to impact their lives today. It describes some specific manifestations of this pattern of cycling between extreme modes of functioning and offers a middle ground. Because, when we function in the extremes, there may be a shadow side vibrating beneath. Underneath enmeshment, for example, may be disengagement and vice versa, which is why neither extreme feels like genuine closeness. The model is for use in the psycho-educational component of any treatment setting for lecture and handouts and/or administered as a "self test." Its experiential use is described in The Living Stage.

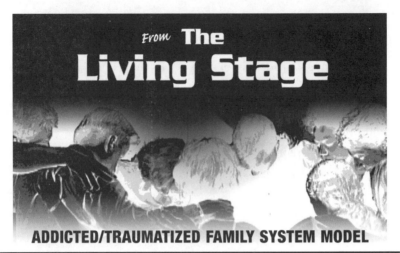

ADDICTED/TRAUMATIZED FAMILY SYSTEM MODEL

EXTREME R.O.F	BALANCED RANGE OF FUNCTIONING	EXTREME R.O.F.
High Intensity	emotional modulation	*Shutdown*
Overfunctioning	balanced functioning	*Underfunctioning*
Enmeshment	healthy-relatedness	*Disengagement*
Impulsivity	balanced self-regulation	*Rigidity*
Grandiosity	healthy self-image	*Low self worth*
Denial	reality orientation	*Despair*
Abuser	talking out rather than acting out	*Victim*
Caretaking	balanced care and concern	*Neglect*

High Intensity vs. Shutdown: Alternating between feeling overwhelmed with emotional vs. physio-logical responses and shutting down.

Overfunctioning vs. Underfunctioning: Alternating between working overtime to fill in what is missing vs. falling apart or barely holding it together.

Enmeshment vs. Disengagement: Alternating between being overclose or fused in identities vs. avoidance, or cutting off leading to disengagement.

Impulsivity vs. Rigidity: Alternating between impulsive behavior that leads to chaos vs. rigid, con-trolling behavior.

Grandiosity vs. Low Self Worth: Alternating between grandiose ideas and fantasies vs. feelings of low self worth.

Denial vs. Despair: Alternating between a state in which reality is denied or rewritten vs. despair, help-lessness (or rage at having life as we know it slip away).

Abuser vs. Victim: Alternating between the role of victim vs. the role of perpetrator.

Caretaking vs. Neglect: Alternating between over concern leading toward enmeshment vs. under-concern leading toward disengagement.

This family and the members in it often attain a dysfunctional balance by moving from one extreme to the other. For example, if they feel overwhelmed by enmeshment in their relationships, they may disengage to get personal space. Or, family members may take on rigid roles i.e. one member is the "impulsive" member while another takes on the role of the "rigid" one. They have trouble living in a balanced, middle ground.

A MODEL OF THE ADDICTED/TRAUMATIZED FAMILY SYSTEM

Living with addiction is traumatizing to the body as well as the mind. And living with trauma can lead to the kind of emotional deregulation that makes us want to turn to substances to regain the sense of calm and regulation that trauma undermines.

Our bodies don't really distinguish between physical danger and emotional stress or crisis. The natural fear response associated with our fight/flight apparatus will cause the body to react to physical or emotional "danger" by pumping out sufficient quantities of what are known as "stress" chemicals such as adrenaline to get our hearts pumping, muscles tightening and breath shortening, in preparation for a fast exit or a fight. These physiological responses give rise to emotions such as fear and anxiety, and the fear and anxiety we feel leads to more physiological reactions. But for those for whom the family itself has become the proverbial "saber-toothed tiger," for whom escape is not really the issue, these chemicals boil up inside and can cause physical and emotional problems.

HIGH INTENSITY VERSUS SHUTDOWN

The addicted/traumatized family may cycle between states of emotional constriction and intense outbursts or acting out behaviors. Swings between high intensity and shutting down or dissociating characterize the trauma response and can become central to the operational style of the family and become internalized by family members.

Emotional modulation is a skill that is learned from birth through regular exposure to modulating relationships such as parents and family members who teach us by example and their behavior toward us, how to regulate intense feeling states. It can also be learned in recovery, and through therapeutic relationships. It can also be aided through regulating activities like meditation/relaxation, deep breathing and exercise, activities that quiet and soothe the limbic system.

Overfunctioning Versus Underfunctioning

In a maladaptive attempt to maintain family balance, some family members overfunction or overcompensate for the underfunctioning of others. Or addicts and family members may do both, overfunctioning to make up for periods of underfunctioning.

Overfunctioning can wear many hats—parentified children may try to take care of younger siblings when parents drop the ball or strive to restore order or dignity to a family that is rapidly slipping. Spouses may overfunction to maintain order while the addict falls in and out of normal functioning.

Still others in the system may freeze like deer in the headlights, unable to get their lives together and make useful choices. The learned helplessness associated with the trauma response, in which one comes to feel that nothing they can do will make a difference, can become an operational style that manifests as underfunctioning.

Unfortunately, a secondary gain of learned helplessness is that others will generally pick up the slack. This learning contributes to learned helplessness becoming seared into place as a quality of personality. And the secondary gain of overfunctioning is that it can lead to outward success, even though it may represent an extreme behavior that interferes with other areas of living.

Balanced functioning is the obvious inbetween of over- and underfunctioning. Balance is when we do what is appropriate to the circumstance and when we have conscious choice around the degree to which we function.

Enmeshment Versus Disengagement

Enmeshment or fusion is generally seen as an attempt to ward off unconscious fears of abandonment. It is a relational style in which identities become confused and fused, it lacks healthy boundaries and discourages differences or disagreement, seeing them not as healthy and natural but disloyal and threatening.

Disengagement is the other side of enmeshment. Family members think the solution to keeping pain from their inner worlds from erupting is to avoid subjects, people, places and things that might trigger it. In addition, the mistrust that grows out of this continual relationship discomfort can make family members withdraw into their own emotional worlds, which further isolates them.

Balanced relatedness is neither a withdrawal from another person nor a fusion with them. It allows each person a reasonable sense of their own autonomy in the presence of the family system.

IMPULSIVITY VS. RIGIDITY

When emotional and psychological pain cannot get talked out, it is often acted out instead. Impulsive behavior can lead to chaos, wherein a pain-filled inner world surfaces in action. Painful feelings that individuals find too hard to sit with explode into the container of the family and get acted out. Rigidity is an attempt to manage that chaos both inwardly and outwardly. Adults in an addictive/traumatizing family system may tighten up on rules and routines in an attempt to counteract or ward off the feeling of falling apart inwardly or outwardly.

Family members need to find a middle ground where strong feelings can be talked over, or even explode momentarily but then be talked through, toward some sort of tolerable resolution.

GRANDIOSITY VERSUS LOW SELF-WORTH

Feelings of low self-worth and shame can plague those within the addicted/dysfunctional family system. Daily assaults on one's self esteem and healthy connection with others erode confidence. Not feeling normal, experiencing themselves as different from other families and hiding the truth of family dysfunction can all contribute to those in an addicted family system feeling bad about themselves.

Grandiosity is a common defense against feelings of worthlessness. Family members may not understand how to take regulated, baby steps toward getting their lives together. Frustrated and disheartened, they may take refuge in grandiose ideas of themselves and their plans in life as a way of warding off ever-growing unconscious fears that something is wrong.

A healthy self-image can tolerate the normal flux in positive and negative feelings about the self without sinking into pervasive feelings of worthlessness or boomeranging into grandiose fantasies. A healthy self-image or good self-esteem is probably one of the most important components of emotional immunity and well-being.

DENIAL VERSUS DESPAIR

Denial is a dysfunctional attempt to put a good face on a bad situation by denying the ever-growing despair that is engulfing family members. Reality gets rewritten as family members attempt to bend it toward making it less threatening and more in line with their sense of "normal." This bending of reality is part of the "crazy making" world of the addicted/traumatizing family in which family members lose their grasp on what constitutes normal functioning. Family members often collude in this denial, and anyone who attempts to turn the spotlight onto the harsh reality of addiction or dysfunction may be perceived as disloyal. They risk being cut off if they get too close to the underlying despair that the family does not want to look at. The family may "kill the messenger" by making them the problem, a phenomenon known as scapegoating.

Reality orientation, or an ability to live "life on life's terms," is an important measurement of recovery.

ABUSER VERSUS VICTIM

Trauma seems to seek a culprit, someone upon whom to externalize, or take out, painful emotions, i.e., a victim. Abuse is part of the impulsivity that characterizes families in which feelings are acted out rather than talked out. Bouts of rage and physical and/or emotional abuse are often part of an addicted/traumatized family system. Children who are abused, i.e. victims of abuse, may turn into the school bully or become abusive to younger siblings, taking out their own feelings of humiliation and helplessness by becoming the abuser. This identification flipping can make the dynamic intergenerational. For example, an abused child or the victim of abuse may "identify with the aggressor," internalizing the role of the abuser. Then, when the roles are flipped and the child becomes a parent, they become what they beheld, the abused child becomes the abusing parent.

Both the role of the victim and the abuser can become personality styles. The perennial bully, the person who shoves other people around physically, emotionally and psychologically, or the perennial victim who sees themselves as the one who never gets the breaks and slips into a kind of helplessness, are both unregulated life roles. Paradoxically, each extreme covers up a sense of helplessness by behaving in an entitled manner. The chronic bully pushes for what he wants through force, and the chronic victim through helplessness.

Learning the skills of emotional literacy—understanding that what happened "wasn't your fault but it is your responsibility to heal it and move on"—is necessary here.

- Tolerating one's own painful emotions without acting out
- Listening to another's without over-reacting
- Naming and processing feelings, learning to think about what one is feeling
- Constructing a balanced life with balanced roles

Caretaking Versus Neglect

In caretaking we assuage or own anxiety by over-responding to another person's inner or outer needs. We project our own anxious feelings onto someone else and set about fixing in them what may need fixing inside of us. Caretaking can also be a symptom of unresolved grief, a displacement of painful emotions onto something outside the self.

Neglect can take the form of under-responding to the physical needs of another person or negating their emotional or psychological self. Children who have been neglected can have a hard time in therapy. They have nothing large and obviously abusive to point to as the "problem." Instead they are often left feeling overly needy, unlikable or undeserving.

Some parents in addicted/traumatized family systems do both; they have trouble modulating their level of care. They care in a great flurry then collapse in exhaustion and frustration.

Balanced care of self and others is part of living a healthy life. Balanced, attuned care of children allows them to internalize this skill to be used toward themselves and others.

ADDICTED/TRAUMATIZED FAMILY SYSTEM MODEL
SELF ASSESSMENT ON A CONTINUUM

Directions: Place an X anywhere along the line that best represents
your personal range of functioning.

Extreme Range of Functioning	Balanced Range of Functioning	Extreme Range of Functioning
High Intensity		*Shutdown*
Over-functioning		*Under-functioning*
Enmeshment		*Disengagement*
Impulsivity		*Rigidity*
Grandiosity		*Low self-worth*
Denial		*Despair*
Abuser		*Victim*
Caretaking		*Neglect*

From *The Living Stage: A Step by Step Guide to Psychodrama, Sociometry and
Experiential Group Therapy,* Tian Dayton Ph.D., HCI 2004.

For further information on this subject see *Trauma and Addiction, HCI*

CONTINUUM FOR ADDICTED FAMILY SYSTEMS

GOALS:

1. To provide an experiential way of working with the family systems model.
2. To concretize the dynamics of the addicted/traumatized family.

STEPS:

1. On large pieces of paper, write the dynamics from the Addicted/Traumatized Family Systems Model. For example, write "high intensity" on one sheet and "shut down" on the other.

2. Place the papers with the inverse characteristics opposite each other with a long distance between. For example, place "high intensity" at one end of the stage or working area and "shut down" on the opposite side. Do the same for each of the characteristics. At the end you will have "high intensity" with "overfunctioning" under it and "impulsivity" under that. On the opposite side will be "shut down" with "underfunctioning" under that and "rigidity" under that and so on.

3. Invite group members to walk over to the set of characteristics they feel most warmed up to and locate themselves in the space between the two characteristics that they feel best represents "how much" or "where they are." Tell them to "Locate yourself on an imaginary line that connects these two characteristics in the place that best represents where you are in relationship to those qualities: e.g. more shut down, more intense or balanced in the middle."

4. Ask group members to share a couple of sentences as to why they are standing where they are standing. Repeat this for a second choice if the group wishes to, or for as many choices as it wishes to explore.

5. Next, ask group members to walk over to someone who shared something with which they resonate or identify.

6. Invite group members to share a couple of sentences describing why they are choosing this person.

7. Move into psychodramas that concretize the family system in which this dynamic got set up or return to seats for continued sharing.

VARIATIONS:

This is a hybrid between a locogram and a spectrogram because neither completely fits the bill. This can be used as an experiential exercise after a presentation of the addicted/traumatized family system model so that those learning about the disease can further explore its affect on their personality while opening the door for sharing, identification and support.

The director can vary the criterion questions if she wishes to, e.g., which set of characteristics felt the most unmanageable to you growing up? Which set of characteristics feel most unmanageable today? Which set of characteristics do you feel gets you into trouble today? Which do you fear most? Which do you resent the most?

To add journaling to this continuum, ask group members to return to their seats and choose a category that they feel warmed up to and write a journal entry about what is coming up for them. After they have written their entries, they can be shared in the group, dyads or subgroups, and then the group can continue to share and process around these issues.

22

Specific Exercises for
Working with Addiction

Note to reader: Most of the exercises in this book are designed to appropriately address the fallout from addiction and the process of recovery, such as those in Section II, Special Issues. The following exercises are directed at those addiction issues typically dealt with in early recovery and in treatment centers. Many, however, may be adapted as the clinician sees fit. See Appendix I for more exercises that can be used with this population.

EXPERIENTIAL CHECK-INS AND WARM-UPS

Experiential check-ins vary the talk format for checking in. They include talking but have the added advantage of helping clients to engage in and focus their check-in because group members are asked to make choices as to where they are standing and share why they chose stand there. Experiential checkins get clients out of their chairs, engaged in the process and connected with each other. Throughout the book, many of the spectrograms and locograms can be used as, or adapted for, experiential check-ins.

LOCOGRAM FOR RECOVERY

GOALS:

1. To allow group members to concretize where they feel they are in their recovery process.
2. To create group cohesion and provide a warm-up or group check-in.
3. To provide a way for people, particularly those in early stages of recovery, to track themselves.
4. To create an atmosphere that encourages openness and identification and promotes bonding and support.

STEPS:

1. Using the format for a locogram (see chapter six, Sociometry) designate areas on the floor to represent whatever you would like to explore as a group. Perhaps there are four areas representing these categories:
   - I feel very solid in my recovery.
   - I'm feeling neutral in my recovery.
   - I'm feeling shaky in my recovery.
   - Other (this is an ever-present designation in sociometry that allows group members to write in their own criteria).
2. Invite group members to stand at the location that best represents where they feel they are at this moment.
3. Invite group members to share a couple of sentences about why they're standing where they're standing.
4. Repeat steps two and three, if desired.
5. Use this as a warm-up to action or as an experiential exercise that leads to further group processing. If used as a warm-up, ask if anyone is "warmed up to work" and proceed with any of the selection methods outlined on page 26, Selecting a Protagonist. If using as its own exercise, simply return to seats and continue processing.
6. Move into psychodramatic work or return to seats for further processing.

VARIATIONS:

The group can put anything in these "locales" they wish to explore. For example, in an early recovery group: "I'm on the edge of picking up," "I'm white-knuckling it," "I'm staying sober a day at a time," and "other" might be used. In an ACOA-codependent group (which may also include people in long-term sobriety) designations such as "I'm feeling numb or emotionally constricted inside," "I have rumblings of strong feelings, but I'm not sure what they're all about," "I'm feeling able to put words to my feelings and express them clearly," and "other" might be used.

You can adjust this to the needs of your group by working out what the group wants to explore together, figuring out the criterion as the group leader or adapting other people's suggestions or work. For example, you might put Terry Gorski's stages of recovery (see page 416) onto the floor and ask group members to stand in the space that best represents where they feel they are in their process. In all cases people may move around during the sharing process if sharing one thing leads them to identify with something new, and they may create their own category by standing in "other."

Group members can also stand "between" categories if they are pulled by more than one.

Another variation is to put these categories on large pieces of paper on the floor in the center of the group and ask group members to pick up the one they identify with and share about why they identify.

To add journaling to this locogram, ask group members to return to their seats and choose a category they feel warmed up to and write a journal entry about what is coming up for them. After they have written their entry, it can be shared in the group, dyads or subgroups, and then the group can continue to share and process around these issues.

SOBRIETY CHECKLIST/LOCOGRAM

GOALS:

1. To allow group members to concretize where they feel they are in their recovery process.
2. To create group cohesion and provide a warm-up or group check-in.

STEPS:

1. Using the format for a locogram (see chapter 6, Sociometry) designate areas on the floor to represent recovery basics. Use any from the list, but no more than four or five, that might apply for your population.

2. Designate areas on the floor to represent any of the following that apply to your group or use your own criterion. Ask the group, "Which areas are you feeling solid in?"
   - Going to meetings
   - Getting enough rest
   - Having a sober social life/ relationships
   - Eating well
   - Exercising
   - Other _____

3. Invite group members to stand in the location that best represents an area they feel they need to strengthen. "Which of these areas do you feel you need to strengthen?"

4. Invite group members to share a couple of sentences about why they're standing where they're standing. Repeat this step if desired, or go to step five.

5. Return to seats for further processing.

VARIATIONS:

The therapist or group may wish to come up with their own categories to place on the floor. The themes above are common but they can be adjusted for the population. To add journaling to this locogram, ask group members to return to their seats and choose a category they feel warmed up to and write a journal entry about what is coming up for them or a letter to themselves from their higher self, giving them sage advice about their current situation, e.g., "Reverse roles with your higher self and write yourself a letter. . . ." After they have written their entries, they can be shared in the group, dyads or subgroups, and then the group can continue to share and process around these issues.

SOMETHING TO SHARE

GOALS:

1. To provide an experiential check-in.
2. To engage group members in their own process of truth-telling.

STEPS:

1. Using the locogram format (see Locogram, page 111), designate areas of the floor that represent:
   - I want to share.
   - I can take it or leave it.
   - I am not feeling like I want to share.
   - Other _____

2. Invite group members to stand in the area that best represents where they are at this moment.

3. Invite group members to share a sentence or two about what they want to share, why they don't want to share or why they feel neutral.

4. Ask group members if anyone said something they especially identify with or anything they especially did *not* identify with, and invite them to walk over to that person and place their hand on his or her shoulder and share with the person why they choose him or her.

5. Return to seats for continued sharing and processing, or move into some form of action based on what came out of the sharing.

VARIATIONS:

After step three, the director may ask group members if anything has changed for them since the sharing began and invite them to move to another spot if they choose and share from there. Doubling may be used during this process.

To add journaling to this locogram, ask group members to return to their seats and choose a category they feel warmed up to and write a journal entry about what is coming up for them or write a soliloquy from themselves in the category. After they have written their entries, they can be shared in the group, dyads or subgroups, and then the group can continue to share and process around these issues.

FEELING FLOOR CHECK

GOALS:

1. To offer an experiential alternative to a "Feeling Check."

2. To provide a way to sociometrically identify a range of emotions and process them in group.

3. To expand a constricted or limited range of affect and develop emotional literacy.

STEPS:

1. On large pieces of paper write "feeling" words such as angry, sad or anxious, frustrated, content, happy, hopeful, always leaving a few pieces of paper blank for the group members to write in their own.

2. Place the words a couple of feet apart, scattered around the floor.

3. Ask participants to "stand on or near" the feeling that best describes their mood of the moment.

4. Say, "Whenever you are warmed up, share in a sentence or two why you are standing where you're standing."

5. After all who wish to have shared, allow the group to repeat the process and stand on another feeling then share as before.

6. At this point you can (a) repeat this process a time or two more or (b) invite the group members to place a hand on the shoulder of someone who shared something that moved them in some way. If you go with option (b), group members can share directly with the person why they chose him or her. The entire group can do this at once.

7. Next you can move into a psychodrama, another form of experiential therapy, or sit down and share about the entire process and what came up throughout.

VARIATIONS:

Group members can share so the entire group can hear them, or if the group is large, they can share with those who are standing on the same word they chose. The word choosing can go on as long as it is useful, depending on the needs of the group. Generally, the group is saturated by the third choice and needs to move into the sociometric-choosing phase.

To add journaling to this locogram, ask group members to return to their seats and choose a feeling they are warmed up to and mentally reverse roles with that feeling and write a journal entry "as" that feeling. After they have written their entries, it can be shared in the group of dyads or subgroups, and then the group can continue to share and process around these issues.

EXPERIENTIAL EXERCISES FOR EXPLORING ISSUES RELATED TO ADDICTION AND CODEPENDENCY

ADDICTED FAMILY SYSTEM ROLES

GOALS:

1. To provide a way to work experientially with family roles.

2. To allow those from addicted systems to explore collective roles in a slightly distanced manner.

STEPS:

1. On large pieces of paper write the family roles as outlined by Sharon Wegscheider-Cruse: addict, enabler, hero, lost child, scapegoat, mascot, other.
2. Scatter these papers around the floor.
3. Invite group members to stand near the role they feel most identified with.
4. Invite group members to share about why they are standing where they are standing. Repeat this process for another role they identify with, or move to step five.
5. Next, ask group members to walk over and stand by one of the roles they least identify with and share about that.
6. After this process either return to seats for continued processing or move into psychodramatic work.

VARIATIONS:

These roles are collective or sociodramatic. They are generic in that many families stratify along these lines. Putting them into a sort of locogram can be a useful way to explore them and to deepen awareness as to how playing the role has affected the person. Identifying with more than one role also allows group members to keep from designating themselves, or being designated, as playing only one role when they may, in fact, have played or identified with other roles as well. If you move into action, have the protagonist choose role players to represent roles and let them talk, as themselves, to the role(s).

This can be followed with a psychodramatic journal entry "as" one or more roles in which the group member mentally reverses roles with a family role and writes from this perspective. The journaling can then be shared with the group.

FAMILY SCULPTURING

GOALS:

1. To get a visual picture of the nature and quality of connectedness or lack of connectedness in a family system.
2. To concretize family dynamics that aren't necessarily in full light of awareness.

STEPS:

1. After the group is warmed up, invite the protagonist to choose role players to represent all those involved in her family system, including herself. Note: This step can be preceded by the client reversing roles with each person involved in the sculpture and "showing" a moment of that person, e.g., how are they standing, what are they saying?

2. Next, ask the protagonist to locate the role player playing them, wherever on the stage that feels right to her.

3. Next, ask the protagonist to locate the rest of the role players representing the family system in whatever relationship to herself that feels right, e.g., if they are distant locate them far away; if they are close, locate them close and so on.

4. Once all role-players are placed in their positions, stand outside of the sculpture and look at it with the protagonist. Ask the protagonist to share what comes up in her from looking at this sculpture.

5. If the protagonist/client feels she wishes to, invite her to double for anyone in the sculpture that she feels warmed up to, including herself.

6. If you wish the sculpture to move into action, invite the protagonist to talk "to" anyone in the sculpture, role-reverse and so on, or you can skip step six and move to step seven.

7. Invite the protagonist to make some closure statements to the sculpture as a whole and to herself standing inside the sculpture.

8. If the protagonist wishes to make some corrective adjustment to the sculpture at this point, she may do so by rearranging the sculpture to reflect the way she may wish things had been or want things to become.

9. Again, ask the protagonist to make some closure statements to both the family as a whole and herself inside the sculpture.

10. Return to seats for continued sharing, de-roling and processing.

VARIATIONS:

To add journaling to this exercise invite group members to journal about what comes up for them through participating in or witnessing the sculpture.

This exercise can be preceded by a social atom and done as an action sociogram (see page 90).

TWO DIFFERENT WORLDS

FAMILY SCULPTURES OF SOBER AND USING WORLDS OF ADDICTION

GOALS:

1. To get a visual picture of the shift in family or object relationships between the alternating sober and using worlds that the addicted family experiences.
2. To concretize the crazy-making dynamics that occur when the family flips between two worlds, when thinking, feeling and behavior are different for each.

STEPS:

1. Ask the protagonist to reflect on the two different realities he experienced if his family alternated between two different worlds, the sober and the using worlds. If the protagonist cannot tune in to two different worlds, he can sculpt the family that presents itself to the world and the family behind the scenes or underneath the "looking good" family.
2. Invite the protagonist to choose role-players to represent all those involved, including himself. Note: This can be preceded by the client reversing roles with each person involved in the sculpture and "showing" a moment of that person, e.g., how are they standing? what are they saying? (See Selecting Auxiliary Egos page 30).
3. Next, ask the protagonist to first locate the role player playing him, wherever on the stage that feels right to him.
4. Next, ask the protagonist to locate the rest of the role players for each sculpture representing the family system in whatever relationship feels right, e.g., if they are distant locate them far away, if they are close, locate them close and so on. Ask the protagonist to pay special attention to how relationships might shift between the two worlds and to shape his sculptures to reflect that shift.
5. Once all role players are placed in their positions, stand outside of the two sculptures and look at them with him. Ask the protagonist to share what comes up for him while looking at this sculpture.
6. If the protagonist feels he wishes to, invite him to double for anyone in the sculptures that he feels warmed up to, including himself.
7. Invite the protagonist/client to make some closure statements to the sculpture as a whole and to himself standing inside the sculpture. Note: If the protagonist wishes to

make some corrective adjustment to the sculptures at this point, he may reorganize the sculptures to reflect the way he would feel less torn inside, more integrated and at peace.

8. Again, ask the protagonist to make some closure statements to both the family as a whole and himself inside the sculpture.

9. Return to seats for continued sharing, de-roling and processing.

VARIATIONS:

This sculpture can be moved into psychodramatic action if the clinician feels comfortable doing so.

This can be done as a journaling exercise by following the instructions for Two Different Worlds in the Social Atom chapter seven.

People feel crazy when families alternate between two different worlds each with its own thinking, feeling and behavior, or in families with members who say one thing and do another— in other words, who don't walk their walk or demonstrate the morality and values they espouse. Also, the shifting dynamics between sober and using worlds can cause family members to question reality and their own perceptions. Concretizing the differences can allow clients to see themselves "as if in a mirror" so they can gain clarity, compassion and insight.

Two sculptures can also be done, one representing the family presented to the world and another representing the family as it is privately. All families have private and public "faces," but in addicted families these two "faces" can be very different because addicted families may try to "look good" in order to hide what's really going on.

Trauma also can have a significant "before and after," that is, there is life before the trauma and life after it, and the trauma can dramatically affect and change life. Object relationships can significantly shift. This sculpture can be done to reflect these two worlds but only with considerable training, great caution and only in an ongoing therapy situation where there will be many weeks to work through what comes up.

For psychodramatic journaling see "Two Different Worlds" page 98.

TWELVE-STEP TIME LINE

GOALS:

1. To provide an experiential approach to working the steps.
2. To motivate group members to work the steps as they deepen their understanding through education and sharing with others.
3. To provide an exercise that allows group members to identify with those working the same steps they are on (or stuck on the same steps) and to learn from those further along in the process or help beginners.
4. To create a vehicle through which to explore the twelve steps that supports the natural teaching and learning, giving and taking of the program.

STEPS:

1. Write down each of the twelve steps, along with their appropriate number, on sheets of paper.
2. Place the steps onto the floor along an imaginary line with plenty of room between each step as determined by the size of the group (between two and four feet apart, for example).
3. Ask whichever criterion questions are appropriate, and after each question invite group members to stand close to the step that best represents their response. After each question, ask group members to share a couple sentences about why they are standing where they are standing. They may share with the group at large, with those standing next to them, with those on their step or close by, or a combination of any of these. Possible questions might be:
   - Which step are you currently working on?
   - Which steps do feel blocked around?
   - Which step do you anticipate with pleasure?
   - Which step do you dread?
4. At any point in sharing on a particular question, the director might ask, "Who in the group said something that you feel you can learn from?" or, "Who in the group said something that moved you?" Then say, "Walk over to that person and place your hand on his or her shoulder and share why you chose him or her."
5. Return to seats for further sharing and processing, or follow one of the suggestions below.

VARIATIONS:

After the sharing, or whenever the group feels ready, they can move into psychodramas around the issues that were awakened relative to whatever step they feel warmed up to. If this is the case, use any of the four ways of choosing a protagonist that feels right to the group.

It can be difficult to engage clients with twelve-step programs. Some see the usefulness immediately, while others resist. This exercise offers a fairly nonthreatening way to introduce twelve-step concepts into the therapeutic process without being overly directive. It gives clients a way to explore their issues about attending program in a nonprescriptive manner consistent with program's "attraction not promotion" philosophy.

To add journaling to this twelve-step continuum, ask group members to return to their seats and choose a step they feel warmed up to or blocked in, then write a journal entry about what is coming up for them. After they have written their entries, they can be shared in the group, dyads or subgroups, and then the group can continue to share and process around these issues.

SPECTROGRAM FOR LIVING WITH ADDICTION

GOALS:

1. To bring a relationship with a substance or behavior into greater awareness.
2. To allow secrets, hidden emotions and thoughts to come to the surface.

STEPS:

1. Using the spectrogram format designate one wall to represent "very much," the opposite wall to represent "very little," and the middle of the floor to represent "50 percent."
2. Using a few of the criterion questions below, or ones you have formulated on your own, ask the group to answer questions by locating themselves along an imaginary line in the place that best describes or shows where they feel they are at the moment (see Spectrogram in chapter six, Sociometry).
   - How much do you feel this substance or behavior has affected your life?
   - How much sadness do you feel relative to this?
   - How much anger do you feel relative to this?
   - How much shame do you feel relative to this?
   - How much loss do you feel relative to this?

- How much confusion do you feel relative to this?
- How derailed do you feel your life has been by this?
- How much regret about the past do you feel relative to this?
- How much anxiety about the future do you feel?
- How much hope do you feel?
- How much strength or personal growth do you feel?
- How much faith do you have?

3. As with a spectrogram, allow group members to share if and when they wish to in response to each criterion question. Limit the sharing so there is plenty of time for all who wish to do so to share. Use only as many questions as the group can handle, generally four or five are plenty.

4. Use this as a warm-up to psychodrama, an exercise in and of itself, or a springboard for sharing.

VARIATIONS:

This can be done for anyone who feels that a substance or addictive behavior has influenced his life, e.g., addicts, ACOAs or codependents. The group leader can come up with the questions, the group can decide what questions they would like to explore, or a combination of both. Use a mix of positive and negative questions. Group members can also be allowed to double for each other throughout the process if desired.

To add journaling to this spectrogram, ask group members to return to their seats and choose a category they feel warmed up to and write a journal entry about what is coming up for them. Or ask them to choose someone either from their lives or from books, movies, media, politics or clergy, or even God, mentally reverse roles with that person and write themselves a letter of encouragement and advice from that person. After they have written their entries or letters, they can be shared in the group, dyads or subgroups, and the group can continue to share and process around these issues.

THE DEVELOPMENTAL TIME LINE USING PAPER AND PENCIL

GOALS:

1. To provide a visual context in which to identify developmental progression.
2. To allow clients and therapists to identify where development may have been arrested or gotten off track.
3. To identify points of strength and resilience.

STEPS:

1. On a sheet of paper, ask clients to make a vertical line representing their developmental progression and divide it into five-year intervals.
2. In the appropriate place along the line ask clients to enter:

   • Life traumas, losses and painful experiences
   • Positive life experiences or their own positive life choices

After this information has been entered, ask participants to share their time lines with the group.

VARIATIONS:

It would be useful to put the life traumas and losses in one color and the positive experiences or choices in another color so each can be seen clearly. The idea is to identify points in development where progress may have gone off track and to see the disease progression. The other important feature is to consolidate strength through identifying resilience-building experiences and relationships and claiming positive personal choices that lead toward wholeness and wellness.

Clients will get a clear picture of at what ages their losses occurred, where reenactment patterns are repeated throughout life, and where things either may have gone off course or their positive actions helped them to move forward. This time line helps clients to recontextualize split-off experience into a coherent whole.

THE DEVELOPMENTAL TIME LINE IN ACTION

GOALS:

1. To concretize the process of development and allow clients to get a clear picture of their own emotional and psychological development and put their lives into a progressive context.
2. To allow clients and therapists to identify where developmental arrests may have occurred.

STEPS:

1. Place cards along the floor in a linear progression that represent five-year intervals.
2. Invite group members to use any of the selection processes that are appropriate to select a protagonist.
3. Using the Paper-and-Pencil Time Line as a map, invite the protagonist to choose group members to represent themselves at any and all points along the time line that the protagonist deems significant. (Note: This means that there will be many representations of the self along the time line).
4. Invite the protagonist to "talk to himself," moving through his time line from the beginning of his life. The protagonist can go to the points along the time line where he feels warmed up to do work or move through it in a linear fashion, as he wishes. The protagonist may reverse roles with himself at any stage of development wherever appropriate as he moves through his time line.
5. Invite the protagonist to end the work in any way that feels appropriate to him.
6. Return to seats for continued sharing.

VARIATIONS:

Each protagonist's work will be different. Some protagonists will wish to move forward in a systematic way as they move along their time lines, integrating as they go. Others will move to parts of their life wherein they feel the greatest developmental arrests or blockages and do vignettes. This can be a very integrating experience.

To add journaling to this time line, ask group members to return to their seats and choose a stage of development they feel warmed up to, mentally reverse roles with themselves at that stage and write a journal entry "as" themselves at that stage of life. After they have written their entries, they can be shared in the group, dyads or subgroups, and then the group can continue to share and process around these issues.

THE EMPTY CHAIR

GOALS:

1. To concretize an interpersonal or intrapersonal act hunger or open tension.
2. To provide an experiential vehicle where open tensions can be brought to completion, words can be spoken, feelings expressed.

STEPS:

1. Invite the protagonist to set up two chairs facing each other, or to set up one chair and the protagonist can stand.
2. Invite the protagonist to place a part of herself, another person or perhaps a substance or behavior into the empty chair, i.e., designate what the empty chair represents.
3. Invite the protagonist to say what she needs or wishes to say to whatever is in the chair. Use role reversal wherever appropriate.
4. If this is done in a group, there may be other group members who have strong identification with what is being said by the protagonist and feel they may be able to bring the protagonist closer to her own truth through brief doubling. Invite the people who feel this way to stand behind and slightly to the side of the protagonist and be her "double." Doubles can spontaneously self-select, double for the protagonist in her own role or while in a role reversal and sit down after they have spoken.
5. When you feel the protagonist has spoken fully, say, "Say the last thing you need to say," and end the action.
6. In the group, share whatever identification members may feel or what came up for them in watching the action. In this way everyone gets a chance to do personal work and share from his or her own experience. Keep the sharing on a personal basis; it is not a time for advice giving or questioning.

VARIATIONS:

The empty chair is very useful for resolving grief issues. Feelings that were never expressed, good-byes that were not said, can be dealt with easily with this very versatile and powerful technique. It is also a very useful format through which to have a conversation with a part of the self or to say good-bye to a substance or behavior. Multiple empty chairs can be used to represent several roles. This can also be used in one-to-one therapy. This technique was adopted by and used greatly in the Gestalt movement.

BIDDING FAREWELL TO THE SUBSTANCE

GOALS:

1. To provide concrete ways of saying good-bye to a substance.
2. To honor the loss of substance as a grief issue.
3. To use as a follow up to the teaching sculpture "The Disease Progression" (see page 146).

STEPS:

1. Give clients a pen and paper.
2. Invite group members to write a letter saying good-bye to their substance.
3. When all are finished, invite group members to share their letters. This can be done:
   - in the group, in dyads or in small groupings;
   - to an empty chair;
   - to a role player or an empty chair representing the substance.
4. When all who wish to have read their letters, return to seats for continued sharing.

VARIATION I:

Letters can be written in terms of the development of the romance or to any or all roles. The following is a sample of the progression. In this case proceed with a locogram, see Variation II:

1. **"The Seducer." Falling in love:** The stage at which you finally find the thing that's going to change your life: "You're wonderful! Where have you been all my life? How did I ever get this far without you?"
2. **"The Companion." Honeymoon:** "This time I've really got what I've always needed. You're all I need toget by."
3. **"The Betrayed." Disillusionment:** "You're letting me down, getting me into trouble, causing problems in my life. You're not fixing my life the way you used to."
4. **"The X." Farewell:** "This is not working out, so I'm leaving you. I know you think I can't make it without you, but I'm willing to try."

VARIATION II:

The four categories representing the development of the Romance can be done as a locogram. (see page 112). E.g. designate areas on the floor to represent "falling in love, "honeymoon," disillusionment," "farewell" and "other." Invite group members to stand in the section that best represents where they currently are and share about why they are standing there.

This is used by Joseph Kern, Ph.D., director of treatment for the Nassau County Department of Drug Addiction.

PSYCHOLOGICAL DEFENSES

GOALS:

1. To teach about psychological and emotional defenses.
2. To allow clients to self-identify, that is, identify their own defenses and take responsibility for working with them.
3. To provide a safe format for sharing the deep feelings beneath the defenses.

STEPS:

1. On sheets of paper, write the defenses the group wishes to examine or the therapist wishes to examine in the group. They may be denial, dissociation, intellectualization, rationalization, minimization, self-medication, splitting, displacement, repression, undoing (you do something you feel bad about, then do the opposite so you feel better), projection, self-medication (with a behavior), shutting down, "other," and so on.
2. Scatter these papers around the floor.
3. Invite group members to stand near the defense they most identify as one they might use.
4. Invite group members to share why they are standing where they are and ask them if they can also share about the feelings they may be defending against, e.g., "I use projection when I can't sit with my own feelings about myself," or, "I want to make them about other people so I can get rid of them; get them out of me onto another person," or, "I use intellectualization when I am feeling overwhelmed with intense emotion," and so on.

5. Repeat this process another time or two. You may also allow group members to double for each other throughout the process. This will allow them to identify with each other and to give voice, through the double, to the emotions and thoughts lying beneath the defenses.

6. Next invite group members to walk over to someone who said something they identify with and share with that person why they chose him or her.

7. After group sharing has drawn to its natural closure, ask the group members to take their seats for continued sharing and processing.

VARIATIONS:

It is useful for clients to eventually begin to understand their own defenses and take responsibility for them so they can work with them. This exercise allows that to begin to happen in a nonthreatening, even playful manner. Group members may extend this exercise by putting their defense into an empty chair or choosing a role player to represent it and do a vignette. In working with defenses it's important to understand that the goal is never to strip someone of their defenses or get rid of them before a person is strong enough to "defend" himself in a more functional manner. Defenses have served a purpose and should be respected.

After a role play is done, the protagonist can choose a reformed auxiliary to play a healthier version of the defense or an alternative to it. Do this in a well-bonded ongoing group.

To add journaling to this locogram, ask group members to return to their seats and choose a defense they feel warmed up to and write a journal entry about what is coming up for them. After they have written their entries, they can be shared in the group of dyads or subgroups, and then the group can continue to share and process around these issues.

EXPLORING RESISTANCE TO SOBRIETY

GOALS:

1. To provide a way to concretize both the sober and the using roles.
2. To articulate both the resistance and the wish for sobriety.

STEPS:

1. Put two chairs on the stage.
2. Designate one chair the sober self and the other the using self.

3. Invite anyone in the group to double for each role.

4. From the double role, group members can speak the inner life of each role and articulate the struggle of both the sober and the using self.

5. After all who care to have shared, move into action or return to seats for sharing and processing.

VARIATIONS:

If the group wishes they can extend the exercise by talking "to" the sober chair or using chair. The director may call for role reversal to deepen the scene if desired. The group can heckle from the sidelines to normalize the feelings of loss. The addict feels so much grief letting go of the substance that comments from the side can pull him out of his isolation. Comments such as, "You'll never make it without me" and "You'll be back" and so on can allow the addict to confront the voices in his head and talk back to them. Role players can also play both selves and the group can double etc.

This is a variation on an exercise created by Rebecca Walters, M.S., TEP., director of child and adolescent treatment at Four Winds Hospital and The Hudson Valley Psychodrama Training Institute.

SOCIOMETRY OF NEGATIVE CORE BELIEFS

GOALS:

1. To make core beliefs conscious and examine them.

2. To trade negative core beliefs for positive ones.

STEPS:

1. Invite group members to come up with negative core beliefs they live by unconsciously or otherwise. For example: "Nothing will ever go right for me," "No one will ever love me." You need only three to five core beliefs. After you have that many, move to step two.

2. Invite group members to walk over to the core belief they identify with and share a sentence why they are standing there. Repeat this step if desired.

3. Ask group members to walk over to the person who shared something they identified with and place a hand on their shoulder.

4. When choices have been made, allow the subgroups to share how these core beliefs play out in their lives.

5. This can be moved into action through some form of selection or return to seats for sharing.

6. As part of sharing ask group members to reframe the core belief into a positive. For example: "Some things may not go right for me but most will."

VARIATIONS:

This process can be done for more than one core belief, if the group wishes. The core beliefs can also be written on large pieces of paper and spread on the floor or put onto the wall. Group members can then stand near the belief they most identify as their own and share. Then they can stand on another one and share or walk over to someone with whom they identify and share with that person why they chose him or her, or both.

To add journaling to this locogram, ask group members to return to their seats and choose a core belief they feel warmed up to and write a journal entry about what is coming up for them. After they have written, their entries can be shared in the group of dyads or subgroups, and then the group can continue to share and process around these issues.

RELAPSE ISSUES

Relapse is not necessarily uncommon. Many addicts relapse in their journey toward complete sobriety. According to Terence Gorski, an expert in relapse, "Relapse is more than just using alcohol and drugs. It is the progressive process of becoming so dysfunctional in recovery that self-medication with drugs and alcohol seems like a reasonable choice" (Gorski 2004). In examining relapse, we need to rewind the clock and understand what kind of thinking, feeling and behavior made using seem like a "reasonable choice." Following are some exercises that sociometrically address issues of relapse. They are psychoeducational in approach, designed to increase awareness around relapse issues and triggers while engaging clients emotionally as well as intellectually.

LOCOGRAM FOR RELAPSE TRIGGERS

GOALS:

1. To allow group members to concretize where they feel they are in their recovery process
2. To create group cohesion and provide a warm-up or group check-in.

STEPS:

1. Write the following categories on sheets of paper and scatter them around the floor:
   - Somatic issues, not eating properly, poor sleep or physical problems
   - Skipping meetings
   - Getting back with the old gang
   - Seeing something on TV or in a movie
   - Music
   - Relationship issues
   - Anniversary reaction. For example, getting sober, divorce, death, job loss, job gain, relationship issue, etc.)
   - Disappointment and discouragement in recovery; a feeling that "life will never be what I want it to be"
   - Other (this is an ever-present designation in sociometry that allows group members to create their own category)
   - Age-correspondence reaction (see chapter 14 on Grief)
2. Invite group members to stand in the location that best represents where they feel they are at this moment.
3. Invite group members to share a couple of sentences about why they're standing where they're standing.
4. Repeat that process a few times, until the group reaches a saturation point.
5. Use this as a warm up to action or as an experiential exercise that leads to further group processing. If used as a warm up ask if anyone is "warmed up" to work and proceed with any of the selection methods outlined in Selecting a Protagonist on page 21. If using as its own exercise, simply return to seats and continue processing.

VARIATIONS:

Adapt this locogram as criterion questions for the issues appropriate to your population. Participants may also double for each other. This exercise is adapted from material used by Sharon Matthew, B.S. CAC, clinical coordinator of Women's Extended Care Program at Caron Foundation in Wernersville, Pennsylvania.

To add journaling to this locogram, ask group members to return to their seats and choose a category they feel warmed up to and write a journal entry about what is coming up for them. After they have written their entries, they can be shared in the group, dyads or subgroups, and then the group can continue to share and process around these issues.

Following are additional variations for the locogram used by Chris Stamp, CSAC, CET, ADS, at Freedom Institute in New York City:

- Isolating
- Getting angry often
- Issues around friends
- Shutting down or spacing out

- Being busy, busy
- Compulsive thinking and feeling
- Hanging out in clubs and bars
- Being mistrustful

THINKING, FEELING AND BEHAVIOR

GOALS:

1. To concretize the thinking, feeling and behavior that is part of one's relapse cycle.
2. To provide a psychoeducational approach that will engage a group around exploring those issues.

STEPS:

1. Using the locogram format, invite the group to reflect on their relapse concerns, designating areas of the floor to represent "thinking," "feeling," "behavior" and "other."
2. Invite group members to stand in whichever area they feel most in touch with at the moment as it relates to their relapse or fear of relapse, e.g., what thoughts get you in or out of trouble, what feelings, what behaviors?
3. Ask group members to take turns sharing a sentence or two about why they are standing where they are standing.
4. Next, invite them to move to a new area and repeat step three.

5. Next, repeat steps three and four one more time, or ask group members to identify someone who said something they identified with, walk over to them and share with them why they identified, move into psychodrama, or both.

6. Return to seats for sharing and processing.

VARIATIONS:

Participants can be allowed to double for each other throughout the process.

If you wish to do this as a journaling exercise, place these three categories (thinking, feeling, behavior) on a sheet of paper and mentally reverse roles with each category and journal "as" that category, e.g. "I am thinking, thinking, thinking about . . .", "I'm feeling . . ."; etc.

RELAPSE: THE PROGRESSIVE PROCESS

GOALS:

1. To provide an experiential format through which to explore relapse.

2. To provide an experiential way of educating people in recovery about the relapse process.

STEPS:

1. Designate a line running down the middle of the room to represent a "progressive process."

2. On cards write Terry Gorski's stages of the progressive process of relapse as follows:

- Getting stuck in recovery
- Denying that we're stuck
- Using other compulsions
- Experiencing trigger event
- Becoming dysfunctional on the inside
- Becoming dysfunctional on the outside
- Losing control
- Using addictive thinking
- Using addictive substances
- Losing control over use

3. Place the cards along a progression.

4. Invite group members to stand at the point along the line that might represent where they feel they are or fear they could get stuck.

5. Invite group members to share about why they are standing where they are.

6. Repeat this process one or two more times if the group wishes to share from more than one area.

7. Next, invite the group to walk over to someone who said something they identify with and share with that person why they chose him or her, or walk over to someone from whom they would like support or guidance.
8. Allow time for group members to share in the natural groupings that may have formed.
9. Return to seats for continued sharing and processing, or move into experiential work.

VARIATIONS:

This is a useful way to help clients to discuss relapse issues in the context of the group. This exercise is more than enough to stand on its own to stimulate sharing and discussion. It can also be a warm-up to psychodramatic work. To add journaling to this locogram, ask group members to return to their seats and choose a category they feel warmed up to and write a journal entry about what is coming up for them. After they have written their entries, they can be shared in the group, dyads or subgroups, and then the group can continue to share and process around these issues.

CENTERING

GOALS:

1. To help the addict or codependent to learn functional rather than dysfunctional ways to self-soothe.
2. To teach the client breathing techniques so she can regulate her physiological systems.

STEPS:

1. Ask group members to sit up straight in their chairs with hands resting on their knees or lie on the floor with palms facing the ceiling.
2. Ask group members to uncross any crossed legs or arms.
3. Invite group members to go to their breath and observe how they are breathing. Are they taking shallow breaths, breathing in with only the top of their lungs, or are they taking deep, diaphragmatic breaths?
4. Now ask the group to begin to breathe mindfully. Say, "Breathe in and out easily and completely. Allow your whole body to breathe. Take a slow breath in (on the count of eight) and let a slow breath out (on the count of eight, without pausing between inhalation and exhalation)."

5. Now ask group members to mentally scan their bodies to see if there is anywhere where they are holding onto tension. Say, "Direct your attention to any areas of your body where you may be holding tension, and ask your mind to ask your body to release it."

6. Invite group members to imagine as they are inhaling that they are breathing in a peaceful, soft light and a sense of tranquility, and as they are exhaling they are releasing tension and worry.

7. As they inhale and exhale, encourage group members to imagine they have a reservoir of calm within them that they are expanding and from which they can draw throughout their day. Whenever it seems appropriate, ask group members to bring their attention back into the room and open their eyes. Ask them how they feel.

VARIATIONS:

It can be helpful to play some ambient sound or music in the background to aid in relaxation and also to dim the lights if possible. This can be used as a warm-up to a guided imagery.

Help group members to become able to use this centering technique daily. Invite them to spend ever expanding amounts of time in their "centers" as they get accustomed to centering themselves. Self soothing is a primary, developmental task that all children and adults need to master in order to be able to calm the nervous system and regulate emotion. As clients become adept at centering, they will experience increasingly deeper and longer states of calm and they will become more adept at "sitting with" and exploring their inner world.

23

Breaking the Chain
of Family Dysfunction:
Working with Couples

"The players of the therapeutic stage are the inhabitants of the private house. If a person lives alone the procession of sensations, feelings, and thoughts of a private, personal world can take place as in a dream without resistance. But when two persons live together and meet one another daily, then the true dramatic situation begins, leading to joy or suffering. It is this situation which produces the conflict. It turns the lonely inhabitants of the house into a community."

J. L. Moreno

Many people in our society live with the false perception that having a meaningful relationship should come easily. Perhaps this stems from the idea of a "perfect" relationship created by television, the movies, Madison Avenue or pop psychology. In reality, and quite to the contrary, having a good relationship is one of the most significant accomplishments of a lifetime and takes more work than we may imagine—and then some. Dysfunctional or otherwise, most of us have a wish to find the idealized partner who will make all pain go away, who will fill in all our empty spots, give us the life we've dreamed of and transform us into the person we long to be. This wish needs to be understood, accepted and, at least to some extent, relinquished so we can engage in a relationship with the real person we're partnered with.

Those who have grown up with dysfunctional relationship models are at a real disadvantage as they have not seen a reasonably imperfect but functional relationship modeled. They don't understand from experience what to focus on and what to ignore—what constitutes a normal range of dissatisfaction, what needs to be just put up with, and what needs to be looked at and resolved so that it doesn't poison love.

ACOAs and adult children of trauma (ACOTs) haven't seen enough of how a couple functionally "rights" itself, how it restores its equilibrium. Couples have a way or righting themselves after, for example, a conflict, much in the way individuals right themselves after a stressful day.

ACOAs, ACOTs and addicts "don't know what normal is" (Woititz 1980). And this not knowing makes having intimate relationships tricky. The positive side of this is that they may have a clear sense of what they don't want to do. Their pain may make them unusually motivated, open to learning and working things through. This can change a bad setup into a good one and open the door to a deep and passionate relationship that is conscious and in which both partners are willing to roll up their sleeves and work it till it works.

In this chapter we will discuss the physical, emotional and psychological setup that those from addicted or abusive homes bring into their partnerships, as well as what areas of relationship become affected when one or both partners become addicted themselves.

When ACOAs or ACOTs grow into adulthood and find partners, the feelings of vulnerability and dependence that characterize any intimate relationship can trigger old emotions from early, dependent relationships—their childhood experiences get warmed up. The intensity of intimacy and all that goes along with it can unconsciously trigger old memories. As we discussed in the chapter Group Therapy, research today reveals that it's not nature versus nurture but nature and nurture that shapes our beings. Each tiny interaction, for example, between a parent and child, can affect the wiring of the growing child, laying down neural pathways that become hardwiring (Schore 1994). This hardwiring evolves into a neural relationship map that is followed by the adolescent or the adult as she cultivates her own relationships. People who grow up in dysfunctional homes are wired for the types of relating they learned in their families of origin. They may become hypervigilant, constantly scanning the environment (or their relationship) for signs of problems, and they are mistrustful in relationships. They are often black and white in their thinking, feeling and behavior, mirroring the all-or-nothing response to trauma. Denying or misunderstanding the presence of the emotional and psychological setup they carry from childhood prevents them from working through it and all too often means that they pass their pain onto yet another generation. Even if they don't drink or drug, the emotional and psychological patterns persist unless they get the help they need to repattern themselves for new kinds of behaviors.

FIGHTING AND THE PREVIOUSLY TRAUMATIZED COUPLE

Memory tends to be state dependent. That is, when we're triggered by conflict, we tend to be flooded with matching memories. When conflict arises, as it does in any intimate relationship, old memories of abusive scenes, withdrawal or chaos can be unconsciously stimulated, making everything in the present feel confusing and hard to deal with. These childhood memories lie in wait for a stimulus to trigger them back to the surface. Yelling, criticism, humiliation, or something as seemingly subtle as a change in eye movement or vocal tone can send the previously traumatized person into a pattern of reactions that has its origins in the past; as the program slogan says, "If it's hysterical, it's historical." The trauma survivor may react to a trigger situation with an intensity of emotion that belongs to another time and place, which can make whatever is happening in the present confusing and difficult to work out.

Trauma is stored in the body, in the fascia that wraps itself in and around the musculature and in the brain that sends messages to those muscles to tense up when triggered or in the midst of conflict. A previously traumatized person may respond to being frightened with an exaggerated response. The fear they feel around conflict may produce unusual physical tension, heart pounding, sweating, shuddering, teeth chattering, queasy stomach and head or body aches. Their physical reactions may then stimulate more flashbacks or disturbing visual images. These disturbing images, in return, stimulate more intense physical reactions, creating a vicious circle, pulling them deeper and deeper into a reactive state. If their frustration, sense of helplessness and disturbing images give way to a rage state then the brain gets hijacked, and any thought of getting out calmly is lost. During a rage episode, the cortex gets overwhelmed by the parts of our brain that are associated with traumatic memory storage. (So much for reasoning or rational behavior.)

Couples with a history of addiction and trauma can bring this setup into their relationships with them. This can lead them to avoid conflict or, alternatively, to live in it or both. But couples who cannot work through and resolve the inevitable conflicts that are part of any relationship seriously undermine their capacity for intimacy and happiness. Part of the trauma response can be an attempt to depersonalize what feels overwhelming or frightening. This unconscious drive to depersonalize obviously doesn't bring a couple any closer together. They deal with each other in ways that are distancing rather than intimacy building. The past is re-created in the present, and if there is no understanding or processing of these historical issues, the present comes to mirror the past as the torch of dysfunction gets passed down. Essentially, each member of the partnership gets triggered, and their psyches freeze. However, they don't see the scared, frozen child standing in front of them but the angry, distancing, controlling or blaming adult. The more they trigger each other the more they revert to their defenses. Rather than heal their early wounds they continue to hurt or retraumatize each other. If they can back up and, when they get triggered, slow down, tune into their inner worlds and figure out what's really going on and why they are feeling so reactive, they may be able to discuss their issues rather than dump them on each other. Couples have an opportunity to be deep healers for each other if they can use these moments of conflict constructively rather than destructively. This doesn't mean that conflict doesn't occur; it means that the couple is willing to work with it in order to deepen intimacy and understanding rather than use it as fuel for distance and disconnection. We choose our partners with our unconscious as well as our conscious minds. The issues they bring often tend to mirror at least some of what we carry inside of ourselves. In choosing our partners we may also be choosing to see a part of ourselves.

People who have grown up with addiction or trauma may exhibit some of the following characteristics when they become adults and enter their own intimate relationships. They may:

- Avoid commitment and intimate relationships because they unconsciously fear another interruption of the affiliative bond, or rashly jump into relationships without sufficient time to get to know someone (fear of abandonment).
- Recreate relationship dynamics that mirror their original trauma (reenactment).
- Have trouble staying present in intimacy.
- Have problems regulating intense emotions.
- Unconsciously project unhealed pain and anger from the original trauma into present-day intimate relationships (transference, projection).
- Become enmeshed in intimate relationships in an unconscious attempt to protect against abandonment (fusing).
- Distance their partner when they enter a dependent relationship (withdrawal, isolation).
- Respond to situations that trigger them by shutting down and withdrawing, or with an intensity of emotions more appropriate to the original traumatic situation (triggering).
- See their partners in intimate relationships as alternately all good or all bad (splitting).
- Misread signals from others, overreacting to signals that threaten to stimulate old pain (alexithymia).
- Lose the ability to let go and be playful in intimate relationships (loss of spontaneity or the ability to fantasize, symbolize).
- Lose the ability to trust and have faith in intimate relationships (interruption of affiliative bonds).
- Lose their capacity to accept support (numbness, shutdown, unresolved pain).
- Engage in sensation-seeking behaviors or raging (high intensity/shutdown).
- Self-medicate with drugs and alcohol (self-medication).

According to Stephanie Covington, Ph.D., of the Institute for Relational Development in La Jolla, California, some of the factors a therapist will need to identify in clients during treatment are:

1. The capacity to have observer ego and self-regulation
2. Family-of-origin patterns
3. Communication styles
4. The individual's defensive structure
5. Each person's ability to seek self-needs from others

MENDING A WOUNDED RELATIONSHIP

Couples who have grown up with or experienced addiction or trauma in their own relationship may need work in some of the following areas:

Intimacy: People who have self-medicated with a substance or been locked in their own trauma reactions have been emotionally unavailable for the subtle nuances of intimacy. The modulated give-and-take, each person retaining and maintaining his or her self while integrating the presence of another, trust levels, comfort with openness, honesty and constant negotiation that are all a part of intimacy may have been undermined by the pressure of addiction or trauma. The couple for whom addiction has played a central organizing role in their relationship may need to learn to rebuild intimacy from the bottom up. In treatment, the "self" of each partner will need to be reaffirmed. Each person may need individual therapy in order to rebuild the self before they are in a position to have a successful partnership or while they are rebuilding one.

Commitment: Broken promises, unreliability and ambivalence about commitment have taken their toll. Victims of addiction and trauma have often lost faith in love and in their ability to stay in long-term partnerships. They may alternate between fear of abandonment and/or engulfment. They may fear they will have to give up the self to stay in a relationship. They may feel they do not have what it takes to make a relationship work in the "real" world. Treatment will require that they keep their words and fulfill their commitments in a responsible manner so integrity and reliability can return or be built in their relationships.

Communication: Good couple communication implies a willingness and ability to connect in meaningful, intimate ways. Traumatized people have trouble with self-regulation and modulated connection. Good communication requires that each partner can tune in on his or her own inner world, articulate it in an emotionally literate manner, and listen to his or her partner do the same. Partners need to accurately read each other's subtle signals. They need to learn to listen to each other without being triggered into attacking, withdrawing, or experiencing explosions and implosions of emotions and psychological intensity that shut down communication. Couples therapy will be, in part, a retraining of good communication skills.

Resolving Transference Issues: Partners may project their unhealed pain onto the other in the form of transference reactions. When unresolved pain gets triggered they may overreact to the partner who triggered it, seeing him or her as the source of their current pain, not recognizing that their intense reactions may well have historical components. Couples need help in separating the past from the present so they can understand their sore spots from childhood that may be causing them to overreact in the present.

Accepting Love and Support: Closeness, in any intimate relationship, ebbs and flows. But for those who have been deeply wounded, that ebb and flow can become hard to tolerate. They will need to learn that it's natural to move in and out of a certain level of closeness.

The addict has often learned to turn to a substance for intimacy and comfort rather than his partner. The codependent may have been isolated from the addict and learned not to "need" anything that might lead to further pain or disappointment. ACOAs may have learned to withdraw into themselves for safety or that intimacy leads to pain and alienation. The couple may fear that allowing closeness to "feel too good," i.e., to "let it in," will only lead to more hurt when it inevitably disappears again, as it did during addiction or loss. They may unconsciously attempt to prevent further abandonment by either maintaining a cool distance or fusing to ward off a sense of aloneness.

Boundaries: Boundaries for ACOAs and addicts may have been rigid or rubber, depending not on a realistic sense of self and relationship but on surviving day-to-day dysfunction. In a chaotic partnership where patterns of fusing versus disconnection and aggression versus withdrawal are the norm, it is difficult to know where one person leaves off and the other begins. Boundaries set in this emotional climate were arbitrary and inconsistent. The treatment will require a methodical rebuilding of self and relationship. Boundaries will then be about maintaining a sense of self while in deep connection with another and allowing the other person to do the same through attunements, respect and negotiation.

Addicts have forfeited the ability to say "no" to themselves and/or to modulate their use of a substance. The substance itself has dictated terms of involvement, invading both the personal and relationship world with the force of a natural disaster—mowing down everything in its path. The enabler or ACOA has also, all too often, given up the words "no" or "enough" or "not now" for long periods of time. Setting meaningful limits, which are a natural outgrowth of a genuine connection with self and a realistic understanding of the dynamics of the relationship, will need attention.

Modulating Emotion: Psychological and emotional trauma interferes with our ability to self-regulate. The emotional climate of the relationship becomes characterized by extremes of shutdown and withdrawal, alternating with emotional intensity or high affect (Van der Kolk 1994). When intense emotional extremes are the rule, the couple may seesaw between conflict and withdrawal. Self-regulation is slowly restored through therapeutic relationships of all levels. It will take time to acquire the new neural wiring that will allow each person in a partnership to become regulated within the self and the partnership.

Trust and Faith: ACOAs and ACOTs may carry a certain loss of trust and faith in intimate relationships. The addict or trauma victim often loses trust and faith in self, others and life. People in or from addicted or traumatized relationships have often lost faith in the relationship's ability to repair and renew itself. Their pain-filled partnerships, especially if addiction has been part of them, may have invaded many aspects of their lives, throwing not only their marriage but other areas of their life out of balance. A low level of chaos may have become a pattern that will need to modulate over time. Initially, the couple may perceive calm and order as boring, or it may make them feel even anxious or mistrustful. Eventually, they will need to restore faith in an orderly, predictable world and partnership.

Having Fun: Spontaneity and relaxation for the addict have been dependent upon a substance-induced state. And ACOAs or ACDOTs can tend to be "terminally serious," due to trauma's numbing response or from fusing chaos and fun in their childhood minds. For the codependent, spontaneity may mean out-of-control or living on the edge of chaos. In the recovering relationship, the addict and codependent or ACOT need to consciously learn to engage in activities that bring pleasure, to plan fun into their lives in whatever way feels meaningful to them. Dinners, socializing and shared hobbies can all be ways of restoring pleasure and play.

Self-Soothing: Over the course of treatment, couples will need to learn to self-soothe without the use of chemicals or acting-out behaviors. They may need to include learning that will help them reregulate their limbic systems to a calmer set point. They may need to actively explore alternate ways of self-soothing such as yoga, exercise, relaxation, meditation and other such leisure activities. It will help if they can recognize that each has to have his or her own manner of keeping happy and comfortable.

Sexuality: ACOTs may have trouble relaxing and letting go. Sex while under the influence of a substance is different from sex while sober. The addict will need to relearn enjoyment and ease with sober sex. Because the codependent partner felt emotionally distant from the addict, the codependent may have withdrawn sexually. Sex while the addict was high may have gratified the codependent physically, but felt humiliating, or it may have been the reverse, and sex while under the influence may have felt freer and more arousing for one or both partners, or both may have been true. Healing in this area will require patience and practicing new behaviors. Masters and Johnson–type tapes and sex therapy are useful to the recovering couple. Less emphasis on intercourse with more time given to fore-play and after-play can extend the pleasure of sex and reduce the anxiety

around performance. Dates and romance need to be consciously sched-
uled and enjoyed.

Realistic Expectations: Couples may have nursed the fantasy that sobriety
would solve all their problems and be very disappointed when it doesn't.
In fact, removing the medicator will inevitably create some problems and
make those that were being avoided or medicated feel more acute. The
couple must learn to have patience and realistic standards. Intimate partnerships cannot meet all personal needs. Part of healing may entail figuring out which needs can be met within the partnership and which needs
are unrealistic to meet there.

ACOA and ACOT couples may have unrealistic expectations of what
partnerships can do for their lives. They may also move through cycles of
high expectation and disappointment that mirror their childhood wishes
for the family becoming magically better, then being bitterly let down
when conflict reemerged.

Couples therapy can help the couple deepen their understanding of the
particular dynamics that are undermining healthy partnership and
strengthen the dynamics that promote good relatedness.

How the Couple's History Plays Out in Parenting

Parenthood stresses out the most solid and well-regulated among us. What
doesn't get triggered in the partnership will surely get triggered somehow along
the line during parenthood. ACOAs, ACOTs, and recovering addicts need help
in parenting, not only to learn what to do to raise their children but also to
resolve their past issues so their dysfunctional patterns of relating don't get
passed down to yet another generation. These parents may:

• Have trouble tolerating their children having experiences of rejection.
• Overreact to their children's intense childhood emotions.
• Read their own historical hurts as their children's, projecting their experi-
ences of childhood onto their children.
• Experience more than the natural amount of irrational guilt in relationship
to their children.

- Have trouble establishing healthy boundaries with their children.
- Have a difficult time negotiating the vicissitudes of intimacy with their children and establishing an overall evenness in relating.
- Overprotect their children even when it is not in their children's best interests.
- Not know what normal is and consequently have trouble understanding what behavior to accept or foster as normal in their children and what behavior to discourage.
- Have trouble having relaxed and easy fun with their children.
- Have impulsive features they act out in their parenting.
- Feel somewhat different from other families.
- Attempt to overcontrol or undercontrol family life and the lives of their children, mirroring the black-and-white, all-or-nothing dynamics of trauma.
- Have trouble generating healthy family rituals and allowing for the natural ebb and flow that accompanies them. They may become too important or minimized as to importance.

The good news in all of this is that nothing leads to more happiness than conscious living. We humans tend to value what we've lost. ACOAs, ACCOTs and addicts, when they find recovery, learn to live again. They learn to live from a conscious place where they are constantly "minding the store," so to speak, growing and developing the skills to meet life's new challenges. Those who make it to the other side in recovery often value life and relationships and experience deep appreciation of and joy in what they have. At the end of the day, this allows them to love life and people in very special ways.

Incorporating Concepts from Psychodrama and Solimetry into Couples Work

The following are some psychodramatic techniques that can be used in couples therapy.

The techniques don't necessarily require mounting an experiential approach. Rather they are ways of employing some basic concepts into the couple situation.

Doubling

Doubling allows partners to tune in on their own and their partner's inner world. During an exchange where therapists feels this might be of benefit, ask one person to stand behind his or her partner's chair and "double" for what he or she feels is going on inside them, thus training the ability to tune-in on the inner world of their partner. If there is a point at which the couple does not understand the other's feelings, for example, the therapist can ask them to "stand behind your partner and double for him." The therapist can check out with each to see if the doubling is close to the mark or needs revising. Each partner can also double for themselves in order to tune in on deeper layers and their partner can get a flavor of the inner workings of the other member of their partnership.

Role Reversal

Ask partners to "reverse roles," to physically change places with each other during a discussion when they may be having trouble seeing the other person's point of view and continue the exchange. This allows each person to experience the role of the other so that empathy and understanding can build. Invite the couple to reverse roles at any point during a communication that you, as therapist, might find useful in order for each partner to gain a clearer under-standing of the other person. Sometimes they may not be capable of a true role reversal; in such cases remind them that a role reversal is truly standing in the shoes of the other person momentarily, than reversing back into the position of the self.

RELATIONSHIP DIAGRAM

GOALS:

1. To concretize the subroles within the partnership.
2. To understand which subroles within the partnership are compatible and which are not harmonious.

STEPS:

1. Using circles to represent females and triangles to represent males, place the name of each member of the partnership in the appropriate symbol (with some space between large symbols).

2. Next, work with the couple in deciding which subroles you wish to explore, and as you decide upon each one, represent it by locating it as a small circle or triangle, depending upon whether it is the subrole of a woman or a man, just outside of the large symbol representing the person. Some examples of subroles might be: intellectual companion, hobby companion, sexual partner, physical companion (nonsexual physical companionship), coparents, financial companion, humor companion, social companion, friends, lovers, life planners/strategizers, playmates and so on, depending upon the couple.

3. As you add each subrole use the following key to reflect whether there is mutual compatibility, compatibility on one side and not the other, or lack of compatibility between the partners in each subrole. There will be two lines with directional arrows for each set of subroles, one from partner 1 to partner 2 and vice versa.

Mutual Compatibility_____Green line

One way compatibility _____Yellow line

Mutual noncompatibility_____Red line

4. Examine these levels of compatibility with the couple and work with each category, analyzing what works, what doesn't work and why. Then develop strategies for understanding how to increase mutual compatibility and work with less than compatible areas. Some needs can and should be met within the partnership while others may be met from outside sources.

VARIATIONS:

A possible alternative to charting with lines can be to use numbers (1–10) to reflect each partner's level of compatibility and/or satisfaction within each subrole. Each partner can have their own number next to the symbol of each subrole.

EXERCISES FOR COUPLES GROUPS

Locogram

In each corner of the room put an aspect of the relationship, e.g., sexuality, communication, fun, conflict and so on. Ask group members to mill around and first go to an area they feel is going well in their partnership and share about why they are standing where they are standing, then stand in the area where they feel stuck. Let them share with the group or each other. This can be used as a springboard for sharing or psychodramatic work at the director's discretion.

Sociometric Identification

Do the previous exercise. After a few members of a couples group have shared about relationship issues, then the rest of the group can place their hands on the person who best describes an issue they identify with. Then they can share with the person they chose why they chose them. This can be used to build group cohesion and clarify central themes that seem to arise in the group.

ROLE REVERSAL INTRODUCTION

GOALS:

1. To create an exercise that immediately puts each member of the partnership in his or her partner's shoes.
2. To maximize empathy and minimize blame and projection.

STEPS:

1. Ask the couple to reverse roles with each other.
2. In role reversal ask each member of the couple to take turns standing behind and introducing his or her partner to the group, for example, Mary, as James, introduces Mary. When Mary, as James, has introduced herself, reverse and have James, as Mary, introduce himself.
3. When each has been introduced, move to the next couple and repeat this process.
4. When all couples have introduced each other in role reversal, return to seats for continued processing and sharing. As there is no clear protagonist, sharing may revolve around how it felt to do the exercise and any member-to-member identification that may arise.

VARIATIONS:

I came up with this variation when working at the Onsite Couples Program and have programmed it into Caron's couple's weekend as well. Faced with a room of couples that I knew may spend a great deal of time talking about each other, I thought this might be a way to break through resistance and get the couple reflecting on themselves in a nonpunitive manner. As the introduction progresses we learn not only about James but how Mary sees James. Mary, as James, introducing herself tells us many things in a short time: how Mary sees herself, how Mary sees herself through James's eyes and how well the members of the couple understand each other. It also and obviously acts as a deterrent against dumping as each of them are going to be introducing themselves, and it promotes the willingness to be honest about the self or makes the lack of it obvious. The director may interview Mary in the role of James or visa versa in order to deepen the exploration but sparingly, only where it is needed to move something forward.

Psychodramatic Partner

We all carry the idealized image of the partner we wish we had, the person who can magically make our life work out and our dreams come true, in whose presence our needs will be met, we will be valued all the time and we can be the best person we're capable of being, even without work. Or the image of our sexual fantasy, our knight in shining armor or the woman of our dreams. These idealized images can cause us to become disappointed and disillusioned when we discover that our partners are only human. In psychodrama we give the partner their idealized person on the stage to interact with in real rather than imagined form. In couple's therapy this may not be advisable, but introducing the concept in a nonthreatening manner can open the door to an awareness of the ideal that may be being projected onto the relationship and getting in the way of loving what is there.

Psychodramatic Child

Many parents hold very definite ideas of the child they wish to have, the idealized version of themselves or the person they want to claim as their own. These idealizations may not match up with the real person who is their child and may keep them from effectively working with, parenting, and even appreciating and loving who their child is. This is not to say that parents are simply supposed to accept anything a child is. It is saying that a parent's love works best when it is unconditional and that children have a better shot at actualizing their real potential if parents are willing to be realistic about who their children actually are. In psychodrama we give the parent their "psychodramatic" or idealized child in concrete form so the parent can deal with the fantasy directly, understand it and relinquish it, and continue the scene with the real child (represented by a role player). In couples work, this can be introduced as an idea if it seems appropriate, that is, if one or more members of the couple cannot get past this image to the authentic child so the child feels seen and loved for who he or she is.

Part IV:

The Experiential Model

24

The Experiential Model:
What It Is, How to Use It

There are two consistent concerns generally voiced by the therapists I've trained over the past two decades. One is, "When do I start using experiential techniques in the recovery process. When is it safe?" and the second is, "Do I have enough training to use psychodrama and experiential therapy without re-traumatizing my clients?" "The Experiential Model" attempts to address these very appropriate and valid concerns. For those working with sober addicts, ACOAs and clients who have lived with addiction or trauma, this model can be adapted to suit treatment facilities, private clinics and private practice.

The Psychoeducational Component, or the first part of the chapter, consists of the approach that I have been developing over the last two decades combining experiential approaches with educational material in order to make education more engaging and connecting for groups.

The Developmental Model, or the second part, is a model built on psychodrama's developmental model. I have adapted it through adding psychodynamic and addiction theoretical concepts. The purpose of this model is to place dysfunction into a developmental framework so that therapists and clients can clearly see where being addicted or living with addiction may have impacted psychological and emotional development and resulted in developmental delays, arrests or problems with attachment.

The Psychoeducational Component

The addictions field, generally speaking, recognizes that patients, including both addicts and codependents, need to learn about the disease that has taken over their lives in order to understand and take ownership of their healing process. Some of the concerns often expressed when working with staffs at clinics and treatment facilities are, "How do we make the psychoeducational component of our program engaging and interesting? How do we encourage member-to-member bonding and support? How do we teach about the addicted family system, relapse prevention, trauma, grief and other recovery issues in a manner that will engage clients? How do we get clients unstuck? How do we encourage clients to become curious about their own issues and take responsibility for their own recovery?"

People whose lives have been ravaged by addiction need to know why that might have happened. Questions like, "What happened to me?" and "What happened to my family?" often plague the person in recovery. Sociometry, along with theory bases that address issues faced in recovery, offers a way to incorporate teaching points with a living, experiential process, one that allows clients to integrate thinking, feeling and behavior.

Sociometry has been a core component of my own approach to programming. The reason that I incorporate so much sociometry is that staff who lack extensive training in psychodrama are hesitant, and rightly so, to use it. However, trained clinicians can usually incorporate sociometric processes such as spectrograms and locograms, along with near-psychodramatic techniques such as letter-writing and psychodramatic journaling, with more manageable amounts of training. These experiential approaches allow the client to get involved in his or her own therapeutic process. They take the work to another level, promoting a deeper experience of the self and a contained vehicle for connecting with others. They also perform some of therapy's most important tasks:

- They allow clients to take ownership of their own healing process, to get involved in their own self-exploration.
- They create an atmosphere where trust can be built, support can be given

and accepted, and relationship connections can be made and practiced.

• They bring the body and behavior into the therapeutic process.

• They provide a contained vehicle through which clients can experience emotions related to an issue, where they can think about what they feel.

• There are built-in opportunities to share laughter as well as pain, to restore the experience of pleasure and joy.

• They create opportunities to practice behaviors, to act "as if" until new behaviors can coalesce and solidify.

• They act as a warm-up for psychodramatic journaling or psychodrama and deepened and more meaningful group sharing and processing.

Most of the exercises in this book can be part of a psychoeducational component. The exercises in Part II, Special Issues, can be used as clinicians see the need, and the exercises in the chapter on addicts and ACOAs are designed specifically for the psychoeducational component of treatment, or for use by private clinicians in addressing issues surrounding addiction and codependency. These approaches, according to those clinicians who use them, "engage clients," "take the work to another level," "bond and connect the group," "build social skills and emotional literacy," and "allow clients to begin to see their own issues in a less defensive manner, because everyone is busy sharing and identifying." Clients are more likely to share the truth because they are actually standing on it. Clients often wake up to their inner truth if their body or physical movement enters the process. It gets them up out of their chairs and into the process.

This is a culturally sensitive approach, as the actual content of what is shared is client-driven and naturally emerges out the particular treatment population. And the exercises themselves provide for many quiet, personal interactions that allow people to enter the process easily and naturally.

SAMPLE SESSIONS

Following are examples of how exercises can be combined for use in treatment settings as a psychoeducation approach.

Working with Loss: Example #1

- Give a brief lecture on grief (see chapter on Grief).
- Do a locogram on the four stages of grief (see page 282). **Note:** This can also be done for saying good-bye to a substance, i.e., where are you in grief process?
- Or do the Loss Chart (see page 283).
- Do psychodramatic journaling/letter writing, empty chair, or go into psychodramatic work.
- And/or return to seats and continue group sharing and processing.

Working with Loss: Example #2

- Give a brief lecture on grief (see chapter on Grief).
- Administer a grief self-test or a grief spectrogram using criterion questions—choose only a few at a time—from the self-test (see page 279).
- Do psychodramatic journaling/letter writing or the empty chair. And/or return to seats and continue group sharing and processing

Doing Family-of-Origin Work

- Do a family-of-origin social atom (see page 90).
- Share the social atom in group.
- Do an action sociogram (see page 93) of one of the social atoms or a sculpture (see page 387) of one of the social atoms.
- And/or do psychodramatic journaling and/or return to seats and continue group sharing and processing.

Teaching About the Addicted/Traumatized Family System Model

- Give a brief lecture on the addicted/traumatized family system model (see chapter 21).

• Do the continuum for addicted family systems (see page 379).

• Move into psychodramatic vignettes or psychodramatic journaling.

• And/or continue sharing and processing.

Working with the Romance with Addiction

• Present a brief lecture on the addictive process (if desired) then do a teaching sculpture on Romance With Addiction or The Disease Progression (see pages 146 to 148).

• After the teaching sculpture has been brought to closure you may:

• Do a letter-writing exercise (see Bidding Farewell to the Substance page 397).

• Do a locogram (See locogram page 112).

• Do vignettes or monodramas saying good-bye to the addictive substance or behavior (see The Empty Chair page 396).

• Do vignettes (see Exploring Resistance to Sobriety page 399).

• Continue sharing and processing until closure is adequate and group equilibrium is restored.

Working with Addiction Issues

• Do a Spectrogram for Living With Addiction (see page 392)

• After the useful amount of questions have been explored, return to seats for continued sharing and processing; do psychodramatic journaling or some form of role-play

• Continue sharing and processing

Working with PTSD Issues: Example

• Give a brief lecture on the characteristics of Adult Children of Addiction and Trauma or show a film such as *Bob's Story*.

• Do the Trauma Time line (see page 256) or do a spectrogram using the symptoms from Adult Children of Trauma and Addiction (see page 240).

• Do psychodramatic journaling and/or return to seats and continue group sharing and processing.

Working with Anger

• Give a brief lecture on anger including what happens to the body when angry.
• Do the Anger Floor Check (see page 318), leading to sharing in pairs or small groupings that form through the sociometric choosing process in the second half of the exercise.
• Or do the Anger Map (see page 319).
• Return to seats for group sharing and processing or use exercises as warm-ups for vignettes, spiraling or psychodrama.

Working with Depression

• Give a brief lecture on depression and/or
• Do the Depression Self Test or use the questions to do a Spectrogram Exploring Depression
• Return to seats for continued sharing and processing, do psychodramatic journaling (see variations) or move into some form of role play and then continue sharing.

Working with the Twelve Steps

• Give a brief talk on the twelve steps
• Do "The Twelve-Step Time Line" (See page 391)
• Return to seats for continued sharing and processing, do psychodramatic journaling or vignettes (see variations), then continue sharing.

Working with Relapse Issues

• Do a brief talk on relapse
• Do Locogram for Relapse Triggers or Relapse: The Progressive Process

- Return to seats for continued sharing and processing or add journaling or vignettes (see variations) and then continue sharing and processing

Working with Resilience

- Give a brief lecture on resilience and its benefits.
- Have clients write a letter thanking someone who was a bonded, supportive relationship, or do an exercise thanking someone using an empty chair, or using a role player to represent him or her (see page 334).
- Continue group processing and sharing.

Working with Forgiveness Issues

- Give a brief lecture on forgiveness and its blocks and benefits, or show a film such as *The Process* (see About the Author page).
- Administer a forgiveness self-test or a spectrogram using criterion questions from the self-test (only a few at a time), or do a forgiveness locogram (see page 346) or a locogram examining myths about forgiveness (see page 345).
- Return to seats for continued sharing and processing, or do one of the following extensions or do one of the following:
- Do empty chair work, placing the part of one's self that we cannot seem to forgive or someone else we can't forgive in the chair.
- Do letter writing to the self or another person then share the letters as instructed in Letter Writing (see page 196).
- Continue group sharing and processing.

Note: For the average therapeutic session the same format can be used without the lecture component.

Working With Guided Imagery and Self-Soothing

- Do a Guided Imagery or play a cassette tape "Deep Relaxation" or "Letting Go" or "A Visit with My Inner Child"(see About the Author page)

• Share what came up in group or do psychodramatic journaling, reversing roles with whatever is being released, e.g., numbness, hurt or the "inner child," and journal as that aspect of self. Then share the journaling in group and continue sharing.

• Or the "Deep Relaxation" tape can be used on its own to learn how to physically relax and breathe deeply and evenly.

Note: Visit *tiandayton.com* for "recovery resources" that are listed in these sections. Resources include free downloads, handouts and audio and video tapes.

There is material in each of the chapters in Special Issues that can be developed into lectures for the psychoeducational component, along with experiential exercises based upon the lecture material. Work the exercises into your program as your team sees fit and according to your programming needs and goals. For example, anger is an issue that emerges during recovery. Sudden outbursts of anger or rage can be symptoms of unresolved grief or PTSD. When these symptoms of anger and rage are persistent they usually have an historical component that needs to be examined in therapy. The chapter on anger provides material to focus issues of anger that can be used at the discretion of the therapist or treatment team. There is material for a didactic portion along with exercises that incorporate the ideas used in the lecture into an experiential format.

Films are used by many treatment centers to illustrate issues related to treatment. They can provide access to up-to-date information or give clients a story to relate to and identify. If the story is particularly moving it's advisable to share what comes up afterwards. The sharing can include a sociometric element by asking questions like: "Who in the film did you identify with? "Who in the film warmed you up to your own issues? Who in the film can you double for? Reverse roles with? Who do you not identify with? Who triggers you?" Sharing or psychodramatic journaling can revolve around exploring these questions. (See combining psychodramatic journaling with film, pg. 190)

Incorporating experiential approaches into a psychoeducational format broadens the possibilities for engagement and connection, getting clients involved in their own healing process.

THE DEVELOPMENTAL COMPONENT

We don't see things as they are, we see them as we are.

—Anaïs Nin

When I was a little girl my brother, sisters and I used to go sliding on a toboggan down a hill. In my child's mind it appeared to be the size of a small mountain. When I grew up, revisited that hillside and saw it through the eyes of an adult, I couldn't believe how much it had shrunk. I kept thinking it must have been a different hill, that the real hill had somehow moved somewhere else. But it wasn't the hill that was different, it was I.

Another salient feature of my sliding capers was the fact that we were Greek, and this meant that we did absolutely everything, including slide down a hill, in a top-down sibling order. First Nick, the oldest, then Kutzi, then Eve and finally me, the baby of the family. So how I experienced sliding was greatly influenced by my age at the time of sliding, and my relative size in relationship to the world and my family position. Nick steered, Kutzi hung onto Nick, Eve always bit her lip, and I just hung on to anything till we hit the bottom of the hill. It was great (mostly).

There are a variety of factors that impact development. Our parents, their life circumstances and social network, our genetic predisposition, our size, gender, ordinal position, level of capability, intelligence, height, weight, and so on all work together to define the parameters of the world in which we develop into adulthood. The stage at which a trauma happened, for example, may be as important as the trauma itself in understanding its impact on the personality. The resources available to support the traumatized person also greatly determine the intensity and persistence of the symptoms. Children who have been traumatized by abuse, neglect or addiction may experience some form of developmental arrest in self or self-in-relation that may affect them throughout life. It is most useful to have a developmental model to identify at what point along the developmental continuum these blocks or gaps might be.

Developmental theories sometimes create the erroneous assumption that the stage of separation/individuation means that we are, in some basic way, no longer a part of where we came from. But the stage of separation is primarily one of self-definition and individuation; one in which we become clearer on where our family leaves off and we begin. Though no one is truly separate, that is, all of us are an incorporation of our experiences and parts of those who raised us in very fundamental ways, we do follow, as does practically any living thing, a growth pattern of gradual self-definition.

Developmental stages are constantly overlapping and co-occurring. We never outgrow our need for doubling, mirroring, auxiliary egos or role reversal in our lives and we are constantly moving through new layers of self-development. These stages are simply meant to provide an overview of what needs to happen on the road to full selfhood, a road I might add, that is the one that allows for full "otherhood," as well. That is, we can't really "see" someone else unless we can "see" ourselves.

In this developmental model we are applying theoretical concepts and techniques of psychodrama to mimic skills learned at different stages of development. Many of these can be incorporated into group process fairly easily. Psychodrama outlines four universes or stages that a person passes through on his or her way to adulthood. They remain co-occurring states within the self throughout life.

1. **The Universe of the Double:** The basic holding experience, oneness with the mother, feeling seen and heard; identifying and naming feeling states.
2. **The Universe of Mirror:** Awareness of a separate self, different from the mother or primary caretaker.
3. **The Universe of the Auxiliary Ego:** Awareness of others; seeing the self as a person among other people.
4. **The Universe of Role Reversal:** Consolidation of one's own identity and acceptance of others as distinct in their own right.

Each of these stages can be actively trained in recovery. The Developmental Model:

• Provides a developmental theoretical framework through which to conceptualize the process of healing and recovering from "less than optimal" early, relational and family experiences.

- Provides clients with an actual, corrective experience in the here and now for missed developmental stages and demonstrates developmental learning.
- Builds skills that can allow those recovering to tolerate greater amounts of intimacy, both with themselves and others.
- Provides for the types of relational experiences that can enter into the biology of clients, rewiring neural systems toward greater regulation.
- Builds emotional intelligence and emotional literacy.
- Offers the person not fully trained in psychodrama experiential approaches to incorporate into the group process.

STAGE ONE: DOUBLING

The stage of the double is the holding experience, feeling seen and understood from the inside out. A person in this stage feels as if someone is accurately "picking up on" their essence. Recent research reveals that the mother's and infant's right brains are structured to exchange affective information from brain to brain. There is not only a "heart-to-heart" but a "brain-to-brain" connection between mother and baby. Perhaps what's known as "mother's intuition" has a biological component. Problems in this early dyad can actually become part of one's neurological wiring.

Doubling enters the experiential process in a concrete way through "doubling" for another person (see page 36, Techniques of Psychodrama). Doubling is a skill that develops both an awareness of self and empathy for another person. Groups in early sobriety can benefit greatly from incorporating doubling into their group therapy. If, for example, a therapist recognizes that a client is struggling to say what is inside of him but that self-disclosure is blocked for some reason, the therapist may say to the client, "Would you like to stand behind your chair and double for yourself? Or would you like to receive some doubling from others in order to get closer to what's going on for you?" This very simple maneuver helps clients to:

- Feel seen and understood by another person (build empathetic bonds).
- Make memories that contain blocked feeling states conscious.
- See that what's going on inside may be different from what they are

presenting on the outside (better understand defensive structure).

• Let other group members see them more fully which, in groups, tends to raise their sociometric status (more people can identify with them).

• Get in touch with what's really going inside of them, a cornerstone for emotional literacy.

• Build, practice and consolidate a sense of self.

• Build an empathetic inner voice that helps calm and regulate the inner world.

• Help clients use their "thinking" to decode what they're feeling by doubling "for themselves" or receiving doubling from another.

The next aspect of doubling is to double for another person. As group members witness another member of their ranks struggle to articulate what is going on inside, they may spontaneously stand behind the person who is struggling and "double" for him or her." They do this by standing behind that person's chair and speaking out what they imagine is going on within their fellow group member. The therapist can say, "Does that feel right? If not, correct it." This allows group members to:

• Build inner strength and strengthen empathic bonds.

• Build empathy for another person.

• Give help to another in coming toward awareness.

• See and understand others, become empathic and practice building skills of empathy.

• Give caring and support.

• Separate the self from the self of another.

• Clarify possible distortions in thinking and feeling.

There can be more than one double; the task of the double is to help the group member to come to the threshold of her own awareness, not to impose his version of a feeling or circumstance. As soon as the person being doubled connects with her own truth the double should sit down; otherwise the double's inner drama can get confused with the drama of the person being doubled.

Because the double actually stands behind a person, there is a somatic connection that can mirror early attachment experience. For this reason, it is important to keep the doubling ego syntonic. It should feel "right."

STAGE TWO: CONCRETIZING MIRRORING

The stage of the mirror is the beginning of seeing the self as a person unattached to another, someone in his own right, who occupies his own physical space. It is a moment in development when it first dawns on children that they are physically unattached, that is to say they occupy a separate body from their parent's. It is a stage that begins in the first year and continues throughout development.

Clients may come into treatment feeling unseen and misunderstood in fundamental ways. If this is the case, they may lack the sense of being "doubled" in a way that makes "mirroring" difficult for them to hear. They may hear mirroring as attack and advice as criticism. It may be that they haven't felt sufficiently valued and understood by their primary caretakers to have good feelings planted firmly enough in their inner world so that they trust the mirroring they are getting is coming from a caring place. Mirroring falls not on deaf ears, but on wounded ones.

Therapists need to be good enough doubles for their clients so the client will be able to tolerate mirroring as it comes, without having to either dig in and resist, or adopt an inauthentic self, or comply to avoid feeling abandoned.

Naturally this therapeutic process will be as imperfect as parenting itself. No one is a good enough double for everyone nor a tender enough mirror to say things in a way that is always useful and usable, but this is a general model to follow. And if there are empathic failures, that is, if the client experiences mirroring as too harsh or wounding, the therapist and group can work it through and attempt to use it as a moment of growth and healing, one in which misunderstanding can be worked through toward understanding. Each one of these moments of working through can represent a maturational moment and a strengthening of the client's ability to live successfully in intimate connection.

Mirroring enters the recovery process in a concrete way most significantly through group process. One of group's strengths and why group is so important to healing is that, as we are having the experience of being doubled so that we can strengthen our core sense of self, we are also being mirrored, getting feedback from others as to how they experience us. Luckily, within the group itself, there are many possibilities for doubles and mirrors. Other concrete devices for mirroring are the use of a "stand in" viewing the self "as if in a mirror" and, for a later stage of recovery, the developmental time line can be used to consolidate a sense of self. When therapists or group members mirror too harshly it can repeat the experience of being wounded for the client. When there isn't enough mirroring, the client may have trouble self-defining and tolerating differences in a genuine manner.

STAGE THREE: CONCRETIZING THE AUXILIARY EGO

The stage of the auxiliary ego is one of beginning separation and individuation, although it is not a true sense of individuation. The child is beginning to see people as separate from her, though still as extensions of herself, not as separate people in their own right. She is testing and experimenting with others to see how they fit into her world, what they can and cannot do for and with her. Seeing people as having their own sets of emotions, thinking and behavior that may have little or nothing to do with her is yet to come. At the auxiliary ego stage the child is still emotionally undifferentiated in so far as recognizing that the world does not necessarily revolve around her. She may think that another person's behavior always has something to do with her. She may assume that she knows what they are thinking and why they are thinking it.

Slowly there is a dawning of awareness, a sort of pulling of the self out, bit by bit, and housing it as an identity of its own. Not so much a clear separation but a consolidation. The word separation can be confusing because it implies that we simply leave something behind, when actually we're also taking something with us. What we're altering is our ability to see ourselves not only as an incorporation of those who raised us but as having an identity of our own and a sense of self that is psychically located within us.

The auxiliary ego enters the experiential process in a variety of ways. In psychodrama, the most obvious is in choosing someone from the group to play the role of someone from our own lives. In this sense, we are recreating not the separate individual being played but our version of him or her. We are working with the protagonist's distortion, as it were, with her point of view exclusively. People who've been traumatized sometimes live in their distortions of reality, their versions of what happened, their own frozen inner worlds. By allowing these particular worlds to emerge on the stage through social atoms on paper or we can reexamine the sense and meaning that may have been made out of circumstances and slowly bring it toward balance.

Another way that the auxiliary naturally enters the process is through sociometry and group psychotherapy. Unlike in psychodrama where we're dealing with the protagonist's personal set of real people represented by auxiliaries; in sociometry and group psychotherapy we're dealing with real people. The triadic system is especially subtle and useful in this way. Through psychodrama the protagonist's personal or surplus reality is represented and acknowledged. Her inner world is seen as she sees it from the inside. Then through sharing more doubling and bits of mirroring enter the process, slowly and gently bringing her from her possibly entrenched point of view, toward others. Then through sociometric exercises and group therapy, the auxiliary enters as other people share their own, separate points of view and open their own individual selves to one another. All of this gradually moves toward role reversal.

STAGE FOUR: CONCRETIZING ROLE REVERSAL

In role reversal the sense of self is intact enough so that we can temporarily leave it, stand in the shoes of another, and return safely home. It is a state of intersubjectivity, the state or process of being in relationship; a simultaneous recognition of one's own self and the self of another in dynamic relationship. The other person, like ourselves, has his own subjectivity, his own mind working from his own point of view. He is not taking care of us in the way, for example, a mother might, putting us first. He is operating on his own behalf in the world, as are we. This ability to be in a state of intersubjectivity can be seen both as a developmental accomplishment and a constantly evolving state of relatedness.

The stage of role reversal heralds a genuine and true separation and individuation. The self, at this point, is consolidated enough so that it remains basically intact while in the presence of others; we can be aware of our own self and the self of another person simultaneously. We can hold on to a sense of self while in the presence of another while allowing him to also maintain his sense of self. This stage allows for an ability to be in another person's presence but not defined by what that other person does or doesn't do.

One of the most important techniques and significant contributions of the method of psychodrama is role reversal. In role reversal we actually stand in the shoes of the other person, see the world through his eyes, feel as him, think as him and act as him. Role reversal enters the experiential process as the concrete act of reversing roles during a psychodrama. This simple but profound technique:

- Builds empathy.
- Allows us to genuinely approach the experience and point of view of the other.
- Provides insight into the part of another person that we carry as self.
- Releases us from a "caught" position vis-à-vis another; helps us to separate our own identity from his.
- Enhances our ability to stay alive and intact while engaged with another.
- Consolidates a sense of self and a sense of the other.

Role reversal can also be used, if indicated, during group process. For example, if two people are in a conflict or unable to see each other's points of view, the therapist can invite them to reverse roles and continue their discussion. The therapist can also invite group members to double for each member of the dyad or each person while in role reversal. (See appendix "Experiential Conflict Resolution: Using Role Reversal and Doubling to work with Conflict" page 475).

DEVELOPMENTAL ARRESTS
WITH ADDICTS AND CODEPENDENTS

Addicts may experience an arrested emotional development that can occur when a substance interferes with their ability to meet normal developmental markers. Emotions provide valuable information that lets us understand who we are and how we respond to the world around us. Healthy emotions help us to make healthy decisions. Healthy emotional maturation comes in part from feeling, processing and learning from emotions. Addiction interferes with this emotional processing as emotions are medicated rather than felt. This population tends to grow up in recovery, revisiting developmental stages where natural, normal development may have become blocked. A therapist may find herself sitting in a group with several adults, but will need to be sensitive to the points of development of any given individual.

Codependency, also, might be seen as an incomplete individuation, one in which a person's sense of self has not become fully consolidated. Consequently that person may have trouble hanging on to a sense of self while in the presence of others because her own sense of self is not fully integrated. They may fuse with, borrow or mistake another person's self for their own. They may project their own, uncomfortable emotions onto another person, identifying those feeling states in the other and disowning them within the self. They may alternate between rigid walls versus no boundaries as they lack a well-developed sense of modulation. They may be stuck around the auxiliary ego stage and may have a weakly individuated sense of self, still seeing others as extensions of themselves rather than separate individuals in their own right. In addition, the way that women react when traumatized, i.e. the "tend and befriend" may, if this response becomes maladaptive through constant and cumulative stress, contribute to the kind of identity fusion that is often part of codependency.

Developmentally speaking, we incorporate others along the path of developing a self; this is normal and natural. But these incorporations, for better or worse, become part of us and need to be understood and worked with as our own. People who get locked in codependent behaviors may need to rework parts their own developmental stages so that they understand who they are and what forces are at work in their own personalities. Otherwise they may tend to project their own inner world onto others, thinking it belongs to the other and not them, or adopt the inner world of the other and mistake it for their own. This is tricky territory, because any close relationship is a co-state, one in which the selves of two or more people naturally mingle and interweave. When those involved have a clear and consolidated sense of self, the co-state can be alive and nourishing.

When they do not, the co-state can be a sort of tug-of-war. It is no accident that the concept of codependency arose from the addictions field. The developmental arrests that occur through addiction and trauma can actually create families of unindividuated people, in which healthy, consolidated selves may have trouble naturally emerging and being nurtured. The co-states in these families may alternate between the dynamics of enmeshment versus disengagement or overclose versus underclose that we discussed in The Addicted/Traumatized Family Model (see chapter 19).

Both addicts and codependents will need to rigorously seek out healthy external modulators in order to repair their own internal structure. Maintaining healthy group norms, beginning and ending on time and keeping regular appointments are all a part of retraining in this area. If they adhere to the prescribed group norms, twelve-step programs also serve, over time, as good internal/external modulators

Luckily, as humans we are capable of constant neuronal growth. Though that growth may not be as rigorous as in childhood, and though there is atrophy as well, we still have the ability to change and grow throughout life. We can expand our inner and outer network, incorporate new experiences, lay down new wiring and expand our consciousness. And perhaps one of the most significant areas in which we can grow is spiritually. We can "grow soul" as Matthew Fox, theologist and writer, puts it. We can expand who we are and lengthen and widen our vision of life and relationships. We can deepen our capacity for love and develop a kind of wisdom that comes with culling insights from living consciously.

A developmental model is important if we are to recover fully. Most people who live with trauma and addiction, whether addicts, codependents or ACOAs, have historical issues that need to be dealt with. There are always exceptions, but in my experience, they are few and far between. It is folly to imagine that our problems have no origins and that our childhood doesn't shape and inform the adults we become. One of the gifts of recovery is that, "it's never too late to have a happy childhood." It is never too late to extend a loving and compassionate hand to the hurting child that lives within us or to take the confused, inner adolescent or young adult by the arm and walk them to safety, sanity and serenity.

Neurological breakthroughs clearly illustrate the helplessness of the infant to understand and deal with threat and the child's inability to decode sensory input and ascertain the level of threat of a given circumstance. And throughout childhood there continues to be a lack of ability to make clear sense of a painful and confusing situation until around age eleven. But the adult in recovery can take the lead and reach out to all those parts of self through role-play and psychodramatic journaling. It can provide the opportunity for each of these aspects of the developing self to have a voice, to become embodied or concretized and move from the then and there into the here and now; to revisit and reinvigorate the self through role-play on the stage or the written page.

The self emerges from the roles we play and can be explored and strengthened through clinical role-play. The developmental approach creates concrete opportunities to experience new roles and/or explore and extend existing ones. Role repair can also extend beyond the therapy group. The same flower may thrive or wither depending upon the conditions in which it is placed. So it is with human beings. Therapists can help clients to connect with life roles that actualize the self in positive ways. The writer, mentor, speaker, hiker, volunteer, spiritual seeker, friend or partner are all examples of roles that may "grow self" and expand a client's role repertoire. In therapy and outside of therapy, we want to find roles in which the client can begin to thrive.

25 Staying Alive While Living: The Survival of the Creator

*The greatest, longest, most difficult and unique of all wars man has ever waged . . .
sounds its call to you. . . . It is not a war against nature, it is not a war against other
animals, it is not a war of one human race, nation, or state. . . . It is not a war of one
social class against another social class. It is a war of man against ghosts. Ghosts
that have been called, and not without reason, the greatest makers of comfort and
civilization.*

They are the machine, the cultural conserve, the robot.

*The critically weakest point in our present-day universe is the incapacity of man to
compete with machine-like devices. . . .*

*Two forms of robots have emerged, one a helper of man and builder of his
civilization — the other a menace to its survival and a destroyer of man.*

—J. L. Moreno
Psychodrama, Volume 1

Prophetically, Moreno feared what he called "the robot." The machine that would replace our own alive and creative process with a "cultural conserve." Everywhere, we see sectors of our population striving toward images of the ideal life, the ideal self, seeing lives not as works in progress, alive in the moment, but as larger-than-life images of perfection; frozen, trapped in a moment. But this stilled image creates a shadow side that inevitably becomes culturally repressed.

Never have there been more people obsessed with being thin, and never have we been more obese.

We see evidence of a loss of personal spontaneity and creativity everywhere in this image of conserved bits of life, the life where the kind of imperfection that is part of the human condition is airbrushed out. When, as a culture, we worship at the altar of perfection that an unconscious, money-driven media spews forward, we give up our own spontaneity and creativity, all that makes us unique and alive. And we make a Faustian bargain. We are being sold a bill of goods about a life that no one lives. Our aliveness is being sacrificed to the film clip, the three-minute sound bite. But life is not lived in five- to seven-minute segments. Life is a process of imperfect and incomplete engagement with the moment, and the more we can engage with our own moment-to-moment aliveness, our own spontaneous process of living, the more we can connect with ourselves and each other.

We do not see in the film, for example, the impulses of the spontaneous moments of creativity that went into making it. The warm-up, that led up to the preserved moment, the mistakes, mishaps and miscalculations that were all a part of the experience of creation. We see instead, a finished product, produced and reproduced. And then, when we want our lives to resemble these conserves, there is a natural distortion. This is because life contains all of those moments of frustration and failure, excitement, trial and error, disappointment and renewal of effort. When the conserve rules we may be left feeling like failures for not being able to get our lives to look like something that doesn't really exist anywhere. Something that is an illusion, that cannot and should not be lived because it is without true reality and humanity. When we worship conserves, rather than continue our own process of growth and exploration so that we can remain ever adaptable to our circumstances, we may find ourselves trying to cram ourselves into a mold wherein we lose our personal creativity. We stop listening to our inner voice and eventually, lose touch with it altogether. Eventually, we lose the confidence that we can be the creator of our lives. Then, helpless, we look to others to tell us how to live and who to be. We give up the role of the creator.

But we cannot leave pieces of our inner world and the relationships of our hearts on a cutting-room floor. We cannot edit our lives for presentation to a public that exists mostly in our minds without losing ourselves in the process. We cannot learn the subtleties of a relationship from relationships with objects. We need to connect with what is living, not what is dead. The inner and the outer cannot meet in harmony if we get stuck in the outer, intoxicated by our own image like Narcissus gazing into the pond, paralyzed by a picture of perfection that can fade away with a strong breeze. We need to reclaim our souls as our own doorway into eternity. We need to stand at the center of our own experience and own it, so that we can use our own creativity to enrich our experience of living; so that we see our lives as our own, creative journey; so that we do not become isolated, not only from others, but from ourselves, disengaged with the moment. Without a rich inner world that we are in charge of, the outer world becomes a replacement for what is missing rather than a kingdom to be explored.

Our children are spending a frightening amount of their developing hours with machines that have programmed, stereotypical responses. Today we understand that hardwiring within the child is developed in concert with their primary caretaker and their environment. Machines do not teach children human sets of responses. They do not smile in response to a smile, say ouch when hit or cry when hurt. What are we hardwiring into our children when they spend their precious, growing hours with technological devices in lieu of people or nature or something that has a soul, that is alive? Children need movement, sensorial and relational experience in order to develop normally. Television has been used with genius in erasing illiteracy and with little conscience in stereo-typing personhood, dumbing down life and selling it to the highest bidder.

Albert Einstein felt that "the greatest challenge in life is to stay alive while living." Our lives are ever-evolving tales of loss and redemption. Over and over and over again we hang in the balance, walk the tightrope, live in the paradox of losing the self to find it. Life is full of death and rebirth. Aristotle has left us with his profound words that have echoed their call through the ages to any daring to take up the challenge, "The unexamined life is not worth living." Zerka Moreno, moving thought into action has responded to this with her own twist, "If the unexamined life is not worth living, then the unlived life is not worth examining." Psychodrama calls to us to stand at the center of our own experience and work with it in all of its complexity: its pain, disappointment, divine inspiration and joy, its strength and its weakness—to step out onto the stage and examine the inner workings of our own experience, to show and tell our own story.

Psychodrama has the power to reach deep into our psyches. The thoughts that rule our lives from their seemingly safe places within us, can be accessed through psychodrama so that wounds, rather than fester in darkness, can come to the light of the stage for healing. Because what we don't know, can hurt us; to know allows us to choose freedom; it "gives us the courage to dream again," it allows us "to stay alive while living." What was learned in action must be unlearned in action, our beings, each and every one of us, has been coproduced. We cannot heal only in isolation but through role-players willing to take a journey with us into and through the complicated labyrinths of our psyches as we pour our inner worlds in all their poverty and richness, onto the stage.

How shall the birth, the goodness, the truth, the lie, the murder, the gossip, the hate, the fear, the horror, the pain, the stupidity, the madness, the recognition, the knowledge, the withdrawal, the death, the mourning, the salvation, the limitless variations and combinations of these processes one with another, how shall they all be saved? And they should all be saved as they are all genuine, spontaneously emerging and belonging parts of living.

It can be done through the last theatre—the therapeutic theatre.

The persons play their own life before them. Life and fantasy become the same in identity and time. Rather than overcome reality, they bring it forth and re-experience it. They are the master: not only as fictitious beings, but also of their true existence. How else could they give birth to it once more? Because it is just this which they do. The whole of life is unfolded, with all its mutual complications, in the dimension of time. Not one moment, not one instance is extinguished from it; each moment of boredom is retained, each question, every fit of anxiety, every moment of inner withdrawal, comes back to life. It is not only that they come back and re-enact their dialogues, but their bodies, too, come back rejuvenated. Their nerves, their heartbeats, they all play themselves from birth on, as if recalled by a divine memory. . . . All their powers, deeds, and thoughts appear on the scene in their original context and sequence, replicas of the phases through which they have once passed. The whole past is moved out of its coffin and arrives at a moment's call. It emerges for relief and catharsis in order to heal itself. It is also driven by the love for its own demons yearning to unchain themselves. In order that they may be driven out from their cages, they tear up their deepest and most secret wounds, and now they bleed externally before all the eyes of the people (J. Moreno 1964).

It is in the psychodrama that we can meet ourselves and in sociometry and group psychotherapy that we can meet others. It is experiential and imitates life, beginning with the resolution of the intrapersonal and extending outward toward resolution of the interpersonal. It is alive and in the moment, flexible enough to adapt itself to the pressing need of the moment and the particular person or population that presents itself. It is theoretically broad enough to address both sickness and health, pathology and normalcy, sorrow and joy, laughter and tears.

And as we take this leap of faith into the vast and far-reaching dimensions of our own self, to our surprise we find that in seeing the self we see the other, and in seeing the other we see the self. We see that we are brothers and sisters under the skin, joined each to the other by our common humanity. Moreno invites us to return to the Garden of Eden, to go to the place of integration and unity before the saint and sinner became forever separated, to restore the spontaneity of the creator:

> There is a way, simple and clear, in which man, not through destructiveness nor as a part of social machinery, but as an individual and a creator, or as an association of creators, can fight back. He has to find a strategy of creation, which escapes the treachery of conservation and the competition of the robot. This strategy is the practice of the creative act, man as an instrument of creation changing his products continuously. Spontaneity, as a method of transition, is of course as old as mankind, but as a focus of itself it is a problem of today and tomorrow. If a fraction of one-thousandth of the energy which mankind has wasted in the conception and development of machine-like devices would be used for the improvement of our cultural capacity during the moment of creation itself, mankind would enter into a new age of culture, a type of culture which would not have to fear any possible increase of machinery, nor the robot races of the future. Man will have escaped without giving up anything that machine civilization has produced, into a Garden of Eden (J. Moreno 1964).

Glossary of Terms

acquaintance volume. The number of individuals with whom an individual is acquainted at any given time throughout the individual's lifespan.

act hunger. A compelling inner drive toward action, a hunger for act completion. A human being's natural drive toward action.

action sociogram. A social atom moved into action. A scene that is concretized. A sculpture.

affect. Emotional content; the feeling atmosphere, e.g., the affective atmosphere.

aristo tele. The form of tele in which one individual is able to exert a strong influence on many individuals through their high tele standing, somehow "aristocratic." The surplus of tele choices that can be shared.

audience. The members of a group; witnesses; those observing the action on stage. In the Greek theater, the audience experienced a spectator catharsis through identifying with action on the stage and the central human concerns being acted out through role-play.

autodrama. A psychodrama that does not have a director.

auxiliary egos. Role players representing the roles in the protagonist's drama, other than the protagonist, but chosen by the protagonist.

catharsis. The purging of strong emotion. The cleansing or purifying of a thing. An Aristotilian term meaning the purging of violence within the soul through dramatic enactment.

catharsis of abreaction. A catharsis against something, e.g., an expulsion of anger.

catharsis of integration. The experiencing and purging of strong emotion that leads toward integration of split off affect and new insight and understanding and/or a shift in perception.

chain. A chain of choices or an open series of choices, e.g., *a* chooses *b* who chooses *c* and so on.

choice. An expression of preference; a choosing of one thing over another momentarily or for a period of time.

cleavage. The discrepancy between the stated values of a system and the unstated ones, or the overt elements of a group and the covert ones.

clusters. Small groupings within a larger group, psychological or emotional groupings that become drawn together because of related or perceived related elements.

codependency. The constellation of pathological symptoms that becomes pervasive and persistent, resulting from living with the symptoms associated with addiction; a cluster of symptoms that can come to have a life beyond living with addiction that is pathological in nature; a form of personal and relational functioning that can be the direct result of trauma or incomplete individuation and self-defining..

codependent. The person who is in a corelationship with an addict; adapted from the term coaddict, sometimes used to refer to the person living with the addict. The meaning has been expanded to include the cluster of symptoms that represents incomplete individuation in which the sense of self becomes fused with another, projected outward and/or is not adequately consolidated or experienced within the self.

cohesion. The bonded aspects of a group; a force that holds groups or varied parts together.

concretization. The movement from the abstract into the concrete form; the process, in psychodrama, of selecting role players to represent people, ideas, aspects of self, nonhuman entities or anything that the protagonist wishes to encounter, in concrete form, on the stage.

creative visualization. Using the natural visualizing quality of mind to envision desired life circumstances.

criterion. The established basis for exploration; the agreed-upon areas of exploration in a choice-making process.

cultural conserve. That part of culture that has been conserved and can be repeated over and over again. e.g., Beethoven's Fifth Symphony; cultural symbols and ideals.

deconserving. The gradual removal of stereotyped thinking, feeling and behavior from a person's personality.

director. The person directing or facilitating the protagonist's drama, generally the therapist.

double. The people who identify with the protagonist and can act as a voice for his or her inner world.

doubling. The act of spontaneously standing behind the protagonist and speaking out or "doubling" for what one imagines is going on within the inner world of the protagonist.

ego-dystonic. Something that is disturbing to one's sense of self, that doesn't feel right to the sense of self.

ego-syntonic. Something that feels in sync with one's sense of self; something that feels right, synonomous.

emotional intelligence. A type of intelligence that is emotionally driven; the ability to integrate emotions into thinking and behavior in a coherent, intelligent manner and use them to inform same.

emotional tracking. Learning to track the path of emotions within the self, e.g., when triggered, tracking the powerful emotions toward their possible source within the self system.

empathy. Understanding, care or compassion toward another person.

enactment. The concretization of the protagonist's drama; the action phase of the psychodrama.

encounter. The direct, face-to-face meeting of two people able or willing to comprehend each other both inside and out.

family-of-origin social atom. A social atom that represents the family of origin.

future-projection social atom. A social atom of an imagined future outcome.

genogram. A paper and pencil three-generation representation of family members.

The Living Genogram. A three-generation representation of family members that allows symbols to be placed at the closeness or distance that represents the emotional closeness or distance of the relationship and can be moved into action.

hypervigilant. Constantly scanning the environment for signs of danger; an active state of anxious anticipation.

intergenerational patterns. Psychological, emotional and/or behavior patterns that get passed down through the generations.

intersubjectivity. A state of relatedness between two people; an awareness of the other and the self as two separate subjective entities co-occurring; the name given to the study of the intersubjective state.

interviewing. Asking questions of the protagonist before the enactment in order to gather information, or interviewing the protagonist in their own role or in role reversal as someone else in order to gather information or allow a spontaneous response from the role being played.

introject. The part of another person that is taken into the self and gets incorporated as an aspect of the self.

introjection. The process of taking in another person as an aspect of the self.

isolate. That sociometric position that represents not choosing or being chosen.

journaling. Using writing to express the inner world; a personal, free and unstructured form of writing for the purpose of elucidating emotions and thoughts.

limbic system. The physio/biological system that regulates emotional states, mood, sleep and appetite cycles.

linkage. The connection that exists between two persons or two subgroups.

locogram. From the Latin root *locus*, meaning place or location. Locating places on the floor to represent particular criteria.

matrix of all identity. The world that infants are born into that is their undifferiented universe in which they experience themselves as one with all that surrounds them.

matrix of all reality. The universe that one differentiates into which allows for both a sense of self and a sense of other.

milling. Moving or walking around the room.

mirror technique. This is when the protagonist chooses a role player to stand in the scene and represent him. The protagonist then stands outside the scene and watches himself "as if in a mirror."

model scene. A prototypical episode from a patient's past, either real or imagined or both, which captures key elements and can be used in the therapy process for exploration.

monodramas. A monodrama, from the Greek word *monos,* meaning only or one, is a drama in which there is only one player, e.g., the protagonist talks to an empty chair.

mutual pairs. A sociometric term describing when two people choose each other; they have a mutual attraction.

mutuality. The experience of reciprocity.

near-psychodramatic techniques. These are techniques such as letter writing that are not necessarily played out on stage but do represent a talking to or as the other or to or as the self.

negative. A state of feeling that may include rejection, repulsion, lack of positive feeling.

neutrality. A state reflecting neither positivity nor negativity but a dispassionate in-between, e.g., one can go "either way."

open tensions. Unresolved situations that live inside the psyche in an unfinished state and produce internal tension.

personal tele. The type of tele that is not based on role but the essence of the real person-to-person connection.

pivotal person. "A person whose sociometric position is located between two key persons or groups" (Hale 1986).

positive. A state of feeling content, satisfied, good; an absence of negativity.

post-traumatic stress disorder. The cluster of symptoms that represents the disorder that emerges after a traumatic circumstance has been experienced. Symptoms may take time, even years, to emerge or become full blown or may become cumulative.

present-day social atom. A social atom representing one's present-day life, relationships and circumstances.

projection. When a person projects the contents of their inner world outward and sees it as belonging to someone or something outside the self; a disowning of what is undesirable to feel, getting rid of it by projecting it elsewhere.

protagonist. The person whose psychodrama or story is being played out on the stage.

psychodrama. A drama that is being played out on stage for therapeutic purposes; a dramatic exploration of intrapersonal or interpersonal worlds through role-play.

psychodramatic journaling. An adaptation of the theory, methology and techniques of psychodrama to the written page.

psychodramatic roles. Roles that exist in the imagination or the "surplus reality" of a person.

psychodramatic trance. A semitrance state that the protagonist and/or role players sometimes enter in which the "as if" falls away and becomes the "as." May be akin to an hypnotic state or a dreamlike state in which the brain is able to rapidly scan its contents, create coalesce symbolic meaning.

psychological social atom. The smallest number of people or range of relationships required to achieve sociostasis.

renactment dynamic. A repeating psychological or relationship pattern; an unconscious reenactment of relational patterns that may have been painful.

role. The tangible form the self takes; the roles played out in a psychodrama as representations of the self representations of other people or qualities.

role analysis. Analyzing a role in depth, a paper-and-pencil activity that examines the inner and outer dimensions of a role that may or may not lead to action.

role cluster. A group of related actions encompassed under a role name, for example: 'parent'.

role creating. The third stage of psychodramatic role development in which the person is infusing the role with their own spontaneity and creativity, where they are creating the role anew with new adequate responses and inventions.

role creation. The last stage of role development according to Moreno. The stage when the role is well enough internalized into the self system so it can be created anew by the person who has internalized it.

role playing. The dramatic enactment of a role for purposes of personal and group demonstration or exploration; the second stage of psychodramatic role development in which the role becomes infused with a measure of a person's spontaneity and creativity but has not fully moved to role creation.

role prescriptions. Recommendations of specific role shifts, e.g., "Spend less time in the role of partier and more in the roles of worker, sober person, exerciser; or develop the role of writer, grandparent and mentor and reduce the roles of boss and CEO."

role repertoire. The number of roles available to a person; part of their "repertoire" of available roles.

role reversal. The process of physically leaving the self temporarily and standing in the role of another person, standing in their shoes, thinking, feeling and behaving as them.

role taking. The first stage of role development, a stage essentially of modeling, taking in the role from another directly, imprinting.

role training. Identifying, exploring and practicing possible options and new, adequate responses in a particular role.

roles in ascendance. Roles in a state of becoming more "central and significant" (Hale 1986).

roles in descendance. Roles in a state of becoming less significant, more peripheral.

scene setting. When protagonists set the scene for their own dramas. Scene setting can involve anything from moving role players into position to incorporating props or furniture into the scene. It is part of the protagonists' warm up and helps them enter the full drama as memory is state dependent, i.e., memory is stimulated when in circumstances similar to those where it germinated.

sculpture. A still or frozen action sociogram; when role players represent roles on stage in a still picture that may or may not be moved into action.

self-system. The dynamics within the self; a dynamic picture or set of representations of the functioning self.

sharing. The third phase of a psychodrama after warm-up and enactment, during which both role players and audience members share what it was like to play a role and what came up for them from their own lives as a result of witnessing or participating in the drama.

social atom. A paper-and-pencil charting or diagramming of the significant relationships in a person's life, reflecting the closeness, distance or sense of relatedness present in the relationships represented.

social expansiveness. The number of relationships that a person is able to sustain.

social network. A person's network of social connections.

social roles. Roles that are interpersonal in the family, social, work or larger community.

sociodynamic laws. "Science of the structures of social aggregates" (Hale 1986).

socio tele. The type of tele that is based on the roles played, e.g., tele between those in the roles of student and teacher, or employer and employee, or biking companions.

sociodrama. A drama in which the role players represent the collective role, e.g., all nurses, all children, all adults, all Greeks, all Turks.

sociodynamic effect. "Distribution of choice in favor of the more highly chosen, as against less chosen. When the number of choices allowable increases, an even greater distance between highly chosen and the unchosen becomes evident" (Hale 1986).

sociogram. "The visual representation of the placement of individuals within a group, and the interrelations of the individuals" (Hale 1986).

sociometric choosing. A process by which group members make choices among each other that represent the patterns of attraction, rejection, neutrality or particular criterion being explored. Also referred to as the sociometric test.

sociometric star. The person most highly chosen in response to a given criterion question.

sociometric test. An investigation of the nature and quality of choice activity among the group members.

sociometry. The systematic study of group dynamics; a method through which the nature and quality of connectedness from person to person, group to group or nation to nation can be concretized, explored and examined and from which conclusions can be drawn that enable groups to explore the level, nature and quality of their relatedness.

soliloquy. When the protagonist speaks out what is going on inside of them, usually done while momentarily leaving the drama and walking along while talking; sometimes referred to as a "walk and talk."

somatic roles. Roles that involve the body or soma, e.g., the role of the eater, sleeper, runner, sexual being and so on.

spectrogram. A sort of imaginary graph laid out on the floor on which patients can indicate their response to a particular question in terms of degree, e.g., "I am 10 percent or 30 percent or 90 percent (or anything in between) glad to be here."

spiraling. A psychodramatic technique referring to beginning with a scene from the present day then spiraling back in order to explore the *status nascendi,* or origin of conflict represented in the scene or source of a reenactment dynamic.

spontaneity. "Operates in the present and is an unconservable energy which propels the individual toward an adequate response to a new situation or a new response to an old situation" (Hale 1986).

stage. The designated area upon which the enactment portion of a psychodrama takes place.

status nascendi. The point at which a particular conflict or complex began; the origin of a problem that gets repeated in the present.

surplus reality. All reality that is not three dimensional, that is carried in the psyche; that part of our world that we carry inside of us that, though not visible, informs all of who we are and what we do.

tele. The simplest unit of feeling between two people; an unspoken connection that can be positive, negative, neutral and all in between.

tele reach. The distance that our tele can reach; the tele range of a particular individual.

time line. A concrete representation of time, e.g.: numbers from 0 to 100 that represent the possible span of one's life.

time regression. A regression into the past of one's life; a psychodrama representing a past situation or issue.

transference. The phenomenon of transferring the content and dynamics from a previous role relationship onto a role relationship in the present.

twelve-step program. A self-help, nonprofessional, anonymous healing program that is open to anyone who has the problem represented by the particular program e.g., alcoholics anonymous, alanon, narcotics anonymous, gamblers anonymous, etc.

vignette. A short form of a psychodrama; a small psychodrama that does not have to be fully mounted nor include scene-setting, that can be very brief or can expand as indicated.

warming-up process. The process of generating a sense of readiness for an encounter or situation.

Appendix

THE MAGIC SHOP, HOLIDAYS, WORKING WITH MASKS,
DIRECTING EXERCISES, THE LIVING GENOGRAM AND MORE

This appendix has six subcategories. First, we have the Magic Shop and psychodramatizing a dream; next are exercises that in some way combine art with psychodrama using masks and next collage; after that are psychodramatic exercises that are very popular with groups but did not fit tongue-and-groove into the categories in the body of the book; then we have specific exercises to use at holidays, always a tender time in the lives of recovering people. In the next section, I've included exercises that can be used in training and supervision groups. These exercises focus on teaching basic theoretical concepts experientially, breaking down directing skills and teaching them one at a time and working with countertransference issues in supervision. Next is an exercise in experiential conflict resolution and lastly, I have included what I call the Living Genogram. This is my own adaptation of the genogram toward experiential use or psychodramatic enactment and/or journaling.

- The Magic Shop
- Psychodramatizing a Dream
- Incorporating Art and Creativity
- Exercises and Warm-ups
- Holidays

- Monodrama
- Introducing the self from the role of another
- Exercises for Training, Directing and Supervision
- Experiential conflict resolution: The encounter using role reversal and doubling to work with conflict
- The Living Genogram

THE MAGIC SHOP

GOALS:

1. To create action insight by therapeutically acting out a wish or desire.
2. To concretize not only what a client wishes to gain or acquire in life, but what she might need to let go of to actualize that wish.
3. To provide a circumstance in which several people might be able to do a meaningful piece of personal works in a controlled, therapeutic environment.
4. To allow playfullness to enter the therapeutic process.

STEPS:

1. The director sets up a "magic shop" on stage. The director may use or wear props—or not—as desired to create the atmosphere.
2. Either the director or someone chosen from the group takes on the role of shopkeeper.
3. The shopkeeper introduces the group to some of the variety of items in the shop, showing and telling about various items such as self-esteem, confidence, playfulness, faith, which are "imaginary items, with values of a nonphysical nature. These are not for sale but they can be obtained in barter, in exchange for other values to be surrendered by the members of the group, either individually or as a group" (J. Moreno 1964). For example, a client may enter the magic shop with a strong desire for inner peace. The shopkeeper may point out that unless the client is willing to surrender something, inner peace may not be obtainable. The shopkeeper may ask the client what she is willing to give up, e.g., addiction to drugs and alcohol, sexual acting out, gambling, etc.
4. One by one, group members enter the magic shop and barter with the shopkeeper for qualities they wish to acquire with those they are willing to surrender. The shopkeeper may explore in some depth what exists behind both the desire and what is being relinquished. This can be done in simple, straightforward dialogue, with input from the group or by using vignettes. The qualities can be concretized with an empty chair or

role-player and a brief scene can ensue. Clients may need to say "good bye" to a sub-stance or behavior, for example, concriticized by an empty chair or a role player who can try to "hang on" or cajole the client. Doubling and role reversal can be used. In each case, clients should ideally reach either some sense of resolution over a course of action or an opening as to what they may need to consider if they wish to move toward their desires. They may conclude, after role oplay, that they aren't ready to give some-thing up for some reason or another.

5. After all clients who wish to participate have taken their turns, invite the group members to share what they experienced during the process, including any new aware-ness they may have, resistance, losses, longings or dreams.

VARIATIONS:

Psychodramatists can do the magic shop using creativity and playfulness. The director may wear a costume piece, and act like a real salesperson, pointing out the benefits of various quali-ties and how the store is overstocked with some and understocked with others. It offers a vehicle for group bonding with a wide emotional range, from play to meaningful work.

PSYCHODRAMATIZING A DREAM

GOALS:

1. To provide a way to concretize a dream and explore it through role play. To allow the symbolic representations of dreams to be concretized and experienced through role reversal.

2. To deconstruct the meaning of a dream as it relates to the self.

STEPS:

1. Allow group members to present a dream if they have one that is meaningful to them.

2. Once the dream has been introduced ask the group member if they wish to move it onto the stage.

3. Invite the protagonist to cast auxiliaries to play each aspect of the dream, the people and animals in it as well as non living elements that seem significant such as a bright blue sky, a rock, a road, wall or any element that the protagonist wishes to include.

4. Ask the protagonist to place each element, person or animal in the dream where they best approximate the protagonists vision of the dream.

5. Allow the enactment to proceed by inviting the protagonist to talk wherever he feeels warmed up to begin.

6. Continue to allow the dream sequence to unfold as the protagonist moves around the stage and interacts with the representations of his internal world. The idea is to talk *to* and reverse roles *with* all elements of the dream so that the protagonist can make the unconscious elements of the dream conscious. He can talk to representations of himself and reverse roles and talk back to himself from the particular representation.

VARIATIONS:

All elements of a dream are seen to be representations of the self. Psychodrama allows these elements to be concretized so that the protagonist can encounter them in full and deconstruct their meaning as it relates to him. He can tease out the messages and meaning in the dream. Note: Generally this grows out of a group member spontaneously sharing about a dream they had recently, keep having or used to have as a child.

THE SOCIOMETRY OF MASKS

GOALS:

1. To offer an alternative way to warm up to internal material.

2. To provide emotional distance from internal issues.

STEPS:

1. Lay masks out all around the floor. Use masks that illustrate a variety of affects such as warmth, aggression, lightness of spirit, sadness, anger, etc.

2. Invite group members to choose a mask they feel warmed up to, that they identify with at the moment, and to stand beside it.

3. Ask group members to share why they are standing where they're standing in a couple of sentences. Or they may double for the masks they have chosen.

4. At this point you can (a) ask group members to repeat this process by choosing another mask, or (b) invite group members to choose someone in the group who said something

they identified with, place their hand on that person's shoulder and share with that person why they chose him or her.

5. By this time someone is generally warmed up to do some psychodramatic work. If this is the case and the group wishes to do this, move into psychodrama. Or the group can simply return to their seats for continued sharing and processing.

VARIATIONS:

This is a very full and rich experience that allows group members to identify with something outside of themselves, something that can encourage a creative connection with emotion. It appeals to the imagination, encourages spontaneity and allows for some emotional distance by identifying with a representational mask rather than the self directly. Allow the group to identify with as many masks as they wish to before making sociometric choices among group members. Once they have expressed certain identifications others may surface. Group members can create their own masks, if desired, and share about the mask they made. Or they can make two masks, e.g., one mask of the part of themselves they present to the group and another part they have not yet shown the group, for example. Or a part of themselves they really like and a part they might like to change or a role they wish to expand and a role they wish to reduce and so on.

This exercise can also be done with pictures of art instead of masks, paintings of some sort, for example, that represent different emotional states. They might be an agressive animal, a passive figure, a hero type, a lost or sad looking soul or person, abstract images and so on. Another variation is to mix costume pieces with masks. Symbolic pieces such as swords, sceptors, crowns, pom-poms, magic wands, devil ears, angel wings as well as abstract pieces such as silver masks, transparent objects or scarves are wonderful, evocative stepping off points for group members to create around. Psychodramatic journaling can be used by asking group members to journal "as" the mask.

COLLAGES

GOALS:

1. To provide a creative arts vehicle to "show and tell" their story.

2. To provide a vehicle for self-exploration that encourages creativity and spontaneity.

3. To coalesce and concretize aspects of the self, drawing from outside stimuli.

4. To facilitate group cohesion in a manner that can include playfulness.

5. To reignite the feeling of playing and losing one's self in a creative project.

STEPS:

1. Spread many different kinds of magazines on the floor along with scissors, glue and some sort of tag board or large, heavy paper. Select magazines that involve all forms of personal, behavioral and emotional expression with as wide a range of images as possible, i.e., beauty, home, automobile, science, fashion, art, etc.

2. Give the group a specific focus. For instance, say, "Look for images that (a) express who you are, (b) express where you want to go or who you want to become in life, (c) express a side of you that you rarely show, (d) express the self you are in the process of building, (e) tell the story of your life, or (f) tell the story of your inner world or inner journey." Encourage them to use pictures, words, headlines—whatever they need to tell their story.

3. After everyone has more or less completed their collage, ask them to share it. If the group is small, they can share with the entire group. If the group is large, they can have the option of breaking down into small groups.

4. After everyone has had ample opportunity to share their story pictures, come back into the large group. At this point you may (a) continue to share new awareness about the self, (b) reframe, helping participants to see through a different lens, to find new meaning in their struggle, to identify life lessons they have learned or strengths they have gained, (c) identify resilience skills that they used throughout their lives, such as creativity, ingenuity, strength, humor, strong will, ability to access mentors or helpful relationships, spiritual faith, artistic talent, intuition, or whatever other resilience skills they may identify that helped them to get to where they are today, (d) identify skills that they may need to cultivate in order to actualize new goals, or (e) consider what self-concepts, outdated belief systems or self-destructive life patterns they may need to work through and let go of in order to actualize new life goals or a more expanded self.

VARIATIONS:

This can be used as a warm-up for action by asking participants, after step #3, if any one is warmed up to doing a particular psychodrama from doing this exercise or a warm-up to psychodramatic journaling by asking participants to write letters to themselves or journal about what comes up around doing the collage after doing this exercise then share them in the group.

LOCOGRAM FOR RETURNING TO GROUP AFTER A BREAK

GOALS:

1. To allow group members to concretize their experience of returning to group after a break.
2. To create group cohesion and provide a warm-up or group check-in.

STEPS:

1. Using the format for a locogram (see chapter seven, Sociometry), designate areas on the floor to represent the following:

   - I'm glad to be back in group
   - I'm ambivalent about being back in group
   - I'm neutral about being back in group
   - I wish I were somewhere else
   - Other

2. Invite group members to stand in the location that best represents where they feel they are at this moment.

3. Invite group members to share a couple of sentences about why they're standing where they're standing.

4. Use this as a warm-up to action or as an experiential exercise that leads to further group processing. If used as a warm-up, ask if anyone is "warmed up" to work and proceed with any of the selection methods outlined in Selecting a Protagonist. If using as a stand-alone exercise, simply return to seats and continue processing.

5. Move into psychodramatic work or return to seats for further processing.

VARIATIONS:

Group members may be invited to double for each other throughout the sharing process. (This exercise was created by Calixte Stamp, CASAC, CET, who uses it at Freedom Institute in New York City).

THE LIAR'S CHAIR

GOALS:

1. To bond the group.
2. To increase spontaneity.

STEPS:

1. Set a chair in the center of the group or stage and designate it as the "liar's chair."
2. Invite any group member who feels warmed up to sit in the chair and tell an obvious lie (see Variations for example).
3. Let other group members take turns telling "lies" until everyone who wishes to has taken a turn. The "lies" can get as deep as the group wishes to go; each group will be comfortable with their own level.
4. Return to seats and continue sharing, warming up or ask if anyone feels warmed up to do a psychodrama.

VARIATIONS:

The group can incorporate doubling, talking *to* themselves in the liar's chair, or as themselves in the role of liar. The exercise can be light and fun or deepen as the group is moved. Chris Stamp uses it this way: "This can be fun and a way to get things said that are not being expressed directly. I introduce the liar's chair by taking a seat and telling an obvious lie, staying neutral from what is happening in the group. Often I proclaim from the chair how much I love filling out my tax return and paying my taxes. I then invite the group to try sitting in the chair, just to see what comes up once they are sitting. Henry, a middle-aged man who had been in the group for two weeks and hardly ever spoke, very shy, and had made very little contact with the other members, got up after most of the group had shared from the chair and anxiously sat in the chair. He looked at the group and said, 'I really love being here.' The group roared with laughter, and Henry had begun to become part of the recovery process."

HOLIDAYS

THANKSGIVING

GOALS:

1. To create a locogram that addresses holiday issues experientially.
2. To address holidays, which can be difficult for recovering people.

STEPS:

1. Following the locogram format designate areas of the floor to represent the following:
   - boisterous, arguing, perhaps drinking heavily
   - quiet, no real feeling of celebration, perhaps depressed
   - superficial, well-behaved, appearing to celebrate and have a good time
   - happy, pleasant and joyous
   - "other"

2. Invite group members to stand in the place that best represents their experience of their family of origin's holidays.

3. Invite group members to share a sentence or two about why they are standing where they are standing. Repeat steps 2 and 3 if appropriate or desired by the group, some clients will have had more then one style.

4. Next ask group members to place their hand on the shoulder of someone they feel they can get feedback from to help them handle the upcoming holiday. This creates lots of ideas on how to handle the holidays and/or to stay sober.

5. Move into psychodramas or return to seats for continued sharing and processing.

VARIATIONS:

1. Designate four corners to represent: 1) lonely/fearful; 2) warm/excited; 3) numb/indiffer-ent; 4) other. As the director, make a doubling statement: "In the present I feel . . ." then ask group members to go to the corner that represents how they feel (see steps 2–5). Note: This can be adapted for other holidays.

VALENTINE'S DAY VARIATION:

2. Using the locogram format (see page 112) put the following categories into corners. On Valentines' Day I feel:
   - Alone

- Aware of my path of self-care/Love
- Reminded of lost relationships through addictions
- Unlovable
- A sense of love within myself
- Other

Invite the group to share as usual, e.g., "I am standing here (or in-between choices) because I feel . . ."

At the end of sharing, ask clients to form a circle with one hand over their hearts and share one Valentine's gift they give to themselves.

This exercise is created by Chris Stamp, CSAC, CET, ADS, of Freedom Institute, New York City.

MONO DRAMA
Dialogue with the self (example)

GOALS

1. To bring forward the inner self at various stages.
2. To work out unfinished business from the past.

STEPS

1. Ask group members to close their eyes and relax, and then to contact a point in their lives when some major change took place or something important was going on. Ask them to summon up the person they used to be, the one to whom they would like to speak.
2. Choose a protagonist and ask her to bring that person onto the stage into an empty chair.
3. Ask the protagonist to reverse roles and show the group how that person sits and looks. She may begin talking from that role or from where she is today.
4. Ask the protagonist to speak from her current vantage point knowing what she knows now.
5. Encourage the protagonist to speak freely to this part of himself, reversing roles if he chooses.

6. Ask the protagonist to end the scene in any way she chooses.

7. Let the group share with the protagonist what came up for them.

VARIATIONS

This exercise can be done over and over again for a variety of powerful moments at any age in the life of the protagonist. It is useful in individual or group therapy and offers people a way to empower themselves by contacting themselves at moments in their lives that they feel a need or pull to encounter.

The protagonist can reverse roles with the other person represented by the empty chair and the director can *interview* them.

A mono drama can be done with the empty chair representing anything agreed upon by the protagonist and director, eg an aspect of self, another person, a pet, a deceased person, a drug, a stage of life, a job, a family and so on. It simply is a scene with only one player.

INTRODUCING THE SELF FROM THE ROLE OF ANOTHER

Goals:

1. To share personal information with the group.

2. To get in touch with feelings associated with the self.

STEPS:

1. Set up an empty chair in the group.

2. Ask group members to imagine a person they would like to have introduce them to the group. Then ask them to reverse roles with that person.

3. Have the protagonist stand behind the chair, using the empty chair to represent himself. Then, in role reversal, he introduces himself (represented by the empty chair) to the group. For example, "I am Jack's Uncle Bill, and I would like to introduce Jack to you and tell you about him.

4. The group leader can ask the protagonist to reverse roles with himself in the chair if it seems appropriate.

5. The group leader may question (interview) the protagonist in either role. Questions that

require only short answers are best. (Eg. "Why do you think Jack brought you here? Tell us a little about your nephew" and so on.

6. When the protagonist is finished, thank him and let him sit down.

7. Allow time for group sharing.

VARIATIONS:

Reversing roles and asking interview questions of either role deepens the action in this exercise quite a bit, and it becomes a mini-psychodrama. The group leader can double for the protagonist if it seems helpful. Group members may use anyone they choose to "introduce them". Perhaps someone who saw them in a positive light, was important to them for some reason or someone who just doesn't understand them. Any of these roles provide rich connections to explore.

EXERCISES FOR DIRECTING/TRAINING OR SUPERVISION GROUPS

WARMUP TO ROLES

GOALS:

1. To discern who is feeling warmed up to be a director, protagonist and so on in a seamless manner that provides for self-identification through action.

2. To provide an action format through which group members can share with the group their reasons for wishing to be in a particular role.

STEPS:

1. Using the locogram format, identify parts of the floor to represent:

   • Director   • Audience

   • Protagonist   • Other

   • Auxiliary ego

2. Invite group members to stand in the designated area that best describes which role they would like to be in at this moment. They can, of course, change their minds as the process progresses.

3. Invite group members to share why they have chosen to stand where they are standing.

4. After all the sharing is completed and group members are satisfied that they are where they wish to be, invite those who wish to be protagonists to share a sentence or two about what they would like to work on, unless they have already shared enough for the group to move directly into choosing.

5. Invite group members to choose who they wish to be protagonist by placing their hands on the shoulder of that person.

6. If a clear protagonist is chosen ask the protagonist to choose a director from among those who have identified themselves as wishing to direct.

7. Proceed with the drama as usual.

8. Share with the protagonist as usual, and after all has been shared invite the group and the protagonist to share with the director as well in order to provide sharing and feedback.

VARIATIONS:

Group members can be allowed to double for one another during the locogram process, allowing for insecurities, needs, wishes and so on, around directing or being in any role, to find voice.

PRACTICING THE BASICS

GOALS:

1. To provide small group-breakdowns in which to practice the roles and techniques of psychodrama.

2. To give many in the group practice in each role in a relaxed unthreatening manner.

STEPS:

1. Invite group members to break into groups of three.

2. Invite the threesomes to divide themselves into three roles: the protagonist, the director and the double.

3. Invite the threesomes to do monodramas using an empty chair.

4. The person who is doubling will double for the protagonist and the protagonist in role reversal. Each time the person doubles, he can check in with the protagonist to see if

the doubling worked to give voice to the inner world of the protagonist and if it helped the protagonist come to the threshold of her own awareness. Was it too much, too little or in a useful, adequate range? The protagonist can say a simples yes or no so as not to break her concentration.

5. Invite the group to change roles and repeat the process until each person has had an opportunity to be the double.

6. Return to seats for continued sharing and processing.

VARIATIONS:

Obviously the person directing will also be getting practice in the role of director, the small groups can give feedback and sharing to the person in the role of director as well as the person in the role of double. The role of protagonist also has its responsibilities. The protagonists should engage fully in the moment and do their best to be authentic and engaged. Feedback can also be given to the protagonist if desired by the group.

The next extension of this exercise would be to add an auxiliary ego and do vignettes using one auxiliary. The auxiliary ego, too, has responsibilities. If the auxiliary ego is added, feedback and sharing can go to them, as well. One more possible role to add is a "witness." The witness can be added before choosing an auxiliary ego or afterward. The witness can also be allowed to double or can just be allowed to hold the role of the audience or group member and share about that experience in the processing after each drama.

PSYCHODRAMATIC-CONCEPTS LOCOGRAM

GOALS:

1. To make basic theoretical concepts alive and engaging.
2. To create an opportunity to illustrate theoretical concepts by weaving them into the choice-making process.

STEPS:

1. On large sheets of paper, write one basic theoretical concept per sheet. Use the basic concepts from section one: spontaneity/creativity, surplus reality, concretization, act hunger, open tension, tele, and so on. **Note:** These can be laminated.

2. Place the papers around the floor or stage and invite group members to self-identify with a concept in the here and now. Use criterion questions like these: "In which of these areas are you feeling an issue today?" or "Which concept illustrates your growing edge today?" or "In which of these areas are you feeling blocked (or expansive)?"

3. Invite group members to stand near that concept and share a sentence or two about why they are standing where they are standing.

4. Invite group members to go through the same procedure with either a new criterion question or an extension of the first one.

5. Group members may repeat this process as many times as useful or can make a sociometric choice as to who may wish to move into psychodrama, having been warmed up by the exercise.

6. Move through psychodrama as usual, then return to seats for processing and sharing.

VARIATIONS:

In doing these with groups it may also happen that, for example, one person may move from one concept to another as she examines areas in which she has issues and come to understand how those issues weave together through theoretical concepts. For example, Jill may feel blocked in her spontaneity, then become aware of an act hunger or open tension that she wishes to share, and so on.

Throughout the process students will ask for clarification of terms and should feel encouraged to do so.

PSYCHODRAMATIC-TERMS LOCOGRAM

GOALS:

1. To make learning psychodramatic terms and techniques experiential.

2. To ground terms both cognitively and emotionally.

STEPS:

1. On separate sheets of paper write one term per paper, e.g., role reversal, interview, soliloquy, doubling and so on (see Psychodramatic Techniques page 36).

2. Invite students to walk over to one of the terms that they feel they understand and stand next to it.

3. Next, ask whoever feels warmed up to do so to give a brief description of the term and/or demonstrate the term. Note: students may use another group member to demonstrate, if necessary.

4. Continue until all those who care to have done a term.

5. Next, invite students to walk over to a term that they feel less clear about.

6. Invite whoever feels warmed up to do so to ask for clarification from other group members.

7. Invite anyone who wishes to, to offer clarification.

8. Move into psychodramas if anyone wishes to or return to seats for continued sharing and processing.

VARIATIONS:

Groups can also play terms charades. Write all terms on small pieces of paper and put them into a container. As each person is up, he or she picks a term out of the container and demonstrates it as the group guesses which term is being demonstrating. **Note:** The group member can use others in the group to demonstrate, if needed.

CONCRETIZING COUNTERTRANSFERENCE THROUGH VIGNETTES OR SPIRALING

GOALS:

1. To provide an experiential format for concretizing the analysis of the therapist while treating their clients.

2. To concretize and work through countertransference dynamics so that it doesn't contaminate treatment.

STEPS:

1. Invite group members to "present" a case in which they are experiencing their own countertransference.

2. Invite whoever feels warmed up, or whomever the group selects sociometrically, to choose role-players to represent herself and her client and set the scene.

3. Move the scene into action.

4. Ask her to observe the "office" scene briefly and move in and out of it to double for herself or her client in order to deepen her awareness of what might be going on underneath. She can also enter the scene as herself and role reverse with her client to gain a deeper sense of what the client is experiencing with her.
5. The exercise can stop here if all involved feel the exploration has been sufficient, or the protagonist/therapist can explore her own countertransference issues further by asking herself what material from her own past might be getting "warmed up."
6. Once an issue from the past of the protagonist/therapist's life is clear, the director can assist her in spiraling back into a model scene from the past and doing some psycho-dramatic work to resolve the issues that are getting triggered.
7. When the scene comes naturally to closure, the director can help the protagonist/therapist to spiral back up to the present day, where her countertransference with the client is occurring, or the "office scene."
8. The protagonist/client can role-play some new ways of dealing with her client based on the new insights and awarenesses that she has gained from her psychodramatic exploration.
9. Return to seats for continued sharing and processing.

VARIATIONS:

Members of the group can also be invited onto the stage for step seven in order to do some "role training" for the protagonist if all involved wish to gain some other perspectives on ways in which the situation can be handled. The protagonist can stand outside of the scene and watch various approaches being role played. This is an adaptation of an exercise used by Jacqueline Siroka, MSW, TEP, codirector of the Sociometric Institute, New York City.

Moreno (*Psychodrama Vol. I*) writes about the origins of the word *transference* in regards to the transference from the patient onto the analyst, "The prospective practitioner may have become free from transference in regard to that particular psychiatrist who analyzed him. But that does not mean that he has become free from transference in regard to any new individual he may meet in the future. He would have had to gain the armor of a saint. His armor may falter any time a new patient marches in, and the kind of complexes the patient throws at him may make a great difference in his conduct. Every new patient produces a spontaneous relationship with the psychiatrist and no educational analysis which has been carried out at one time can preview and check all the emotional difficulties emerging on the spur of the moment. In my opinion the self-analysis of the psychiatrist is not a sufficient check on this process. Therefore the first recommendation which we made in the first days of psychodramatic work was that the psychiatrist who participates in the procedure—just as well as the patient—has to be analyzed by others during the treatment."

HELP FOR THE HEALERS

GOALS:

1. To bring relief and support to those in the helping professions.
2. To create awareness around countertransference issues that may be impacting treatment negatively.

STEPS:

1. Ask group members to get out of their seats and begin milling around the room.
2. As they mill, give the following instructions in a clear, audible voice:
   - Feel your body moving through space.
   - Tune in on your present state of mind.
   - How are you feeling?
   - Go to your breath.
   - Breathe in and out easily and completely.
   - Now reflect upon your work.
   - What areas of your work do you feel strongest in?
   - What areas of your work do you feel weakest in?
   - Speak them out now.
   - Look at those you pass by.
   - Make eye contact.
   - What are your biggest fears about being a therapist or psychodramatist?
   - Walk over to that person and share your areas of strength and weaknesses.
   - Look at people as you pass them.
   - Who could you share these fears with?
   - Make eye contact.
   - Choose a partner.
   - Share your fears—each take a turn.
   - Good.
   - Back to milling.
   - Next, what unresolved pain do you feel gets touched off most frequently in your work?
   - Make eye contact.
   - Find a partner to share with.

- Share this with a partner.
- Now, with your partner, find another pair of people and share further about an area of your own issues that gets touched off in your work.

3. Invite participants to move into psychodramatic work (see Variations) or continue to share in the large group or subgroups.

VARIATIONS:

This exercise can be used in training new students so that they can get their fears and worries off their chests and get some support and sharing.

Countertransference issues can be the source of some burnout in therapists. This exercise provides a comfortable format for working with these issues with the support and identification of others. It can be used as a springboard for psychodramatic work. The issue with the client in the here and now can be put onto the stage, then the protagonist can spiral back to the issue that gets touched off in his own life and structure that personal scene. When that scene is fully played out the protagonist can spiral back into the present and replay the scene with his client with new insight and understanding.

After the sharing it might be a good idea to check in with therapists as to whether or not they are doing their own personal care, whether it be maintaining their own recovery programs, getting the rest and exercise they need, eating well, taking time to enjoy leisure activities, or nourishing their own relationships. Ignoring the self does not enhance helping others. Therapists need to have a very good regime of self-care to counteract the intensity of caring for others.

EXPERIENTIAL CONFLICT RESOLUTION: THE ENCOUNTER
USING ROLE REVERSAL AND DOUBLING TO WORK WITH CONFLICT

GOALS:

1. To use role reversal and doubling to create empathy, tolerance and understanding.
2. To provide an experiential vehicle for resolving conflict.

STEPS:

1. When and if a conflict arises between two people, invite them to work with it experientially.

2. If both parties agree, either put two chairs on the stage or work from wherever the two people are already sitting in group.

3. Invite each party to use any or all of the following devices as they continue their "talk" wherever they feel they are appropriate.

- **Doubling for the self:** Each party can double for themselves.
- **Group Doubling:** Each person in the conflict can receive doubling from and or all group members to the extent that is useful.
- **Doubling for Each other:** Each person can attempt to double for the other person in the conflict.
- **Role Reversal:** The two members of the conflict can reverse roles.

4. Eventually, when each party clearly seems to have worked through their major blocks to communication and seems able to talk in a less conflictual manner, they may continue their exchange in a less heated manner.

5. Bring the encounter to a closure, even if this means agreeing to disagree.

6. Allow the group to share what came up for them witnessing this encounter.

VARIATIONS:

The purpose of the role reversal is to actually attempt to stand in the shoes of the other party, to "get" where they are coming from so that empathy and tele can guide each party toward some level of understanding of the other's point of view. If the role reversal is not genuine that is, if the parties cannot "change places" momentarily with the other, it can be assumed that more work needs to be done from the position of the self in order to help each person get unstuck from a frozen position. This work can be done through the various forms of doubling listed in the steps. Eventually, the doubling should allow each party a deepened understanding of the underlying motivations both within themselves and within the other person.

THE LIVING GENOGRAM

Getting the Generational Picture

"The development of the genogram was greatly influenced by Moreno's concept of the Social Atom" (Marineau 1989, 158). The genogram is an instrument from the family systems field that can illuminate patterns that get passed down through generations. It is an invaluable tool for providing family history.

I have adapted the genogram to psychodrama, that is, moved it from the paper to the stage as the Living Genogram. In this process, the genogram is completed on paper then put into psychodramatic action.

The Living Genogram is a genogram brought to life through the use of role-play in the same way that a social atom becomes an action sociogram. It combines the family systems tool of the genogram with the psychodramatic method of role-play. It brings what was on paper into space, giving it concrete form and dimension, allowing clients to obtain a three-generational visual picture of the family system that they grew up in. The full genogram need not become an action sociogram in one session. It can act as a treatment map that both brings into focus areas that need work and provides a way of understanding how issues of trauma and addiction have manifested through generations of unhealthy dynamics. When clients are permitted, through the use of the Living Genogram, to see the whole picture, they can:

- Sense where their unfinished business lies by observing their feelings as they explore the various relationships in their sculptures.
- Have an opportunity to make mental time lines for where they need to go in their personal work.
- Get a sense of the origin of their transferences, attractions and rejections as well as noticing act hungers and open tensions by actually taking a walk through or revisiting their own pasts.
- Have the opportunity to identify patterns of generational dysfunction. This can help to free the self from the pathological grip of a pain-filled system. At the same time, through self-defining and separating, clients can view a system now separate with perspective and compassion.
- Recognize the gifts and strengths they may have gained from the family system along with those from whom they received support.

THE LIVING GENOGRAM

GOALS:

1. To act as a segue between the field of psychodrama and the broader mental health field, connecting family systems theory with psychodrama.
2. To bring the genogram to the psychodramatic stage where its contents can be made visible through the casting of role-players to represent people in the genogram or the use of a warm-up to focused work through vignettes or family enactments.
3. To provide a visual picture of a personal history.
4. To add a surplus reality element to the traditional genogram.

STEPS:

1. Provide paper and writing utensils.
2. Using the symbols for the social atom (a forerunner of the genogram, see page 87) create a genogram. (Note: The genogram uses squares to represent men, in the Living Genogram, we use triangles to be consistent with the social atom.)
3. The next step is to make it "Living" by rearranging the symbols on the genogram, "not how it was, but how it felt. Rearrange the symbols by placing yourself anywhere on the page that feels right, then others on your genogram in whatever way feels accurate or appropriate.
4. Choose role-players to represent the people on the genogram, including a stand-in for the self.
5. Place role-players on stage to reflect distance or closeness, triangles, covert and/or overt alliances.
6. Step outside of the genogram and look at it. "How does it feel?" "Is there anyone you wish to double for, including yourself? If so do so."
7. Next ask "is there anyone in your family system that you wish to say something to? If so do so." The protagonist can talk to or reverse roles with anyone in contained vignettes.
8. Invite the protagonist to "rearrange this genogram so that it reflects the way you wish it had been."
9. Return to seats for continued sharing and processing.

VARIATIONS:

When the genogram is put into action, it can be done so through vignettes. The client chooses someone to play or represent herself, then is free to move in and out of the picture through role reversal or she can speak from her position outside of the genogram which can make the psychodramatic portion a bit more contained and manageable. Step 7 can be skipped entirely and the protagonist can enter the genogram only through doubling and (if desired) talking to herself (her stand in) from outside the sculpture. Then proceed to step 8 or 9.

This exercise allows the protagonist to give concrete form to the family that lives in her imagination or surplus reality and to get a visual picture of the intergenerational family system. Some of the questions to be explored are:

- Where are some of the triangles in this family system?
- Along what generational lines does family addiction and dysfunction seem to travel, and what does that indicate in terms of risk categories?
- What are the types of addiction in this family?
- What are some of the strengths that continue to show up through the generations?
- How did the gender roles in this family system get played out?
- Who do you feel close to, distant from, affectionate toward, antagonist toward?
- How does it feel to look at your Living Genogram, to look at your family?
- Where are you the most comfortable; the most uncomfortable?
- Where do you feel that you have unfinished business?
- Who do you wish to talk to in this genogram?
- Who do you feel you do not wish to talk to?
- Who do you wish to thank?
- How might the dynamics you observe be playing out in your life today?

Psychodramatic journaling may be added by doing the living genogram on paper then using the above questions as journaling topics.

Bibliography

Abraham, Karl. 1955. *Clinical Papers and Essays on Psychoanalysis.* New York: Brunner/Mazel, Inc.

Ackerman, R. J. *Children Of Alcoholics: A Guidebook For Educators, Therapists and Parents* (2nd ed.). Holmes Beach, FL: Learning Publications.

Ackerman, R. J. *Perfect Daughters.* 1989. Deerfield Beach, Fla. Health Communications.

Allen, J. 1996. "The Renfrew Perspective." Summer, 2(2).

Amen, Daniel G. 1998. *Change Your Brain, Change Your Life.* New York: Three Rivers Press.

American Psychiatric Association. 1994. *Diagnostic and Statistical Manual of Mental Disorders,* fourth edition. Washington, DC: American Psychiatric Association.

Axline, M. Virginia. 1947. *Play Therapy.* New York: Ballantine Books.

Baill, Cori. 2002. "Menopause Management: How to Tame Your Raging Hormones." *Speaking of Women's Health,* August 10.

Baker-Miller, J., with I. P. Stiver and T. Hooks. 1997. *The Healing Connection.* Boston: Beacon Press.

Bannister, A. 1997. "The Healing Drama: Psychodrama and Dramatherapy with Abused Children." London: Free Association Books.

Bard, Arthur S., and Mitchell G. Bard. 2002. *Understanding The Brain.* Alpha, A Pearson Education Company.

Beasley, D. 2000. "Fight Versus Flight." ABC News Internet Ventures.

Benson, H. (1996) (with Marg Stark). *Timeless Healing: The Power and Biology of Belief.* New York: Scribner.

Black, C. 1981. *It Will Never Happen To Me.* Denver: Medical Administration Co.

Blatner, A. 1987. *The Foundation of Psychodrama.: History, Theory and Practice.* New York: Springer Publishing Co.

Blatner, A. 1994. "Psychodramatic Methods in Family Therapy" (pp. 235-246). In C.E. Schaefer & L.J. Carey (Eds.), Family play therapy. Northvale, NJ: Jason Aronson.

Blatner, A. 1994. "Tele: The Dynamics of Interpersonal Preference." In P. Holmes, M. Karp, & M. Watson (Eds.), Psychodrama since Moreno: Innovations in theory and practice. London: Routlege, 1994.

Blatner, A. 1995. "Drama in Education as Mental Hygiene: A Child Psychiatrist's Perspective." Youth Theatre Journal, 9, 92-96.

Blatner, A. 1996. "Acting-in: Practical Applications of Psychodramatic Methods." (3rd Ed.). Springer Publishing Co.

Blatner, A. 1999. "Psychodrama." In D. Wiener (Ed.), Beyond talk therapy. Washington, DC: American Psychological Association

Blatner, A. 2000. "Foundations of Psychodrama: History, Theory and Practice." (4th Ed.). New York: Springer.

Blatner, A. 2000. "Psychodramatic Methods for Facilitating Bereavement" (Chapter 2, pp. 42-51). In P. F. Kellermann & M. K. Hudgins (Eds),. Psychodrama with trauma survivors: Acting out your pain. London & Philadelphia: Jessica Kingsley-Taylor & Francis.

Blatner, A. 2001. "Psychodrama." (Chapter 51, pp 535-545). In R. J. Corsini (Ed.), Handbook of innovative therapies (2nd ed.). New York: Wiley.

Blatner, A. 2002. Psychodrama. In: Play Therapy with Adults, edited by Charles E. Schaefer, Hoboken, NJ: John Wiley & Sons.

Blatner, A. & Blatner, A. 1997. The Art of Play: Helping Adults Reclaim Imagination & Spontaneity. (Revised 2nd ed.) New York: Brunner/Routledge- Taylor & Francis.

Blume, S. B. 1985. "Psychodrama and the Treatment of Alcoholism." In S. Zimberg, J. Wallace, & S. B. Blume (Eds.), Practical approaches to alcoholism psychotherapy (2nd ed., pp. 87-108). New York: Plenum Press.

———. 1983. Acting-In. Practical Applications of Psychodramatic Methods. New York: Springer Publishing Co.

Boeree, C. George The Emotional Nervous System.

Bowlby, J. 1973a. Attachment and Loss, Vol. I: Attachment. New York: Basic Books, a Division of HarperCollins Publishers.

———. 1973b. Attachment and Loss, Vol. II: Separation, Anxiety and Anger. New York: Basic Books, a Division of HarperCollins Publishers.

Bradshaw, John. 1988. Healing the Shame That Binds You. Deerfield Beach, FL: Health Communications, Inc.

Brazelton, T. Berry and Stanley Greenspan. 2000. The Irreducible Needs of Children: What Every Child Must Have to Grow, Learn and Flourish. New York: Perseus Books.

Briggs, Dorothy Corkille. 1975. Your Child's Self-Esteem. New York: Doubleday.

Brody, Jane. 2004. "Often Time Beats Therapy for Healing Grief." New York Times, Jan. 27.

Buchanan, D. R. 1984. "Psychodrama. In T.B. Karasu" (ed.), The Psychiatric Therapies. Washington, D.C.: The American Psychiatric Association.

Buchanan, D. R. "The Central Concern Model." Group Psychotherapy, Psychodrama and Sociometry.

Butler, K. 1997. "The Anatomy of Resilience." The Networker, Mar./Apr., p. 25.

Canadian Newswire, 2003. "Research Breakthrough in Understanding Treatment-Resistant Depression: A pioneering research study using brain imaging has yielded new clues to help sufferers from severe depression who do not respond to conventional treatment." October 3.

Carnes, P. J. 1997. The Betrayal Bond. Deerfield Beach, FL: Health Communications, Inc.

Carpi, J. 1996. "A Smorgasbord of Stress-Stoppers." Psychology Today, Jan./Feb.

Center for Substance Abuse Treatment. 1994. "Assessment and Treatment of Patients with Coexisting Mental Illness and Alcohol and Other Drug Abuse: Treatment Improvement Protocol (TIP)" series number nine. DHHS Publication No. (SMA) 94-2078. Washington, D.C.

Center of Addiction & Mental Health [DATE]. "Best Practices - Concurrent Mental Health and Substance Use Disorders Prepared by the Centre of Addiction & Mental Health." Ottawa, ONT Publications, Health Canada, Ottawa, Ontario, K1A 0K9 Tel: (613) 954-5995 Fax: (613) 941-5366; www.cds-sca.com.

Chelston, G. Addiction, Affects and Self-Object Theory.

Childre, Doc. 2001. Forgiveness—A Real Stress Buster. HeartMath LLC.

Cohen, P. 1999. "The Study of Trauma Graduates at Last." *The New York Times*, May 8.

Conway, Jim and Sally. 2000. "Women at Midlife: Finding Your Identity." *Midlife Dimensions.*

Corey, G. 2004. Psychodrama (Chapter 8, pp. 204-237). In Theory and practice of group counseling (6th Ed.). Belmont, CA: Brooks/Cole-Thomson Learning.

Corsini, R. J., Shaw, M. E., & Blake, R. R. 1961: Roleplaying in Business and Industry. New York: The Free Press of Glencoe.

Cousins, Norman 1979. *Anatomy Of An Illness as Perceived by the Patient.* New York: Norton; New York: Bantam (1981).

Covington, Stephanie. 1997. *Helping Women Recover Curriculum: A Program for Treating Addiction.* Center City, MN: Hazelden.

Crosby Ouimette, P., Brown, P.J, Najavits, L.M. 1998. "Course and Treatment of Patients with Both Substance Use and Posttraumatic Stress Disorders." *Addictive Behaviors.* Vol 23(6), 785-796

Curtin, Paul J. 1985. *Tumble Weeds.* Stroudsburg, PA: Quotidian.

———. 1987. *Resistance And Recovery for Adult Children of Alcoholics.* Delaware Water Gap, PA: Quotidian.

Czikszentmilahyi, M. 1990. *Flow: The Psychology of Optimal Experience.* New York: HarperCollins Publishers.

Damasio, Antonio. 1995. *Descartes' Error: Emotions, Reason and the Human Brain.* New York: Avon Books.

———. 1999. *The Feeling of What Happens.* New York: Harcourt, Inc.,

Danieli, Y. 1984. "Psychotherapists' Participation in the Conspiracy of Silence About the Holocaust," *Psychoanalytic Psychology,* p. 23–42.

Darwin, C. (1872) 1965. "The Expression of Emotion in Man and Animals." Reprint. Chicago: Univesity of Chicago Press.

Dass, Ram and Paul Gorman. 1987. *How Can I Help?* New York: Alfred A. Knopf.

Dawson, J. 1993. "Deep in the Human Mind." *Minneapolis Star-Tribune,* May.

Dayton, T. 2004. The Drama Within: Psychodrama and Experiential Therapy. Deerfield Beach, Fla: Health Communications, Inc.

Dayton, T. 2000. *Trauma and Addiction.* Deerfield Beach, Fla., Health Communications.

Dayton, T. 1997. *Heartwounds.* Deerfield Beach, Fla., Health Communications

DeBeauport, E. 1996. *The Three Faces of Mind.* Wheaton, IL: Quest Books, an imprint of Theosophical Publishing House.

Denney, Melita and Osborne Phillips. 1980-1983. *Creative Visualization.* St. Paul, MN: Llewellyn Publications.

DeNoon, D. 2004. "Anger Hurts Men's Hearts: Hostile, Angry Men at Risk of Early Atrial Fibrillation." Web MD Medical News.

Dimberg. U.E. Ohman, A. 1996. "Beyond the Wrath: Psychophysiological responses to facial stimuli. *Motivation and Emotion.*

Deutsch, C. 1982. *Broken Bottles, Broken Dreams: Understanding and Helping ACOAs.* New York: New York Teachers College Press.

———. 1993. *Healing Words.* San Francisco: Harper San Francisco,

Dossey, Larry. 1988. *Be Careful What You Pray For . . . You Just Might Get It.* San Francisco: Harper.

Dowrick, Stephanie. 1997. *Forgiveness and Other Acts of Love.* New York: Viking.

Driesen, Jacob L. 2003. *Depression and the Brain.*

Elam, Kier. 1980. *Semiotics of Theater & Drama.* New York: Routledge Chapman & Hall.

Eil. 1984. *The Family.* New York: Center for Family Learning.

Elkind, David. 1981. *The Hurried Child.* Reading, MA: Addison-Wesley.

Enright, Robert. 2000. *Forgiveness Is a Choice*. Washington, D.C.: International Forgiveness Institute, APA Books.

Erickson, J. M. 1988. *Wisdom and the Senses: The Way to Creativity*. New York: W.W. Norton & Co.

Estes, Nada J. and Edith M.Heinemann. 1982. *Alcoholism*. St. Louis, Toronto, London: The C.V. Mosby Company.

Faber, Thomas F. 1986. *Alcohol and Culture: Comparative Perspectives from Europe and America*. New York: New York Academy of Science.

Fals-Stewart, W. (2003). "The Occurrence of Intimate Partner Violence on Days of Alcohol Consumption: A Longitudinal Diary Study." Journal of Consulting and Clinical Psychology, 71, 41-52.

Fals-Stewart, W., & Birchler, G. R. (2002). "Behavioral Couples Therapy for Alcoholic Men and Their Intimate Partners: The comparative effectiveness of master's- and bachelor's-level counselors." Behavior Therapy, 33, 123-147.

Fals-Stewart, W., Birchler, G. R., & O'Farrell, T. J. (1996). "Behavioral Couples Therapy for Male Substance-Abusing Patients: Effects on Relationship Adjustment and Drug-Using Behavior." *Journal of Consulting and Clinical Psychology, 64, 959-972.*

Farmer, C. 1995. Psychodrama and Systemic Therapy. London: Karnac Books.

Feuerstein, George. 1978, 1989. *The Yoga-Sutra Of Pantanjali*. Rochester, VT: Inner Traditions International, Ltd.

Fine, L. J. 1979. "Psychodrama." R. J. Corsini (ed.), *Current Psychotherapies* (2nd ed.). Itasca, IL: F. E. Peacock.

Fisher, Ruth. 1988. *Time For Joy—Daily Affirmations*. Deerfield Beach, FL: Health Communications, Inc.

Fitzhenry, R. I. 1993. *The Harper Book of Quotations*. New York: HarperPerennial, a Division of HarperCollins Publishers.

Flannery, R. B. 1986. "The Adult Children of Alcoholics: Are They Trauma Victims with Learned Helplessness?" *Journal of Social Behavior and Personality*, vol. I, no. 4.

Fox, Jonathan (ed.) 1987. *The Essential Moreno: Writings on Psychodrama, Group Method & Spontaneity*. New York: Springer Pub.

Fox, J. & Dauber, H. (Eds.) 1999. Gathering Voices: Essays on Playback Theatre. New Paltz, NY: Tusitala.

Franklin, Jon. 1988. *Molecules of the Mind*. New York: Dell Publishing Co.

Freedman, D., R. Pisani, and R. Purves, 1978. *Statistices*. New York: Norton.

Freud, Anna. 1963. *Psychoanalysis for Teachers and Parents*. New York: Norton,

Freud, Sigmund. 1957. *On Dreams*. New York: Norton.

———. 1957. *A General Selection from the Works of Sigmund Freud*. New York: Doubleday.

———. 1900. "The Interpretation of Dreams." *Standard Edition*, 4 and 5. London, Hogarth Press, 1953.

———. 1913. "The Claims of Psycho-analysis to Scientific Interest." *Standard Edition*, 13: 164-190. London, Hogarth Press, 1957.

Fried, M. N. and H. Fried 1980. *Transitions: Four Rituals In Eight Cultures*. New York: W.W. Norton.

Fuhlrodt, R. B. (ed.). 1990. *Psychodrama: Its Application to ACOA And Substance Abuse Treatment*. (Available from Perrin & Treggett Booksellers, P.O. Box 190, Rutherford, NJ 07070. 1-800-321-7912.)

Galsworthy, J. 1996. *Forsyte Saga*. New York: Simon & Schuster.

Gant, Linda, Ph.D. 2003. "Art of Therapy and Trauma." *Counselor Magazine*.

Gass, M. 1997. Rebuilding Therapy: Overcoming the Past for a More Effective Future. Westport, CT: Praeger.

Gawain, Shakti. 1989. *Return to the Garden*. San Rafael, CA: Publisher

Geary, David C. 1998. *Male, Female: The Evolution of Human Sex Differences*. Washington, D.C.: APA Books.

Gershom, J. 2002. *Psychodrama in the 21st Century*. New York: Springer.

Gilligan, C. 1993. *In a Different Voice: Psychological Theory & Women's Development.* Cambridge, MA: Harvard University Press.

Goertz, C. 1973. *The Interpretation of Cultures.* New York: Basic Books.

Goldman, E. E. and D.S. Morrison. 1984. *Psychodrama: Experience and Process.* Dubuque, Iowa: Kendall/ Hunt.

Goleman, D. 1998. *Working with Emotional Intelligence.* New York: Bantam Books.

Goodman, Elaine and Walter. 1979. *The Family Yesterday, Today, Tomorrow.* New York: Farrar-Straus and Gidroux.

Grady, D. 1998. "Hardest Habit to Break: Memories of the High." *The New York Times,* October 27.

Gray, R. M. 1999. "Addictions and the Self: A Self Enhancement Model for Drug Treatment in a Group Setting." New York: Presentation at NASW and Addiction Conference 1999 at Rutgers University.

Greenberg, I. A., (ed.). 1974. *Psychodrama Theory and Therapy.* New York: Behavioral Publications.

Greenspan, Stanley I and George H. Pollock. 1980. *The Course of Life.* Washington: U.S. Dept. of Health and Human Services.

Greenspan, S. "Building Healthy Minds." 2000, Persus Publishing.

Grinker, R. R. 1985. *Men Under Stress.* New York: Irvington Publishers.

Guilford, J. P. 1977. *Fundamental Statistics in Psychology and Education.* (3rd ed.) New York: McGraw Hill.

Hainstock, G. Elizabeth. 1978. *The Essential Montessori.* New York: Signet.

Hale, A. E. 1986. *Conducting Clinical Sociometric Explorations: A Manual for Psychodramatists and Sociometrists.* City: Publisher.

Hare, A. P. & Hare, J. R. 1996. J.L. Moreno. Series, "Key Figures in Psychotherapy". London & Thousand Oaks, CA: Sage.

Hartnoll, Phyllis. 1985. *The Theatre: A Concise History.* New York: Thames Hudson,

Hay, Louise L. 1984–1987. *You Can Heal Your Life.* Santa Monica, CA: Hay House.

Hayden-Seman, J. 1998. Action Modality Couples Therapy: Using Psychodramatic techniques in helping troubled relationships. Dunmore, PA: Jason Aronson.

Hayes, W. L. 1973. *Statistics for the Social Sciences.* New York: Holt, Rinehart & Winston.

Hendricks, C. Gaylord and Kathryn Hendricks. 1983. *The Moving Center.* New Jersey: Prentice Hall.

Heran, J. L. 1992. *Trauma and Recovery.* New York: Basic Books, a division of HarperCollins Publishers.

Hibbard, S. 1987. "The Diagnosis and Treatment of ACOAs as a Specialized Therapeutic Population." *Psychotherapy* (Winter), vol. 24.

Hobson, Allan J. date. *The Dreaming Brain.* New York: Basic Books, Inc. Publishers.

Hoel, P. G. 1960. *Elementary Statistics.* New York: Wiley and Sons.

Hoey, B. 1997. Who Calls the Tune? A Psychodramatic Approach to Child Therapy. New York: Routledge-Taylor & Francis.

Hollander, C. E. 1978. *A Process For Psychodrama Training: The Hollander Psychodrama Curve.* Denver, CO: Snow Lion Press.

Holmes, J. 1993. *John Bowlby and Attachment Theory.* New York: Routledge.

Horowitz, M. J. 1997. *Stress Response Syndromes.* Northvale, NJ: Aronson.

Howard, Pierce J. 2000. *The Owner's Manual for the Brain.* Atlanta: Bard Press.

Hudgins, M. K. 2002. Experiential Treatment for PTSD: The Therapeutic Spiral Model. New York: Springer.

Isaacs, K. 1998. *Uses of Emotion.* Westport, CT: Praeger Publishers.

Johnson, D. R. 2000. History of Drama Therapy (pp. 5-15). In, P. Lewis & D. R. Johnson (Eds). Current approaches in drama therapy. Springfield, IL: Charles C. Thomas.

Johnson Institute. 1986. *Intervention.* Minneapolis, MN.

Joseph, R. 1999. "Environmental Influences on Neural Plasticity, The Limbic System, Emotional Development and Attachment." *Child Psychiatry and Human Development,* 29, 187-203.

Kalsched, D. 1996. *The Inner World of Trauma.* New York: Routledge.

Karp, M., Holmes, P., & Bradshaw-Tauvon, K. (Eds.) 1998. Handbook of Psychodrama. London & New York: Routledge-Taylor & Francis.

Kellermann, P. F. 1992. Focus on pychodrama: The Therapeutic Aspects of psychodrama. London: Jessica Kingsley-Taylor & Francis.

Kellerman, P. F. 1983. Resistance in Psychodrama. *Group Psychotherapy, Psychodrama And Sociometry,* 36, 30–43.

Kinney, H. C., Brody, B.A., Kloman, A.S. & Gilles, F.H. 1988. "Sequence of central nervous system myelination in human infancy. *Journal of Neuropathology and Experimental Neurology.*

Kipper, D. A. 1986. Psychotherapy Through Clinical Role Playing. New York: Brunner/ Routledge-Taylor & Francis.

Kipper, D. A. 2001. Surplus Reality and the Experiential Reintegration Model in Psychodrama. International Journal of Action Methods: Psychodrama, Skill Training and Role Playing. 53,137-152.

Kipper, D. A., & Ritchie, T. D. 2003. The Effectiveness of Psychodramatic Techniques: A Meta-analysis. Group Dynamics: Theory Research and Practice 7 (1), 13-25.

Kleber, R. 1987. "Psychotherapy and Pathological Grief Controlled Outcome Study." *The Israel Journal of Psychiatry and Related Sciences,* 24.

Klein, M. 1940. "Mourning and Its Relation to Manic Depressive States." *The International Journal of Psychoanalysis,* 21.

Krystal, H. 1968. *Massive Psychic Trauma.* Madison, CT: International Universities Press.

Kuman, V. K. & and T. W. Treadwell, 1985. *Practical Sociometry For Psychodramatists.*

Lachman, Frank. *Infant Research and Adult Treatment: Co-Constructing Interactions,* 2002, Analytic Press, Inc.

Lacoursiere, R. 1980. "Traumatic Neurosis in the Etiology of Alcoholism." *American Journal of Psychiatry* 137.

Landy, Robert, *Personna and Performance,* Guilford Publications, Inc., 1996.

———. Drama Therapy; *Concepts, Theories, Practices,* 1994, Charles C. Thomas.

Langone, J. 1985. *The War That Has No Ending.* Discover.

Lazarus, R.S. 1991. "Progress on a cognitive—relational theory of emotion." *American Psychologist.*

Lazarus, R.S. & McCleary, R.A. 1951. "Autonomic discrimination without awareness: A study of subception. *Psychological Review.*

Ledoux, Joseph. 2002. *The Synaptic Self.* New York: Viking Penguin Group.

Ledoux, J. 1996. *The Emotional Brain.* New York: Simon & Schuster.

Leshner, Alan. Addiction/Recovery Guide: Addiction Is a Brain Disease.

Leshner, A. 1998. "Drugs, Minds and Brains." American Academy of Addiction Psychiatry Ninth Annual Meeting (Winter 1999 newsletter insert from the AAAP).

Leveton, E. 2001. A Clinician's Guide to Psychodrama (3rd ed.). New York: Springer

Lickliter, R. & Gottlieb, G. 1986. "Visually imprinted material preference in ducklings is redirected by social interaction with siblings." *Developmental Psychobiology.*

Lifton, R. J. 1964. "On Death and Death Symbolism, the Hiroshima Disaster." *American Psychiatric Journal.*

Lindemann, E. 1944. "Symptomatology and Management of Acute Grief." *American Psychiatrist.*

Lynch, J. 1985. *The Language of the Heart.* New York: Basic Books, a Division of HarperCollins Publishers.

Marano, first name 1999. "Depression Beyond Serotonin." *Psychology Today,* March/April.

Marineau, R. F. 1989. *Jacob Levy Moreno 1989–1974: Father Of Psychodrama, Sociometry and Group Psychotherapy.* London and New York: Tavistock/Routledge.

Marlin, E. 1989. *Genograms: A New Tool for Exploring the Personality, Career and Love Patterns You Inherit.* Chicago: Contemporary Books.

Marty, P. 1963. "Las Pensee Operatoire." *Revue Francaise de Psychanalyse,* 27.

McDougall, J. 1989. *Theaters of the Body.* New York: W.W. Norton & Co.

McGoldrich, M. 1985. *Genograms in Family Assessment.* New York: W.W. Norton & Co.

Middleton-Moz, J. 1993. *After the Tears.* Deerfield Beach, FL: Health Communications, Inc.

Miller, W. R. 1990. "Spirituality: The Silent Dimension in Addiction Research." *Drug and Alcohol Review,* 9, 259 - 266.

Miller, W. R. 1998. "Researching the Spiritual Dimensions of Alcohol and Other Drug Problems." *Addiction,* 93, 979 - 990.

Moe, Jerry, *Conducting Support Groups for Elementary Children K-6*, Hazelden, 1991 Kids Power: Too Imagin Works, 1996.

Moreno, J. 1964. *Psychodrama.* Vol. 1 Ambler, PA: Beacon House.

———. 1969. *Psychodrama.* Vol. 3. Ambler, PA: Beacon House.

Moreno, J. 1999. Acting Your Inner Music: Music Therapy & Psychodrama. St. Louis. MMB Music

Moreno, J. L. 1934. Who Shall Survive? A New Approach to the Problem of Human Interrelations. Washington, D.C.: Nervous & Mental Disease Publishing.

Moreno, J. L. 1946-1969. Psychodrama, Vol.1, 2 & 3 (last two with Z. T. Moreno). Beacon, NY: Beacon House.

Moreno, Z. T., Blomkvist, L. D. & R,tzel, T. 2000. Psychodrama, surplus reality, and the art of healing. London & New York: Routledge-Taylor & Francis

Nemiah, J. 1978. "Alexithymia and Psychosomatic Illness." *Journal of Continuing Education in Psychiatry.*

———. 1970. "Affect and Fantasy in Patients with Psychosomatic Disorders." *Modern Trends in Psychosomatic Medicine,* vol. 2.

Norden, M. 1995. *Beyond Prozac.* New York: HarperCollins Publishers.

Nunnally, J. C. 1925. *Tests and Measurements: Assessment and Prediction.* New York: McGraw Hill.

———. 1978. *Psychometric Theory.* New York: McGraw Hill.

O'Gorman, P. 1994. *Dancing Backwards in High Heels.* Center City, MN: Hazelden Educational Materials.

Oliver-Diaz, P. 1985. "Self-Help Groups Through Children's Eyes," *Focus on Family and Chemical Dependency,* vol. 8, no. 2.

Olsson, P. A. 1989. "New Uses of Psychodrama." *Journal of Operational Psychiatry,* vol. 14, no. 2.

Ornstein, R. 1990. *The Healing Brain.* New York: The Guilford Press.

Oschman, J. L. 1995. "Somatic Recall." *Massage Therapy Journal,* Summer.

Pace. 1997. *Psychiatric Times,* Mar.

Pendagast, E. G. 1984. *The Family.* New York: Center for Family Learning.

Pennebaker, J. W. 1997. *Opening Up: The Healing Power of Confiding in Others.* New York: The Guilford Press.

Pert, C. 1997. *Molecules of Emotion.* New York: Scribner.

———. 1998. "The Psychosomatic Network: Foundations of Mind-Body Medicine." *Alternative Therapies,* July, vol. 4, no. 4.

Pesso, A. 1997. Pesso System/Psychomotor Therapy. In C. Caldwell (Ed.), Getting in touch: a guide to body-centered therapies. Wheaton, IL: Theosophical Publishing House.

Piaget, J. 1981. "Intelligence and Affectivity: Their Relationship During Child Development." *Annual Reviews.*

Pitman, R. K. 1991. "Psychiatric Complications During Flooding Therapy for Post-Traumatic Stress Disorders." *Journal of Clinical Psychiatry,* 52.

Pitzele, P. 1998. Scripture windows: Toward a practice of Bibliodrama. Los Angeles: Alef Design Group.

Pollock. G. H. 1989. *The Mourning-Liberation Process.* Madison, CT: International Universities Press.

Presnall, Lewis. 1977. *Alcoholism, the Exposed Family.* Salt Lake City, UT: Utah Alcoholism Foundation.

Raimundo, C. 2002. Relationship capital: true success through coaching and managing relationships in business and life. Australia: Pearson Education.

Rando, T. A. 1993. *Treatment of Complicated Mourning.* Chicago: Research Press.

Rocha do Amaral, Júlio and Jorge Martins de Oliveira. 1998. "Limbic System: The Center of Emotions," 1999. Child Psychiatry and Human Development, Sept. 10, 1999.

Røine, E. 1997. Psychodrama: group psychotherapy as experimental theatre. London: Jessica Kingsley-Taylor & Francis

Rosenthal, Norman E. "The Emotional Revolution."Seacaucus, N.J. Citadel Press/Kingston Publishing. 2002. Stern, Daniel N. The Present Moment. Norton, London. (2004)

Russell, P. 1979. *The Brain Book.* New York: Plume.

Sacks, J. M., Bilaniuk, M. & Gendron, J. M. 2003. Bibliography of psychodrama: Inception to date. *www.asgpp.org/02ref/index.html.*

Satir, Virginia. *The New Peoplemaking.* Palo-Alto Science and Behavior Books, Inc. 1988.

Scategni, W. 2002. Psychodrama, group processes and dreams: Archetypal images of individuation. (Translated from the Italian). New York: Brunner-Routledge/Taylor & Francis

Schore, A. N. 1994. *Affect Regulation and the Origin of the Self.* Hillsdale, NJ: Lawrence Erlbaum Associates Publishers.

Schore, A. N. (in press.) "The Right Brain, The Right Mind and Psychoanalysis." Guildford Press.

Seligman, M. 1975. *Helplessness: On Depression, Development, and Death.* San Francisco: Freeman, Cooper & Co.

Shapiro, E. R. 1994. *Grief As a Family Process.* New York: The Guilford Press.

Skog, S. 1999. *Depression: What Your Body's Trying to Tell You.* New York: Wholecare.

Smith, Deborah. 2002. "Major National Studies of Women's Health Are Providing New Insights." *Monitor on Psychology* (vol. 33), May 5.

Smith, D. 2003. "Placebo Alters Brain Function of People with Depression." Vol. 33, No. 3.

Solms, M. 1996. "Towards an Anatomy of the Unconscious." *Journal of Clinical Psychoanalysis,* 5: 331-367.

Spiegel, M.R. 1961. Schaem's Outline Series. *Theory and Problems of Statistics.* New York: McGraw Hill.

Stanton, Annette L. 1999. "Psychotherapy May Be as Useful as Drugs in Treating Depression, Study Suggests." *APA Monitor Online* (vol. 30), September 8.

Starr, A. 1977. *Rehearsal For Living: Psychodrama.* Chicago, IL: Nelson Hall.

Steiner, C. 1997. *Achieving Emotional Literacy.* New York: Avon Books.

Steinglass, Peter. 1987. *The Alcoholic Family.* New York: Basic Books.

Sternberg, P. & Garcia, A. 2000. Sociodrama: Who's in your shoes? (2nd ed.) Westport, CT: Greenwood Publishers.

Straussner, S.L.A. 1997. "Group Treatment with Substance Abusing Clients: A Model of Treatment During the Early Phases of Outpatient Group Therapy." *Journal of Chemical Dependency Treatment,* 7, 67-80.

Swanson, Naomi G. "Women Face Higher Risk at Work than Men." *Monitor on Psychology,* 31.

Sykes, Mary Wylie. 2003. The Limits of Talk: Bessel Van der Kolk Wants to Transform the Treatment of Trauma." *The Psychotherapy Networker.*

Tauvon, K. 1998. *The Handbook of Psychodrama. Principles of Psychodrama.* New York: Routledge.

Taylor, G. 1984. "Alexithymia: Concept, Measurement and Implications for Treatment." *American Journal of Psychiatry,* June, vol. 14, no. 6.

Thagard, Paul and Allison Barnes. 1996. "Emotional Decisions." Proceedings of the *Eighteenth Annual Conference of the Cognitive Science Society.*

The American Society for Group Psychotherapy & Psychodrama (ASGPP): *www.asgpp.org.*

The Journal of Group Psychotherapy, Psychodrama, & Sociometry. Published by Heldref, 1318 18th St, Washington, DC 20006. www.heldref.org.

Thoresen, Carl E. 1999. *Spirituality and Health: Is There a Relationship?*

Toffler, A. 1970. *Future Shock.* New York: Random House.

Tomasulo, D. J. 1998. Action methods in group psychotherapy: practical aspects. Accelerated Development-Taylor & Francis.

Tronick, E.L., Bruschweiler-Stern, N., Harison, A.M., Lyons Ruth, K., Morgan, A.C., Nahum, J.P., Sandler, L. and Stern, D. N. 1988. "Dyadically expanded states of consciousness and therapeutic change." Infant Mental Health Journal.

Turnbull, C. 1990. *Liminality: A Synthesis of Subjective and Objective Experience.* Cambridge, MA: Cambridge University Press.

Vaillant, George E. 2002. *Aging Well.* New York: Little, Brown and Co.,

Van der Kolk, Bessel. 1987. *Psychological Trauma.* Washington, D.C.: American Psychiatric Press, Inc.,

Van der Kolk, B.A., and Fisler, R.E. 1994. "Childhood abuse and neglect and loss of self-regulation." Bulletin of the Menninger Clinic, 58: 145-168.

Vaughn, S. C. 1997. *The Talking Cure.* New York: G.P. Putnam's Sons.

Verhofstadt-DenÈve, L. 1999. Theory and practice of action and drama techniques: developmental psychotherapy from an existential-dialectical viewpoint. London & Philadelphia: Jessica Kingsley-Taylor & Francis.

Walsch, Neale Donald. 1999. *Forgiveness—The Greatest Healer of All.* Hillsboro Publishing.

Walsh, F. 1998. *Strengthening Family Resilience.* New York: The Guilford Press.

Wiener, D. J. & Oxford, L. K. (Eds.) 2003. Action therapy with families and groups. Washington, DC.: American Psychological Association.

Weiner, H. B. 1975. "*Living Experiences with Death—A Journeyman's View Through Psychodrama.*" *Omega,* 6 (3), 251–274.

Weisaeth, L., and Van Der Hart, O. 1966. "History of trauma in psychiatry." *In Traumatic Stress:The Effects of Overwhelming Experience on Mind, Body, and Society,* ed B.A. van der Kolk, A.C. MacFarlane, and L. Weisaeth. New York, Guildford Press, pp. 47-74.

Werner, E. 1989. "Children of the Garden Island." *Scientific American,* April.

Werner, H. 1963. *Symbol Formation.* New York: Wiley.

Williams, R. 1993. *Anger Kills.* New York: Harper Paperbacks, a division of HarperCollins Publishers.

Winnicott, D. W. 1981. *The Child and the Outside World.* London: Pelican Books.

Woititz, J. 1983. *Adult Children of Alcoholics.* Deerfield Beach, Fla: Health Communications, Inc.

Wolin, S. J. 1993. *The Resilient Self.* New York: Villard Books, a Division of Random House, Inc.

Worrell, J., & Remer, P. 1992. Feminist perspectives in therapy. New York: Wiley

Wright, Rusty. 2000. "Forgiveness Can Be Good for Your Health." *Probe Ministries.*

Wycoff, J. 1991. *Mindmapping: Your Personal Guide to Exploring Creativity and Problem-Solving.* New York: Berkley Books.

Yablonsky, L. 1976. *Psychodrama: Resolving Emotional Problems Through Role-Playing.* New York: Basic Books.

Yakovlev, P.I. & Lecours, A.R. 1967. "The myelogenetic cycles of regional maturation of the brain." *Regional Development of the Brain in Early Life.* A Minkow. Oxford: Blackwell.

Yalom, I. 2002. The gift of therapy. New York: Harper & Row.

Yalom, Irvin D. 1970, 1975 and 1985. *The Theory and Practice of Group Psychology.* New York: Basic Books, a division of HarperCollins Publishers.

Young, M. E. 2001. Learning the art of helping: Building blocks and techniques (2nd ed.). Upper Saddle River, NJ: Prentice-Hall.

Zohar, Danah. 1991. *Quantum Self: Human Nature and Consciousness Defined by the New Physics.* New York: HarperTrade.

About the Author

Tian Dayton, Ph.D., TEP, holds a doctorate in clinical psychology, a master's in educational psychology and is a board-certified trainer in psychodrama, sociometry and group psychotherapy. She is the director of the New York Psychodrama Training Institute at Caron, New York, where she offers training in psychodrama, sociometry and group psychotherapy and consults in program development. Dr. Dayton is a fellow of the American Society for Psychodrama, Sociometry and Group Psychotherapy and an executive editor of the society's *Journal on Group Therapy, Psychodrama and Sociometry* and serves on the professional standards committee. She is the winner of the society's scholar's award. She is also a board member of the National Association for Children of Alcoholics (NACOA).

Dr. Dayton has trained professionals throughout the country, for the past two decades, in the New York area and at New York University in the use of psychodrama, sociometry and experiential methods to treat addiction, trauma and grief.

Dr. Dayton has written many books and numerous articles. Her books include recovery bestseller *Forgiving and Moving On, Trauma and Addiction, Heartwounds: The Impact of Unresided Trauma and Grief on Relationships, Drama Games* and *The Drama Within,* and her work has been featured in a docudrama on psychodrama called *The Process.* She has been one of the pioneers in adapting experiential methods for treating issues surrounding addiction and trauma. She is a regular guest expert on TV and radio and has appeared on NBC, MSNBC, CNN, *John Walsh, Montel, Geraldo, Rikki Lake,*

Gary Null and many more. She lives in Manhattan with her husband of thirty years and near her two grown children.

To learn more about Dr. Dayton's training groups call (212) 371-3220 *4399, or for information on consulting, program development or training in your facility, call (212) 787-7914 or visit *tiandayton.com*.

Videotapes and Audiotapes

Also available on *tiandayton.com* are the following videos and tapes for use in treatment centers and clinics The following films can be used as part of a psychoeducational program and/or training tapes: *The Process,* a docudrama using psychodrama to tell powerful stories on addiction, loss and forgiveness; *Bob's Story,* which investigates the disease underneath the disease, relapse issues and the connection between trauma and addiction through psychodrama; *The Hurting Family,* which illustrates sculpturing the dysfunctional family system from the social atom, *Letterwriting;* vignettes on addiction, adoption, abuse, relationship issues and physical ailments; and *Psychodrama Basics: A Psychodrama Training Tape.*

The following audiotapes can be used at home or in groups as guided relaxations, guided imageries or as "homework": for learning the techniques of relaxing and self self-soothing, three guided imagery tapes, *A Visit with My Inner Child, Releasing Numbness,* and *Turning It Over.*

To learn more about how to become a psychodramatist log on to ASGPP (*ASGPP.org*) or an experiential therapist call ASET (773) 848–2738 or go to: *www.ASETonline.com.*

Other Books by Tian Dayton, Ph.D., TEP

Affirmations for Parents

The Magic of Forgiveness

The Quiet Voice of the Soul

The Soul's Companion

It's My Life: A Power Book for Teens

Journey Through Womanhood

Sign up to receive a free daily affirmation or e-letter
via e-mail at *tiandayton.com.*

OTHER BOOKS BY TIAN DAYTON PH.D., TEP
THAT SUPPORT THIS PROCESS:

Trauma and Addiction

Those with symptoms of PTSD often self-medicate with drugs and alcohol to quell their inner pain. This book describes the complicated relationship between trauma and self-medication using research, descriptive material and case studies. It is a popular textbook for those in the addictions field and can be given to clients so that they can better understand their disease process.

Heartwounds: The Impact of Unresolved Trauma and Grief on Relationships

This book paints a clear and moving picture of how PTSD related issues and unresolved grief get played out in intimate relationships. Addiction can be a form of pathological mourning in which obsessive use of substances or behaviors mask symptoms of unresolved grief and anger. And, in the reverse, addiction leaves pain and anger in its wake. It gives therapists an overview of current research and clients the information, and case study examples they can readily use to gain the insight and motivation needed to heal their relationships.

Daily Affirmations for Forgiving and Moving On

This recovery bestseller is a favorite with those who want daily inspiration in their recovery process. Written in the first person, readers experience the material as an inner voice of support and understanding. Complicated psychological information is broken down into a simple, daily, user-friendly format.

Daily Affirmations for Parenting

Parents who have grown up with dysfunction or addiction are at risk for passing their unresolved issues down through the generations. This book provides encouraging, uplifting readings to turn this dynamic around, one day at a time. The pages offer a brief refuge; containing insight and inspiration to help with the important job of parenting.

The Magic of Forgiveness

Forgiveness is increasingly being recognized a pathway out of the kind of emotional and psychological pain that repeats and repeats itself throughout life. Forgiveness of self and others helps to mobilize blocked energies toward positive life goals. This book breaks the process of forgiveness down into stages, each stage including simple exercises. The stages, which include anger, resentment and sadness, help clients to understand that forgiveness is a process not an event and requires us to face the often deep and painful feelings that stand in our way of inner peace.

Drama Games

Popular with teachers and therapists this book includes simple and easy-to-follow exercises that can be done with adults in treatment or young people.

The Drama Within

This book outlines the basics of psychodrama and sociometry and includes over one hundred exercises and warm-ups.